CW00596981

TRAVEL & LEISURE

Paris

by Nadine Frey

Macmillan • USA

MACMILLAN TRAVEL
A Simon & Schuster Macmillan Company
1633 Broadway
New York, NY 10019

Find us online at **http://www.mgr.com/travel** or on
American Online at Keyword: **Frommer's**

ISBN: 0-02-860695-7
ISSN: 1088-4815

Editor: Peter Katucki
Production Editor: Trudy Brown
Digital Cartography by Ortelius Design
Design by Amy Peppler Adams—designLab, Seattle

SPECIAL SALES
Bulk purchases (10+ copies) of Frommer's and selected
Macmillan travel guides are available to corporations,
organizations, mail-order catalogs, institutions, and charities
at special discounts, and can be customized to suit individual
needs. For more information write to: Special Sales,
Macmillan General Reference, 1633 Broadway, New York,
NY 10019.

Manufactured in Singapore

CONTENTS

LIST OF MAPS

Dedicated to my mother, Maria Lyons Frey

About the Author
Nadine Frey is a graduate of Princeton University and the Columbia School of Journalism. From 1983 until 1988, she was the Milan bureau chief of *Women's Wear Daily* and *W.* She has lived in Paris since 1988 and writes frequently for magazines and newspapers about fashion, travel, and the arts.

Acknowledgments
Many colleagues and friends helped bring this book to life by sharing their own knowledge of Paris and its institutions. Among those, Christopher Petkanas gave generously and freely of his time and knowledge. I would also like to thank my father, Donald Frey, and my sister, Lisa Frey; Alec Lobrano, Diane Pernet, and Vincent La Rouche, all of whom were unstinting in sharing both files and experiences; and my editor at Macmillan, Peter Katucki. Sandra Hoff at the French Tourist Board was a tireless source of information. Many thanks to Susan Bouchet for her resourcefulness in researching and fact-checking the manuscript. I would also like to thank my husband, Jean-Marc Martin, and Alexis and Amory for living good-humoredly with this project the many months that I did.

An Additional Note
Please be advised that travel information is subject to change at any time—and this is especially true of prices. We therefore suggest that you write or call ahead for confirmation when making your travel plans. The authors, editors, and publisher cannot be held responsible for the experiences of readers while traveling. Your safety is important to us, however, so we encourage you to stay alert and be aware of your surroundings. Keep a close eye on cameras, purses, and wallets, all favorite targets of thieves and pickpockets.

INTRODUCTION

THOSE WHO KNEW PARIS MORE THAN 30 YEARS AGO, inntroduys before President de Gaulle, remember the city for its shades of gray—the prevailing atmosphere one of exquisitely faded charm. The water was hazardous, plumbing was often antediluvian, and the franc was a precarious currency.

All that has changed. The *Mairie,* or town hall, has taken the townscape firmly in hand. Buildings are regularly cleaned and restored; monuments have been regilded. Planning controls prevent unwarranted demolitions and inappropriate developments. The avenue des Champs-Elysées has polished its position as an important—if no longer quite classy—business and touristic thoroughfare. Street-cleaning operations have been impressively, and quite visibly, streamlined—smart, green-uniformed workers push smart, green brooms and even the city trash bins are green to tie in with the color scheme.

Improvements to the open spaces have also helped the environment. A number of small parks and squares, many dating from the 19thC, now have playgrounds, benches, and well-tended flower beds. Parisians are apartment-dwellers and courtyard-tenders, and their need for green space has been recognized.

Throughout the 1980s and into the 1990s, this prospering, confident Paris was seized by an urge to build on a grandiose scale. The government of the late President François Mitterrand—determined to put France and the French capital at the cutting edge of urban renewal—financed numerous costly, ambitious, architecturally challenging projects: the Opéra Bastille; the Cité des Sciences at La Villette; and the Grande Arche at La Défense, surrounded by a huge, gleaming "Manhattan-sur-Seine" complex of skyscrapers. Most breathtaking in its scope and daring was the transformation of the Musée du Louvre, symbolized by I. M. Pei's glass pyramid thrusting through the Cour Napoléon.

Projects planned years ago will soon be realized, such as the transformed Jardins du Tuileries, the new Musée de la Mode et du Textile in the Louvre, and the Bibliothèque de France. President Jacques Chirac continues his own schemes to improve the cultural heritage—with plans to restore the Pompidou Center, the Grand Palais, as well as the Musée Guimet, all of which will be under construction in 1996 and 1997. Following the lead set by the government's *grands travaux,* or major works, private money has funded other major schemes, including the Grand Ecran Gaumont, now the largest cinema screen in Paris, and the Cartier Center, now an important venue for the contemporary arts.

While the city powders its face, its population flees to the suburbs to make ends meet—an exodus only partially stemmed by attractive housing subsidies. Not surprisingly, abject poverty has become more visible in Paris. The cardboard-box-dwellers are in evidence in many central areas, and beggars, many tragically young, frequent the métro stations.

President Chirac, a neo-Gaullist with a strong vision of France's world role, maintains his country's commitment to the European Union. But his first year in office was characterized by confusion and uncertainty as he attempted to cut the country's unprecedented 12% unemployment rate and slash public spending at the same time, resulting in the largest civil disobedience in France since 1968. His problems were compounded by a series of deadly terrorist attacks that struck Paris in the fall of 1995, aggravating the feeling of disarray in the capital.

Will an increasingly divided French electorate continue to support ambitious public works, with so many citizens out of work and the country's much vaunted social security system in serious debt? The politicians' message seems to be that France and its capital must remain at the center of the civilized world: A reasonable goal, to be sure, but one that unavoidably means investing taxpayer money on a lavish scale, with an eye to the long, not the short, term.

If this vision of France as a great economic and cultural power is to survive through the 21stC, the country's fast-changing yet timeless capital must continue its drive to reinvent itself. Witnessing the city in the midst of its current adventure is both to admire, and understand, something of the spirit propelling France today.

An Overview of the City

What might be called "Greater Paris"—that is, the entire metropolitan area—covers 479 square kilometers (185 square miles) and has a population of just over 9 million. But with only a few exceptions, including Disneyland Paris, this guide focuses on the city proper.

Cut in two by the Seine, and surrounded by the beltway, or ring road, known as the *Périphérique,* the city of Paris covers only 106 square kilometers (41 square miles). Though just over 2 million inhabitants are crammed into this small area, by a miraculous sleight of hand, Paris still gives an impression of spaciousness.

The city is divided into 20 *arrondissements,* or administrative districts. Each arrondissement has its own urban ambiance, lifestyle, even a distinct accent. Within the arrondissements, and often overlapping them, are *quartiers* (quarters), such as **Montmartre, Montparnasse,** and the **Latin Quarter.** This seeming inconsistency was the work of Napoléon III, who intentionally drew arrondissement boundaries to split existing villages and lessen their revolutionary tendencies.

The **Seine** divides the city into **Rive Droite** (Right Bank) and **Rive Gauche** (Left Bank) with the 2 islands, **Ile de La Cité** and **Ile St-Louis,** in the middle. The Right Bank is conspicuous by its affluence and smartness and its high concentration of imposing buildings, large shops, museums, and theaters. The districts of bright lights (and red ones) are also mostly concentrated on the Right Bank. The Left Bank has its share of fine buildings and some dazzle, but on the whole its charm is more subtle, romantic, and bohemian.

From a visitor's point of view, the districts of greatest interest are the 1er to the 9e, with a few pockets in outlying places. Much of this central area is superb walking territory. The districts on the outskirts beyond the Périphérique do not belong to Paris proper, except for the **Bois de Boulogne** and **Bois de Vincennes,** but there are places of interest, such as **La Défense,** the **Flea Market** at Clignancourt, and **St-Denis** basilica.

Identifying the Arrondissements & Postal Codes

On maps and in common usage, the 20 arrondissements are shown by a numeral followed by the raised letters *er* or *e* representing *premier, deuxième, troisième,* etc. The

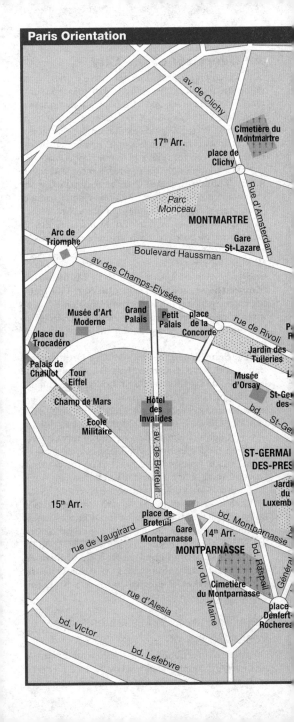

av. de Clichy

Cimetière du
Montmartre

17th Arr.

place de
Clichy

Rue d'Amsterdam

Parc
Monceau

MONTMARTRE

Gare
St-Lazare

Arc de
Triomphe

Boulevard Haussman

av des Champs-Elysées

Musée d'Art
Moderne

Grand
Palais

Petit
Palais

place
de la
Concorde

rue de Rivoli

P
P

place du
Trocadéro

Jardin des
Tuileries

L

Palais de
Chaillot

Tour
Eiffel

Musée
d'Orsay

Champ de Mars

Hôtel
des
Invalides

St-Ge
des-

bd.

St-Ge

Ecole
Militaire

av. de Breteuil

ST-GERMAI
DES-PRES

Jardi
du
Luxemb

15th Arr.

place de
Breteuil

bd. Montparnasse

rue de Vaugirard

Gare
Montparnasse

14th Arr.

MONTPARNASSE

bd. Raspail

av. du Maine

Général

rue d'Alesia

Cimetière
du Montparnasse

place
Denfert
Rocherea

bd. Victor

bd. Lefebvre

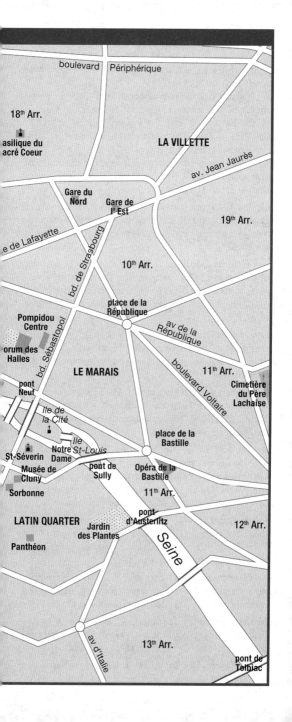

1er is in the center of the city, and the numbers are arranged in a spiral that works outward in a clockwise direction.

Postal codes are easy to decipher. Usually, in postal addresses, the number of the arrondissement is preceded by the Paris code 750. For example, the 9e is 75009, the 18e is 75018. The postal code precedes the word Paris and is generally written 75009 Paris.

The following list describes briefly the most significant *quartiers,* with their corresponding, often overlapping arrondissements.

Opéra Quarter (part of 1er, 2e, and 9e)   An area of grand architecture, smart shops, and highbrow culture. Glossy and expensive, but somewhat fraying at the edges.

Les Grands Boulevards (part of 9e and 10e)   Just east of the smart Opéra Quarter; strong magnet for shoppers, with a good range of restaurants, hotels, and cafes. The big cinemas are on the boundary of the 9e and 10e.

Les Halles (part of 1er)   A touristy, mostly pedestrian area following massive redevelopment, filled with shops, restaurants, sights cultural and otherwise, and the **Forum** itself.

Le Marais (3e and part of 4e)   An old, gracious district, now very fashionable. Blessed with many fine 17thC mansions (*hôtels*), museums, narrow rambling streets, and a strong flavor of the past.

Ile de la Cité & Ile St-Louis (part of 1er and 4e) The first is the historic heart of Paris containing the **Conciergerie, Palais de Justice, Sainte Chapelle,** and **Notre-Dame.** Busy and touristic. The Ile St-Louis, by contrast, is charming, quiet, and residential.

Latin Quarter (5e)   This area, originally known as the Université, has remained the learned quarter of Paris. Youthful, cosmopolitan, colorful, bohemian, with a large student population.

St-Germain (6e and part of 7e)   A quarter with a wide boulevard, tiny side streets, old buildings, and a thriving cafe life. Intellectual, artistic, and elegant.

Montparnasse (straddling 14^{ea} and 15^e)   Cosmopolitan, former bohemian colony, torn apart by redevelopment, but retaining some of its old character.

Eiffel Tower, Les Invalides & Environs (remainder of 7e)   Quiet, mainly residential area dominated by the axes of the **Champ-de-Mars** and Hotel des Invalides complex.

Palais de Chaillot & Environs (16e)   Cluster of museums set in an opulent residential arrondissement.

Avenue des Champs-Elysées & Rue du Faubourg-St-Honoré (8e)   Busy with tourists, businesspeople, and professional workers; expensive, classy stores; embassies.

Parc de Monceau & Environs (straddles 8e and 17e)   Stolid and residential.

Montmartre (18e)   Often referred to as the "Butte"; location of the **Sacré-Coeur** basilica. Rambling, picture-postcard quaintness, side by side with neon-lit but shabby razzle-dazzle.

Belleville/Ménilmontant (straddling 19e and 20e)   Its former dilapidated charm now largely eroded by redevelopment. Strong North African flavor. Notable mainly for Père Lachaise cemetery.

Bastille/Bercy (12e)   Both areas transformed by redevelopment. With the Opéra Bastille completed in 1990 and formally opened in 1991, the works at Bercy added the Viaducs des Arts to the recent Palais Omnisports and the Ministère des Finances.

Tolbiac (13e)   Until now an area of little distinction, the Tolbiac has suddenly become the focus of attention, as the swathe of land below the Gare d'Austerlitz reemerges to house the TGB (Bibliothèque de France).

DINING

Dining Out in Paris

Cooking in France is regarded not as a necessity but as an art, and its leading exponents, such as Paul Bocuse, Michel Guérard, Alain Ducasse, and Alain Senderens, are held in godlike esteem. They are the modern-day successors of the immortalized 19th- and early 20th-C chefs Carême and Escoffier, masters of haute cuisine.

Although lavishly appointed and witheringly expensive restaurants dot the Paris landscape, they are not necessarily purveyors of haute cuisine. Haute cuisine is that magic chemistry of art and science that sets the standard for cooking all over the world. The ingredients are often many and costly, the preparation calling for a large and rigorously-schooled team of professionals, and that creative magic that only a few chefs can bring to the art of cooking. At best, the earth should move. It's also said that at least one dish should break all the rules, such as Senderens' famous coupling of foie gras with cabbage. Remember, too, that even the most sophisticated and daring of chefs should be judged by their simplest dishes—a plain roasted chicken, for example.

One of the most important culinary revolutions in France took place not so long ago. Begun after World War II by such chefs as Alexandre Dumaine, André Pic, and Fernand Point, it was termed simply nouvelle cuisine. (The term *nouvelle cuisine* had in fact been used in the 1740s during a similar culinary sea change.)

The 5 main tenets of nouvelle cuisine were that produce should be fresh and of the highest quality; under- rather than over-cooked whenever possible; undisguised by rich, often difficult to digest sauces; imaginatively combined with other ingredients; and attractively presented in smaller, more manageable portions.

Nouvelle cuisine was not a total culinary revolution, because although the ideas were different, the methods remained the same; it was, and remains today, a far-reaching adaptation of classic French cooking to the requirements of the late 20thC.

As everyone knows, the abuses of nouvelle cuisine—crazy concoctions and miserly portions—gave it a bad name, so much so that people today often speak of its death or demise (if they speak about it at all). Yet, the fact is that much of what you find in contemporary French restaurants—new, inventive combinations of the freshest seasonal ingredients that burst with flavor in your mouth—is influenced by nouvelle cuisine. The point is that this new way of cooking was indeed a revolution, not a fad, and as such it has changed and will continue to change the culinary landscape for years to come.

At the same time, it would be a mistake to imagine that nouvelle cuisine, however influential, has swept traditional French cooking entirely aside. On the contrary, classic dishes—*coq au vin, gratin dauphinois,* and whole stuffed cabbage—today are enjoying a new popularity. The quest for all things authentic has invigorated many a French restaurant in the nineties, with a strong emphasis on regional specialties and rib-sticking *cuisine bourgeoise:* everything from chicken with calvados and apples (Normandy) to aïoli (Provence), choucroute (Alsace), and cassoulet (Gascony). The modern Parisian is as interested in ferreting out an authentic *bouillabaisse* or a real *pissaladière* as he or she is the latest innovations of 3-star cooking.

The selection of restaurants that follows focuses on French cuisine, but there are many other cuisines to try. Moroccan and Vietnamese cuisine, in particular, are well represented in Paris.

Choosing a Place to Eat

If you can be persuaded to eat your main meal at midday, you can benefit from exceptional prix-fixe "menus" at many of the city's culinary palaces. In addition, restaurants with months-long waiting lists will often have tables available at lunchtime.

Brasseries are restaurants-cum-cafes that—with their moleskin banquettes, long bars, and outdoor tables—decorate most of the city's large boulevards. A brasserie meal can be both lively and inexpensive, especially if the people-watching is good and there's a soul-satisfying *blanquette de veau* accompanied by a *pichet* of house wine set out on your table (a few accommodating places are listed below).

That said, the sad truth is that it isn't an absolute given that eating at an indiscriminately chosen brasserie will have anything over eating at the lowest-rent fast-food joint. Dismayingly, your pickings at many a brasserie melts down to a nest of wilted green lettuce smothered in gooey industrial vinaigrette, blandly overcooked vegetables, and that tough and salty staple, *steak frites.*

A cheese omelet or a simple but tasty ham-and-cheese sandwich served on a baguette, ubiquitously called a *sandwich mixte,* are available at almost any brasserie and are safe bets when you don't know the establishment.

The same goes for the city's many cafe-restaurants. Look carefully at the menu in the window. If the chef takes any trouble, there will be a few *plats du jour, specialités,* or unusual dishes. A drab list of easy-to-cook steaks and microwaveable stews bodes ill.

The Restaurant Menu

The set-menu offers good value at more expensive restaurants, though the choice of dishes may be limited, and the portions smaller than regularly priced meals.

Fortunately, the service charge now has to be included, by law, in the quoted price. The days of deciding exactly how much to tip have passed.

A full, 5-course meal in France begins with an *entrée* (or appetizer), often quite elaborate and very often vegetable-based, followed by a main course, salad, cheese, dessert, and coffee. A *ménu dégustation,* or tasting menu, offers small portions of many—sometimes as many as 9—courses and is designed to show off the chef's range of expression.

Choosing & Ordering Wine

Although there is much talk about asking the advice of a wine waiter (*sommelier*), in fact there are hardly two dozen Paris restaurants that have one who is properly qualified. The good news is that a restaurant need not have a sommelier to keep a good wine list. Try asking advice from the owner, who is not infrequently the person who greets and seats customers, and is probably also the one who buys the wines.

Although wine waiters often get a bad rap for over-selling, a new generation of sommelier is much more user-friendly. Their job is not to steer you to the most expensive wine in the cave, but to the wine that is well-matched to your budget, and to what you're ordering. Before asking for advice, look at the wine list, so that you understand the price range and qualities offered. There are invariably some bargains, but these are not always easy to find. On average, the mark-up is about 2.5 times higher than the price you would pay in a wine store. When you know nothing about the subject, either ask, or turn to the Bordeaux and order the third least expensive wine on the list.

French wines are classified into *Appellation d'Origine Contrôlée* (AOC), *Vin Délimité de Qualité Supérieure* (VDQS), *Vin de Pays,* or *Vin de Table,* but none of these titles bring an absolute guarantee of quality. They simply mean that each category must conform to certain criteria of origin, vinification, and grape variety. The criteria are more strict for AOC than VDQS, and so on down the scale, and prices reflect this. Good value, however, can be found in each category.

Vin de Pays, literally "country wine," offers the best value in many restaurants. These wines have a less prestigious provenance, but are made according to strict rules.

The reputation of the grower, château, or *négociant* (middleman) is another extremely important factor. If a name is not familiar, it is often wiser to choose according to the year, because a good vintage VDQS can often be of better quality and value than a mediocre vintage of an AOC. Some wine in the lower categories is blended by the shippers and often does not carry vintage dates.

VDQS is being slowly phased out, leaving AOC and *Vin de Pays* as the 2 categories. If you want only a half-bottle (*demi bouteille*), your choice is likely to be restricted. *Vin de Table* is commonly served in carafes or jugs called *pichets.*

Wine & Food

Rules are made to be broken, and you can always be adventurous and allow yourself to be guided by your palate and pocket. When eating regional food, however, you may want to pick a wine from the same area. Some partnerships are enshrined in gastronomic legend: red Bordeaux with lamb, Muscadet with shellfish, Riesling with choucroute. Others are less obvious but equally enjoyable: In the Loire Valley they enjoy salmon with a light red, such as Chinon or Saumur Champigny. Dishes from Provence, with their emphasis on fruity

olive oil, tomato, and herb flavors, are well matched by
Provençal and Rhône wines. The cuisine of the Lot
and Dordogne, built around rich foods such as preserved duck, goose, and truffles, is complemented by
the red wines of Bergerac, Cahors, and Duras.

How to Use This Chapter

Our selection of restaurants has been made to give you
a varied range of prices and cuisines throughout Paris.
Nearest métro stations are given, as well as stars showing restaurants representing good value in their own
class.

Restaurants are listed alphabetically, for speed of
reference. They're also listed by arrondissement.

The prices corresponding to our price symbols are
based on the average cost of a meal for 1 person, without wine. Tax is included (now an astonishing 20.6%),
as well as a service charge. Although actual prices will
inevitably increase as time passes, our relative price categories are likely to remain the same.

Price Chart

$$$$$	Very Expensive, More than 500F
$$$$	Expensive, 301F–500F
$$$	Moderate, 201F–300F
$$	Inexpensive, 120F–200F
$	Cheap, Under 120F

Restaurants by Arrondissement

1er

Café Marly. **$$/$$$**
Café Richelieu. **$/$$**
Chez Issé. **$$$$**
L'Ecluse. **$/$$**
Gaya. **$$$**
Gérard Besson. **$$$$**
★★★ Le Grand Véfour.
    $$$$$
Pharamond. **$$$/$$$$**
Au Pied de Cochon. **$$$**
★★ Restaurant du Palais-
    Royal. **$$$**
La Terrasse Fleurie. **$$$$**
Toupary. **$$**
Willi's. **$$**

2e

★ Le Vaudeville. **$$$**

3e

L'Ambassade d'Auvergne.
    $$$
★ Anahi. **$$/$$$**
★ Au Bascou. **$$**
★★★ Chez Nenesse. **$$/$$$**
★ Chez Omar. **$$**

4e

★★★ L'Ambroisie. **$$$$$**
★★ Benoît. **$$$$**
Bofinger. **$$$**
Ma Bourgogne. **$$**
Brasserie de l'Ile St-Louis. **$$**
Le Dôme Bastille. **$$**
Le Grizzli. **$$**
★ L'Impasse. **$$**
La Taverne du Sergent
    Recruteur. **$$**

5^e

Le Balzac. **$$**
★ Campagne et Provence. **$$$**
Dodin Bouffant. **$$$$**
Institut du Monde Arabe. **$$$**
Au Pactole. **$$$**
Toutoune. **$$**

6^e

★★★ Les Bookinistes. **$$$**
Brasserie Lipp. **$$$**
Casa Bini. **$$$**
Le Chat Grippé. **$$$**
Le Cherche Midi. **$$/$$$**
★ La Closerie des Lilas. **$$/$$$**
Crèmerie-Restaurant Polidor. **$/$$**
L'Ecluse. **$/$$**
★★ L'Epi Dupin. **$$**
La Hulotte. **$$/$$$**
Jacques Cagna. **$$$$$**
Lapérouse. **$$$$**
★ Marie et Fils. **$$/$$$**
La Méditerranée. **$$$$**
★ Le Petit St-Benoît. **$$**
Le Petit Zinc. **$$$**
Le Procope. **$$$**
★★ La Rôtisserie d'en Face. **$$**

7^e

★ L'Arpège. **$$$$$**
Bistrot de Paris. **$$/$$$**
Chez Ribe. **$$**
Aux Fins Gourmets. **$$**
★ Jules Verne. **$$$$$**
La Petite Chaise. **$$**
★ Le Télégraphe. **$$$**
Thoumieux. **$/$$**

8^e

L'Appart. **$$/$$$**
L'Avenue. **$$$**
Bateaux-Mouches. **$$$$**
Café Indochine. **$$/$$$**
Cercle Ledoyen. **$$$**
Chez Edgard. **$$/$$$**
Daru. **$$$**
L'Ecluse. **$/$$**
La Fermette Marbeuf 1900. **$$$**
Laurent. **$$$$$**

Ledoyen. **$$$$$**
Maxim's. **$$$$$**
Au Petit Montmorency. **$$$$**
Régence. **$$$$$**
La Table du Marché. **$$$**
★ Taillevent. **$$$$$**

9^e

Chartier. **$**
Au Petit Riche. **$$$**
Ty-Coz. **$$$**

10^e

Brasserie Flo. **$$**
Julien. **$$/$$$**
★★ Da Mimmo. **$$$**
Terminus Nord. **$$**

11^e

★★★ Les Amognes. **$$**
★ L'Astier. **$$**
Chardenoux. **$$/$$$**
Chez Paul. **$$**
L'Ecluse. **$/$**
Mansouria. **$$**

12^e

★★★ Square Trousseau. **$$$**
Au Trou Gascon. **$$/$$$**

14^e

La Coupole. **$$$**
Le Dôme. **$$$$**
Natacha. **$$$**
Le Pavillon Montsouris. **$$$**
★★★ La Régalade. **$$**

15^e

★★ La Dinée. **$$$$**
Morot-Gaudry. **$$$$**
★★★ L'Os à Moelle. **$$**
★ Le Petit Plat. **$$$**
Pierre Vedel. **$$$**
★ Restaurant du Marché. **$$$**

16^e

★ L'Auberge du Bonheur. **$$/$$$**
★ La Butte Chaillot. **$$$**
★ Chalet des Iles. **$$$**
Au Clocher du Village. **$$/$$$**
Le Pré Catelan. **$$$$$**
Prunier-Traktir. **$$$$**

★★ Relais du Parc. **$$$**
★★★ Robuchon. **$$$$$**
Le Vivarois. **$$$$$**

17e

★ Les Bouchons de François
   Clerc. **$$/$$$**

Chez Fred. **$$**
Guy Savoy. **$$$$$**

18e

★ A. Beauvilliers. **$$$$/
   $$$$$**
Le Maquis. **$$$**

Restaurants by Cuisine

*French/The Top Tables
of Paris*

★★★ L'Ambroisie. **$$$$$**
★ L'Arpège. **$$$$$**
★ A. Beauvilliers. **$$$$/
   $$$$$**
★★ Benoît. **$$$$**
★★ La Dinée. **$$$$**
Dodin Bouffant. **$$$$**
Gérard Besson. **$$$$**
Le Grand Véfour. **$$$$$**
Guy Savoy. **$$$$$**
Jacques Cagna. **$$$$$**
★ Jules Verne. **$$$$$**
Lapérouse. **$$$$**
Laurent. **$$$$$**
Ledoyen. **$$$$$**
Maxim's. **$$$$$**
Morot-Gaudry. **$$$$**
Au Petit Montmorency. **$$$$**
Le Pré Catelan. **$$$$$**
Régence. **$$$$$**
★★★ Robuchon. **$$$$$**
★ Taillevent. **$$$$$**
La Terrasse Fleurie. **$$$$**
Le Vivarois. **$$$$$**

*French Bistros (Moder-
ately Priced)*

L'Amognes. **$$**
L'Appart. **$$/$$$**
★ L'Astier. **$$**
★ L'Auberge du Bonheur.
   $$/$$$
Bateaux-Mouches. **$$$$**
Bistrot de Paris. **$$/$$$**
Bofinger. **$$$**
★★★ Les Bookinistes. **$$$**
★ Les Bouchons de François
   Clerc. **$$/$$$**
Brasserie Flo. **$$**
La Butte Chaillot. **$$$**
Cercle Ledoyen. **$$$**
★ Chalet des Iles. **$$$**
Chardenoux. **$$/$$$**
Chartier. **$**

Le Chat Grippé. **$$$**
Chez Edgard. **$$/$$$**
★★★ Chez Nenesse. **$$/$$$**
Chez Paul. **$$**
Chez Ribe. **$$**
Au Clocher du Village.
   $$/$$$
Crèmerie-Restaurant Polidor.
   $/$$
★★ L'Epi Dupin. **$$**
La Fermette Marbeuf 1900.
   $$$
Aux Fins Gourmets. **$$**
La Hulotte. **$$/$$$**
★ L'Impasse. **$$**
Julien. **$$/$$$**
Le Maquis. **$$$**
★ Marie et Fils. **$$/$$$**
Natacha. **$$$**
L'Os à Moelle. **$$**
Au Pactole. **$$$**
Le Pavillon Montsouris. **$$$**
★ Le Petit Plat. **$$$**
Au Petit Riche. **$$$**
★ Le Petit St-Benoît. **$$**
Le Petit Zinc. **$$$**
La Petite Chaise. **$$**
Pharamond. **$$$/$$$$**
Pierre Vedel. **$$$**
★★★ La Régalade. **$$**
★★ Restaurant du Palais-
   Royal. **$$$**
★★★ Square Trousseau. **$$$**
La Taverne du Sergent
   Recruteur. **$$**
★ Le Télégraphe. **$$$**
Toupary. **$$$**
Toutoune. **$$**
★ Le Vaudeville. **$$$**

*Regional French
Cuisine*

Auvergne
L'Ambassade d'Auvergne.
   $$$

Basque
★ Au Bascou. **$$**
Burgundy
Ma Bourgogne. **$$**
Lyonnais
Chez Fred. **$$**
Mediterranean
La Table du Marché. **$$$**
Provençal
★ Campagne et Provence.
$$$
Southwestern
Le Grizzli. **$$**
★ Restaurant du Marché. **$$$**
Thoumieux. **$/$$**
Au Trou Gascon. **$$/$$$**

Seafood
Le Dôme. **$$$$**
Le Dôme Bastille. **$$**
Gaya. **$$$**
La Méditerranée. **$$$$**
Prunier-Traktir. **$$$$**
Ty-Coz. **$$$**

Spit-Roasted
La Rôtisserie d'en Face. **$$**

Cafes/Brasseries—
Open All Day
L'Avenue. **$$$**
Le Balzar. **$$**
Brasserie de l'Ile St-Louis. **$$**

Brasserie Lipp. **$$$**
Café Marly. **$$/$$$**
Café Richelieu. **$/$$**
★ La Closerie des Lilas.
$$/$$$
La Coupole. **$$$**
Au Pied de Cochon. **$$$**.
Le Procope. **$$$**
Terminus Nord. **$$**

Wine Bars
L'Ecluse. **$/$$**
Willi's. **$$**

Foreign
Cambodian
Café Indochine. **$$/$$$**
Italian
Casa Bini. **$$$**
Le Cherche Midi. **$$/$$$**
★★ Da Mimmo. **$$$**
Japanese
Chez Issé. **$$$$**
Middle Eastern
Institut du Monde Arabe. **$$$**
Moroccan
Mansouria. **$$**
North African
★ Chez Omar. **$$**
Russian
Daru. **$$$**
South American
★ Anahi. **$$/$$$**

Critic's Choice

For a romantic dinner out, there isn't a restaurant in Paris that can beat the intimate and softly lit **L'Ambroisie,** located in the wonderfully romantic place des Vosges. You'll have the meal of a lifetime, as well. Or try **A. Beauvilliers,** perched on a hill in Montmartre, where the service is attentive and the interior is decorated like a charming private home. A lush and glorious spot to wow someone is **Le Grand Véfour,** located just off the exquisite Palais-Royal.

For a typically Parisian night out, try dining at **Chez Nenesse,** a small bistro, classic in look, in the Marais. Afterwards, stroll the quiet cobblestoned streets, stopping in at one of the old-style cafes dotting the area.

If you're in the mood to celebrity gaze, try **Natacha,** where you may spot the likes of actress Béatrice Dalle or director Wim Wenders. Hollywood and French film stars eat here so often it's like the canteen on a film set. Or, to see the stylish arbiters of fashion—from supermodels to designers—air-kissing over a meal, try the **Café Indochine,** or settle into the plush banquettes at the **Café Marly.**

For an evening of celebrating, the atmosphere is always reliably festive at **La Coupole.** Or drink champagne to your heart's content at **Les Bouchons de François Clerc,** where the Taittinger Brut is only 121 francs a bottle.

The best place to dine with a view is the **Jules Verne,** in the Eiffel Tower, where the cooking is getting better and better. Or, for a cheaper meal, try the Lebanese specialties at the restaurant in the **Institut du Monde Arabe.**

Restaurants A to Z

L'Ambassade d'Auvergne

22 rue du Grenier-St-Lazare, 3e. ☎ 01-42-72-31-22. AE, MC, V. Open daily. Métro: Rambuteau. **$$$**. AUVERGNE/FRENCH.

Many Parisian cafe-owners hail from the Auvergne. When they have something to celebrate, they will, as often as not, head for this invitingly rustic "embassy" of Auvergnat tradition to savor the dishes of their childhood—such as *jambon d'Auvergne,* a stuffed *poitrine d'agneau,* or the traditional *aligot* (cheese whipped into potatoes). The Auvergnat cheeses are superb, as is the welcome, the family atmosphere . . . and the food.

★★★ L'Ambroisie

9 pl. des Vosges, 4e. ☎ 01-42-78-51-45. AE, MC, V. Closed Sun, Mon. Métro: Bastille. **$$$$$**. FRENCH.

Master chef Bernard Pacaud's L'Ambroisie has a Michelin 3-star rating. Partly due to the setting on place des Vosges, and the beauty and intimacy of the interior, this is one of the most romantic of Paris's gastronomic temples. Built toward the end of the 16thC, the house was refashioned by François-Joseph Graf, who brought to its high-ceilinged dining room a Venetian elegance. An immense tapestry dominates the tranquil, flower-decorated space. Pacaud's cooking is a feast of invention, as in the feuilletine of lobster tails seasoned with sesame and served in a curry sauce, or a millefeuille with rhubarb for dessert. Book weeks ahead.

★★★ Les Amognes

243 rue du Faubourg St-Antoine, 11e. ☎ 01-43-72-73-05. MC, V. Closed Sun, Mon. Métro: Faldherbe-Chaligny. **$$**. FRENCH.

This little restaurant, belonging to Thierry Coué, a pupil of Alain Senderens, offers an inventive take on classic French cuisine. Virtually everyone comes here for the 4-course "menu" that's one of the city's real culinary bargains. The service is impeccable. Perfect for an elegant dinner out at a budget price.

★ Anahi

49 rue Volta, 3e. ☎ 01-48-87-88-24. MC, V. Reservations advised. Open daily. Métro: Arts et Métiers. **$$/$$$**. SOUTH AMERICAN.

The 2 sisters who turned this former charcuterie into an outpost for South American cuisine bustle about their cozy restaurant creating a familial atmosphere. Specialties include guacamole served with big pieces of homemade toast, wonderful Argentinean grilled steaks, and jumbo shrimp served with a spicy sauce. The margaritas are heavenly.

L'Appart

9 rue du Colisée, 8e. ☎ 01-53-75-16-34. AE, V. Reservations advised. Open daily. Métro: Franklin-D-Roosevelt. **$$/$$$**. FRENCH.

Thanks mostly to a reliable selection of lighter dishes, all attractively priced, this restaurant—cozily designed to resemble a chic Parisian apartment—has built a faithful following among well-heeled young Parisians out for a night on the town. A new bar area has seating around a cozy fireplace. Then too, it's a welcome oasis in the midst of all the touristy places that overrun the nearby Champs Elysées. Ask for a table upstairs.

★ L'Arpège

84 rue de Varenne, 7e. ☎ 01-45-51-47-33. AE, D, MC, V. Closed Sat and Sun for lunch. Métro: Varenne. **$$$$$**. FRENCH.

Young chef Alain Passard has been the dauphin on the Paris culinary scene since he opened here in 1986. His exquisitely inventive cuisine—the house specialty is the canard Louis Passard—are a treat, and the wine list is top notch. The expensively redesigned interiors have a smart, pale, modernist look that is coolly fragile but oddly impersonal, too. There's nothing very Parisian-looking about the place, which, at these prices, is sure to disappoint some.

★ L'Astier

44 rue Jean-Pierre Timbaud, 11e. ☎ 01-43-57-16-35. MC, V. Reservations advised. Closed Sat, Sun, Aug. Métro: Parmentier. **$$**. FRENCH.

A gem of an old-style bistro with a familial air and tables crammed together in what you will either find cozy or cramped, depending on your definition of personal space. The servings are hearty and scream home-cooking, especially the pâtés and lamb stews. There's something life-affirming in the sheer size of that runny cheese plate being handed over from table to table at the end of a meal. L'Astier is out in the middle of nowhere, but you get more than your money's worth, especially if you go for one of the good house reds.

★ L'Auberge du Bonheur

Bois du Boulogne, allée de Longchamp, 16e. ☎ 01-42-24-10-17. AE, MC, V. No reservations in summer. Wheelchair access. Summer, open daily; winter, lunch only; closed Sat. Métro: Porte Maillot. **$$/$$$**. FRENCH.

Tucked inside the city's largest park, this garden restaurant is still (surprisingly) an insider's find. The setting is strictly rural, with the tables set out on gravel surrounded by trees, and a branch brushing your shoulder. This is a place for grilled steaks—the house specialty is the côte de boeuf for two—and hearty sautéed potatoes. In winter, the tables move inside, near the fireplace. On warm evenings there's

Right Bank Restaurants

often a wait—it's a good idea to show up before 8:30pm. It's a long walk from the métro, so you may want to take a cab.

L'Avenue

41 av. Montaigne, 8e. ☎ 01-40-70-14-91. AE, MC, V. Reservations advised. Open daily; closed Aug. Métro: Franklin-D-Roosevelt. **$$$**. CAFE/BRASSERIE.

Ladies who shop for a living rest their Ferragamo pumps at this smart restaurant/tea salon/brasserie for tea or a light lunch. You can ring up a good-sized bill ordering those vaguely Italian, vaguely "international cuisine" meat

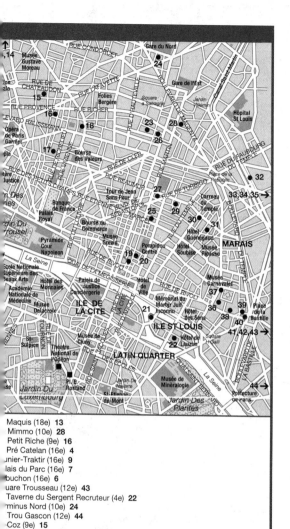

and fish dishes on the menu (designed by illustrator Pierre Le Tan), but you're much better off sticking to the perfectly acceptable and reasonably priced club sandwich or fresh tomato and mozzarella salad. The whole place is drowning in good taste, not surprising given that it's owned by the largest luxury conglomerate in the world (Moët Hennessy–Louis Vuitton) and was designed by celebrity decorator Jacques Grange.

Le Balzar
49 rue des Ecoles, 5e. ☎ 01-43-54-13-67. AE, MC, V. Open daily;

closed Aug. Métro: Cluny-La-Sorbonne. **$$**. CAFE/ BRASSERIE.

Owner Jean-Pierre Egurreguy took over this 1930s classic in 1987 and had the good sense not to change anything about it (except to install some welcomed air-conditioning). Solid, traditional fare—skatefish poached in butter, liver pan-cooked with sautéed potatoes—is served in this old-fashioned Latin Quarter brasserie by dashingly expert waiters in waistcoats and long aprons. The clientele to be found eating here (or having a drink in the small cafe section) includes academics and members of the literary and publishing worlds.

★ Au Bascou

38 rue Réaumur, 3ᵉ. ☎ 01-42-72-69-25. AE, MC, V. Reservations advised. Métro: Arts-et-Métiers. **$$**. BASQUE.

Since 1992, new owner Jean-Guy Loustau has revved up the southwestern cuisine in this casual but very good bistro that attracts a local crowd as well as itinerant trendies from the nearby Marais. Inside, the place can get pretty crowded and smoky, but chef Jean Marie Toyos's Basque country cooking—including a *morue fraîche à la mode de Biscaye* served with onions and tomatoes and *piment doux*—doesn't disappoint. The terrace is festive, when it's warm enough.

Bateaux-Mouches

Pont de l'Alma, 8ᵉ. ☎ 01-42-25-96-10. AE, MC, V. Lunch 1pm; dinner 9:30pm. Reservations required. Jacket and tie required at dinner. Closed Mon lunch. Métro: Alma-Marceau. **$$$$**. FRENCH.

Eating on a Bateaux-Mouches cruiser as it chugs up and down the River Seine is a romantic and remarkably neat way to combine traffic-free sightseeing with good classical food. Two options available: a 300F lunch trip and a 500F dinner outing (jacket and tie required). Both prices include a full meal (count on traditional fare—*filet de boeuf* in a béarnaise sauce, etc.) plus wine and coffee. Totally touristy and not cheap, but the boat ride is special, particularly after dark. Go. You may be surprised at how much you enjoy it.

★ A. Beauvilliers

52 rue Lamarck, 18ᵉ. ☎ 01-42-54-54-42. AE, V. Reservations required. Closed Sun, Mon lunch. Métro: Lamarck-Caulaincourt. **$$$$/$$$$$**. FRENCH.

One has the sense here of being a guest in a calm and beautiful 19thC private house, and that is precisely the effect that owner Edouard Carlier has striven to create. The restaurant is filled with lovely things: antique silver, porcelain, flowers, and Carlier's own superb collection of prints. The house itself stands on the hillside of Montmartre. The food, served either indoors or on the small but extremely pretty terrace, matches the surroundings—Carlier aims for top quality, and always seems to achieve it. A rich crowd, most of whom look like they just got in from Monte Carlo. Probably the most pleasant spot to enjoy an evening in Montmartre.

★★ Benoît

20 rue St-Martin, 4ᵉ. ☎ 01-42-72-25-76. No credit cards. Reservations advised. Wheelchair access. Closed Aug. Métro: Hôtel de Ville. **$$$$**. FRENCH.

The acknowledged classic of Parisian bistros, Benoît is

postcard perfect: gleaming brass, immaculate red banquettes, starched linens. The menu is ferociously traditional—they still serve dishes like cassoulet or a cold *pot au feu salade*—which is why Paris society likes to give private parties here. Try the prized, black-footed chicken of Brest, one of the few French foods outside of cheese and wine that has been awarded AOC status. (For an explanation of AOC, *Appellation d'Origine Contrôlée*, see "Choosing & Ordering Wine," above in this chapter.)

Bistrot de Paris

33 rue de Lille, 7e. ☎ 01-42-61-16-83. AE, MC, V. Reservations required. Closed Sat lunch, Sun. Métro: rue du Bac. **$$/$$$**. FRENCH.

This fashionable classic bistro is the jewel in the crown of restaurant supremo Michel Oliver. The close-set tables are packed, the conversation animated, the Art Nouveau decor ravishing, and the food first-class—such as the *croustillant d'agneau aux aubergines*. But, this is such a place for regulars that you may feel vaguely left out. The bill undoubtedly reflects not only the food but the famous faces to be found eating here.

Bofinger

5-7 rue de la Bastille, 4e. ☎ 01-42-72-87-82. AE, D, MC, V. Reservations advised. Wheelchair access. Never closes. Métro: Bastille. **$$$**. FRENCH.

Some 132 years old in 1996, this is reputedly the oldest brasserie in Paris. There's that familiar background roar you get in all busy brasseries come evening; the bustle gives the place a certain energy. The beautiful Art Nouveau interiors and moleskin banquettes are the perfect background for late-night post-opera or -theater suppers, especially when you're studying them across a huge plate of oysters or, what the hell, a heaping dish of choucroute (they have 4 varieties). Reserve a table on the ground floor under the exquisite glass roof.

★★★ Les Bookinistes

53 quai des Grands-Augustins, 6e. ☎ 01-43-25-45-94. AE, MC, V. Reservations advised. Closed Sat lunch and Sun. Métro: St-Michel. **$$$**. FRENCH.

A stone's throw from the Pont Neuf, this is one of Guy Savoy's 5 baby bistros. Dishes are careful orchestrations of prime ingredients—milk-fed pork served in its own terrine, tuna carpaccio with baby vegetables and grilled parmesan—that are meant to dazzle, and do. With pale lemon-colored walls and wood floors, Les Bookinistes aims to be fashionable—and is, though not enough to be scary. Well-dressed gallery owners from the Left Bank and fashionable young professionals flock here.

★ Les Bouchons de François Clerc

22 rue de la Terrasse, 17e. ☎ 01-42-27-31-51. AE, MC, V. Wheelchair access. Closed Sat lunch and Sun. Métro: Villiers. **$$/$$$**. FRENCH.

A kind of thunderous roar was heard throughout the restaurants of Paris when François Clerc opened his restaurant here selling *grands crus* at wholesale prices. For example, a Calon Ségur St-Estèphe 1988, 122F; Champagne Taittinger brut, 121F. The fine cuisine, including *tournedos de thon* (tuna) served with foie gras, and the wine couldn't go down any easier at these prices. The best place to sit is on the terrace, where 6 tables of 6, prettily set with white china and linens, are flanked by flower boxes on a tiny pedestrian walkway.

Ma Bourgogne

19 pl. des Vosges, 4e. ☎ 01-42-78-44-64. No credit cards. Open daily; closed Feb 1–Mar 7. Métro: Bastille. **$$**. BURGUNDY.

The rule about eating on the place des Vosges is simple: Unless you're splurging for haute cuisine at L'Ambroisie, you skip all the other non-sense and go straight to Ma Bourgogne. Traditional bistro fare—from a good *sandwich mixte* (ham and cheese) to copious salads, steak tartare, Burgundy specialties, and ice cream by Berthillon. The inside is smoky and claustrophobic, but the tables outside afford an unbeatable view of the stunning 17thC arcade balustrading what is probably the most beautiful square in the city.

Brasserie Flo

7 cour des Petites-Écuries, 10e. ☎ 01-47-70-13-59. AE, D, MC, V. Reservations advised. Open daily; serves until 1:30am Métro: Chateau-d'Eau. **$$**. FRENCH.

One of Jean-Paul Bucher's 6 Paris restaurants (see also La Coupole, Julien, Terminus Nord, and Le Vaudeville), Brasserie Flo reflects his Alsatian origins in its food and drink, with beer drawn from the barrel. The turn-of-the-century decor, with its stained-glass panels, leather-covered bench seating, and landscapes painted by Morel de Tangry, was entirely cleaned and restored in 1994. There is a very good late-night bargain: a 112F menu that includes

a quarter bottle of wine, available after 10pm.

Brasserie de l'Ile St-Louis

55 quai de Bourbon, 4e. ☎ 01-43-54-02-59. No credit cards. No reservations. Closed Thurs lunch, Wed and Aug. Métro: Pont-Marie. **$$**. CAFE/BRASSERIE.

An institution of sorts, this brasserie is popular with Anglo-Saxon kids as well as Parisians looking for an inexpensive place for an impromptu lunch. Glasses of beer and Riesling are the standbys here, as well as dishes such as *tarte à la oignon* and *salade de pommes de terre avec saucisse*—which are mostly unremarkable, though generously piled on. This is a good place to come for a salad and a dish of Berthillon sorbet (they have been selling it for 30 years) on a hot afternoon of sightseeing, if you can snag a table on the terrace.

Brasserie Lipp

151 blvd. St-Germain, 6e. ☎ 01-45-48-53-91 (telephone reservations not accepted). AE, D, MC, V. Open 8am (for breakfast) to 12:45am (main meals from noon). Closed Aug. Métro: St-Germain-des-Prés. **$$$**. CAFE/BRASSERIE.

This delightfully intact turn-of-the-century brasserie attracts the capital's intellectual, political, and showbizzy elite in far greater swarms than any other Parisian restaurant, however chic. The previous owner, Roger Cazes, died in 1987, and the Lipp is now run by his nephew, M. Perrochon. Following the tradition of his uncle, Perrochon is famously careful in seating clients. The unknowns usually get sent up to the 1st floor (where the occasional celebrity is to be spotted), but beware: It is perfectly possible to be turned away, even if the place is not full. Dogs are allowed—provided that they have the right owners. Impeccable service by long-aproned and long-serving waiters, reliable plats du jour, and the herd instinct explain Lipp's phenomenal success.

★ La Butte Chaillot

110bis av. Kléber, 16e. ☎ 01-47-27-88-88. AE, MC, V. Open daily. Métro: Trocadéro. **$$$**. FRENCH. Top chef Guy Savoy is a prolific spawner of offshoots of his own eponymous 2-star establishment (see also Les Bookinistes), and here's another of his children (see "Dining Large on a Budget," below). However you feel about 3-star chefs slumming it in cheaper digs, this is one of the best food values in the city. Some of the more succulent entries now include a spit-roasted Brest chicken and crispy dorade with a Provençal gratin of vegetables. It attracts cigar-smoking 30-year-olds and their stylish companions.

Café Indochine

195 rue du Faubourg St-Honoré, 8e. ☎ 01-53-75-15-63. AE, D, MC, V. Reservations advised. Open daily; closed Sat lunch. Métro: Ternes. **$$/$$$**. CAMBODIAN.
Almost a club for the fashion crowd in the area. Cambodian delicacies—crêpes vapeurs stuffed with duck or shrimp, poulet grillé au satay—and a lot of air-kissing against a decor inspired by French Indochina.

Café Marly

93 rue du Rivoli, 1er. ☎ 01-49-26-06-60. AE, MC, V. Reservations advised; no reservations taken for the terrace. Open daily, 8am–2am. Métro: Palais-Royal/Musée-du-Louvre. **$$/$$$**. CAFE/BRASSERIE.
A fashion hot spot that snagged the single best cafe location in Paris: the Louvre courtyard. Sit on the balustraded terrace and watch the moonlight on I. M. Pei's pyramid; alternately, ogle models at the next table. Inside, the velour chairs, Pompeian burgundy-and-gilt walls, and handblown chandelier set off the historically classified boiserie. The menu is a quick spin around the world: a little sushi, a club sandwich, a pasta dish, grilled sole; but the point here isn't the food, it's all about those high-powered media lunches taking place all around you. Reserve a table in the front room, for the view. In summer, come right before 8pm to snag one of the good tables outside. The service is friendlier than you'd expect in such a boiler room of fashion.

Café Richelieu

109 rue de Rivoli, 1er. ☎ 01-47-03-99-68. AE, DC, MC, V. No reservations. Wheelchair access. Closed Tues and national holidays. Métro: Palais-Royal/Musée-du-Louvre. **$/$$**. CAFE/BRASSERIE.
Opened in November 1993, this cafe inside the recently re-opened Richelieu wing of the Louvre has an unbeatable view of the pyramid in the museum courtyard. With its tasty selection of pains au chocolat, cheesecake, and other pastries, it's a good place to break for coffee when visiting the museum. Architect Jean-Michel Wilmotte, who also recently spruced up the lamplights and benches on the Champs Elysées, pulled together a team of designers to furbish the interior. Daniel Buren—who put all those little columns in the Palais-Royal—ran blue and white stripes all

over the walls, the tables, the chairs, even the coffee cups. Photographer Francis Giacobetti provided the black-and-white portraits that plaster the walls, and Jean Pierre Reynaud inset the vaulted ceiling with ceramic tiles to evoke Fra Angelico's *L'Annunciation.* This is the place to go to study that museum catalogue or read the *Herald Tribune.* At dinnertime, the livelier place to be is downstairs, at the Louvre's Café Marly (see above).

★Campagne et Provence

25 quai de la Tournelle, 5e. ☎ 01-43-54-05-17. MC, V. Closed for lunch Sat and Mon, all day Sun, Aug. Métro: Maubert-Mutualité. **$$$**. PROVENÇAL. Paris—like the rest of the world—has gone Provence-mad in the past few years; this restaurant is one of the better of the endless southern cousins that have recently descended on the city. Formerly owned by Giles Epie, the restaurant has changed hands, and the new chef, Patrick Jeffroy, serves up some of the best Provençal-style cooking you'll find in Paris today, including dorade grilled with pastis-flavored fennel and rabbit cooked in a *tapenade.* The small interior is all de rigueur pastels—still, it's not very impressive. Though purists might not appreciate a certain "updating" of classic dishes, the place is always lively.

Casa Bini

36 rue Grégoire-de-Tours, 6e. ☎ 01-46-34-05-60. AE, D, V. Closed Sat and Sun lunch, Aug. Métro: Mabillon. **$$$**. ITALIAN. An elegant pasta hot-spot for Parisian literati. Tuscan dishes and nouvelle-style pasta dishes, including pasta with baby vegetables and *tagliolini au citron.*

Cercle Ledoyen

Carré des Champs-Elysées, 8e. ☎ 01-47-42-23-23. AE, D, MC, V. Reservations advised. Closed Sun. Métro: Champs-Elysées-Clemenceau. **$$$**. FRENCH. Located on the ground floor of the Parisian institution **Ledoyen,** (see below), this is the budget restaurant of the establishment, which is set back from the street and located in a glitzy mansion. The pluses are that you get to pull up to the same gorgeous building with the sweeping drive, and choose from an array of dishes overseen by the only female among Paris's top chefs, Ghislaine Arabian. All the starters are one price, ditto the main courses and desserts; so a whole meal is really a steal. The problem is, the menu is somewhat limited, and if you are quite picky there's no guarantee you'll find something you like. The very grand interiors are by Jacques Grange; in the summer, the tables go up under parasols out in the equally grand, very manicured garden. Bourgeois French families out for lunch with grand-mère like to come here.

★ Chalet des Iles

Lac du Bois de Boulogne, 16e. ☎ 01-42-88-04-69. AE, D, MC, V. Reservations required. Open daily. Métro: rue de la Pompe. **$$$**. FRENCH. A romantic ferry boat takes you across the lake to the island where this restaurant is located. There is a superb terrace in the summer, but the chalet's large glass windows make it equally appealing in the cold months. Dishes—shrimp curry flavored with mango and celery and a raspberry cheesecake—are pleasant enough but the unusual setting is why everyone comes here. The boats goes back and forth every few minutes so you never have to wait very long. The small cafe next door, having the same owners, is a nice place to come for a drink when spending the day in the park in summer.

Chardenoux

1 rue Jules Vallès, 11ᵉ. ☎ 01-43-71-49-52. AE, MC, V. Reservations advised. Closed Sat lunch and Sun. Métro: Charonne. **$$/$$$**. FRENCH.

Not far from the Bastille, this is an excellent Parisian bistro with a historically classified interior. The engraved glass, marble bar, carved woodwork, and ceiling moldings date from 1904, when the restaurant first opened. Owner Bernard Passavant serves up food in the classic tradition, including a roast saddle of lamb seasoned with thyme and *rognon de veau rôti entier*. Reliably good food in a traditional setting.

Chartier

7 rue du Faubourg-Montmartre, 9ᵉ. ☎ 01-47-70-86-29. MC, V. No reservations. Open daily. Last orders 9:30pm. Métro: rue-Montmartre. **$**. FRENCH.

This is Paris's sole-surviving mid-19thC bouillon decor (bouillons were popular restaurants, or soup kitchens), and the management seems to have no intention of changing the format or their most precious asset, an unspoiled historic decor. The unassuming facade is easily missed; it's down an alleyway opposite the Cité Bergère just before the boulevard Montmartre.

Chartier has fed Paris's working classes since the 1800s, and prices don't seem to have risen much since then. There's a line to get in, and don't hope for more than a couple of sliced tomatoes and a piece of roasted chicken, but the price couldn't be cheaper, and the bohemian atmosphere, not the food, is what it's all about. Chartier serves more than a thousand meals a day—you feel quite rushed—and really, what else would you want to know?

Another branch, of equally good value, is Le Drouot, at 103 rue de Richelieu, 2ᵉ (☎ 01-42-96-68-23).

Le Chat Grippé

87 rue d'Assas, 6ᵉ. ☎ 01-43-54-70-00. AE, MC, V. Reservations advised. Wheelchair access. Closed Mon and Sat lunch. Métro: Port-Royal. **$$$**. FRENCH.

Le Chat Grippé is a small, elegant, and well-regarded establishment in the hinterland of the Luxembourg Gardens, an area not over-endowed with restaurants. The menu changes seasonally and is geared to market availability; recent entries included a *langoustine rôtie à la crème de petit pois* and a *croustillant d'agneau aux fleurs de courgettes*. Two tasting menus are available at dinner.

Le Cherche Midi

22 rue du Cherche Midi, 6ᵉ. ☎ 01-45-48-27-44. No credit cards. Reservations advised. Open daily. Last orders midnight. Métro: Sèvres-Babylone. **$$/$$$**. ITALIAN.

The Italian cantine of the smart left-bank set. Smoky and packed—but nonetheless a pretty little restaurant where the food is good. It offers a small but consistently good-quality menu with a variety of fresh pastas (3 are made in-house daily) and carpaccio served with mushrooms, celery, and parmesan.

Chez Edgard

4 rue Marbeuf, 8e. ☎ 01-47-20-51-15. AE, D, MC, V. Reservations required. Closed Sun. Métro: Franklin-D-Roosevelt. **$$/$$$**. FRENCH.

Perhaps the most startling thing about this excellent if rather noisy restaurant, which is located in the plush business quarter of avenue George-V, is its wide spectrum of prices. The food is not the bargain it once was, but you can still enjoy a 3-course meal for an extremely reasonable price. The fare is simple but imaginative, with the accent mostly on seafood—in winter they bring it from Brittany.

Chez Fred

190bis blvd. Pereire, 17e. ☎ 01-45-74-20-48. AE, D, V. Closed Sun. Métro: Ternes. **$$**. LYONNAIS.

A cozy bistro serving good, solid traditional Lyonnais dishes (terrines, coq au vin, etc.). Chez Fred is a great favorite with television and showbizzy personalities, though the popular owner has recently departed.

Chez Issé

56 rue Ste-Anne, 1er. ☎ 01-42-96-67-76. MC, V. Reservations advised. Closed Sat and Sun, Mon lunch. Métro: Pyramides. **$$$$**. JAPANESE.

The best restaurant in Paris for grilled fish, sushi, and sashimi, at non–sushi-bar prices. Designers like Issey Miyake and Kenzo and executives from Shiseido keep the newly decorated rooms (spare furnishings and pale woods) crowded.

★★★ Chez Nenesse

17 rue de Saintonge, 3e. ☎ 01-42-78-46-49. V.

Reservations advised. Closed weekends year-round, and the entire month of Aug. Métro: Filles-du-Calvaire. **$$/$$$**. FRENCH.

Everyone is always looking for that cozy, unspoiled Parisian bistro—well, voilà. A tiny gem with high ceilings, wood floors, and white tablecloths, totally lost in the heart of the Marais, that's about as old-fashioned Parisian as you can get. A sturdy menu of traditional French fare turns up a few inventive surprises: Try the asparagus and langoustine salad when in season or the saddle of lamb with fresh mint.

★ Chez Omar

47 rue de Bretagne, 3e. ☎ 01-42-72-36-26. No credit cards. Reservations advised. Closed Sun lunch. Métro: Arts et Métiers. **$$**. NORTH AFRICAN.

An extremely hip, fashionable following comes here for a good inexpensive couscous (especially vegetable or chicken) and excellent grilled lamb. The tables are almost poised on top of each other, the noise is airport-level, but Omar greets everyone like family.

Chez Paul

13 rue de Charonne, 11e. ☎ 01-47-00-34-57. AE, MC, V. Reservations advised. Open daily. Métro: Bastille. **$$**. FRENCH.

A Parisian institution that offers home-cooking at relatively painless prices.

This small and aggressively unpretentious bistro stars lots of local atmosphere and is usually packed with neighborhood regulars. The goat-cheese salad and cold fish platter are good values; watch out for huge portions. A few tables are set outside in warm weather.

Chez Ribe

15 av. de Suffren, 7e. ☎ 01-45-66-53-79. AE, D, V. Closed

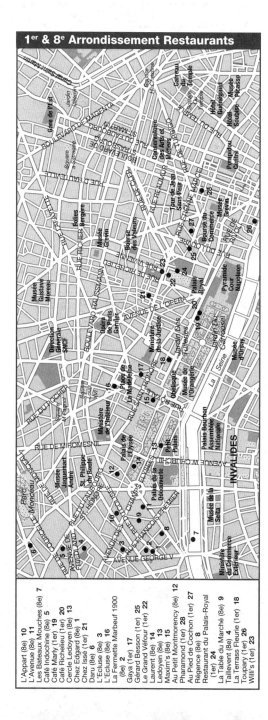

1er & 8e Arrondissement Restaurants

Sat lunch and Sun. Métro: Bir-Hakeim. **$$**. FRENCH.
Bistro Parisian-style, it offers 10 starters and 10 main course menu options—including *carré d'agneau* and aïoli—on a very reasonably price-fixed menu.

Au Clocher du Village

8bis rue Verderet, 16e. ☎ 01-42-88-35-87. No credit cards. Closed for lunch Sat and Sun year round, entire month of Aug. Métro: Eglise d'Auteuil. **$$/$$$**. FRENCH.

A picture-postcard place with the atmosphere of an old auberge, located in a charming little village square. Lace curtains, old posters on the walls, wine presses hanging from the ceiling, the place positively oozes charm. The food is excellent (try the *agneau* sautéed with apricots), well-prepared, classic French cuisine—leaving you glad to have had a taste of the "real France."

★ La Closerie des Lilas

171 blvd. du Montparnasse, 6e. ☎ 01-43-26-70-50. AE, D, MC, V. Wheelchair access. Open daily. Métro: Port-Royal. **$$/$$$**. CAFE/BRASSERIE.

La Closerie has always been, and is still, the haunt of literati, artists, and plain hacks. Nowadays, they tend to congregate in the bar and brasserie section, whose prices are lower than in the restaurant proper, where a pleasant terrace—recently enlarged—accommodates an altogether more bourgeois crowd, and the food is appropriately classical.

La Coupole

102 blvd. du Montparnasse, 14e. ☎ 01-43-20-14-20. AE, D, MC, V. Open 7:30am to 2am. Closed Christmas eve. Métro: Vavin. **$$$**. CAFE/BRASSERIE.

La Coupole is Paris's largest brasserie, and an institution; its 600 seats continue to be sought-after, from prelunch to the early hours. It probably serves the most varied crowd of customers to be found in any Paris eating place—politicians and movie-producers to photographers and students—all appreciative of the excellent exposure afforded by La Coupole's open plan with its long, broad aisles. Intelligently refurbished and part of the Flo group, La Coupole offers good-quality fare. Go for the ambiance, but do not expect a tranquil meal; this is food-consumption at its noisiest.

Crèmerie-Restaurant Polidor

41 rue Monsieur-le-Prince, 6e. ☎ 01-43-26-95-34. No credit cards. No reservations. Métro: Odéon. **$/$$**. FRENCH.

Polidor gives away a 3-course set meal for a fantastically low price. Little has changed in this 150-year-old *bouillon* since the days of Verlaine, Valéry, and Joyce: There are still lace curtains, numbered napkin lockers (some in use), a spiral staircase, and even waitresses in turn-of-the-century dress. Good *cuisine bourgeoise, ragoûts,* and *blanquettes.*

Daru

19 rue Daru, 8e. ☎ 01-42-27-23-60. V. Closed Sun, Aug. Métro: Courcelles. **$$$**. RUSSIAN.

White Russians, many of them taxi drivers, used to recall the "good old days" over a glass of vodka and a *zakouski* in this grocery/snack-bar opposite the Russian Orthodox Church. Although most of them have since departed this world, the Daru remains a repository of Russian tradition, boasting a score of Russian and Polish vodkas. There is also tasty food for every purse, from tarama and borscht to smoked salmon and caviar.

★★ La Dinée

85 rue Leblanc, 15e. ☎ 01-45-54-20-49. AE, MC, V. Reservations advised. Closed Sun lunch and Sat. Métro: Balard. **$$$$**. FRENCH.

Persnickety French food critic Guy Pudlowski made this smart and spacious bistro his big find for 1995; now reservations are more advised than ever. Young chef Christophe Chabanel likes a blend of traditional and exotic, wittily and often beautifully served, such as the pan-cooked foie gras with artichokes. A menu offering very good value is available at dinner.

Dodin Bouffant

25 rue Frédéric-Sauton, 5e. ☎ 01-43-25-25-14. AE, D, MC, V. Closed Sat lunch and Sun. Métro: Maubert-Mutualité. **$$$$**. FRENCH.

One of the finest restaurants in the capital—and certainly one of the best values for quality food. A winter specialty is game, particularly hare. The restaurant offers wonderful fish combinations, a sumptuous and utterly fresh *plateau de fruits de mer,* and unusual meat dishes—everything market-fresh.

Le Dôme

108 blvd. du Montparnasse, 14e. ☎ 01-43-35-25-81. AE, D, MC, V. Closed Sun, Mon, and Aug. Métro: Vavin. **$$$$**. SEAFOOD.

A huge, bustling cacophonic restaurant, specializing in impeccably prepared fish, that is a Montparnasse institution. They serve one of the freshest *bouillabaisses* (a Provençal fish stew) you'll find north of Marseilles, and the oysters—from the fish shop next door—are as fresh as they come in Paris. The next door Bistrot du Dôme (1 rue Delambre, 14e, ☎ 01-43-35-32-00; métro: Vavin; **$$**; AE, MC, V; reservations advised; open daily) is a cheaper alternative offering up daily specials, and the atmosphere is quite informal and lively. Or try Le Dôme Bastille (below).

Le Dôme Bastille

2 rue de Bastille, 4e. ☎ 01-48-04-88-44. AE, MC, V. Reservations advised. Open daily. Métro: Bastille. **$$**. SEAFOOD.

A pretty and comfortable 2-story Dôme offshoot that just should be a little cheaper to feel right. Nonetheless, the grilled sea bass and langoustines are top-rate. Some of the starters, like the meat-stuffed vegetables, are mostly puzzling: play it safe here and stick to fish, like the baby clams in a thyme-broth. Or skip a starter and make a meal of a main course and a dessert—the bill will be all the more reasonable and you won't have missed much. The bottles on the short but well chosen wine list are all priced at 98F. Walk on the wild side and order a Bordeaux, such as a young Côtes de Bourg, with your *dorade.*

L'Ecluse

Four branches:
15 quai des Grands-Augustins, 6e. ☎ 01-46-33-58-74. Métro: St-Michel
64 rue François-1er. ☎ 01-47-20-77-09. Métro: George-V
15 pl. de la Madeleine, 8e. ☎ 01-42-65-34-69. Métro: Madeleine
13 rue de la Roquette, 11e. ☎ 01-48-05-19-12. Métro: Bastille
For all: AE, MC, V. Open daily year-round. Last orders 1:30am. **$/$$**. WINE BAR.

Throughout this wine-bar chain, the good selection of vintage wines available at reasonable prices can be accompanied by excellent cold dishes: *carpaccio*, foie gras, smoked salmon, *saucisson sec*, goat cheese, and a superbly rich and sticky chocolate cake that connoisseurs travel far to sink their teeth into. The "grands crus" here are open and can be drunk by the glass.

★★ L'Epi Dupin

11 rue Dupin, 6e. ☎ 01-42-22-64-56. V. Reservations advised. Closed Sat lunch and Sun. Métro: Sèvres-Babylone. **$$**. FRENCH.
A low-key and charming new restaurant with a 153F set price for a 4-course meal— a very good value given the quality of the food. Successful inventions include the *pissaladière* (a thin crust topped with tomatoes, onions, and paper-thin slices of tuna), and a sautée of lamb and potatoes, topped with parmesan and served inside a whole grilled eggplant skin. The desserts are somewhat sweet, but after they've brought out the 2-foot-wide wheel of brie and carved you a slice, you won't be hungry enough to care. The room is soothingly pretty, with half-timbered walls and a cozy banquette along one wall. In warm weather, they have tables outside, and the street is quiet, if unglamorous.

La Fermette Marbeuf 1900

5 rue Marbeuf, 8e. ☎ 01-53-23-08-00. AE, D, MC, V. Open daily year-round. Métro: Alma-Marceau. **$$$**. FRENCH.
A superb Art Nouveau restaurant with a stunning glass roof, La Fermette was recently taken over by the Blanc brothers, owners of Procope and Pied de Cochon

(see "Cafes & Tea Salons" below). This busy and rather noisy eating place offers highly-quality classic French cuisine— *côte de boeuf bordelaise, barbue aux graines de sesame grillées*— with regular seasonal changes. It caters to a mixed bag of business and media people.

Aux Fins Gourmets

213 blvd. St-Germain, 7e. ☎ 01-42-22-06-57. No credit cards. Closed Sun, Mon, Aug. Métro: rue du Bac. **$$**. FRENCH.
A cheerful little bistro that prides itself on being unmodernized—one of the few remaining bastions of yellowing lincrusta wallpaper and banquette seating—and where one feels totally at home, sitting elbow-to-elbow with the French, who are out in force at this excellent outlet for the country cuisine of the southwest. Huge helpings of *cassoulet* and *gigot*, filling desserts, and a generous cheeseboard made a warm impression, as did the low final price.

Gaya

17 rue Duphot, 1er. ☎ 01-42-60-43-03. AE, MC, V. Closed Sun. Métro: Madeleine. **$$$**. SEAFOOD.
Another of the Parisian baby bistros, this one belongs to the tonier Gourmand-Prunier located next door. (Yet another offspring, also called Gaya, is in the 7e, at 44 rue du Bac, ☎ 01-45-44-73-73.) Relatively new, Gaya attracts a crowd of smart and well-heeled young professionals tucking into the just-fish menu. Not terribly lively, and expensive for an offshoot restaurant.

Gérard Besson

5 rue Coq-Héron, 1er. ☎ 01-42-33-14-74. AE, D, MC, V.

Reservations advised. Wheelchair access. Closed Sat lunch and Sun. Métro: Palais-Royal/Musée-du-Louvre. **$$$$**. FRENCH. Gérard Besson, whose career took in a period at Jamin, has a classical yet very personal style that contrasts refreshingly with the striving-after-effect of which some innovative chefs are guilty. He also lays down his own wines, with a stock of some 45,000 bottles.

★★★ Le Grand Véfour

17 rue de Beaujolais, 1ᵉʳ. ☎ 01-42-96-56-27. AE, D, V. Closed Sat, Sun, Aug. Métro: Bourse. **$$$$$**. FRENCH. If you walk out of the Palais-Royal at its north end, you can spy this softly lit restaurant tucked under the arcade. Founded in 1784, this is simply one of the world's most beautiful restaurants. The decor dates from the Directoire, and so much of it is extant it is classified as a historical monument. This is the world-famous Le Grand Véfour, formerly home ground of much-traveled author and cook Raymond Oliver, now the property of Jean Taittinger, of champagne fame. The excellent food, created by Guy Martin, is full of winning surprises, like a ravioli de foie gras with an emulsion of truffle-flavored crème fraîche.

Le Grizzli

7 rue St-Martin, 4ᵉ. ☎ 01-48-87-77-56. AE, MC, V. Closed Sun. Métro: Châtelet, Les Halles. **$$**. SOUTHWESTERN FRENCH. Owner Bernard Areny and chef Patrick André have kept the southwestern culinary tradition well-stoked in this century-old bistro—which means hearty portions and meats cooked on a heated slate (*sur ardoise*). A blackboard announces the day's specials;

for something lighter, try the cold ratatouille served with a poached egg. Imagine a big ham set out for carving, bistro chairs, white tablecloths, salamis strung from a dumbwaiter, and you'll get the picture.

Guy Savoy

18 rue Troyon, 17ᵉ. ☎ 01-43-80-40-61. AE, MC, V. Métro: Charles-de-Gaulle-Etoile. **$$$$$**. FRENCH. Guy Savoy has many offshoots around the city (see box below), but this is his namesake restaurant established in 1987. Born in southeastern France, Savoy is one of cooking's great entrepreneurs. Spring is always announced with a market garden stew featuring zucchini, artichokes, peas, and more in crushed tomatoes, tarragon, and olive oil. The winter version is a swankier version of a classic *potée*—cabbage, carrots, and onions with truffles shaved over the top. There is always a main course composed strictly of vegetables, such as a ragout of mushrooms and artichokes. Impeccable ingredients, pre-paration, and presentation. The one complaint here is that Guy occasionally descends into the soulessness of 3-star cooking. Recently redecorated in soft beige and green, the restaurant is quite impersonal and businesslike—you feel like you're in one of those places where powerful people have power dinners on one of the power spokes of the Champs Elysées.

La Hulotte

29 rue Dauphine, 6ᵉ. ☎ 01-46-33-75-92. AE, D, MC, V. Closed Sun, Mon, Aug. Métro: Odéon, Pont-Neuf. **$$/$$$**. FRENCH. This restaurant's snug little upstairs dining room—recently refurbished—is a haven of reliability in the shark-infested

waters of Latin Quarter catering. A basket of brown bread served, unusual for Paris, with a little dish of butter and a jug of good cheap wine will keep your hunger and thirst at bay while you wait for a very reasonable *filet d'agneau à l'estragon*. Follow that with one of their excellent desserts and you'll leave contented.

★ L'Impasse

4 impasse Guéménée, 4e.
☎ 01-42-72-08-45. MC, V.
Reservations advised. Closed Sat and Mon for lunch, Sun, Aug.
Métro: Bastille. **$$**. FRENCH.
An unpretentious restaurant on a tiny side-street in the Marais that offers up uncomplicated cooking (salads, *boeuf bourguignon*, *filet de veau*) in a homey atmosphere, with genuinely friendly and accommodating service. A few tables on the street in summer.

Institut du Monde Arabe (Restaurant Fakhr el Dine)

1 rue des Fossés-St-Bernard, 5e.
☎ 01-46-33-47-70. AE, D, V.
Wheelchair access. Closed Sun eve, Mon. Métro: Cardinal Lemoine, Sully-Morland. **$$$**.
MIDDLE EASTERN.
This widely acclaimed new building has attracted international attention. The south facade overlooking the visitor entrance is composed of geometric shapes that open and close according to the light. The 9th-floor restaurant, by contrast, is set within a sweeping terrace that has views of the river through walls of glass and metal. The views equal that at La Tour d'Argent but at half the price. The food, mainly good Lebanese-Arab specialties, should be taken as part of an overall experience.

Jacques Cagna

14 rue des Grands-Augustins, 6e.
☎ 01-43-26-49-39. AE, CB, D, MC, V. Reservations required. Jacket and tie required. Closed Sat lunch, Sun, 3 weeks Aug.
Métro: St-Michel. **$$$$$**.
FRENCH.
This and L'Arpège are the 2 haute cuisine palaces of the Left Bank. While L'Arpège is probably better in terms of sheer culinary mastery, Jacques Cagna is located in a 17thC townhouse that's one of the most beautiful restaurant settings in Paris. The period Dutch paintings, oak beams, and terra-cotta walls are all cozily lit by soft lighting—a rarity in Parisian restaurants. Cagna's *poularde de Houdan* is served in 2 stages (the wing followed by the leg), accompanied by wild mushrooms and is out of this world. At lunch, the special 270F menu is one of the better gastronomic bargains in town.

★ Jules Verne

Tour Eiffel, 2e étage (2nd floor), 7e
(access via private lift). ☎ 01-45-55-61-44. AE, D, V. Reservations required, allow 2 months. Open daily. Métro: Champ-de-Mars Tour Eiffel, Bir-Hakeim. **$$$$$**.
FRENCH.
Getting better and better, with Alain Reix getting more and more adventurous in his cooking—as in a delicate turbot grilled with green apples—Jules Verne is more popular than ever. Built on a 500-square-meter (598-sq.-yd.) platform, between the great wheels and the pulleys of the tower's elevator mechanism, and sitting 123 meters (135 yd.) above the city, the restaurant offers breath-taking views in every direction. Even the ceiling offers glimpses, through glass panels, of the metal structure

up to the top of the tower, some 150 meters (164 yd.) higher. Reserve—possibly weeks ahead. For the best of all views, ask for the intermediate room (salle intermédiaire) between the bar and the room facing the Palais de Chaillot. From here, the panorama takes in every conceivable sight. Once considered a tourist trap, but no more, the Jules Verne is outpacing everyone's expectations.

Julien

16 rue du Faubourg-St-Denis, 10e. ☎ 01-47-70-12-06. AE, D, MC, V. Wheelchair access. Closed Christmas Eve. Last orders 1:30am. Métro: Strasbourg-St-Denis. **$$/$$$**. FRENCH.

Jean-Paul Bucher, owner of 6 top Parisian eating places, has single-handedly done more than anyone to save authentic restaurant decors from the modernizer's axe. Although both Brasserie Flo and Le Vaudeville are splendid, the jewel in Bucher's crown must be Julien, which sports some of Paris's most fabulous Art Nouveau designs, including a number of murals by Alphonse Mucha. It's much favored by a lively crowd of young professionals. The food is classical and straightforward—*escalope de foie gras, choucroute*—with a slight Alsatian bias.

Lapérouse

51 quai des Grands-Augustins, 6e. ☎ 01-43-26-68-04. AE, D, MC, V. Wheelchair access. Closed Sun, Mon lunch, Aug. Métro: St-Michel. **$$$$**. FRENCH.

The decor of this restaurant facing the Seine is that of a bourgeois interior of the 19thC, with its concealed doors, overladen woodwork, and private rooms for 2 to 8

diners, often frequented by politicians and writers. The cuisine is classic—*brochette de langoustines, ris de veau à l'oseille, feuilleté aux poires*. A memorable place to dine.

Laurent

41 av. Gabriel, 8e. ☎ 01-42-25-00-39. AE, D, V. Wheelchair access. Closed Sat lunch, Sun. Métro: Champs Elysées Clemenceau. **$$$$$**. FRENCH.

Well-bred opulence is the keynote of this distinguished establishment, occupying a delectable pavilion in the parkland setting off avenue des Champs-Elysées. All white-and-gold stucco on the outside, Second-Empire elegance inside, Laurent has a garden at the back where one can feast under the chestnut trees on a summer's day. The menu is composed of fine, classic dishes, including a satisfying *foie gras de canard* with spicy black beans. Philippe Bourguignon, one of the top sommeliers in France, will offer discreet advice on choosing the 600-strong wine list. Service is exceptionally good. In the evening, candlelight and a pianist add to the festive atmosphere.

Ledoyen

1 Carré des Champs-Elysées, 8e. ☎ 01-47-42-23-23. AE, D, MC, V. Reservations required. Closed Sat, Sun, Aug. Métro: Champs-Elysées-Clemenceau. **$$$$$**. FRENCH.

For almost 2 centuries, this classic restaurant has been a standard bearer for elegant dining. Wielding the pots is the blond Ghislaine Arabian, noted for her tradition of cooking with beer—as in her turbot roasted in a beer sauce and fried onions. The elegant setting, in a private mansion not far from the Place de la Concorde, is a plus.

Mansouria

11 rue Faidherbe, 11e. ☎ 01-43-71-00-16. V. Open daily. Métro: Faidherbe-Chaligny. **$$**. MOROCCAN.

A big, oddly plushy place for *tagines, pastilla aux pigeons,* and other Moroccan specialties. More refined than your average couscous joint, with a shop next door selling Moroccan pottery and takeout.

Le Maquis

69 rue Caulaincourt, 18e. ☎ 01-42-59-76-07. D, MC, V. Closed Sun dinner. Métro: Lamarck-Caulaincourt. **$$$**. FRENCH.

The streets bordering that center of kitsch art, place du Tertre, are not a very good area for eating—some of the bad habits of picture-vendors seem to have rubbed off on restaurant owners. A 10-minute walk down the Butte, however, leads to this attractively decorated bistro, which offers an inexpensive set lunch and interesting à la carte food—*lotte au pistou, gigot d'agneau*—that's unfussy and reliable.

★ Marie et Fils

34 rue Mazarine, 6e. ☎ 01-43-26-69-49. AE, MC, V. Closed Mon lunch and Sun. Métro: St-Germain-des-Prés. **$$/$$$**. FRENCH.

A mother-and-son act that brings together a social left-bank crowd. Good food in a cozy bistro—upbeat, casual atmosphere.

Maxim's

3 rue Royale, 8e. ☎ 01-42-65-27-94. AE, D, MC, V. Last orders 11pm. Closed Sun. Métro: Concorde, Madeleine. **$$$$$**. FRENCH.

The reputation of this world-famous restaurant revived when it was taken over a few years ago, in the face of much skepticism, by fashion designer Pierre Cardin. Cardin has maintained and renovated its marvelous Art Nouveau decor, but Maxim's has fallen off the map for serious diners. A starry-eyed crowd of international tourists keeps the place filled.

La Méditerranée

2 pl. de l'Odéon, 6e. ☎ 01-43-26-02-30. AE, D, V. Open daily. Métro: Odéon. **$$$$**. SEAFOOD.

Fish dishes from the South of France are the headliners at this venerable restaurant, which has carried a reputation since the heady days of the early 1960s when Jean Cocteau and Orson Welles were regulars. The menus and crockery all bear the Cocteau logo. For a restaurant that's almost always been overpriced, the situation has gone sadly downhill—dishes are some-times skimpy, many of the fish dishes banal, and the service just careless. Still, it's full of memories and lovely to look at. The front opens up to become a terrace in summer and overlooks a pleasant and none-too-busy square.

★★ Da Mimmo

39 blvd. Magenta, 10e. ☎ 01-42-06-44-47. MC, V. Open Mon–Sat; closed Aug. Métro: Jacques Bonsergent. **$$$**. ITALIAN.

The tacky wall murals and the odd plastic flowers will make you feel you really are in Naples. This is one of Paris's best, though not cheapest, Italian trattorias. Pizzas are excellent, as is the baked pasta with eggplant. Ask your waiter what the fresh fish is that day—he may surprise you and bring out a plate of raw calimari from the kitchen. Try the tiramisu followed by a lemoncello, an after-dinner drink that's out of this world. The crowd here is expat Italians mingled with the odd table of trendies. Service is efficient, if not effusively friendly.

Morot-Gaudry

8 rue de la Cavalerie, 15e.
☎ 01-45-67-06-85. AE, D, MC, V. Wheelchair access. Closed Sat, Sun. Métro: La Motte-Piquet-Grenelle. **$$$$**. FRENCH.

As majestically located as La Tour d'Argent, on the top floor of a shiplike 1920s building, with a wonderful view of the nearby Eiffel Tower, this restaurant is much favored by bigwigs from UNESCO (also nearby). Concoctions here have the stamp of true originality—calf's liver with raspberries, crab *boudin,* red mullet with chanterelles. An excellent and reasonably priced set luncheon menu is deservedly popular with businesspeople. More than 1,000 wines on the list.

Natacha

17bis rue Campagne-Première, 14e. ☎ 01-43-20-79-27. AE, MC, V. Closed Sun year-round, entire month of Aug. Métro: Raspail. **$$$**. FRENCH.
This is Paris's answer to Elaine's—though here, you would and should dare to reserve a table. It's especially popular with the international film crowd, and there's no question that eating here gives you the feeling of being in the thick of the action. The bad part is that the food is less reliable; for example, an artichoke served with a poached egg inside was a nice idea, but the egg was cold. But if your

culinary expectations aren't too high, you'll enjoy the rest.

★★★ L'Os à Moelle

3 rue Vasco-da-Gama, 15e.
☎ 01-45-57-27-27. MC, V. Closed Sun, Mon, and Aug. Métro: Lourmel. **$$**. FRENCH.
Owner and chef Thierry Faucher, 27, worked the ovens at Les Ambassadeurs before setting up his own establishment here in a lost corner of the 15the. The gimmick at L'Os à Moelle is that everyone gets the same cut-price, 6-course tasting menu, spelled out on a blackboard by the door, with all the wines at one price (90F). It's a bit of a novelty act, but the deal is a good one, with a typical menu including a grilled filet of beef, risotto in a black eel sauce, and scallops in cream. When Faucher finally makes the rounds in his chef's toque, he looks like he's just run the Indie 500. Word of mouth put this restaurant on everyone's lips literally overnight, so book in advance.

Au Pactole

44 blvd. St-Germain, 5e.
☎ 01-46-33-31-31. AE, D, MC, V. Closed Sat lunch, Sun. Métro: Maubert-Mutualité. **$$$**. FRENCH.

Lunch is the best time to eat here, because, with luck, the sun will be streaming through the windows of the attractive covered terrace. The decor has bright tones of orange and yellow. Roland Magne is an inventive yet unfussy cook with a penchant for unusual combinations—kid with mint, lamb with violets. His set menu is a wonderful bargain.

Le Pavillon Montsouris

20 rue Gazan, 14e. ☎ 01-45-88-38-52. AE, D, V. Open daily.

Métro: Cité-Universitaire. **$$$**.
FRENCH.

This restaurant, decorated in
Belle Epoque style, is set in a
peaceful pavilion in the Parc
Montsouris. A shady veranda
and a summer terrace facing
banks of flowers in the park,
or a winter log-fire, provide
pleasant settings for dishes such
as *fondant de pommes de terre au
foie gras de canard,* or succulent
veal kidneys roasted with
coriander and basil.

Au Petit Montmorency

5 rue Rabelais, 8ᵉ. ☎ 01-42-25-
11-19. MC, V. Wheelchair
access. Closed Sat, Sun, Aug.
Métro: Miromesnil, Franklin-D-
Roosevelt. **$$$$**. FRENCH.

Chef Daniel Bouché follows
no school of cooking but his
own, and by doing so has
attracted a faithful and rather
chic clientele, who come back
again and again for such
inventive delights as *foie gras
au caramel,* or a deceptively
simple *côte de veau de lait.* The
restaurant has recently been
enlarged, and the decor is
pleasantly old-fashioned—
plants everywhere, ancient
kitchen utensils and en-
gravings on the walls.

★ Le Petit Plat

49 av. Emile Zola, 15ᵉ. ☎ 01-45-
78-24-20. MC, V. Reservations
advised. Closed Sun and Mon.
Métro: Charles-Michel. **$$$**.
FRENCH.

This recently opened bistro
belonging to Jean and Victor
Campreia specializes in an
expertly prepared cuisine at
moderate, though not cheap,
prices. The interior is both
comfortable and pretty, with
tables that are well spaced. This
is liberally interpreted bistro
fare that packs a lot of flavor,
as the *pastilla de canard* served
with carrots or tomatoes
proves. Friendly service.

Au Petit Riche

25 rue Le Peletier, 9ᵉ. ☎ 01-47-
70-68-68. AE, D, V. Wheelchair
access. Closed Sun. Métro:
Richelieu-Drouot. **$$$**. FRENCH.

A quite exceptional decor,
which, with its frosted
windows, large mirrors, and
brass luggage-racks, is
somewhat more Edwardian
than Belle Epoque. Still
divided into a number of small
dining rooms, this fine bistro
accommodates the après-
theater crowd at night. Good,
solid cuisine bourgeoise
without pretension is served
here, and a commendable
selection of Loire wines.

★ Le Petit St-Benoît

4 rue St-Benoît, 6ᵉ. ☎ 01-42-60-
27-92. No credit cards. Closed
Sat, Sun. Métro: St-Germain des
Prés. **$$**. FRENCH.

A real neighborhood place.
The fare is very traditional
French housewife food—
though not always made with
the same care that a wife
would take. Cheap and
fashionable in a quiet way, it
attracts not just tourists but a
steady crowd of left-bank
antiques dealers and book
editors from the St-Germain
area, who sit out on the
terrace in summer.

Le Petit Zinc

11 rue St-Benoît, 6ᵉ. ☎ 01-42-
61-20-60. AE, D, MC, V. Last
orders 2am. Métro: St-Germain-
des-Prés. **$$$**. FRENCH.

Probably the best late-night
restaurant in town; a good set-
price menu and an interesting
carte attracts a varied clientele.
Mustachioed waiters in
traditional long, white aprons
give warmly efficient service.
Gorgeous Art Nouveau decor,
full of scrolls and sinuous
curves. Always busy—
reservations are advised for
dinner.

La Petite Chaise

36 rue de Grenelle, 7ᵉ. ☎ 01-42-22-13-35. AE, MC, V. Wheelchair access. Open daily. Métro: rue du Bac. **$$**. FRENCH.

The patina of 315 years shines in this quaint old inn, which claims to be the oldest restaurant in Paris, especially in the dark and intimate bar. The decor within the dining room is more stark, perhaps a little Puritan, but it has its appeal, particularly for American visitors who come back again and again. The fixed-menu–only policy pays dividends and gives plenty of choice. The cuisine is modest, as are the prices.

Pharamond

24 rue de la Grande-Truanderie, 1ᵉʳ. ☎ 01-42-33-06-72. AE, D, MC, V. Closed Sun, Mon lunch. Métro: Les Halles. **$$$/$$$$**. FRENCH.

This gem of a restaurant is in a historically listed building, with its Art Nouveau mirrors and faïence created for the 1900 World's Fair. It's the last-remaining vestige of the heart of Les Halles market. Always famed for its succulent tripe, *andouillette*, and pig's feet, Pharamond now has a new chef, Jean-Michel Faijean, who prepares a wonderful *coquilles St-Jacques* (scallops).

Au Pied de Cochon

6 rue Coquillière, 1ᵉʳ. ☎ 01-42-36-11-75. AE, D, V, MC. Wheelchair access. Open 24 hr. Reservations only until 8:30pm, then queue. Métro: Les Halles. **$$$**. CAFE/BRASSERIE.

This old landmark of Les Halles has, alas, succumbed to the winds of change, adopting a strange, gaudy Italian style in recent years. The restaurant no longer has the atmosphere of the old Les Halles for which it was once famed—still, it has a

curious charm. Stays open day in and day out. Its customers eat their way through a ton of shellfish every day and 80,000 pigs' feet a year.

Pierre Vedel

19 rue Duranton, 15ᵉ. ☎ 01-45-58-43-17. AE, D, V. Wheelchair access. Closed Sat, Sun May–Oct. Métro: Boucicaut. **$$$**. FRENCH.

Genuine Mediterranean restaurants do not lie thick on the ground in Paris, so all the more reason to be thankful for the existence of this welcoming bistro. Vedel himself, who comes from the fishing port of Sète, naturally feels most at home with seafood (such as an excellent garlicky lobster soup or the *bourride de lotte*), but he also has a talent for inventive vegetable dishes, for example, aïoli and a gamut of combined vegetable mousses. Extremely good value for such quality.

Le Pré Catelan

Route de Suresnes, Bois de Boulogne, 16ᵉ. ☎ 01-45-24-55-58. AE, D, MC, V. Closed Sun eve, Mon, 1 week in Feb. Métro: Porte Maillot (but it's far). **$$$$$**. FRENCH.

Many well-heeled Parisians who hanker after tiptop food in an accessible pastoral setting make their way to this establishment in the Bois de Boulogne. In winter you can dine in front of logs blazing in the vast black-marble fireplace, or in summer in the orangery, surrounded by the splendid gardens.

Le Procope

13 rue de l'Ancienne-Comédie, 6ᵉ. ☎ 01-43-26-99-20. AE, D, MC, V. Last orders 1am. Métro: Odéon. **$$$**. CAFE/BRASSERIE.

The oldest restaurant in Paris, Le Procope opened as a cafe in

Left Bank Restaurants

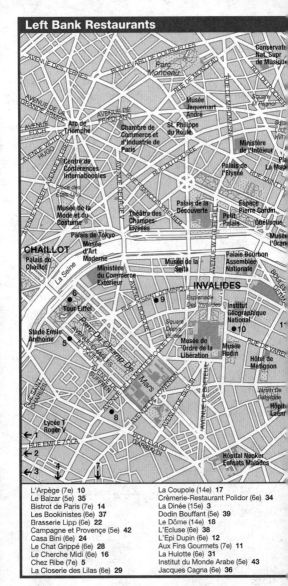

1686. Former patrons include La Fontaine, Voltaire, Benjamin Franklin, Jean-Jacques Rousseau, Robespierre, Napoléon, Balzac, George Sand, and Huysmans. Its 2 floors have retained their warm, original atmosphere.

The fare is traditional *cuisine bourgeoise* with a good selection of seafood.

Prunier-Traktir

16 av. Victor-Hugo, 16e. ☎ 01-44-17-35-85. AE, D, MC, V. Reservations advised. Wheelchair

access. Closed all day Sun and
Mon lunch. Métro: Charles-de-
Gaulle-Etoile. **$$$$**. SEAFOOD.
Opened in 1925, the original
Prunier shut down in 1990;
4 years later, the legendary
seafood site was reborn
under the direction of

Taillevent-owner Jean-Claude
Vrinat. Much of this Art Deco
restaurant—with its mosaic
facade, marble "marquetry,"
and the sculpted wood panels
behind the bar—has been
classified a historical monument. (The maritime-style

interiors were designed by Louis-Hippolyte Boileau, one of the 3 architects of the Palais de Chaillot.) Chef Gabriel Biscay worked at both the Ritz and Lapérouse before landing here. Specializing in oysters and seafood—notably a creamy lobster bisque and a turbot with girolle and morille mushrooms.

★★★ La Régalade

49 av. Jean Moulin, 14ᵉ. ☎ 01-45-45-68 58. MC, V. Reservations required. Closed Sat lunch, Sun–Mon, July and Aug. Métro: Alésia. **$$**. FRENCH.

Chef Yves Candeborde used to mind the stoves at the Hôtel Crillon; here, he serves up elevated country-cooking that is surprisingly good. Watch out for disastrously haphazard service—your main course may arrive before your entree does. The excellent food at the equally excellent prices put this restaurant on the map overnight—and has encouraged a number of other young chefs to go shopping for restaurant space in similarly less expensive neighborhoods. Though it's not centrally located, it's a must-do if you can get a table—reservations often need to be made 3 weeks in advance.

Régence

25 av. Montaigne, 8ᵉ. ☎ 01-47 23-78-33. AE, D, MC, V. Reservations advised. Wheelchair access. Open daily. Métro: Franklin-D-Roosevelt, Alma Marceau. **$$$$$**. FRENCH.

People come to the more expensive of the 2 restaurants at the Hotel Plaza-Athénée (see "Accommodations") to savor the glittering company as much as the food. In summer, tables are set in the inner courtyard, a marvelous ivy-festooned haven of coolness.

The cuisine is a mixture of classical and new styles, including the house specialty, lobster soufflé. The wine list is superb.

★★★ Relais du Parc

Hotel Parc Victor-Hugo, 55 av. Raymond Poincaré, 16ᵉ. ☎ 01-44-05-66-10. AE, D, MC. Reservations required. Wheelchair access. Open daily. Métro: Victor-Hugo. **$$$**. FRENCH.

Joel Robuchon's less expensive offshoot was designed by English decorator Nina Campbell to create a winter garden look. The service is perfunctory, and something that shouts "hotel restaurant" still lingers about the interior, yet, there's an appealing buzz to being here, and the prices are easy on the pocket. Supervised by Robuchon, chef Giles Renault concocts hearty dishes often served in their own individual casseroles. The pan-cooked St-Pierre, served with mashed potatoes, is quite good, as is the oxtail stew in wine sauce; try the latter with a fleshy 1990 red Gaillac from La Cave de Tecou in southwestern France.

★ Restaurant du Marché

59 rue de Dantzig, 15ᵉ. ☎ 01-48-28-31-55. AE, D, MC, V. Closed Sat lunch and Sun. Métro: Porte de Versailles. **$$$**. SOUTHWESTERN FRENCH.

It looks like nothing has been touched in 50 years in this restaurant, which isn't central, but don't let this dissuade you. Christianne Massia, who wears her straw-colored hair in a braid, upholds the belief that cooking done by women is more attached to the soil than that by men. Be that as it may, her bistro with a southwestern accent has many delicacies, including a pastry the thinness of cigarette paper layered and filled with prunes flavored with Armagnac. Other specialties include cassoulet and confit. In her tiny shop next door, she sells great foie gras. Everything's on the blackboard, the place is very friendly, and everyone loves the charm here.

★★ Restaurant du Palais-Royal

110 galerie de Valois, Jardins du Palais-Royal, 1er. ☎ 01-40-20-00-27. AE, DC, MC, V. Reservations advised. Wheelchair access. Closed Sat lunch and Sun. Métro: Palais-Royal. **$$$**. FRENCH.

While the Palais-Royal presents one of the rare opportunities in Paris to dine alfresco in a car-free environment overlooking one of the most beautiful public gardens in Paris, the restaurants (excepting the superb Grand Véfour, see above) actually located under those gorgeous arcades have never lived up to the real estate. The good news is new owners have reclaimed the former "Espace Champagne," given the interiors a smart new look with pale woods and glass doors, and are now serving all sorts of tasty, souped-up classics—such as the cod with bacon and diced tomatoes. In the summer, reserve a table on the terrace, sip a glass of wine from the Loire, and enjoy the smell of all that horticulture.

★★★ Robuchon

59 av. Raymond-Poincaré, 16e. ☎ 01-47-27-12-27. AE, DC, MC, V. Reservations required several weeks in advance. Closed Sat, Sun, July. Métro: Trocadéro. **$$$$$**. FRENCH.

A few years ago, Joël Robuchon left his famed Jamin behind him and moved into this luxurious Belle Epoque townhouse. An elaborate stairway trimmed with historically classified wrought-iron balustrades leads upstairs to the 3 dining rooms—all calling forth a magnificently appointed private house, with an English-style library, sculpted *boiserie,* and ornate silver. Robuchon retired in the summer of 1996 and the reins here have been taken up by another of France's great chefs, Alain Ducasse. Ducasse is a vocal advocate of a return to traditional French cuisine, and tables here continue to be reserved far in advance.

★★ La Rôtisserie d'en Face

2 rue Christine, 6e. ☎ 01-43-26-40-98. AE, MC, V. Reservations required. Closed Sat lunch and Sun. Métro: Odéon, **$$**. SPIT-ROASTED.

This is Jacques Cagna's lower-priced restaurant, located around the corner from his original, tonier home-base. One of the city's most popular spots, it is also one of the most charming, with a sunny, spacious dining room set off with blue, rush-seated chairs and tile floors. As the name indicates, many of the dishes here, such as the lamb, are cooked on a spit (rôtisserie), and the 6-grain bread is made right on the premises. For a grill, the dishes try for more than the merely predictable: sample the vegetable terrine starter and the thick, sizzling grilled tuna.

★★★ Square Trousseau

1 rue Anton Vollon, 12e. ☎ 01-43-43-06-00. AE, V. Reservations advised. Open daily. Métro: Ledru-Rollin. **$$$**. FRENCH.

The address of this bistro-style restaurant behind the Bastille was passed hand to hand among food cognoscenti ever since its opening in the late 1980s; now it's become quite trendy in a low-key way—and happily, owner Philippe Damas and his équipe haven't seemed to have taken any mind. Try the superb house-made foie gras and the market-fresh specials—including a butter-like filet of beef and grilled sea bass. In the summer, the windows facing the little park across the street are open, and the tables spill out on the sidewalk. Damas does a fine job ferreting out small, lesser known vintages—ask him for some recommendations. A good Sunday brunch, too.

La Table du Marché

14 rue de Marignan, 8e. ☎ 01-40-76-34-44. AE, CB, D, MC, V. Reservations advised. Closed Sun lunch. Métro: Franklin-D-Roosevelt. **$$$**. MEDITERRANEAN.

You won't know who the people sitting next to you are, but they might be great screen stars in France. Why would you care? This spacious, elegant restaurant is orchestrated by chef/owner Christophe Leroy—a former student of Alain Ducasse—who also has a restaurant in St-Tropez. The menu here brings the same Mediterranean cuisine to bear. The "chef's selection" of first courses (marinated mushrooms, eggplant parmesan) is a good way to get started. The look is polished and sunny, with a brick oven facing the dining room and wine out on racks.

★ Taillevent

15 rue Lamennais, 8e. ☎ 01-45-61-12-90. AE, D, MC, V. Reservations required. Wheelchair access. Closed Sat, Sun. Métro: Charles-de-Gaulle-Etoile, George-V. **$$$$$**. FRENCH.

Taillevent, named after one of the first great French cooks who lived in the 14thC, is run by Jean-Claude Vrinat, who has made it one of the capital's top 5 restaurants. Vrinat follows new cooking trends and is also always on the look-out for excellent lesser-known wines to fill out his internationally reputed list. He buys some of his cheeses direct from the farm. Taillevent is much frequented by politicians and top businesspeople. The decor in this lovely mid-19thC mansion is suitably discreet. Reserve weeks—even months—ahead.

La Taverne du Sergent Recruteur

41 rue St-Louis-en-l'Ile, 4e. ☎ 01-43-54-75-42. AE, MC, V. Open for dinner only; closed Sun. Métro: Pont-Marie. **$$**. FRENCH.

In the 18thC, when the French army was short of men, it would employ a recruiting sergeant, a sly character who would ply his victims with food and drink until they signed his enlistment papers without objection. This is just the sort of place where you can imagine him at work: leaded windows, stone-flagged floor, heavy wooden beams, and stone arches. At this restaurant, you get similar lavish treatment but without the penalty; make sure that you have a big appetite. No à la carte, only a 4-course, fixed-price menu, including wine, of remarkably good value.

★ Le Télégraphe

41 rue de Lille, 7e. ☎ 01-40-15-06-65. AE, V. Reservations advised. Open daily. Métro: rue du Bac, Solférino. **$$$**. FRENCH.

Only a stone's throw from the Musée d'Orsay, Le Télégraphe's popularity continues. Publishers, journalists, and politicians gather to talk shop, and in the evenings (when reservations are essential) fashionable young Parisians flock here. The superb decor, by François-Joseph Graf, is its principle charm, although he started with an enviable advantage: This room, the astonishing refectory of a former dormitory for female post office workers, came equipped with arches, arcades, stained-glass windows, and Art Nouveau woodwork. A pleasant veranda overlooks a small garden, and the food is light, if not particularly memorable.

Terminus Nord

23 rue de Dunkerque, 10ᵉ. ☎ 01-42-85-05-15. AE, D, MC, V. Closed Christmas Eve. Métro: Gare-du-Nord. **$$**. CAFE/BRASSERIE.

Cafes and restaurants near stations tend to treat their captive and hurried clientele in less than gentlemanly fashion. A notable exception is the Terminus Nord, another restaurant in the stable of Jean-Paul Bucher (see Brasserie Flo, La Coupole, Julien, and Le Vaudeville). An ideal place at which to eat before taking a train from the station opposite, this brasserie offers food that is good enough to attract swarms of gourmets who have no intention of leaving town. A special menu after 10pm offers very good value.

La Terrasse Fleurie

Hotel Inter-Continental, 3 rue de Castiglione, 1ᵉʳ. ☎ 01-44-77-10-44. AE, D, MC, V. Reservations advised. Wheelchair access. Closed weekends. Métro: Tuileries. **$$$$**. FRENCH.

This year-round terrace restaurant is unusual for a luxury hotel (it's part of the Hotel Inter-Continental; see "Accommodations") in that it offers a set menu, which, in view of its copiousness and high quality, is a very good value indeed. The restaurant itself is small but pretty, extending out in the warm months to a lovely central courtyard. The chef shows a refreshing interest in the kitchen garden, as well as in the recently added Provençal specialties. Try the langoustines roasted with sage butter when available, it's delicious.

Thoumieux

79 rue St-Dominique, 7ᵉ. ☎ 01-47-05-49-75. V. Reservations recommended. Open daily. Métro: Latour-Maubourg. **$/$$**. SOUTHWESTERN FRENCH.

This spacious, vaguely Art Deco brasserie, attached to a hotel of the same name and not far from the Tour Eiffel, has been in the same family for 3 generations, serving good traditional food from the southwest region—country charcuteries, an excellent *cassoulet au confit du canard,* *tête de veau ravigote,* and a very good fixed-menu. Although budget tourists tend to outnumber locals at times, the level of food is excellent for the price, and the service couldn't be nicer or more attentive.

Toupary

Samaritaine, 2 quai du Louvre, 1ᵉʳ. ☎ 01-40-41-29-29. AE, MC, V. Wheelchair access. Closed Sun. Métro: Pont-Neuf. **$$**. FRENCH.

An enormous restaurant on the top floor of the Samaritaine department store, with one of the best views in Paris. Designed by transplanted Atlanta Hilton McConnico, its color scheme (ochre, apricot, electric blue) is reminiscent of his beautiful sets for the movie *Diva*. The restaurant seats 250; the sandwich bar next door is a faster and cheaper lunch alternative. Classic French fare in what couldn't be described as your typical department store eatery.

Toutoune

5 rue de Pontoise, 5e. ☎ 01-43-26-56-81. AE, V. Reservations recommended. Closed Sun and Mon lunch. Métro: Maubert-Mutualité. **$$**. FRENCH.

A cozy bistro with Provençal furnishings and tables covered in Soléiado fabrics, Toutoune offers one of the great culinary bargains of the city. Dinner is a 1-price, 158F affair, offering 4 courses. The wines are incredibly well priced—including champagne at 190F a bottle, not to mention a 1991 Chateau Camensac, a haut médoc that's a *grand cru classé*, for 169 francs. The food—including *sauté d'agneau provençal* and a cinnamon-flavored *tarte au chocolat*—won't disappoint. Some tables are set on a small sidewalk terrace in warm weather. Not the place to go if you're looking for a particularly lively or fashionable evening, but reliable and good.

Au Trou Gascon

40 rue Taine, 12e. ☎ 01-43-44-34-26. AE, D, MC, V. Reservations required. Closed Sat, Sun, Aug. Métro: Daumesnil. **$$/$$$**. SOUTHWESTERN FRENCH.

The acclaimed chef Alain Dutournier, creator of this restaurant, has turned it over to his wife, who has continued in the same style. The restaurant offers a most unusual blend of new ideas and provincial (Gascon) tradition, and an equally rare selection of wines—some 450, ranging from prestigious Bordeaux to humble, little-known crus, all annotated in detail on the city's most compulsively readable wine list. Throw in the amazing collection of Armagnacs and the restaurant's turn-of-the-century decor (a riot of mirrors and moldings), and you have the makings of a memorable meal.

Ty-Coz

35 rue St-Georges, 9e. ☎ 01-48-78-42-95. AE, V. Reservations advised. Closed Mon dinner, Sun. Métro: St-Georges. **$$$**. SEAFOOD.

Chef/owner Marie-Françoise Lachaud's mother is a famous Paris food figure and opened Ty-Coz in the early 1960s. Typical dishes from one of Paris's better known female chefs include a smoked haddock, desalted under cold running water, poached in milk, and served with a light hollandaise sauce learned from her grandmother. Quite dark, gloomy, and wood-beamed—the decor is sincere and not disagreeable for all that. An authentic seafood restaurant where you can find a delicious *lotte au cidre*.

★ Le Vaudeville

29 rue Vivienne, 2e. ☎ 01-40-20-04-62. AE, D, MC, V. Reservations required. Open daily until 2am. Métro: Bourse. **$$$**. FRENCH.

The people who love this restaurant—and there are many of them, some of them really picky about where they go—really love it. The same bustling mood prevails here as found at La Coupole. This 1930s-style marble-and-mirrored restaurant specializing in oysters and platters of fresh seafood is a preferable alternative to many of the city's brasseries because of its more human dimensions. An interesting crowd mix of film, theater, and fashion types mingle with tourists, who have been known to burst into impromptu song.

Le Vivarois

192 av. Victor-Hugo, 16e. ☎ 01-45-04-04-31. AE, D, V. Reservations required. Wheelchair access. Closed Sat, Sun, Aug. Métro: av. Henri-Martin. **$$$$$**. FRENCH.

This is the most unusual of Paris's pantheon of first-class restaurants, frequented by well-heeled gourmands and run by a true eccentric, chef-patron Claude Peyrot, who likes nothing better than to discuss philosophy with his customers. Peyrot is a master at dishes that defy categorization. His aim is not flashy inventiveness but utter perfection of both raw materials and the end-product. By reputation, he succeeds every time.

Willi's

13 rue des Petits-Champs, 1er. ☎ 01-42-61-05-09. Wheelchair access. Open 11am–11pm; closed Sun. Métro: Bourse, Palais-Royal. **$$**. WINE BAR.

Willi's (named after both owner Mark Williamson and Colette's first husband) is a faithful copy of a typical London wine bar, except that the large number of wines (many available by the glass) and the quality of the food are much higher than you would normally expect in Britain. It's crowded with English expatriates and tweedy French Anglophiles.

Dining Large on a Budget

Paris has never offered such good value to travelers in search of a fine meal. Prompted by the recent economic downturn known in France as *La Crise,* top chefs have been spinning off lower-priced secondary establishments—the so-called baby bistros— offering a sampling of their skills at a fraction of the price.

At the same time, new chefs have been staking out terrain in the lower-rent arrondissements, tempting diners out of the center by offering inventive cooking at bargain prices. And many of the city's gastronomic temples—from **L'Arpege** to **Taille-vent**—are offering specially priced menus that promise a taste of French cuisine as only a few chefs in the world can prepare it.

Guy Savoy is one of the engines of the baby-bistro movement. Savoy, whose own eponymous establishment has the Michelin guide's 2-star rating, has made a mini industry out of his annexes: He now counts 6, including the city's first baby brasserie **Cap Vernet** (82 av. Marceau, 8e, ☎ 01-47-20-20-40). His empire stretches from his 3 cozy **Bistro de l'Etoile** offshoots (19 rue Lauriston, 16e,

☎ 01-40-67-11-16; 13 rue Troyon, 17ᵉ, ☎ 01-42-67-25-95; 75 av. Niel, 17ᵉ, ☎ 01-42-27-88-44) to the coolly modern **La Butte Chaillot** (110bis av. Kléber, 16ᵉ, ☎ 01-47-27-88-88) to his most successful: The swooningly charming switch-hitter **Les Bookinistes,** with its menu scribbled on an old-fashioned blackboard set in the middle of a sunny, modern room overlooking the Seine.

The Left Bank also boasts the original offshoot of **Jacques Cagna**'s pricey namesake establishment. His **La Rôtisserie d'en Face** offers spit-roasted foods in a brightly polished, country-style setting. His baby bistro has become so popular that Cagna has gone on and opened 2 other clones on the Right Bank, **La Rôtisserie Monsigny** (1 rue Monsigny, 2ᵉ, ☎ 01-42-96-16-61) and **La Rôtisserie d'Armaillé** (6 rue d'Armaillé, 17ᵉ, ☎ 01-42-27-19-20).

Some baby bistros, such as La Rôtisserie d'en Face, succeed on their own; others are only dim reflections of the more glorious establishment. Such is the case with **Le Cercle Ledoyen,** which has its uses, being inexpensive and superbly located downstairs from the more glamorous **Ledoyen.** But without this hook and the Jacques Grange decor, one wonders if anyone would be there.

And while one offshoot works well, another may do less well: The expensive fish palace **Le Dôme** lucked out with it's first clone, **Le Petit Dôme;** it's second, **Le Dôme Bastille,** while it does offer a good selection of daily fish specials, otherwise has little to distinguish it from the many other midpriced restaurants in Paris.

Look out for young chefs branching out on their own. Eager to establish a clientele and a reputation, they usually offer very good value for the money.

Thierry Coué, who worked with Alain Senderens at Lucas-Carton, moved out behind the Bastille to set up the highly successful **Les Amognes,** where he is very correct about passing on what he saves in rent to the customer.

Equally, Yves Camdeborde's **La Regalade,** in the far reaches of the 14th arrondissement, has been packed since the week it opened when word got out about the deliciously prepared French staples to be sampled in the 1-price, 150F menu.

And Thierry Faucher, who cut his teeth at the Hotel de Crillon's famed restaurant, Les Ambassadeurs, has run up his flag in the 15th arrondissement. His **L'Os à Moelle,** with it's 6-course tasting menu, offers an expansive gastronomic experience which is all the more unique for being served up in a homey, unpretentious bistro setting.

Cafes & Tea Salons

The cafe is one of the most civilized institutions ever invented. It is a living stage, a forum for debate, a club, a home away from home. By and large, the French are proud of their cafe tradition—in most cafes, no one will dream of bothering you if you sit over the same cup for the whole afternoon, although it's polite to settle up those little white tickets slipped under your cup with reasonable speed. That said, a busy cafe on the boulevard St-Michel is obviously going to be a less welcome spot to loiter than a quiet little place on a side street. People spend entire afternoons upstairs at the **Café Flore,** many of them apparently ordering nothing. Cafes with terraces are good vantage points for observing the passersby—the **Café de la Paix** near the Opéra is a good example—but expect to be asked to pay more: You're paying for the real estate.

A 2-tiered pricing system exists at most cafes, depending on whether you drink at the bar or occupy a table. Often, the price difference is quite steep, and you can pay up to 50% less if you choose not to sit on the terrace.

Service charges are included in the bill in cafes. If you wish, you may leave a few francs on the table when you leave.

Left Bank

Montparnasse

It's been a long time since Montparnasse was the center of bohemian life in Paris. Nonetheless, artists, intellectuals, writers, movie people, and hangers-on from every walk of life still gather in **La Coupole** or **Le Sélect Montparnasse** (99 blvd. du Montparnasse), which has hardly changed since it was frequented by Erik Satie, Francis Poulenc, Robert Desnos, and Foujita. Across the way, **Le Dôme** is still cashing in on its reputation as a favorite watering-hole of Modigliani, Stravinsky, Picasso, and Hemingway. A further 5-minute walk along the boulevard is the lively and quirkily authentic **La Closerie des Lilas.**

St-Germain-des-Prés

Two of the most famous of all cafes, **Les Deux Magots**—a *magot,* by the way, is a Chinese miniature figure and not what you might think—and **Le Flore** (170 and 172 blvd. St-Germain, respectively), are to be found, side by side, right in the heart of this district. The list of their customers past and present reads like a roll call of French intellectual life over the last hundred years: Huysmans, Jarry, Barrès, Giraudoux, Sartre, de Beauvoir, Breton, Camus, and the Prévert brothers. Nowadays, however, times have changed, and only the wealthier literati can afford to hold court regularly at the 2 renowned cafes. For a less touristy and less pricey cafe experience in the same neighborhood, go around back of both to **La Palette** (43 rue de Seine, 6e), with lovely Art Deco interiors, where artists, gallery owners, students, and literati still gather.

Down closer to the riverbank, the toniest tea shop in Paris, **Marriage Frères,** has a tea salon upstairs— 2 steps from the antiques shops on the Left Bank— that's a soothing place to take a lunch or late afternoon break. It's found at 13 rue des Grands-Augustins.

Right Bank

Avenue des Champs-Elysées

There is only one cafe of any real interest actually on avenue des Champs-Elysées: **Fouquet's** (no. 99). You can pay a lot just to sit on the terrace among the famous faces, but there's still a genuine buzz at Fouquet's, which has recently been classified a historic monument. It defies reason, but no unaccompanied ladies are allowed at the bar within.

Opéra/Boulevard Haussmann

One of the most celebrated establishments in Paris is, of course, the **Café de la Paix** (12 blvd. des Capucines). It emerged from meticulous restoration a few years ago with its deliciously ornate green-and-gold decor and its clientele (wealthy tourists for the most part) unscathed.

After a day's shopping in rue du Faubourg-St-Honoré, you have your pick of the city's 3 smartest tea salons: **Ladurée** (16 rue Royale) is famous for their world famous chocolate macaroons, of which they sell some 1,000 daily. Just down the street towards the place de la Concorde, the porcelain shop **Bernardaud**

(Galerie Royale, 9 rue Royale) sports its own newly minted tearoom, where you can select both your tea and the china you'd like it served on. And do treat yourself to tea at **Angélina** (226 rue de Rivoli), where Parisians from Marcel Proust to Coco Chanel have come to sample the pastries, including the house favorite: the *mont-blanc,* a delectable concoction of cream and meringue.

Or, for a fashionably modern take on the cafe experience, try the **Café Bleu Lanvin** (15 rue du Faubourg-St-Honoré), located downstairs in the Lanvin shop, where fashion types gather for light and well prepared lunches and snacks.

Les Halles

While Les Halles has few places where you can really dine well, it sports a reasonable number of cafes in which to sit, or to grab a quick bite—try **Le Comptoir** (14 rue Vauvilliers), for a little tapas and a margarita before going out one night. And across from the Pompidou Center, the **Café Beaubourg** (43 rue St-Merri)— owned by Gilbert Costes, who also owns the Café Marly and is one of the young restaurateurs repainting the Parisian cafe scene in our times—is a sleek modern temple with excellent coffee and a lively terrace scene.

Walking on towards the rue du Louvre, try the **Café de L'Epoque** (Galerie Véro-Dodat) located in a beautiful 19thC covered passageway. The adjoining fashionable shops mean that celebrities pop up among the old-time crowd here to enjoy one of the city's best Tarte Tatins. And probably the most stylish terrace in town belongs to the **Café Marly,** in the Richelieu wing of the Louvre facing the pyramid. When the weather isn't cooperative you can still have a drink or tea inside and enjoy the somewhat baroque Olivier-Gagnère designed interiors.

Le Marais

On the beautifully intact 17thC place des Vosges, there is the staidly, if cozily, reliable **Ma Bourgogne,** which serves reasonably good wines. **La Chaise au Plafond** (10 rue du Trésor, ☎ 01-42-76-03-22) is hidden in a tiny impasse, but worth the detour. Destroyed by bombs in 1917—the only thing that was left was a chair stuck in the ceiling, hence the name—the cafe was recently refurbished by Zaza, the owner of the nearby **Petit Fer à Cheval** (another smoky, atmospheric bar in the Marais, with a horseshoe-shaped bar). In the warm months, life spills out onto the terrace, and drinking goes on until 2am. Another lively bar in the area is **Le Majestic Café** (34 rue Vielle-du-Temple), with a slightly faded but decidedly old-world charm.

Montmartre/Pigalle

All self-respecting painters have long since fled place du Tertre in Montmartre, which is now crammed with terrible paintings of sad-eyed children and dogs. Pigalle seems to have become a sex-shop jungle.

In both areas, cafes have turned the exploitation of tourists into a fine art, but as soon as you move away from the bright lights you may find a genuine Montmartre cafe. One such establishment is the delightful **Aux Negociants** (27 rue Lambert), where excellent and inexpensive wines flow freely as regulars converse, conveniently gathered around the tiny, horseshoe-shaped bar.

Bastille

The Bastille area now sports some of the liveliest cafe action in Paris, if you know enough to stay off of the overcrowded rue de la Roquette and rue de Lapp, where teenaged tourists from all parts of the globe gather to make noise. Instead, try the **Café de l'Industrie** (16 rue St-Sabin), a cavernous old cafe full of gamely redecorated (but not too redecorated) banquettes and wood tables where the Gaulloise smoke blows thick and French students and intellectuals still make fevered conversation over glasses of pastis and endless cups of black coffee. Or, for a look at a real zinc bar and something of the way Paris looked a long time ago, drop into **L'Ami Pierre** (5 rue de la Main-d'Or). Tiny and crowded, full of theater folk and neighbors, L'Ami Pierre boasts a wonderful selection of wines by the glass or bottle as well as inexpensive homemade dishes.

ACCOMMODATIONS

Making Your Choice

Few cities have such a deeply varied choice of hotels—from luxury palaces to small *hotels du charme* that are one of Paris's specialties. At either end of the scale, the best preserve an old-fashioned style of management (rapidly dying out here as elsewhere) as well as cleanliness, courtesy, a high ratio of staff to guests, and a quintessentially French atmosphere. On the debit side, however, Paris has its share of downmarket hotels, surly staff, and miniscule rooms, so it's wise to choose carefully and reserve well in advance.

Most importantly, decide in which part of the city you'd like to stay. The *arrondissements* in Paris curl outward like the shell of a snail, with the 1er *arrondissement* roughly in the middle—so in general, staying in one of the lower number *arrondissements* means a more central location. (You can deduce the *arrondissement* in which the hotel is located from the last 2 numbers of the zip code.) The hotels situated generally between the Opéra and the place de la Concorde (1er *arrondissement*) provide easy access to major monuments, such as the Louvre, as well as the busy shopping areas along the Boulevard Haussman and the upscale Faubourg-St-Honoré. Left-bank hotels in St-Germain-des-Prés and the Latin Quarter (5e, 6e, 7e) pack the most charm (though sometimes frayed), often opening onto tiny streets in an area full of cafes. But, aside from the Montalembert, where the rooms are relatively small, there aren't many luxury hotels on the Left Bank. Instead, look for one of the better *hotels du charme*—smaller hotels where services may be light, but you might find yourself in a room with a fireplace (Hôtel de l'Université), or a stunning outdoor garden (Hôtel des Grandes Ecoles). Fashionable types have given up on the St-Germain area in favor of the Marais, located in the 3e and 4e arrondissements around the place des Vosges—a less touristy area, certainly, and full of atmosphere, but also less rich in shops and museums. In addition, the Marais suffers from a stunning dearth of hotel choices, with very few really geared to people traveling on business. And some of the more interesting ones, such as the Hôtel de la Bretonnerie, have rooms so tiny that life inside can pass quickly from charming to exasperating.

Keep in mind that, while it's theoretically interesting to stay in a hotel near the Arc de Triomphe, in practice its main thoroughfare, the Champs Elysées, is today an unremarkable zone of fast-food joints and car showrooms. Unless you're conducting business in this part of town, you may find staying this far west means that you spend a lot of your actual day in taxis or the métro. (This is the one acknowledged drawback to the city's most romantic hotel, the stunning Hôtel Raphaël.)

Reservations

Although Paris boasts close to 2,000 hotels from the French grade of 1 star and up, there can be problems getting a room on short notice: It is best to reserve a minimum of 1 month in advance. Remember that the busiest time is from September to October, when many of the city's most popular hotels are booked a full year ahead of time. If you're booking yourself, the easiest and safest way is to send a fax. If you're reserving at the last minute, use the services of the tourist offices at Orly and Roissy/Charles-De-Gaulle airports, the Gare du Nord, Gare d'Austerlitz, Gare de Montparnasse, Gare de Lyon, Gare de l'Est, the Eiffel Tower, or the main Office de Tourisme (see "Useful Telephone Numbers & Addresses" in "The Basics" for details). Don't be too put-off if all you're offered is a hotel in one of the less central of the 20 arrondissements: The capital has excellent public transportation.

Paris is a busy, often noisy, city. When reserving, ask for a room on the courtyard (*sur cour*) and double check that the windows are double-glazed (*double-vitrage*). Paris's hotels—particularly the small ones—are predominately quirky affairs, and often rooms differ dramatically in size, furnishings, etc. If you prefer a large room, ask for one—and mention that you have a lot of luggage (the French are convinced that Americans all travel with prodigious amounts of luggage). Ditto for a spacious bath, if it matters, or even a high ceiling. Given enough notice, even the tiniest hotel will usually try to accommodate you. Keep in mind that a room with a shower may cost less than one with a bathtub. If you want a shower, ask for one; older rooms may have only tubs.

Price Chart

$$$$$	Very Expensive, More than 2,000F
$$$$	Expensive, 1,001F–2,000F
$$$	Moderate, 601F–1,000F
$$	Inexpensive, 400F–600F
$	Cheap, Under 400F

Hotels by Arrondissement

1er

Castille. **$$$$$**
★★★ Costes. **$$$$$**
★★ Inter-Continental. **$$$$/$$$$$**
Louvre-Montana. **$$$/$$$$**
Meurice. **$$$$$**
★★ Ritz. **$$$$$**
★ Des Tuileries. **$$$/$$$$**

4e

★ De la Bretonnerie. **$$$**
★ Des Deux Iles. **$$$**
Fauconnier. **$**
Fourcy. **$**
★★★ Grand Hôtel Jeanne d'Arc. **$**
Maubuisson. **$**

5e

★★★ Des Grandes Écoles. **$$**

6e

★★★ L'Abbaye St-Germain. **$$$$**
Atelier Montparnasse. **$$$**
L'Hôtel. **$$$$/$$$$$**
Novanox. **$$$**
Relais Christine. **$$$$**
De Seine. **$$$$**
La Villa. **$$$/$$$$**

7e

Duc de St-Simon. **$$$$**
★ Lenox. **$$$**
★ Montalembert. **$$$$**

Quai Voltaire. **$$/$$$**
Solférino. **$$**
De Suède. **$$/$$$**
★★ De l'Université. **$$$/$$$$**

8e

Bradford. **$$$**
★★ Le Bristol. **$$$$$**
★★★ De Crillon. **$$$$$**
George-V. **$$$$$**
Plaza-Athénée. **$$$$$**
Royal Monceau. **$$$$$**

9e

Chopin. **$$**
Grand Hôtel Inter-Continental. **$$$$$**
★ Libertel Lafayette. **$$$/$$$$**
Opéra Cadet. **$$$**
William's. **$$**

12e

Le Pavillon Bastille. **$$$**

14e

★ Lenox. **$$$**
Meridien Montparnasse. **$$$$**

15e

Hilton International Paris. **$$$$/$$$$$**

16e

★★★ Pergolese. **$$$/$$$$**
★★★ Raphaël. **$$$$$**

17ᵉ
Arc de Triomphe-Etoile. **$$$**
Regent's Garden. **$$$**

18ᵉ
Terrass. **$$$/$$$$**

Charles de Gaulle airport
★★★ Sheraton Paris Airport Hotel. **$$$/$$$$**

Critic's Choice

The most romantic hotel in the city is the **Raphaël,** a sort of club for slightly cerebral international celebrities. Fashion pros and fashion victims are most at home in the **Lenox** (the one on rue de l'Université in the 6ᵉ arrondissement—not the one in Montparnasse), though the tiny rooms don't allow room for spreading out a lot of designer ensembles. The *hotel du charme* that still merits the name is the **Hôtel des Grandes Ecoles,** where visiting professors from the Sorbonne sip their café au lait under the spreading shade trees in the garden. Underpaid publishing and media professionals have made a sort of club out of the faded but charmingly quirky, family-run **Grande Hôtel Jeanne d'Arc** in the Marais. The best place to show off for a drink is with a cognac in your hand at the Ritz Bar at the **Ritz Hotel.** The best suite in the city is the Leonard Bernstein suite in the **Hôtel de Crillon:** It's not the biggest suite in Paris, but, with its sprawling terrace and a sitting room where the maestro used to compose, it has the most comfort and cachet. And the swankest pool and gym facilities are to be found in the sultan-ish Ritz Club, in the basement of the **Ritz Hotel.**

Hotels A to Z

Our Recommendations   The selections in this chapter cover a range of prices and neighborhoods, with an emphasis on atmosphere, relative quiet, and good value. The price rating is based on 2 people staying in a double room with bathroom/shower, including value added tax (VAT). Breakfast is extra, unless noted.

Amenities   All the hotels listed below, except for the hostels listed at the end, have telephones in the rooms. Other facilities—gyms, conference rooms, air-conditioning, etc.—are cited only when available. Cable or satellite television, when indicated, means that you'll get stations in English.

Breakfast   French hotel breakfasts, except in the very best hotels (where you pay for the privilege), are the one blot on the nation's gastronomic copybook: Too often, bland croissants or a baguette and individually packed portions of butter and jam are your only choice. Unless you give priority to breakfasting in bed, you'll definitely find better value around the corner from the hotel at a near-by cafe.

Tipping   A service charge is included in the hotel rates. If you're particularly pleased with the service, tip the chambermaid and the concierge a few francs. The amount you tip is dependent on the cost of your hotel; in general, give baggage handlers 10F or 20F (more if you have staggering amounts of luggage).

★★★ L'Abbaye
St-Germain

10 rue Cassette, 75006 Paris.
☎ 01-45-44-38-11; fax: 01-45-48-07-86. 42 rooms, 4 suites.
Métro: St-Sulpice, Rennes.
(Continental breakfast included in room rate). AE, MC, V. **$$$$**.
Located on a short, quiet street close to St-Germain and the Luxembourg Gardens, this magnificent and extraordinary converted 17thC convent shows just what results can be obtained when the ancient and modern are skillfully combined. Contemporary sofas complement 18thC antiques in the downstairs lobby, while the rooms themselves, some with original beams and alcoves, have a quiet charm. The courtesy and helpfulness of the staff are exemplary. With so much to recommend it, however, it can be extremely difficult to find a room here in peak periods. A giant plus here is that there are no rooms on the street—the hotel is situated between a courtyard and a garden and so is exceptionally calm. Reserve a room on the garden if possible, and, if you can get it, try for the much-demanded room number 4 on the ground floor, with it's private terrace.

Amenities: A charming little bar, and a terrace where you can have breakfast; room service for light snacks and drinks available 7am to midnight; TV; A/C.

Arc de Triomphe-Etoile

3 rue de l'Etoile, 75017 Paris.
☎ 01-43-80-36-94; fax: 01-44-40-49-19. 15 rooms, 10 suites.
Métro: Ternes, Charles-De-Gaulle-Etoile. AE, DC, MC, V. **$$$**.
This small, charmingly-run hotel close to the Arc de Triomphe was totally renovated in 1994 by new owner Roger Alvarez, who spiffed up the contemporary furnishings and created new marble baths. The larger rooms can sleep three and give onto the courtyard; all rooms are soundproofed and reasonably quiet. This is a hotel well-suited to the businessperson on a budget, as well as anyone who appreciates a family atmosphere. Alvarez says his motto is "service, service, service," and you will believe him. Special weekend rates and holiday fares are available.
Amenities: Rooms have satellite and cable TV, as well as minibars, safes, and trouser-pressing machines. There's a bar and minilibrary in the

lobby, and no restaurant, but drinks can be served in the room 24 hours a day. The conference room accommodates a maximum of 20 people. A real plus is the ticketing office in the lobby selling tourist passes for the métros, as well as tickets to shows, Disneyland, and so forth. The hotel offers preferential rates in the parking lot across the street.

Atelier Montparnasse

49 rue Vavin, 75006 Paris.
☎ 01-46-33-60-00; fax: 01-40-51-04-21. 16 rooms, 1 suite.
Métro: Vavin. AE, DC, MC, V.
$$$.

In the 1920s, rue Vavin in Montparnasse was a bustling center of literary life in Paris; almost all of that is gone now, though you do have easy access to the big brasserie nightlife found around the corner at restaurants such as La Coupole and Le Dôme. Each of the rooms in this very small hotel has been named after a painter—including Gauguin, Picasso, Matisse, and Modigliani—and the mosaic tiled bathrooms re-create works by these artists. Owner Marie-José Tibble looks for a friendly atmosphere, and creates one. The rooms are in a pleasant contemporary style. *Amenities:* Room service 7am to 10pm for drinks and snacks.

Bradford

10 rue St-Philippe-du-Roule, 75008 Paris. ☎ 01-45-63-20-20; Best Western: 800-528-1234; fax: 01-45-63-20-07. 46 rooms, 2 suites. Métro: St-Philippe-du-Roule, Franklin-D-Roosevelt. AE, DC, MC, V. **$$$**.
Friendliness is one of the best features of this unassuming hotel near rue du Faubourg-St-Honoré and av. des

Champs-Elysées, now part of the Best Western group. The rooms are large and pleasantly furnished, and the authentic 1920s decoration is charming. The rooms whose numbers end with a 6 or 7 are the largest. Most welcome in an area blighted by heavy traffic, is the almost total quiet and seclusion of the street on which it's located. *Amenities:* Satellite TV. There isn't a bar, but drinks are served in the salon, and room service is available until 8pm. You can also order dinner via room service, which is provided by an outside restaurant.

★ De la Bretonnerie

22 rue Ste-Croix-de-la-Bretonnerie, 75004 Paris.
☎ 01-48-87-77-63; fax: 01-42-77-26-78. 28 rooms, 3 suites.
Closed Aug. Métro: Hôtel-de-Ville.
MC, V. **$$$**.
This quiet hotel, housed in a simple, white 17thC townhouse on a quiet, atmospheric street, was redone in the early 1990s and has since become one of the area's most popular layovers for gallerists (the Marais is filled with art galleries and antique shops) and trendy types traveling on a budget. If you're one of those people who believe that 60% of a good hotel room is the bathroom, then this is the place for you: Room 19, for example, is tiled in beige marble, has good thick towels, and offers a spacious corner tub. Though there's lots of charm and many a beamed ceiling, rooms are mostly tiny. That and the lack of a restaurant makes it less than a prime choice for the business traveler, but pickings are slim in the Marais. *Amenities:* Each room equipped with a safe, minibar, and cable TV; room

service (snacks and drinks) from 8am to 8pm; all windows are double-glazed.

★★ Le Bristol

112 rue du Faubourg-St-Honoré, 75008 Paris. ☎ 01-42-66-91-45; Leading Hotels of the World: 800-223-6800; fax: 01-42-66-68-68. 155 rooms, 45 suites. Métro: Champs-Elysées-Clemenceau, Miromesnil. AE, DC, MC, V. **$$$$$**.

The Bristol has the staid and elegant look of an 18thC mansion—in fact, part of it was once the private theater of Madame de Pompadour. Heads of government and high-flying diplomats who have an appointment with the President at the Elysée Palace prefer the Bristol, conveniently located nearby on one of Paris's most exclusive and expensive streets. It also boasts a private entrance from its own garage—allowing celebrities to avoid the paparazzi. This is one of Paris's most discreet luxury hotels, from the elegant Gobelin-tapestries, to the 23 Baccarat chandeliers in the lobby, to the quiet elegance of its teak-decked, top-floor, indoor pool. (It was designed by Casar Pinnau, who designed yachts for Niarchos and Onassis.) The white marble bathrooms, with separate shower and twin sinks, are sumptuous—as can only be imagined when you think that they were restored in 1989 at a cost of $67,000 per room. Ask for a room on the precision-manicured interior garden. Look out for rare bottles (a Chateau Petrus 1980 or a Mouton Rothschild 1958) among the 31,000 bottles in the superb restaurant—a hub for the city's power lunches (if you're dining there in winter, ask for an alcove table—they're the private ones reserved by the city's powerbrokers). *Amenities:* Indoor pool and fitness center with top-of-the-line machines; massage rooms; 6 conference rooms; business center with bilingual secretarial facilities and faxes available for in-room hook-up; a gastronomic restaurant (1 Michelin star) and a bar; parking garage; 24-hour room service; cable TV; A/C.

Castille

33 rue Cambon, 75001 Paris. ☎ 01-44-58-44-58; fax: 01-44-58-44-00. 90 rooms, 17 suites. Métro: Concorde. AE, DC, MC, V. **$$$$$**.

A former annex of the Ritz, this 18thC building was converted into the Hôtel Castille in 1993, making it one of Paris's newest 4-star hotels. A new wing (called the Rivoli wing), designed by celebrity decorator Jacques Grange, opened in 1995. The whole thing is designed in a rich Venetian style that features a lot of rosy ochre, pale Burgundy stone, and *faux marbre*. The hotel is around the corner from the shops lining the Faubourg-St-Honoré and a short walk from the Tuileries Gardens, and features one of the city's prettiest courtyards, all painted in trompe-l'oeil, where Karl Lagerfeld and the girls who work for him at Chanel, which is right down the street, come to have lunch under big snowy umbrellas in nice weather. Rooms are chic and spacious. The turn-of-the-century-style bathrooms have embroidered bathrobes and bath products by Molton Brown. *Amenities:* 24-hour room service; nonsmoking floors; A/C; outlets for faxes and computers in the room; cable TV; minibar; conference/reception facilities. The

Right Bank Hotels

Arc de Triomphe-Etoile (17e)	**2**	Libertel Lafayette (9e)	**18**	
Bradford (8e)	**7**	Louvre-Montana (1er)	**16**	
De la Bretonnerie (4e)	**24**	Maubuisson (4e)	**23**	
Le Bristol (8e)	**8**	Meurice (1er)	**13**	
Castille (1er)	**10**	Opéra Cadet (9e)	**21**	
Chopin (9e)	**19**	Le Pavillon Bastille (9e)	**2**	
Costes (1er)	**11**	Plaza-Athénée (8e)	**6**	
De Crillon (8e)	**9**	Raphaël (16e)	**3**	
Des Deux Iles (4e)	**25**	Regent's Garden (1)	**1**	
Fauconnier (4e)	**27**	Ritz (1er)	**14**	
Fourcy (4e)	**26**	Royal Monceau (8e)	**4**	
George-V (8e)	**5**	Terrass (18e)	**22**	
Grand Hôtel Inter-Continental (9e)	**17**	Des Tuileries (1er)	**15**	
Grand Hôtel Jeanne d'Arc (4e)	**28**	William's (9e)	**20**	
Inter-Continental (1er)	**12**			

restaurant Il Cortile is well-frequented by the nearby fashion houses for its Italian specialties.

Chopin

46 Passage Jouffroy, 75009
Paris. ☎ 01-47-70-58-10; fax:
01-42-47-00-70. 36 rooms.

Métro: Rue Montmartre. DC,
MC, V. **$$**.

One of the hotel's strongest selling points is its quiet aspect. In the center of one of the pretty arcades that branch unobtrusively off the noisy Grands Boulevards, this is a quirky, oddly romantic, and

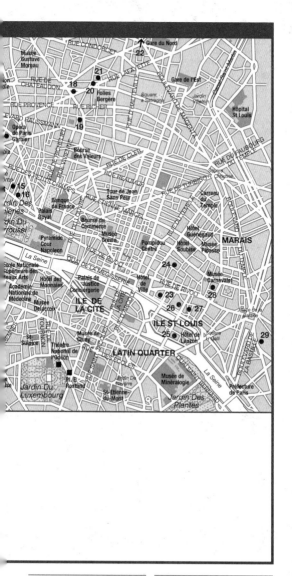

inexpensive place to stay in Paris. The charming mid-19thC Hôtel Chopin stands proudly in the passage Jouffroy, right next to the Musée Grévin and the antiquarian bookstores. It is excellently positioned for trips to the Grands Boulevards and the Opéra Quarter. Most of the rooms are quite small but unobtrusively decorated in old furnishings, with a Chesterfield leather sofa in the lobby, and a lot of art gallery posters. *Amenities:* Except for TVs in the rooms, very little: no bar or room service.

★★★ Costes

239 rue St-Honoré, 75001 Paris.
☎ 01-42-61-54-60; fax: 01-40-
20-96-32. 80 rooms; 5 duplexes.
Métro: Concorde, Tuileries.
AE, DC, MC, V. **$$$$$**.

Jean-Louis Costes, creator of
the now-defunct, Philippe-
Starck-designed Café Costes,
and his brother Gilbert, owner
of the trendy Café Beaubourg
and the even trendier Café
Marly, are two of Paris's most
closely watched style com-
passes. Which is one reason
why all eyes were on Jean-
Louis when he bought a run-
down hotel, the France et
Choiseul, and turned it into a
luxury palace. The hotel's
location is one of the best in
Paris, on the fashionable rue
St-Honoré, equidistant from
the place Vendôme and the
Tuileries Gardens. The most
interesting thing here is
Costes's decision to turn his
back on modernism and return
to a padded, baroque luxury
that French like to call *le style
Rothschild*. The lobby is done
in S-shaped upholstery in a
rich mix of bold patterns; the
neoclassical courtyard is
rimmed with Roman-style
statues, and the rooms are
full of old furniture cut and
reworked to look custom-
fitted.

Every room is different,
and each sports an old-
fashioned luxury—tiled baths,
claw footed tubs, inlaid-wood
wardrobes—mated with high-
tech touches like your own
fax machine (and private line)
and little CD players bolted to
the TV screens. The 5th floor
duplexes all have gabled ceilings and probably pack the
most charm, with views over
the rooftops of Paris. The best
double room is no. 202, with
its baldachin bed, high ceilings,
and an armoire inlaid with
mother-of-pearl. *Amenities:*
Faxes with individual lines in
all rooms. Cable TV and CD
players. Air conditioning.
Restaurant and bar, both with
continuous service from 7am
until midnight; 24-hour room
service; conference facilities. A
48- by 15-foot pool, sauna,
and gym opened in 1996.

★★★ De Crillon

10 pl. de la Concorde, 75008
Paris. ☎ 01-44-71-15-00;
Leading Hotels of the World: 800-
223-6800; fax: 01-44-71-15-02.
123 rooms, 40 suites. Métro:
Concorde. AE, DC, MC, V.
$$$$$.

In a city full of luxury palaces,
the Hôtel de Crillon sits on
top of them all—one of the
great classic hotels of the
world. Its air of quiet excel-
lence is symbolized by the
fact that it displays no
ostentatious signs, only its
name in discreet letters over
the entrance to its magnificent
18thC premises. In one of the
best locations of any hotel in
Paris—overlooking one of the
most famous views in the
world—and formerly an
aristocrat's mansion, it became
a hotel in 1907, and the
sumptuous decor and formal
inner courtyard were
preserved. Its wood-paneled,
stately reception rooms are
now deservedly classified on
the list of national treasures.
The level of service here is
what has made the name of
this hotel: The concierges
here are famous for their
ability to scout out last-
minute reservations to 3-star
restaurants, as well as their
attention to small details, like
lending you an umbrella in a
pinch. None of the doubles
give out onto the place de la
Concorde, but the courtyard
view is very pretty. *Amenities:*
Perhaps the single best hotel
restaurant in Paris, Les

Ambassadeurs, for gastro-nomic cooking. The same chef, Christian Constant, serves bistro fare in the less expensive L'Obélisque. The well-known bar, Le Bar, was designed by Sonia Rykiel and becomes a piano bar in the evening. The tearoom, Le Jardin d'Hiver, features harp music in the afternoons. Rooms are air-conditioned, with cable TV, minibar and 24-hour room service. Eight reception/conference rooms include 3 classified as historical monuments.

★ Des Deux Iles

59 rue St-Louis-en-l'Île, 75004 Paris. ☎ 01-43-26-13-35; fax: 01-43-29-60-25. 17 rooms. Métro: Pont-Marie. V. **$$$**.

The Hôtel des Deux Iles occupies a 17thC building in the quiet street that runs the length of the Ile St-Louis, the smaller and quieter of the Seine's 2 islands. The decor brings a distinctly Indian colonial feel throughout the hotel, with a charming interior garden. The rooms here are not large, but they are all charmingly decorated, and all the beds are new. There isn't a proper bar, though drinks can be served to your room from 8am until 8pm. There's also a sitting room down in the former wine cellar where you can bring your own bottle of wine—the hotel will provide glasses for you to enjoy it in front of the open fire in winter. *Amenities:* Cable TV; A/C.

Duc de St-Simon

14 rue de St-Simon, 75007 Paris. ☎ 01-45-48-35-66; fax: 01-45-48-68-25. 29 rooms, 5 suites. Métro: rue du Bac. No credit cards. **$$$$**.

Quiet, cozy, intimate, welcoming, and discreet are all descriptions that apply to this 19thC hotel, located in a calm street just off boulevard St-Germain. While it's not cheap, the hotel is one of the city's more reputed *hotels du charme*. The Duc de St-Simon is remarkable for its period furnishings, as well as its flower arrangements. New pieces of antique furniture have been gradually added to the rooms, making it a delightful and consequently extremely popular hotel. The quieter rooms are on the garden. *Amenities:* Bar with room service for snacks and drinks from 10:30am until 10pm. TV on request.

George-V

31 av. George-V, 75008 Paris. ☎ 01-47-23-54-00; A Forte Exclusive hotel: 800-225-5843; fax: 01-47-20-40-00. 248 rooms, 50 suites. Métro: George-V. AE, DC, MC, V. **$$$$$**.

Just off avenue des Champs-Elysées, in the city's principal business area, the George-V is grand and unashamedly lavish. Flemish tapestries, sculptures, ormolu clocks, and original paintings (including Renoir's *Le Vase des Roses*) complement the gracious 18thC-style furniture. *Amenities:* The hotel has a delightful bar and a lovely inner courtyard, where in summer, meals are served amid red umbrellas and masses of potted plants as part of the restaurant, Les Princes, which serves traditional cuisine. There is also a deluxe brasserie, Le Grill. Wheelchair access, air-conditioning, minibars, cable TV, 24-hour room service, and conference facilities.

Grand Hôtel Inter-Continental

2 rue Scribe, 75009 Paris. ☎ 01-40-07-32-32; fax: 01-42-66-12-51. 459 rooms, 65 suites.

Métro: Opéra. AE, DC, MC, V. **$$$$$**.

Built in 1862, the Grand Hôtel is a smoothly running mini-metropolis—5 kilometers (3 miles) of hallways—where guests consume 48,000 bottles of champagne a year and the budget for flowers alone is more than $150,000. It overlooks the Opéra, which dominates the view from the front windows. It now aims (although not exclusively) at the upper end of the business market. Air-conditioning and soundproof double-glazing are now universal, and the rooms have received a luxury treat-ment, in a traditional if nondescript range of pastel colors. The restoration of the public areas to their original splendor was carried out in the early 1990s and a spectacular glass atrium now covers the winter garden, which opens onto a statue-lined courtyard.

On the restaurant/bar scale, the Grand Hôtel is like a city unto itself. The restaurant L'Opéra is a palace of haute gastronomy, though the same kitchen serves up quicker (and cheaper) dishes in the Bar Opéra. The Brasserie du Café de la Paix has an elegant terrace, serves haute brasserie food, and has an attractively priced prix-fixe dinner. In the covered courtyard, the Verrerie serves lunch and dinner, with a special chocolate fest here on Saturday afternoons. *Amenities:* Sauna, sun lounge, and gym-nasium; 18 meeting rooms, including the Versailles-like mirrored and colonnaded Salon Opéra, with its 40-foot domed ceiling; A/C; cable TV; minibars; 24-hour room service.

★★★ Grand Hôtel Jeanne d'Arc

3 rue de Jarente, 75004. ☎ 01-48-87-62-11; fax: 01-48-87-37-31. 36 rooms. Métro: St. Paul. MC, V. **$**.

The address of this charmingly quirky but cozily comfortable hotel was passed hand to hand for years; now that's its built its reputation, it's a little hard to get into, but try. The price is right, and the location, a stone's throw from the place des Vosges, is great for both shopping, wandering the historic streets of the Marais, or sipping pastis under the arcades of the place des Vosges. The hotel changed hands a few years ago and was entirely renovated in 1994—though miraculously, prices didn't change much. The blue-and-beige rooms all have a crisp look, though the rooms, including the tiny little downstairs salon with its hand-painted floors and walls, are somewhat blanketed in crocheted lace. The rooms are wildly uneven in size here—but some are really enormous, and so are some of the black-and-white tiled bathrooms. All the "twin" rooms have 2 double beds and can accom-modate families traveling with children. *Amenities:* Cable TV. There's no room service, but the the Bar de Jarentes, an old-fashioned bar the likes of which are hard to find in Paris, is right next door.

★★★ Des Grandes Ecoles

75 rue du Cardinal-Lemoine, 75005. ☎ 01-43-26-79-23; fax: 01-43-25-28-15. 48 rooms. Métro: Cardinal-Lemoine. MC, V. **$$**.

One of the city's truly exceptional *hotels du charme,* the Grandes Ecoles has a cultlike following among everyone from visiting scholars, who appreciate its proximity to the Sorbonne, to thrifty Englishwoman in town for a week of shopping. On the Left Bank not far from the Jardins des Plantes, the hotel's 3 buildings are set back from the street and tucked behind a low gate, facing each other around a graceful tree-lined garden. In summer, everyone has breakfast on the stone terrace hemmed by trim little hedges.

With its flowered wallpaper, matching curtains, crocheted bedspreads, spotless baths, and antique furnishings, the hotel has a quiet air of old-fashioned gracefulness. The hotel is currently undergoing a major renovation: The 2 annexes are being entirely rebuilt. The air is spartan if *gentille,* and amenities are slim. You won't want to stay here if you're in town on business, but you couldn't find a more charming hotel in which to enjoy a romantic stay. *Amenities:* Telephones in the rooms and that's about it. No restaurant facilities other than breakfast, but they will bring you a cup of tea or cold drink to enjoy on the terrace in the afternoon.

Hilton International Paris

18 av. de Suffren, 75015 Paris. ☎ 01-44-38-56-00; 800/445-8667; fax: 01-44-38-56-10. 433 rooms, 29 suites. Métro: Bir-Hakeim, Champ-de-Mars. AE, DC, MC, V. **$$$$/$$$$$**. Close to the Seine and the Eiffel Tower, the Hilton International is considerably more luxurious and expensive than many others in the Hilton chain, and was the first modern hotel built in Paris after the war. *Amenities:* Eleven excellent conference suites, including Le Toit de Paris, which looks out toward the Eiffel Tower. A business center. One restaurant, Le Western, provides all-American Far West

catering, the other, La Terrasse, offers traditional French fare. Two bars. Nonsmoking floor; rooms for the handicapped. Direct access to underground garage (fee). Rooms are air-conditioned, with cable TV, minibars, and 24-hour room service.

L'Hôtel

13 rue des Beaux-Arts, 75006 Paris. ☎ 01-43-25-27-22; fax: 01-43-25-64-81. 25 rooms, 3 suites. Métro: St-Germain-des-Prés. AE, DC, MC, V. **$$$$/$$$$$**. In the heart of the St-Germain Quarter, L'Hôtel has a kitsch if legendary reputation that has earned it the nickname the left-bank Ritz. A favorite with fashion types and the European art world, the hotel can only be described as ornate— antiques everywhere, pink Venetian marble in the bathrooms, and velvet on virtually every surface, from the elevator to the uniforms. You may be given the room containing Mistinguett's own Art Deco furniture (including a leopard-covered bed), the bedroom that Oscar Wilde died in, or the top-floor suite with a flower-decked balcony and a view over the church of St-Germain-des-Prés. You might rub shoulders with any number of personalities (both real and aspiring) from show-biz, fashion, or advertising. This extravaganza is the brainchild of Guy-Louis Duboucheron, who converted it, 25 years ago, from the cheap, sleazy Hôtel d'Alsace that Oscar Wilde knew. This is a very small hotel that prides itself in offering a superb—but above all discreet—service for the discriminating. *Amenities:* There's a winter garden with restaurant, Le Bélier, and an intimate piano bar. Rooms

have cable TV and air-conditioning. Room service available until 2:30am.

★★ Inter-Continental

3 rue de Castiglione, 75001 Paris. ☎ 01-44-77-11-11; fax: 01-44-77-14-60. 450 rooms. Métro: Concorde, Tuileries. AE, DC, MC, V. **$$$$/$$$$$**.

Built in 1878, the Inter-Continental has a certain matter-of-fact bustle to it: This is a hotel for people who go and do and eat and tour—and the hotel staff looks out of breath from keeping up with all of them. The clientele here is largely American, and the prices, while expensive, are still reasonable for the area and the level of services—the hotel employs more than 500 people. Several of its grandly ornate salons are now listed as historic monuments. Completely and intelligently renovated while keeping its original atmosphere almost intact, the hotel is grand but never pretentious—a nice trick. The top-floor rooms afford a majestic view over the Tuileries Gardens. *Amenities:* All the trappings of a modern luxury hotel, including 24-hour room service, a terrific bar, as well as conference rooms complete with secretaries, interpreters, and audiovisual facilities. Rooms are air-conditioned and have cable TV and minibars. The hotel also has a beautiful covered terrace, and its year-round restaurant, La Terrasse Fleurie, is a pretty and intimate place to dine.

★ Lenox

9 rue de l'Université, 75007 Paris. ☎ 01-42-96-10-95; fax: 01-42-61-52-83. 34 rooms, 2 duplexes. Métro: Rue du Bac. AE, DC, MC, V. **$$$**.

A 3-minute walk from boulevard St-Germain and the Seine, the Lenox is one of those rare hotels that stands out, not only in its class, but by any standards, because of a special thoroughbred quality. The rooms are tiny, but the forties-looking furnishings are smart, and the place has an atmosphere of trendy elegance—you feel in the center of things at the Lenox. The staff is friendly, and the service is willing. The cozy little bar off the reception area is a good place to meet someone for a quiet drink. Its sister hotel in Montparnasse (15 rue Delambre, 14e, ☎ 01-43-35-35-50) gives the same excellent value, though it is decidedly less well situated. The whole 5th floor has recently been redone. *Amenities:* Room service from 7:15am to 2pm and 5pm to 2am.

★ Libertel Lafayette

49/51 rue Lafayette, 75009 Paris. ☎ 01-42-85-05-44; fax (Central Reservation Number): 01-44-70-24-51. 97 rooms, 6 suites. Métro: Havre-Caumartin. AE, MC, V. **$$$/$$$$**.

The concept of the Libertel chain is a welcome one: moderately priced hotels featuring modern amenities and small, personal atmospheres that re-create the traditional style of *hotels du charme.* Near the shopping along the Grands Boulevards, the Libertel Lafayette is a new hotel that was decorated by Anne-Marie de Ganay in a typically French style—with cherry woods and linen on the walls, and a sculpted wood fireplace. The old-fashioned *toile de Jouy* fabric used in the rooms underlines a country charm. The 6 suites are conveniently equipped with kitchenettes. *Amenities:* Minibars; cable TV; tea/coffeemakers; 24-hour room service; some rooms A/C; a nonsmoking floor; conference room; 2 rooms especially outfitted for the handicapped.

Louvre-Montana

12 rue St-Roch, 75001 Paris. ☎ 01-42-60-35-10; fax: 01-42-61-12-28. 25 rooms. Métro: Pyramides. AE, DC, MC, V. **$$$/$$$$**.

If you feel like giving yourself a treat but can't afford the luxury hotels that line rue de Rivoli, take a few steps down a side street and try this small but spacious hotel. The Louvre-Montana has almost all the facilities of its more illustrious neighbors, but it won't cost the earth. The hotel was closed for 2 months in 1995 for renovations; the rooms are still traditional looking—lots of woodwork and floral fabrics—but everything from beds to baths has been spiffed up, and some rooms have period furnishings. *Amenities:* TVs (though not cable or satellite); minibars; 24-hour bar and room service.

Meridien Montparnasse

19 rue du Cdt René-Mouchotte, 75014 Paris. ☎ 01-44-36-44-36; Forte Exclusive: 800-225-5843; fax: 01-44-36-49-00. 953 rooms including 35 suites. Métro: Montparnasse-Bienvenüe, Gaîté. AE, DC, MC, V. **$$$$**.

Close to the Montparnasse train station and the brasserie nightlife of the area, this 4-star hotel was built as part of the Montparnasse redevelopment scheme. The building itself, by Pierre Dufau, who also designed part of La Défense, is an elegant white giant, rising 35 stories and contrasting strongly with its unlovely surroundings. With Gare Montparnasse and many

métro lines right outside, the hotel caters with renowned efficiency to its guests, which include tour groups and business executives, who appreciate the hotel's 4-star services and facilities. Prices are excellent for a luxury hotel in Paris, though the hotel isn't particularly well-located and you won't be able to walk to many sites from here. *Amenities:* Twenty-one conference rooms. Three restaurants, Le Montparnasse 25, which serves a decent enough cuisine classique; Justine, a buffet restaurant; the Atlantique, a cafe. Air-conditioning, cable TV, minibars, 24-hour room service. Rooms for the handicapped; 4 nonsmoking floors. Direct access to underground parking (fee).

Meurice

228 rue de Rivoli, 75001 Paris. ☎ 01-44-58-10-10; Leading Hotels of the World: 800-223-6800; fax: 01-44-58-10-78. 152 rooms, 28 suites. Métro: Tuileries, Concorde. AE, DC, MC, V. **$$$$$**.

Opened in 1816 opposite the Tuileries Gardens, the palatial Meurice used to receive almost all the crowned heads of Europe. More recently, the hotel, now part of the Sheraton group, has been patronized by members of the international set. The splendid salons, with their gilded paneling, tapestries, and huge chandeliers, have been added to the list of historical monuments. Le Meurice is its gastronomic restaurant. *Amenities:* Like many of the best hotels, the Meurice now has an excellent Business Center, with conference rooms and secretarial services. Cable TV, 24-hour room service, A/C, minibars.

Left Bank Hotels

★ Montalembert

3 rue de Montalembert, 75007 Paris. ☎ 01-45-49-68-68; fax: 01-45-49-69-49. 49 rooms, 7 suites. Métro: Rue-du-Bac. AE, DC, MC, V. **$$$$**.

Near the Musée D'Orsay and left-bank shopping, in one of the city's most elegant arrondissements, this charming and much sought-after hotel was refurbished in 1991 with great fanfare by designer of the moment Christian Liagre. Though the rooms are notoriously small for a hotel with

these prices, they're modern looking with luxurious details, like smoke-tinted sycamore headboards, Louis-Philippe furnishings, and plump navy-and-white striped duvets on the beds. The best suites provide views of the Musée d'Orsay and the Eiffel Tower. In the public rooms, pale burgundy stone and inlaid wood are used to set-off period furnishings. The contemporary cocktail lounge is a cozy spot for 5 o'clock coffee, with a monolithic fireplace, comfy armchairs, and a selection of newspapers. *Amenities:* A restaurant, the Montalembert, and a bar; small conference room; cable TV and VCRs; A/C; minibar; 24-hour room service. For a fee, the hotel can provide day-passes to a nearby gym.

Novanox

155 blvd. du Montparnasse, 75006 Paris. ☎ 01-46-33-63-60; fax: 01-43-26-672. 27 rooms. Métro: Vavin, Raspail. AE, DC, MC, V. **$$$**.
Straddling the back of the St-Germain-des-Prés area and Montparnasse, the Novanox is a small, personal hotel with a smart, high-tech look to it that makes it all the rage with art directors and models breezing through town for the collections—you can see them gathered in the stainless-steel bar area until the wee hours. The rooms have a trendy retro feel to them, with low-backed rounded stools and chrome-legged vanities. The rooms ending in 1 and 5 give out on to the quieter side-street; rooms 45 and 25, each with enormous black-and-white tiled baths, are particularly desirable. Owner Bertrand Plasmans worked for a spell at the Crillon, and he's picked up some good tricks; the breakfast—with mini croissants served in a basket and a sliced kiwi coddled in an egg cup—are one of the nice touches that make a stay here welcome. But if you're set on staying in the Left Bank, remember that this hotel is practically in Montparnasse—a good stretch from the cafes on the boulevard St-Germain. *Amenities:* A small conference room, though they have or will get you all necessary conference facilities. TV and 24-hour room service from the bar.

Opéra Cadet

24 rue Cadet, 75009 Paris. ☎ 01-48-24-05-26; fax: 01-42-46-68-09. 82 rooms, 3 suites. Métro: Cadet. AE, DC, MC, V. **$$$**
A crisp and ultramodern designer feel makes this hotel just right for the visiting businessperson or for anyone not looking for floral wallpaper but keenly interested in modern amenities and services at good prices. The hotel is just off rue LaFayette, in a market-filled pedestrian street near the Grands Boulevards, and the rooms are generously sized. Take breakfast in your room or in the delightful breakfast room overlooking the courtyard. *Amenities:* Wheelchair access. Room service from 8am to 10pm. There's a bar open all day in the lobby and a conference room for meetings of up to 20 people. Rooms are air-conditioned and equipped with minibar and cable TV.

Le Pavillon Bastille

65 rue de Lyon, 75012 Paris. ☎ 01-43-43-65-65; fax: 01-43-43-96-52. 23 rooms, 1 suite. Métro: Bastille. AE, DC, MC, V. **$$$**.
Up until recently, it was hard to find a hotel as refurbished as the rest of the Bastille area—at least until they opened this hotel a few years ago. Somewhat in the tradition of the Paramount hotel in New York, the Pavillon offers luxury and high design at a moderate price. The hotel is situated on a side street adjoining the place de la Bastille, in a former townhouse with a 17thC fountain in it's pretty front courtyard. The interior, decorated in blue and yellow, has a slightly retro feel, with thirties-style club chairs. Some

of the nice touches include Porthault towels and bathrobes in the bathrooms. *Amenities:* Cable TV. Free minibars in all rooms. No restaurant but 24-hour room service of drinks and snacks. The suite has wheelchair access.

★★★ Pergolese

3 rue Pergolese, 75116 Paris. ☎ 01-40-67-96-77; fax: 01-45-00-12-11. 40 rooms, 1 suite. Métro: Argentine. AE, DC, MC, V. **$$$/$$$$**.

Opened in the spring of 1991, this hotel was designed by architect and furniture designer Rena Dumas (wife of Hermès chairman Jean-Louis Dumas) and strikes a clean balance between modernism and classicism. The dining room tables are by Philippe Starck, and the chrome sinks in the bathroom are designed by Andrée Putman—the whole place has a kind of Calvinist, no-nonsense feel to it. The rooms have blond wood furniture and an unfussy charm. A good hotel for business travelers, but it's in the west of Paris, not far from the Bois de Boulogne, and lacks a truly central location.. *Amenities:* Three small salons and a bar on the ground floor. 24-hour room service. A/C, cable TV, minibar.

Plaza-Athénée

25 av. Montaigne, 75008 Paris. ☎ 01-47-23-78-33; A Forte Exclusive hotel: 800-225-5843; fax: 01-47-20-20-70. 168 rooms, 42 suites. Métro: Alma Marceau, Franklin-D-Roosevelt. AE, DC, MC, V. **$$$$$**.

Ever since its founding in 1911, the Plaza Athénée has been synonymous with a certain kind of cosmopolitanism; rich exiles from Argentina like to stay here, as did Josephine Baker and even

Mata Hari (she was finally arrested in front of the hotel in 1917). Near the Seine and avenue des Champs-Elysées, but away from the noise and bustle, the hotel has everything that you could want in a pleasure palace. Afternoon tea can be taken in the elegant, long gallery, and an inner courtyard, with red awnings and geraniums in the window boxes, is one of the prettiest in Paris. Its hallmarks are gorgeous period-style suites and attractive bedrooms, superb service, an excellent classic gastronomic restaurant, the Régence, and a grill, the Relais-Plaza, a fashionable spot to stop for lunch. Still, outside of the restaurants, the Plaza-Athénée lacks a certain glamor these days, and not for lack of trying. *Amenities:* Besides the 2 restaurants, the Bar Anglais features live music at night. There isn't a gym here, but guests have free use of a nearby health club, and the hotel will pay for your taxi there. Four conference rooms; A/C; cable TV; minibars; rooms with wheelchair access available.

Quai Voltaire

19 quai Voltaire, 75007 Paris. ☎ 01-42-61-50-91; fax: 01-42-61-62-26. 33 rooms, 29 with bath. Métro: rue du Bac, Solférino, Musée d'Orsay. AE, DC, MC, V. **$$/$$$**.

Most rooms in this light, bright little Left Bank hotel afford a superb view over the Seine—a view enhanced by the tall French windows. The front rooms can unfortunately be rather noisy, so if the view of the Seine doesn't matter to you, ask for rooms out back. The establishment has a cultural and literary past. Pissarro painted *Le Pont Royal* from the window of his room, and the hotel was patronized by Charles Baudelaire and Oscar Wilde, as well as Sibelius and Wagner. It has a small, unostentatious bar—a choice meeting place for the lions of modern French literature. *Amenities:* TV on request; room service from 7am to 9pm.

★★★ Raphaël

17 av. Kléber, 75016 Paris.
☎ 01-44-28-00-28; fax: 01-45-01-21-50. 89 rooms, including 45 suites. Métro: Kléber. AE, DC, MC, V. **$$$$$**.

The smallest of the Parisian *palaces* (luxury hotels), the Raphaël has a richly romantic atmosphere that is heightened by dark wood-paneling, heavy tapestries, thick carpets, and a huge seascape by Turner right over the reception area. The suites are movie-star glamorous, but the doubles can be tight for two at these prices. The Raphaël has an artsy, literary cachet—this and its discreet location near place Charles-de-Gaulle and the Arc de Triomphe may be what appeals to the movie stars and producers who stay here regularly. Though this may be the most romantic hotel in the world, it isn't ideal for a busy tourist stay—the location is too far away from the center. *Amenities:* Small conference rooms; A/C; cable TV; minibars; restaurant; 24-hour room service; a bar open all day for lunch as well as cocktails.

Regent's Garden

6 rue Pierre-Demours, 75017 Paris. ☎ 01-45-74-07-30; Best Western group: 800-528-1234; fax: 01-40-55-01-42. 39 rooms. Métro: Charles-de-Gaulle-Étoile. AE, DC, MC, V. **$$$**.

The Regent's Garden lives up to its name by possessing a real garden (as opposed to a court-yard) complete with statues and fountains and where you can breakfast on spring and summer mornings. The building itself, on a quiet street in a residential area not far from Arc de Triomphe, is typical of the showy *grand bourgeois* architecture of the mid-19thC. Its lofty rooms, whose ceilings sport decor-ative moldings, are furnished in appropriate style, with period furniture and large mirrors. *Amenities:* No restaurant or room service, excluding breakfast. Rooms have cable TV.

Relais Christine

3 rue Christine, 75006 Paris.
☎ 01-43-26-71-80; fax 01-43-26-89-38. 51 rooms, 17 suites. Métro: Mabillon, Odéon. AE, DC, MC, V. **$$$$**.

Located in a quiet backwater in the heart of the Latin Quarter, close to place St-Michel, this 16thC building, once a monastery, became many other things, including a publisher's book depot, before transformation into a hotel in 1979. Although it's expensive, the hotel offers excellent value. Its comfortable, spacious, and tastefully decorated rooms—several of which are split-level apartments—are individually furnished with period pieces. Those on the lower floors are rather dim, although 1 ground-floor room has a stone wall and a fine carved door. Rooms give on to either the garden, courtyard, or street; the doubles on the street are the largest, and the street is so small that noise isn't a problem. The rooms on the garden are the smallest. *Amenities:* Private garage; satellite TV; minibar; bar open 24 hours; 24-hour room service; A/C; conference room.

★★ Ritz

15 pl. Vendôme, 75001 Paris.
☎ 01-42-60-38-30; fax: 01-42-60-23-71. 142 rooms, 45 suites.
Métro: Pyramides, Madeleine. AE, DC, MC, V. **$$$$$**

Overlooking the exclusive place Vendôme, this is arguably the most famous hotel in the world, and the Ritz lives up to its reputation, exuding luxury, attentiveness, and just the right amount of glitz. It has not rested on its laurels like many other long-famous hotels, but has been sensitively renovated over a period of years: They kept the huge and splendid original baths whereas the telephones became computerized.

The benefits of staying at the Ritz are many: Unobtrusive service, beautiful period furnishings, a lovely inner garden, several chic bars, and a good restaurant, L'Espadon. For the truly discriminating, it is showier and less discreet than its closest competitor, the Crillon, and can border on a certain kitsch. *Amenities:* The Ritz Health Club, with its vast pool in a Taj Mahal–like setting, including workout rooms, squash courts, saunas, and steam baths. The men's barber shop, overseen by the affable Monsieur Joseph, is where the city's power heads go for a scissored trim. Down in the bowels of the hotel, the Ritz-Escoffier School of French Gastronomy offers pricey cooking classes; you can pay on a one-off basis to attend demonstration classes, and you'll never forget the experience. The new Hemingway Bar is a classy spot for an afternoon cocktail; less inviting is the Ritz Club, a kind of supper club that has never really found its place in the competitive world of Parisian nightclubbing. Conference rooms, wheelchair access, cable TV, A/C, minibars.

Royal Monceau

37 av. Hoche, 75008 Paris.
☎ 01-45-61-98-00; fax: 01-42-99-89-90. 219 rooms, including 40 suites. Métro: Charles-de-Gaulle-Étoile. AE, DC, MC, V.
$$$$$

Between the Arc de Triomphe and the attractive Parc Monceau, this hotel is a favorite with international business clients, but all who can afford the Monceau enjoy its serene elegance and many excellent pluses: Few luxury hotels in Paris boast both a pool and a Michelin-starred restaurant. In addition to the sumptuous rooms and attentive staff, the Monceau also boasts 2 fine restaurants. Offering Italian fare, the well-known Il Carpaccio is situated in the hotel's main building. In a rotunda in the courtyard is Le Jardin (with 1 Michelin star), offering gourmet specialties from southwestern France. In addition, there are 2 elegant cocktail bars, including a piano bar that opens at 9pm. The hotel also features Les Thermes, a fitness club that includes a swimming pool, a sauna and gym, massage, hydrotherapy, and its own separate health-conscious restaurant. *Amenities:* The Royal Monceau is well equipped to cater to the corporate traveler, and has 7 rooms suitable for conference or banqueting functions. Rooms are air-conditioned. Cable TV, minibars, 24-hour room service.

De Seine

52 rue de Seine, 75006 Paris.
☎ 01-46-34-22-80; fax: 01-46-34-04-74. 30 rooms. Métro: St-Germain-des-Prés, Mabillon. MC, V. **$$$$**

In the heart of the bustling St-Germain Quarter, the

Hôtel de Seine is is run with friendliness and great efficiency; the hotel itself is not fancy, but it is, however, well-maintained and one of the city's better-reputed *hotels du charme*. Keep in mind though that prices are fairly expensive for a hotel containing neither a bar, nor restaurant, nor room service; if you are in town on business, this is probably not the place to stay. An easy walk from the *quai*, the hotel is a fine base from which to explore the Latin Quarter or for that other favorite Parisian pastime, cafe-hopping, with a remarkable choice virtually outside your door. Rue de Seine, known for its art galleries, also has a superb open-air food market. As one might expect given its location, the hotel is usually heavily reserved. *Amenities.* Cable TV. Drinks only served in rooms from 7am to 5pm.

★★★ Sheraton Paris Airport Hotel

Charles de Gaulle, Aerogare 2, Terminales C and D, BP 30051, 95716 Roissy Aerogare. ☎ 01-48-62-36-56; fax: 01-48-62-36-55. 242 rooms, 14 suites. AE, DC, MC, V. **$$$/$$$$**.
A brand new luxury hotel conveniently situated inside Terminals C and D at the Charles de Gaulle airport (meaning you can walk there from your plane), right above the newly built RER and TGV (high-speed train) stations, the Sheraton Paris Airport, which opened in early 1996, is shaped like an ocean liner, Its interiors were designed by top-Parisian decorator Andrée Putman, who put a sleek modern touch to everything. *Amenities:* Soundproofed rooms; individually controlled A/C; cable TV and VCR; TV screens give

times and hours of flights; minibar; computer and fax lines; 4 conference rooms; free pressing of 1 suit and free washing of 3 items; gym and sauna; massages; business center. A gastronomic restaurant, Les Etoiles; a brasserie, Les Saisons; and a bar.

Solférino

91 rue de Lille, 75007 Paris. ☎ 01-47-05-85-54; fax: 01-45-55-51-16. 33 rooms, 27 with toilet facilities. Métro: Solférino, Assemblée Nationale. Breakfast included in room rate. Closed 10 days during Christmas. MC, V. **$$**.
The Solférino is a charming, old-fashioned, and modest hotel with prettily and tastefully decorated, high-ceilinged bedrooms; a delightful little sitting room; and a breakfast veranda with dainty cane furniture. The faithful, mainly English and American, clientele are especially appreciative of the warm welcome extended by the Solférino's friendly staff. The hotel is located in St-Germain, tucked between the Seine and boulevard St-Germain. *Amenities:* TV in some rooms only.

De Suède

31 rue Vaneau, 75007 Paris. ☎ 01-47-05-00-08; fax: 01-47-05-69-27. 38 rooms, 1 suite. Métro: Sèvres-Babylone, Vaneau. AE, MC, V. **$$/$$$**.
Cool elegance distinguishes this hotel, and that is just as it should be, since it backs onto the gardens of the Prime Minister's official residence, the Hôtel Matignon. If you want to try to glimpse the man, or simply admire the towering plane trees that grow here, ask for a room on the 2nd or 3rd floor. The hotel also has a large, gently-lit lounge in the

Directoire style and a pretty little inner-courtyard, where morning or afternoon refreshment may be taken. *Amenities:* TV, 24-hour room service.

Terrass

12 rue Joseph-de-Maistre, 75018 Paris. ☎ 01-46-06-72-85; fax: 01-42-52-29-11. 88 rooms, 13 suites. Métro: Blanche, Place Clichy. Buffet breakfast included in room rate. AE, DC, MC, V. **$$$/ $$$$**.

This first-class establishment, perched on an outcrop of the Butte de Montmartre, offers just about the best views of any hotel in Paris. You can see the Panthéon, the Opéra, Les Invalides, the Arc de Triomphe, the Eiffel Tower, and even La Défense from its restaurant terrace and from some of the rooms. Built in 1912 but modernized several times since then, the Terrass is the only 4-star hotel in Montmartre. What's more, the prices are a little lower than for something comparable elsewhere. *Amenities:* A rooftop restaurant, La Terrass Panoramique, is open on the 8th floor terrace from April to September, when it moves back inside to the ground floor. Bar open from 4pm to 2am. Rooms have cable TV, A/C, and minibars.

★ Des Tuileries

10 rue St-Hyacinthe, 75001 Paris. ☎ 01-42-61-04-17; fax: 01-49-27-91-56. 26 rooms, 4 suites. Métro: Pyramides, Tuileries. AE, DC, MC, V. **$$$/$$$$**.

You won't find a much quieter street in the center of Paris than the tiny rue St-Hyacinthe, close to place Vendôme and within easy reach of avenue de l'Opéra and the Tuileries Gardens. The Hôtel des Tuileries occupies a late 18thC townhouse that used to belong to a lady in waiting of Marie Antoinette, who stayed here for a time on the 3rd floor. The Poulle-Vidal family has run the hotel for 3 generations, and they've been discreetly modernizing it for years: Now the rooms all have marble-clad bathrooms. A lot of the furnishings are authentic period pieces; those and the oriental carpets give it the air of an elegant private home. An old-fashioned notion of service still reigns here. *Amenities:* TV; A/C; small conference room; bar; room service (snacks and drinks) from 7am to 8pm.

★★ De l'Université

22 rue de l'Université, 75007 Paris. ☎ 01-42-61-09-39; fax: 01-42-60-40-84. 26 rooms, 1 suite. Métro: rue du Bac. AE, MC, V. **$$$/$$$$**.

Everything here shouts refinement, from the taped classical music playing in the lobby to the gravely mannered staff to the handpicked antiques and tapestries dotting the stone lobby. The establishment, which occupies a 17thC *hôtel particulier* (townhouse) on a sedate street in the heart of the Left Bank, has good-sized rooms, each outfitted with period furnishings. The hotel is reserved well ahead by people who want to stay in quiet style at the antique-dealing and publishing end of the St-Germain Quarter. If you can, reserve room 32, with a fabu-lous mirrored fireplace flanked by armchairs. For a little more, you can have a room with a terrace (no. 52) that has to be one of the most charming rooms in Paris. The hotel is deliberately low-key, like a tony antiques gallery: No one here will run to get a stamp for you, and at these prices, that might be troubling to some. But the intimate beauty and cachet of this hotel are rare even in a city such as Paris. *Amenities:* Satellite TV; individual safe; A/C. No bar. Room service until 8pm. About half of the rooms have minibars.

La Villa

29 rue Jacob, 75006 Paris.
☎ 01-43-26-60-00; fax: 01-46-34-63-63. 32 rooms, 3 suites. Métro: St-Germain-des-Prés. AE, DC, MC, V. **$$$/$$$$**.

In his search to create an avant-garde mood with the ultimate in designer chic, owner Vincent Darnaud took the gamble of entrusting his new hotel's entire design to the young but highly-regarded Marie-Christine Dorner. The result is a sleek temple of modern design in the heart of St-Germain, between boulevard St-Germain and the Seine, blending anthracite-colored marble, burnished metal, plane wood, leather, and sanded and engraved glass. A swirling metal stairway leads downstairs to the highly reputed jazz club in the cellar. Reserve well ahead: La Villa is *très à la mode* among architects and design folk. *Amenities:* Cocktail bar and jazz club with top international performers. 24-hour room service; satellite TV; minibar; A/C; wheelchair access.

William's

3 rue Mayran, 75009 Paris.
☎ 01-48-78-68-35; fax: 01-45-26-08-70. 30 rooms. Métro: Cadet. RER: Gare du Nord. AE, DC, MC, V. **$$**.

An inexpensive and quite unusual little hotel off rue LaFayette, with every room facing out over the tranquil square Montholon. Many of the rooms are irregularly shaped and quite small, but the decor is tastefully modern and the color-schemes quite striking, with an accent on red and purple. The welcome is warm. *Amenities:* Not many but you won't care at this price. Drinks can be served to your room, which has a TV.

Other Alternatives

Apartments

You may prefer to rent your own apartment for a week or so. Speak to **Rothray** (6 rue Bertin, 75001 Paris, ☎ 01-48-87-13-37, fax: 01-42-78-17-72). Owner Ray Lampard, a business executive who has himself lived in a number of capital cities, knows the difficulties of foreign travel. His company offers a friendly, efficient, reasonably priced, and very flexible service (a 7-day minimum stay is required) and there are various apartments, some small and some large, in the **Marais/Halles/Pompidou Center** areas. You can pay in your own currency, by personal check.

Hotel-Hostels

At the other end of the range, you may find that good, clean, friendly hostel accommodation is all that you need. There are a number of hostels run by **MIJE**

(Maisons Internationales de la Jeunesse et des Etudiants), which has 3 good hotel-hostels within the **Marais.**

The rooms have from 1 to 8 beds in them. These hotel-hostels are, in theory, for young people. In practice, anyone over 18 willing to share a room with one or more strangers of the same sex is welcome—though if you're over 35, they insist that you take a double or a single. The rooms have showers, but bathrooms are in the halls, and it's a cash-only operation.

All the buildings are superb 17thC former private houses in quiet locations. They have exposed beams, original floor tiles, stone flagging, and antique furniture. All of the rooms, singles included, cost under 200F and include breakfast. Individuals can reserve 1 week in advance. The central inquiries and reservations number is ☎ 01-42-74-23-45.

Fauconnier, 11 rue du Fauconnier, 75004 Paris. 100 beds. Métro: St-Paul-le-Marais. Location: In a small street by the Seine, opposite the Ile St-Louis.

Fourcy, 6 rue de Fourcy, 75004 Paris. 204 beds. Métro: St-Paul-le-Marais. Location: Behind the Hôtel de Sens/Bibliothèque Forney.

Maubuisson, 12 rue des Barres, 75004 Paris. 90 beds. Métro: Hôtel-de-Ville. Location: Behind St-Gervais-St-Protais church near the Hôtel-de-Ville.

Bed & Breakfasts

Several Paris organizations propose rooms in private homes. This option provides both a reasonably-priced alternative to a hotel stay and can introduce you to life as the Parisians live it. **Café Couette** (8 rue d'Isly, 75008 Paris, ☎ 01-42-94-92-00, fax: 01-42-94-93-12), for example, has a list of 75 families who will open their homes to travelers for a minimum of 2 nights to a maximum of 1 month. Prices vary according to the accommodations, and don't expect anything more than a private room and breakfast, but more than one friendship has been made across the Atlantic this way. The company's employees all speak English, and you can request a stay with English-speaking residents. Prices are 280F for a room with a shared bathroom, 390F for a room with private bath, 520F for a luxury lodging in a large, well-situated apartment.

SIGHTS & ATTRACTIONS

For the latest happenings, get hold of the 2 excellent, free publications available from the Bureaux de Tourisme, *Paris, Ile-de-France, Guide des Musées et Monuments* and *The Paris User's Guide.*

For almost any question you would have about Paris—the time of the last trip of the day up the Eiffel Tower, the name of a wine bar in the 12e arrondissement, as well as for assistance in arranging personal tours—call the friendly bilingual **visitor information hotline** at ☎ 01-44-29-12-12. They couldn't be more helpful.

Many museums close on Tuesday and on some public holidays. Many are also now free or cheaper on Sunday.

If you plan to visit a number of museums, buy a **Carte Musées et Monuments,** on sale at museums and monuments, métro stations, and tourist offices. This card, costing from 60F to 170F for 1, 3, or 5 days, allows you unlimited access to 65 sights, without having to line up for tickets.

Special-Interest Tours

The **American Express Travel Service** (11 rue Scribe, 9e, ☎ 01-47-77-77-37; métro: Opéra) is a valuable source of information for travelers seeking guided tours, as well as reservations for many events and other information. A bilingual toll-free tourist advice and information service is available (Mar–Oct, Mon–Sat 8:30am–8pm, ☎ 01-05-20-12-02).

Paris Vision (214 rue de Rivoli, 1er, ☎ 01-42-60-31-25) offers 2-hour tours of the city delivered in English and other languages for 150F; as well as day-trips to Fontainebleau and Versailles.

For First-Time Visitors	
Arc de Triomphe	Palais-Royal
Eiffel Tower	Musée Picasso
Grand Carnavalet	Notre Dame
Musée d'Orsay	Place des Vosges
Louvre	Tuileries Gardens

Cityrama (4 pl. des Pyramides, 1ᵉʳ, ☎ 01-44-55-60-00) offers 1-hour city tours with headphones on a double-decker bus for 150F; a 3¹/₂-hour "artistic" tour of Notre Dame and Louvre for 260F; and a 4-hour trip including a cruise on the Seine, and a stop at the Eiffel Tower, also for 260F. Day-trips to nearby sites including Fontainebleue and Versailles are also given. This company also offers an individual English-speaking guide with a minivan at 1000F for 3 hours.

Paris Shopping Tour (☎ 01-42-94-13-87) offers a look at some of the main fashion arteries and scouts out lower-priced finds.

Paris-Velo (2 rue du Fer à Moulin, 5ᵉ, ☎ 01-43-37-59-22) conducts special biking tours of the capital every Wednesday night. Guides take you down little-known streets, like the Montaigne St-Geneviève.

Paris Walking Tours (☎ 01-48-09-21-40), run by a British couple, offers classic tours of the Latin Quarter or the Marais—as well as offbeat ones such as "Kings, Courtiers, and Cardinals."

Paris Market Tours (☎ 01-45-35-26-34), led by food journalist Rosa Jackson, takes first-time visitors out to breakfast and then to an open-air market.

Walking the Spirit Tours (☎ 01-42-29-60-12), led by Canadian filmmaker Julia Browne, offers insights into the African American in Paris with a tour that focuses on the entertainers in Montmartre and another specializing in "Intellectuals and Artists" (Richard Wright, Chester Himes).

Paris Contact (☎ 01-42-51-08-40) provides freelance guides, who customize trips to your interests. Their speciality? The secret gardens of Paris, including the vineyards of Montmartre.

Special Moments

Julius Caesar said that before taking a city, you had to see it from on-high. Among the best places to do this are the **Eiffel Tower** and the **Tour Montparnasse.**

Back on terra firma, amble along the **banks of the Seine** in the 6ᵉ arrondissement, then cross to **Notre**

Dame on the **Ile de la Cité.** Try to come in the early morning, and take a seat, before the hordes of tourists descend. Remind yourself that kings of France were crowned here, crusaders started off from here, Parisians slept here with their goats, and at various times in France's history some 10,000 people gathered within these immense walls.

Walk through **Ile Saint Louis,** where the narrow streets are still incised with the gutters that carried away waste in the days before plumbing. Imagine wheat and fish piled in creaking wooden wagons on their way down the **Rue Saint Honoré** and **Rue des Poissoniers** to the crowded markets of the Ile de la Cité.

Another magical place to visit is **Montmartre,** but only in the early morning or off-season, before visitors arrive in search of the Real Paris. Renoir, Modigliani, Pisarro, and van Gogh—these are only a few of the artists who made their home here. The tidy buildings, the steep winding streets, the views of the city below, the greenery—all are part of the Montmartre experience which can't be duplicated anywhere else in the city. One of the prettiest streets to stroll is the **Villa Léandre,** lined with 2-story townhouses with ivy-covered balconies. But almost all of Montmartre is surprising—from the **tiny vineyard** on **Rue Saint-Vincent,** to the **skylit painters' studios** at 1 rue d'Orchampt, to the **windmill,** (stand at the corner of the Rue Lepic and the Rue Girardon) to the bustle of **shops on Rue Lepic.**

Sights & Attractions by Category

Churches

Chapelle Expiatoire
★ Dôme
★★ La Madeleine
★★★ Notre-Dame de
  Paris
★ Sacré-Coeur, Basilique du
St-Augustin
★★★ Sainte-Chapelle
St-Denis, Basilique
St-Etienne-du-Mont
St-Eustache
St-Germain l'Auxerrois
★★ St-Germain-des-Prés
St-Joseph-des-Carmes
St-Julien-le-Pauvre
St-Louis-Les-Invalides
St-Nicolas-des-Champs
St-Roch
St-Séverin

St-Sulpice
Val-de-Grâce

Streets, Squares & Quartiers

Bastille, place de la
Bercy
★ Champs-Elysées,
  avenue des
★ Concorde, place de la
La Défense
Les Halles
★★★ Ile de la Cité
★★ Latin Quarter
★★★ Marais
★ Montmartre
Montparnasse
Opéra Quarter
"Passages"
★★ Pont Alexandre III

★★★ Pont-Neuf
St-Germain Quarter
★ Place Vendôme
La Villette
★★★ Place des Vosges

Famous Homes

Balzac, Maison de
Bourdelle, Musée Antoine
★★ Camondo, Musée
   Nissim de
Le Corbusier, Fondation
Delacroix, Musée Eugène
d'Ennery, Musée
Hugo, Maison Victor
Moreau, Musée Gustave
Pasteur, Musée
Piaf, Musée Edith
Vie Romantique, Musée de la
   (Maison Renan-Scheffer)
Zadkine, Musée

General Interest

Catacombes
★ Cité de la Musique
Egouts (Sewers)
★★ Flea Market
Gobelins
Grévin, Musée
Hôtel des Ventes
★★ Marché aux Puces
Les Martyrs de Paris
Napoléon's Tomb
Opéra Bastille
★★ Opéra Garnier
Palais des Congrès
Paristoric
Pavillon de l'Arsenal
★ Père Lachaise, Cimetière
Publicité, Musée de la
Radio-France, Maison de
Viaducs des Arts

Historic Buildings

★★ Archevêques de Sens,
   Hôtel des
Beaux-Arts, Ecole des
Bibliothèque Nationale
Bourse des Valeurs
★ Comédie Française
★★ Conciergerie
★ Hôtel des Invalides
Hôtel de Ville
Institut de France
Luxembourg Palais du
Observatoire de Paris
★ Opéra Garnier

Palais de Chaillot
Palais de l'Elysée
Palais de Justice
★★★ Palais-Royal
Palais de Tokyo
★★★ Panthéon
Sorbonne
Vincennes, Château de

Science & Technology

★★★ Cité des Sciences
   et de l'Industrie
Techniques, Musée des

Modern (20thC) Buildings & Districts

Le Corbusier, Fondation
La Défense
Disneyland Paris
Forum des Halles
★ Grande Arche de la Défense
★★ Grand Louvre-Pyramid
Hôtel des Ventes
★★ Institut du Monde Arabe
Opéra Bastille
Palais de Chaillot
Palais des Congrès
Palais de la Mode
★ Pompidou Center
Radio-France, Maison
Tour Montparnasse
La Villette

Monuments & Landmarks

★★★ Arc de Triomphe
Arc de Triomphe du Carrousel
Fontaine des Quatre Saisons
Grande Arche de la Défense
Porte St-Denis
Porte St-Martin
★★★ Tour Eiffel

Museums & Galleries

★ Arts Forains
Archives Nationales
Armée
Art Moderne
Art Moderne de la Ville
   de Paris
Arts d'Afrique et d'Océanie
★★ Arts Asiatiques-Guimet
Arts Décoratifs
Arts de la Mode et du Textile
Arts et Métiers
★ Arts Forains
★ Arts et Traditions Populaires
Balzac, Maison de

Beaux-Arts
Bourdelle
★★ Camondo, Nissim
Cernuschi
Chasse et Nature
Cinéma Henri-Langlois
Clemenceau
★★★ Cluny, Thermes
de Cognacq-Jay
Le Corbusier
Crypte Archéologique
de Notre-Dame
Dalí, Espace Salvador
Delacroix
d'Ennery
★★★ Grand Carnavalet
★★★ Grand Louvre
★ Grand Palais
Grévin
Hébert
Henner
en Herbe
Histoire de France
★★ Histoire Naturelle
Homme
Hugo, Victor
★ Institut du Monde Arabe
Jacquemart-André
★ Jeu de Paume
Légion d'Honneur
Marine
★ Marmottan
Mode et Costume
★★ Monde Arabe
Monde de l'Art
Monnaie
Monuments Français
Moreau, Gustave
★★★ Moyen Age
Orangerie des Tuileries
★★★ Orsay
Ordre de la Libération
Palais de la Découverte
Pasteur
Petit Palais
★★★ Picasso
Plans-Reliefs
Police

★★★ Pompidou Center
Poste
Publicité
Radio-France
★★★ Rodin
Sculpture de Plein Air
Techniques
Vie Romantique
Zadkine

Parks, Gardens & Open Spaces

Arènes de Lutèce
★★ Bois de Boulogne
Buttes Chaumont
Canal St-Martin
Champ-de-Mars
Jardin des Plantes
★★ Jardin du Luxembourg
Parc Monceau
Parc de Montsouris
★★★ Tuileries
★ La Villette
★ Vincennes, Bois de

Viewpoints . . . Famous

Arc de Triomphe
Grande Arche de la Défense
Montmartre-Butte
Notre-Dame
Panthéon
Pompidou Center
Sacré-Coeur
Tour Eiffel
Tour Montparnasse

Viewpoints . . . Less Famous

Concorde LaFayette Hotel
(bar)
Galeries LaFayette terrace
Institut du Monde Arabe
(cafeteria terrace)
Parc des Buttes-Chaumont
Samaritaine department store
terrace
Tour Eiffel (restaurant Jules
Verne)

Sights & Attractions A to Z

Note: If you only know the name of a museum in English and cannot find it in this A-to-Z list, try looking it up in the index. Other sights that do not have their own entries may well be included in a district entry; look these up in the index, too.

Andre-Citroën, Parc

Entrances on rue de la Montagne-de-la-Farge and rue de la Montagne-de-L'Esperou, 15ᵉ. Open dawn to dusk. Métro: Balard or Javel.

Recuperated from the site of a former Citroën car factory, the latest entrant to the city's parks is a sprawling $67 million hybrid of outdoor and indoor spaces that sprawls over a full 34 acres (14ha). Unlike either the Bois de Boulogne or the Parc de Vincennes, the Parc Andre-Citroën, which opened in 1992, is a case of nature being marshalled in the strictest sense.

Two immense 50-foot-high glass-walled structures—an orangery and a conservatory housing southern Mediterranean plants—bring the outdoors in, providing a welcome and often handy reprieve from Paris's frequent showers. The rest of it is a sort of contemporary formal garden. Six Serial Gardens are strictly high-concept, with colors and senses (blue/smell, green/sound, orange/touch, red/taste, gray/sight, gold/the 6th sense) artfully linked. There's also a water garden and a wild garden that, sprinkled with cotton thistle and cow parsnip, is vaguely Little House on the Prairie-ish. It's a thinking-person's park of sorts, and though that might not conform to everyone's idea of nature, the whole thing is undoubtedly scrupulously tended and designed with a certain museumlike comfort.

★★★ Arc de Triomphe

Pl. Charles-de-Gaulle, 8ᵉ. ☎ 01-43-80-31-31. Open Apr 1–Sept 30: 9:30am–11pm (6pm on Sat and Sun), Oct 1–Mar 31: 10am–10pm (6pm on Sun and Mon). Closed public holidays. Admission charged. Métro: Charles-de-Gaulle-Etoile.

As much a symbol of Paris as the **Tour Eiffel** or **Notre-Dame,** the Arc de Triomphe is the largest structure of its kind in the world—50 meters (164 ft.) high and 45 meters (148 ft.) wide—and its massive bulk dominates the **place Charles-de-Gaulle,** formerly the place de

L'Arc de Triomphe

l'Etoile, from which the 12 broad avenues radiate to create the star-shape of Paris.

The quickest—and safest—way to reach it, positioned as it is at the center of an immense traffic circle, is by a tunnel that leads from the north side of the avenue des Champs-Elysées.

The ponderous and imposing arch is clean and shining right now, having received a thorough clean-up at the time of the bicentenary celebrations in 1989. In a way, it is surely one of the biggest white elephants ever created. Curiously, an earlier plan for the site was to erect a vast stone elephant containing an amphitheater, banqueting hall, and other apartments.

The present arch was begun in 1806 on the orders of Napoléon, who wanted a monument to French military victories, but it remained unfinished at the time of his downfall. Under the restored monarchy, work on the arch continued spasmodically, and it was finally completed in 1836.

Many artists worked on the decoration of the exterior, which includes 4 huge relief sculptures at the bases of the pillars: *The Triumph of 1810* by Cortot; both *Resistance* and *Peace* by Etex; and *The Departure of the Volunteers* (commonly known, for obvious reasons, by the name of *La Marseillaise*) by François Rude, which is generally considered to be the best of the four.

Higher up are reliefs of battles and a crowded frieze, and engraved around the top are the names of major victories won during the revolutionary and Napoleonic periods. On the inside walls appear the names of lesser victories and of 558 generals.

Set into the ground under the arch is the **Tomb of the Unknown Soldier,** commemorating the dead of World Wars I and II, whose memory is kept alight by an eternal flame—a few years ago, an irreverent person cooked an omelet over it. The arch seems to invite such disrespectful gestures: In 1919 the aviator Godefroy flew under it in an airplane, defying a police ban.

Inside is a **museum of the arch's history,** which runs a continuous audiovisual program in French and English recounting the monument's great moments. But this little collection is no substitute for the real thing, and you must mount to the viewing platform for what is one of the best views in Paris. To the northeast is the **Grande Arche** at **La Défense,** constructed on an axis with the Arc de Triomphe that continues on through **Place de la Concorde** and the gardens of the **Tuileries** as far as the **Grand Louvre** with its pyramid.

Arc de Triomphe du Carrousel

Pl. du Carrousel, 1ᵉʳ. Métro: Tuileries, Palais-Royal/Musée-du-Louvre.

This graceful arch, with its rose-colored marble columns, is linked with the greater **Arc de Triomphe** by the splendid axis formed by the **Champs-Elysées** and the **Tuileries,** culminating now at **La Défense** in the northeast outskirts of Paris.

Completed in 1809, it commemorates Napoléon's victories in 1805 (including Austerlitz and Ulm), which are depicted on 6 marble low reliefs. It was formerly surmounted by the 4 gilded bronze horses from St. Mark's in Venice. When these were returned to Italy in 1815, they were replaced by a bronze group, representing the Restoration, riding in a chariot drawn by 4 horses. The arch once formed the gateway to the Tuileries Palace, which burned down in 1871, and for many years it seemed to float in the gardens between the great jaws of the **Louvre** like a dainty morsel about to be swallowed by a whale.

Massive excavation and rebuilding works have disrupted its peace since 1991. The new formal gardens surrounding the place du Carrousel were designed by Jacques Wirtz.

Archives Nationales: Musée de l'Histoire de France (National Archives: Museum of French History)

Hôtel de Soubise, 60 rue des Francs-Bourgeois, 3ᵉ; Hôtel de Rohan, 87 rue Vieille-du-Temple, 3ᵉ. ☎ 01-40-27-60-00. Open 2–5pm. Closed Tues. Admission charged. Métro: Rambuteau, Hôtel-de-Ville.

How many tumultuous events have started with an innocent-looking document? The Revocation of the Edict of Nantes by Louis XIV removed freedom of worship, and drove thousands of Protestants out of France. The Revocation and the original Edict are both in the Historical Museum of France, and form part of a collection of documents belonging to the National Archives, which are housed in one of the great mansions of the **Marais** district, the Hôtel de Soubise.

Here also are the wills of Louis XIV and Napoléon, the Concordat of 1802 between Napoléon and the Holy See, the Declaration of the Rights of Man, letters by Joan of Arc and by Voltaire—snippets of history skillfully displayed and carefully illustrated with the use of maps, photographs, and captions to create an intriguing scrapbook of the French nation.

The National Archives themselves, which take up 280 kilometers (175 miles) of shelving, have been housed in the Hôtel de Soubise since 1808 and in the adjacent Hôtel de Rohan since 1927.

The documents are temporarily closed to visitors due to a reorganization of the museum, though the archives are available for scholarly research. But there is more to see here than the documents. The **Hôtel de Soubise** itself, with its elegant, colonnaded courtyard, is worth visiting on its own account. It was built between 1705 and 1708 for the Princesse de Soubise, on the site of a medieval mansion, of which 1 tower remains, overlooking rue des Archives. It was sumptuously decorated by some of the greatest artists and craftsmen of the era, including Boucher, van Loo, and Lemoyne.

Leaving the main room of the museum on the 1st floor, formerly the guard room, one passes through a series of private apartments. Particularly worth seeing are the Princess' Oval Salon, with its 8 paintings of the loves of Psyche by Charles Natoire, and also her small bedroom, which now houses a permanent exhibition on the French Revolution.

The **Hôtel de Rohan** (officially called the **Hôtel de Strasbourg**) is around the corner in rue Vieille-du-Temple. As well as being part of the National Archives, it is now frequently used for temporary exhibitions. It was lived in by 4 successive cardinals of Strasbourg who decorated their apartments with rich extravagance. One of the rooms, the Monkey Cabinet, retains its original panels, decorated with animals by Christophe Huet in 1745.

The remainder of the interior is the result of skillful restoration. The courtyard has a fine relief by Robert le Lorrain, *The Horses of Apollo.*

Arènes de Lutèce

Entrances in rue Monge (next door to Hôtel des Arènes) and rue de Navarre, 5e. Open dawn to dusk. Wheelchair access. Métro: Place Monge, Jussieu, Cardinal-Lemoine.

Turning off the street into what you might expect to be an ordinary Parisian park, you walk down a stone corridor and suddenly emerge into a Gallo-Roman amphitheater with terraces for spectators. All but demolished by barbarian invasions in the 3rdC, the arena was rediscovered quite by chance in 1869 during construction work on rue Monge, and was restored 50 years later.

Now it is enjoying a second and quieter lease on life. Surrounded by greenery, it makes an ideal place for watching a game of *boules* or for simply sitting and imagining life in Lutetia—as Paris was known in the Roman era.

Armée, Musée de l'
See Invalides, Hôtel National des.

Art Moderne, Musée National d'
See Pompidou Center.

Art Moderne de la Ville de Paris, Musée d' (Museum of Modern Art of the City of Paris)
Palais de Tokyo, 11 av. du Président-Wilson, Paris 16ᵉ. ☎ 01-53-67-40-00. Open Tues–Fri 10am–5:30pm, Sat and Sun 10am–6:45pm. Closed Mon. Admission charged. Wheelchair access. Métro: Iéna, Alma-Marceau. RER: Pont de l'Alma.

A lively museum, housed in the west wing of the **Palais de Tokyo,** this stately building is a typical example of 1930s style, which once seemed so aggressively modern and yet now bears the hallmarks of another time. Something of the same feeling is also evoked as you enter the museum, and it is helpful to see the paintings in the context of their periods: for example, Raoul Dufy's huge canvas *La Fee Electricite* (The Good Fairy Electricity).

In 1993 a new room, the Salle Matisse, was inaugurated to exhibit 3 versions of the painter's *Danse,* 2 of which belong to the museum.

Other works in this very fine collection dedicated to 20thC art include cubist paintings by Picasso and Braque, canvases of the Fauve school (Matisse, Derain), and paintings by artists of the Paris school (Modigliani, Soutine, Pascin). Temporary exhibitions are also staged.

The museum is also home to ARC (Animation, Recherche, Confrontation), an area devoted to offbeat contemporary exhibitions, lectures, and other cultural events.

Arts d'Afrique et d'Océanie, Musée National des (Museum of African and Oceanic Arts)
293 av. Daumesnil, 12ᵉ. ☎ 01-44-74-84-80. Guided tours by prior arrangement. Open Mon–Fri 10am–noon, 1:30–5:15pm; Sat–Sun 10am–6pm (aquarium 10am–5:15pm). Closed Tues. Admission charged. Wheelchair access. Métro: Porte-Dorée.

This museum, housed in a building put up for the Colonial Exhibition of 1931, contains a superb collection of ethnic art: Benin bronzes, masks from New Guinea, Aboriginal bark paintings, and a particularly fine display of North African Islamic art. Down in the basement is one of the best **tropical aquariums** in Europe, complete with a huge crocodile pit, where admission is free for those under 18.

★★ Arts Asiatiques-Guimet, Musée National des
6 pl. d'Iéna, 16ᵉ. ☎ 01-47-23-61-65. Guided tours. Open 9:45am–6pm. Closed Tues. Admission charged. Wheelchair access (phone

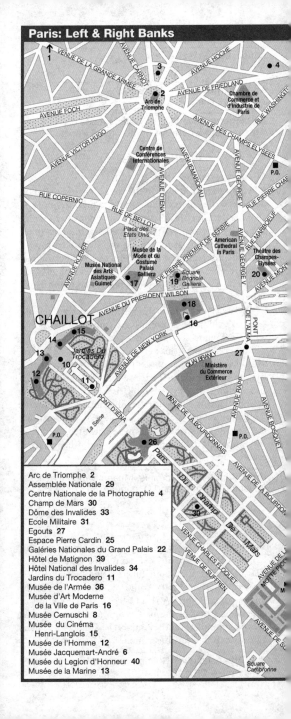

Paris: Left & Right Banks

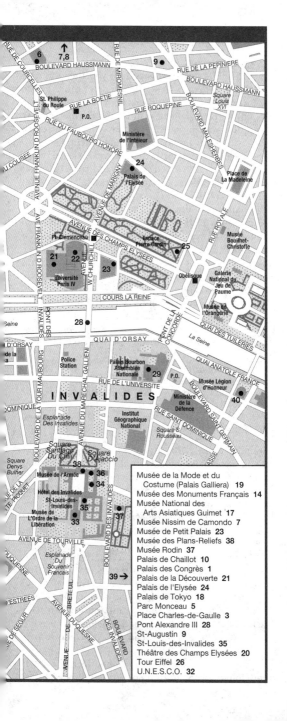

ahead at 01-47-23-61-65 to have the door at 2, rue Boissière opened). Métro: léna.

If the Far East holds any appeal for you, then this treasure house of Asian art—already one of the largest in the world—is a must. Its nucleus is a collection formed by the 19thC industrialist Emile Guimet, whose intention was to gather together objects illustrating the civilizations and religions of the Orient.

Since the museum became a national one, it has been greatly enriched by the addition of other Oriental collections, and now houses a splendid, wide-ranging array of works of art from Afghanistan, Pakistan, India, Vietnam, Laos, Kampuchea, China, Korea, Japan, Thailand, Tibet, and Nepal. The museum is justly renowned for its Kampuchean sculptures, as well as for its magnificent Tibetan tangkas (devotional paintings used for meditation), and ritual instruments reflecting the richly colorful and highly symbolic world of Tantric Buddhism.

Note: The Musée Guimet will close in September 1996 for 1 year while undergoing a $50 million renovation/expansion designed to make it the largest museum dedicated to Oriental art in the world.

Arts Décoratifs, Musée des (Museum of Decorative Arts)

107 rue de Rivoli, 1ᵉʳ. ☎ 01-44-55-57-50. Joint admission if required, with Musée des Arts de la Mode et du Textile and Musée de la Publicité. Open 12:30–6pm, Sun noon–6pm. Closed Mon, Tues, public holidays. Admission charged. Wheelchair access. Métro: Tuileries, Palais-Royal/Musée-du-Louvre.

Founded in the 1870s as part of an attempt to combat mediocrity in the applied arts, this museum presents a panorama of decorative art from the Middle Ages to the 20thC. Housed in the Pavilion Marsan of the **Grand Louvre,** it comprises 220,000 pieces—furniture, ceramics, drawings, silver objects—set out in a series of rooms furnished and decorated in the style of different eras.

Here you can see medieval carvings, chests, and tapestry work, Renaissance stained-glass, elaborate inlaid 17thC furniture, 18thC Vincennes porcelain, and 20thC Art Nouveau paneling. One of the most striking rooms is a complete Second Empire **Italianate salon** with richly painted and gilded wood paneling. From more recent years, the **Art Nouveau** and **Art Deco rooms** are a wonder to behold.

The museum also houses an important **library** of books and documentation concerning the decorative arts, art history, design, and architecture (111 rue de Rivoli, ☎ 01-44-55-59-36, open Tues–Sat 10am–5:30pm, Mon 1:45–5:30pm, closed Sun).

In the same building is the the **Musée de la Publicité,** which stages themed shows of printed publicity material through the ages. The 2 museums, along with the **Musée des Arts de la Mode et du Textile** (see below), are run by the Union des Arts Décoratifs, together with the **Musée Nissim de Camondo.**

Arts de la Mode et du Textile, Musée des

109 rue de Rivoli, 1er. ☎ 01-44-55-57-50. Joint admission if required, with Musée des Arts Décoratifs and Musée de la Publicité. Wheelchair access. Métro: Tuileries, Palais-Royal/Musée-du-Louvre.

Curator Katell Le Bourhis has been waiting a long time for her day in the sun. Brought over with much fanfare a few years ago from the Metropolitan Museum of Art (where she once assisted Diana Vreeland organizing fashion exhibitions), Le Bourhis has seen the opening date of Paris's fashion museum come and go for some time. Now, at least, work has finally started and the Fashion and Textile Museum is expected to open sometime at the end of 1996—though absolutely no one should hold their breath for that. Eventually, it will be situated on 4 floors of the Rohan wing of the Louvre. It is destined to house a permanent fashion collection—the museum has some 7,000 dresses and thousands of accessories in its possession—as well as mount temporary exhibitions.

★ Arts et Traditions Populaires, Musée des (Museum of Folk Arts and Traditions)

6 av. du Mahatma Gandhi, Bois de Boulogne, 16e. ☎ 01-44-17-60-00. Guided tours by prior arrangement. Open 9:45am–5:15pm. Closed Tues. Admission charged. Wheelchair access. Métro: Les Sablons.

Models of fishing boats, Breton peasant costumes, a blacksmith's forge, a clairvoyant's consulting room complete with crystal ball and tarot cards—these and many more curiosities are to be found in this colorful museum dealing with French folk art and culture from the beginning of the Iron Age to the 20thC.

A visit adds another dimension to a pleasant excursion to the **Bois de Boulogne.**

★ Arts Forains, Musée des (Funfair Museum)

50 rue de L'Eglise, 15e. ☎ 01-45-58-65-60. Open Sat and Sun 2–7pm. Admission charged. Métro: Félix Faure.

This is a gaily jumbled reconstitution of a funfair from the Belle Epoque, complete with organ grinders and jesters. A fascinating and unusual place, which groups together 1,522 one-of-a-kind pieces from 1850 to the

present. Huge, richly decorated carousels with pranc-
ing wooden horses; brightly enameled "autodrome" cars
from Germany, precursors of the go-cart; marionettes;
organs; and more all call up the small, often itinerant
European funfair. Children like this place and they don't:
What they're looking for is the real thing, and carousels
you can't ride on are probably more for adults. The
museum is both charming and poetic in equal mea-
sure, somehow sad too, as retired monuments to youth
always seem to be.

Balzac, Maison de

47 rue Raynouard, 16ᵉ. ☎ 01-42-24-56-38. Guided tours. Open
10am–5:40pm. Closed Mon, public holidays. Admission charged.
Métro: Passy, La Muette.

This house is the only survivor of the several Paris homes
lived in by Honoré de Balzac (1799–1850), the author
of the great series of novels entitled *La Comédie Humaine*.
It would no doubt appeal to Balzac's sense of irony to
find it being used as a museum to his memory, for he
considered it somewhat degrading. Fleeing his credi-
tors in 1840, he rented this place in the name of his
housekeeper in order to avoid their attentions, and
remained here for 7 years. It was here that he wrote
some of his last novels, including *La Rabouilleuse, Une
Ténébreuse Affaire,* and *La Cousine Bette.*

Whatever reservations Balzac may have had about
it, to the modern visitor, his house appears an idyllic
place that still possesses the flavor of his era and the
stamp of his personality. It is approached from a terrace
lying below the level of rue Raynouard. Passing through
a gate that seems to lead nowhere, one suddenly descends some steps into the hidden garden of a charming, rustic-looking building with pale turquoise
shutters. It appears to be a single-story cottage but is, in
fact, the top floor of a large house, which has another
entrance on a lower street.

The house is full of fascinating mementoes of
Balzac, including a series of tradesmen's invoices. One
of them is from a glove-maker, and the caption reveals
that Balzac once bought 60 pairs of gloves in a month.
Personal effects on display include his coffee pot—he
often drank 30 cups a day to sustain his prodigious out-
put. Its library has books by and about Balzac.

Bastille, place de la

4ᵉ. Métro: Bastille.

Built between 1370 and 1382, the Bastille served for 4
centuries as a fortress and prison—mainly for powerful

La Place de la Bastille

people who had fallen foul of the king. On July 14, 1789, it was stormed by a revolutionary mob and afterwards demolished, an event still annually celebrated with gusto in France. Now all that remains of the Bastille is a line of cobblestones at the west side of the square, marking out the ground plan of the once formidable building with its projecting towers. Pictures of the Bastille before—and during—its storming and demolition can be seen at the **Grand Carnavalet** museum.

Today, place de la Bastille is a huge, bustling intersection, bounded on the south side by the Arsenal Basin. This contains a boating marina, the **Port de Plaisance de l'Arsenal,** and is surrounded by movie theaters, cafes, and shops. The square is dominated by the **Colonne de Juillet** (July column), a massive memorial surmounted by the gilded, allegorical figure of the **Genius of Liberty.** The column commemorates the Parisians killed in the 3 days of street-fighting of 1830 that brought about the fall of Charles X and replaced him with Louis-Philippe, the "Bourgeois Monarch."

The elephant-shaped plinth of the column contains the remains of 500 victims of the fighting, as well as another 196 who died in the 1848 uprising against Louis-Philippe. Curiously, an Egyptian mummy is also housed there. Their marble-lined crypt can be entered through a door in the plinth.

Beaubourg
See Pompidou Center.

Beaux-Arts, Ecole Nationale Supérieure (School of Fine Arts)
Exhibition entrance at 17 quai Malaquais, 6ᵉ. ☎ 01-47-03-50-00. School open 9am–noon, 2–5pm (library 10am–6pm) Mon–Fri;

Exhibitions also open Tues–Sun 1–7pm. Exhibitions closed Mon,
Aug, public holidays. Métro: St-Germain-des-Prés.

In his *Paris Sketch Book,* 150 years ago, the English
novelist William Makepeace Thackeray wrote of this
building: "With its light and elegant fabric, its pretty
fountain, its archway of the Renaissance, and fragments
of sculpture, you can hardly see, on a fine day, a place
more *riant* and pleasing." His words apply equally well
today.

The former Couvent (convent) des Petits Augustins has housed the School of Fine Arts since 1817.
Although the main buildings date from the 19thC, the
chapel and cloisters are dated much earlier. Although
there is no permanent gallery, temporary exhibitions
of painting and sculpture are held here several times a
year. Simply wandering through the courtyards and
mingling with the students is a pleasure.

Bercy

In the 12e, to the east of the Bastille and the Gare de Lyon, on the
Right Bank. Métro: Bercy

This formerly run-down docklands quarter has been
undergoing major surgery since 1989, following a government plan to revitalize the east of the city (as it has
revitalized the west at La Défense). The first improvement was the **Opéra Bastille,** completed in 1990. In
the second phase, the new **Parc de Bercy** will extend
southeast from the **Palais Omnisports,** covering what
was once an area of old wine warehouses.

Another of the new developments in Bercy was the
Ministry of Finance, which relocated in 1989 from
its offices in a wing of the Louvre to a bold and often-
criticized new building that straddles the road and has
its feet in the water. The new **TGB–Bibliothèque de
France,** still not completed, will be located at Tolbiac
on the opposite bank of the Seine. A new bridge across
the Seine will eventually be constructed at this point,
as well as 2 new métro stations.

Bibliothèque Nationale de France (National Library)

58 rue de Richelieu, 2e. ☎ 01-47-03-81-26. Medallions and Antiques
Gallery open 1–5pm. Mansart and Mazarine Galleries open 9:30am–
6:30pm. Photography Gallery (in the Rotonde Colbert, entered from
2 rue Vivienne) open 1–6pm. All closed Sun, Mon, public holidays.
Admission charged. Métro: Bourse, Palais-Royal/Musée-du-Louvre.

As befits one of the world's greatest collections of books,
manuscripts, prints, maps, medallions, and other treasures, the Bibliothèque is housed in a splendid mansion, the main entrance of which is in rue de Richelieu,
reached via a fine courtyard. The building was created

by Cardinal Mazarin in the 17thC out of 2 adjacent houses, the Hôtel Tubeuf and the Hôtel Chivry, and the resulting complex covers an entire block. After Mazarin's death, the mansion was split between different owners.

Part of it, which had come into the hands of the crown, became the repository of the royal library, later the National Library, which ultimately took over the whole of Mazarin's mansion. Since 1537, a copy of every French book published has, by law, been kept there.

Accredited scholars have access to the library's service departments. Members of the public can view the **medallion collection** on the 1st floor, the temporary exhibitions in the ground floor **Mansart Gallery** and the superb **Mazarin Gallery** at the top of the imposing stairway, and those in the **Rotonde Colbert** photographic gallery. Beyond a glass door, the magnificent Second Empire reading room, with its domed ceiling and cast-iron columns, gives the impression of a Byzantine cathedral.

Note: The National Library has announced its relocation to a site in the east of Paris, fronting the Seine (1 place Valhubert, 13ᵉ). The controversial modern design for the building features 4 20-storey-high, glass-and-steel L-shaped towers that are supposed to resemble open books, facing each other on a 7-hectare (17-acre) site. Work began in 1990 on the new **Bibliothèque de France** by a young French architect, Dominique Perrault; it is expected to be open to the public in 1997. Future use of the beautiful but cramped building in the rue de Richelieu has yet to be decided, though the galleries and exhibition halls are expected to remain.

★★ Bois de Boulogne

To the west edge of Paris, beyond the Périphérique and in the crook of the Seine. See also detailed map on page 94.

"I will not describe the Bois de Boulogne. It is simply a beautiful, cultivated, endless, wonderful wilderness." This was Mark Twain's reaction in *The Innocents Abroad* to the 900-hectare (2,224-acre) park—once a royal hunting forest—on the western outskirts of Paris. Today, the Bois could no longer be described as a wilderness, there are too many roads. Furthermore, it is, in places, rather monotonous, and much of it is haunted by libidinous characters, especially at night. For this reason, it is now closed to cars at night.

However, there are many spots of great beauty, and you must be prepared to seek these out. The most

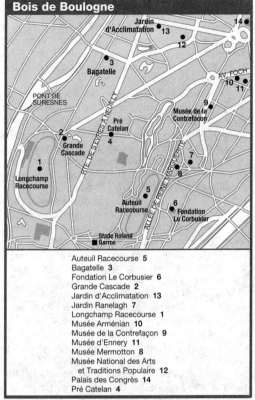

Bois de Boulogne

delightful of all must surely be the **Bagatelle** (open daily, admission charged), a relatively small park-within-a-park where in the 18thC the Count of Artois, the future King Charles X, built himself an enchanting little villa (constructed in less than 70 days on a bet with Marie-Antoinette) surrounded by a romantic and picturesque garden with artificial waterfalls, grottoes, Gothic ruins, and other follies. Later, a second building, the Trianon, was added near the villa. Today, the Bagatelle (the word means trifle) is a place of potent magic, with a renowned flower garden.

The **château de la Bagatelle** is now open for tours (on weekend afternoons mid-Mar–Oct, ☎ 01-40-71-75-23). There is also an elegant restaurant, **Les Jardins de Bagatelle,** where you can sip afternoon tea languidly and dream.

Another appealing oasis in the Bois is the **Pré Catelan,** also a self-contained park. Its attractions include a majestic copper beech with a wider span of branches than any other tree in Paris. In addition, the Pré has a **Shakespeare Garden** containing plants mentioned in the master's works. The **Théâtre de la Verdure** (open-air theater) holds performances here June through September (☎ 01-42-76-47-72 for program details). A first-class restaurant of the same name (**Le Pré Catelan,** see "Dining") is also nestled here.

If you have children with you, the spot to head for is the **Jardin d'Acclimatation,** a children's paradise on the north side of the Bois (open daily, admission charged). A little train runs there from Porte-Maillot. Here you will find a zoo, a go-cart track, merry-go-rounds, a miniature golf course, and a cafe, **La Ferme du Golf,** one of the few places where youngsters can sit in a farmyard and eat an ice cream or pizza, while goats, sheep, and ducks mill around their tables.

Within the Jardin d'Acclimatation is the **Musée en Herbe** (☎ 01-40-67-97-66, open Sun–Fri 10am–6pm, Sat 2–6pm, admission charged), which lets children discover art while having fun. Lively temporary exhibitions are mounted, and there is a supervised studio in which children can paint or draw impressions of what they have seen. The **Musée des Arts et Traditions Populaires** is also nearby.

Other attractions in the Bois include lakes (the **Lac Inférieur** has boating facilities), 2 racecourses (**Auteuil** and **Longchamp**) and Paris's municipal floral garden, the **Jardin des Serres d'Auteuil.**

Perhaps one of the best and most enjoyable methods of traveling about in the Bois is on 2 wheels. However, you may prefer, like the Englishman who broke the bank at Monte Carlo, to "walk along the Bois de Boulogne with an independent air."

Bourdelle, Musée Antoine

16 rue Antoine-Bourdelle, 15ᵉ. ☎ 01-45-48-67-27. Guided tours: Tues 2:30pm only. Open 10am–5:40pm. Closed Mon, public holidays. Wheelchair access. Métro: Falguière, Montparnasse-Bienvenüe.

This charming oasis in **Montparnasse** was for 45 years the home and studio of Antoine Bourdelle (1861–1929), a sculptor of genius who, along with his friend Rodin, helped to give sculpture a new lease on life. Where Rodin's work has the fluidity of emotion, Bourdelle's is characterized by the thrusting harnessed power of the will, seen in such creations as his *Héracles Archer* and *Tête d'Apollon.* These and Bourdelle's paintings, including portraits, landscapes and still-lifes, are displayed in a series of light, spacious rooms and leafy courtyards.

Part of the museum is used for temporary exhibitions by other sculptors. The museum has recently been renovated and expanded.

Bourse des Valeurs (Stock Exchange)

Pl. de la Bourse (entrance on the side of rue Notre-Dame-des-Victoires), 1er. Guided tours compulsory, every half hour from 1:30–4pm. Admission charged. Closed Sat, Sun, holidays. Métro: Bourse.

A serene, 19thC classical building surrounded by Corinthian columns, the stock exchange was extensively restored in 1995. To help visitors make sense of the spectacle of the dealing room floor, which they will witness from a gallery at the end of the tour, they are shown films and receive lectures on the workings of the Bourse and the stock market. The whole tour lasts an hour and is not geared toward foreign visitors with a less-than-good grasp of French. If you have an interest in money matters at this level, and your French can stand the pace, it is a fascinating show.

Buttes Chaumont, Parc des

Rue Manin, 19e. Open daily. Métro: Buttes-Chaumont.

This park is totally unlike any other in Paris and has a strongly romantic appeal. Brilliantly landscaped by Haussmann on a disused quarry site, it has steeply undulating wooded contours and a lake with a rocky island rising dramatically from the center, spanned by 2 high bridges. On the island, one path leads up a flight of steps through a grottolike tunnel to the summit, which is crowned by a small classical temple with an open colonnade. From here, there is a superb view over the city to the north, east, and west, with **Montmartre** and the **Sacré-Coeur** standing out against the horizon.

This is one of the few Parisian parks where you can actually sit on the grass. For children, there are rides in a donkey cart, and a boating lake, and, for adults, on the west side, there is an inviting restaurant, the **Pavillon du Lac** (☎ 01-42-02-08-97, open daily noon–2:30pm only) with tables overlooking the lake.

★★ Camondo, Musée Nissim de

63 rue de Monceau, 8e. ☎ 01-45-63-26-32. Guided tours. Open 10am–noon, 2–5pm. Closed Mon, Tues. Métro: Villiers, Monceau.

Like the nearby **Cernuschi** museum, this private house and its contents have been bequeathed to the nation. Its creator, Count Moïse de Camondo, was a rich collector with a passion for 18thC decorative art. In 1910, he built a house in the style of the Petit Trianon at **Versailles,** where he set out to re-create the atmosphere of an 18thC interior. Thanks to his discrimination and finely tuned visual sense, the effect is one of harmony combined with the highest quality. The furniture is by such master cabinetmakers as Jacob, Riesener, and Saunier, and the tapestries come from the great workshops of **Gobelins,** Beauvais, and Aubusson—one particularly fine set depicts the famous fables of La Fontaine.

Recent work has restored the bedroom of the young count Nissim de Camondo, who died tragically young in aerial combat in 1917, as well as his father's spartan, tiled bathroom, and his closets, all mahogany *boiserie* and green silk moiré—which put a more personal face on this "museum-home" than many others can claim.

Carnavalet, Musée
See Grand Carnavalet.

Catacombes (Catacombs)
1 pl. Denfert-Rochereau, 14ᵉ. ☎ 01-43-22-47-63. Guided tours. Open Tues–Fri 2–4pm, Sat–Sun 9–11am and 2–4pm. Closed Mon, public holidays. Admission charged. Métro: Denfert-Rochereau.

Here is a creepy experience: a walk of three-quarters of an hour through a subterranean necropolis. These are not ancient catacombs like the ones in Rome, but former stone quarries that were filled with the bones cleared from many Parisian cemeteries during the 18th and 19th centuries. They have been open to the public since 1874, but the visitor sees only a small part of the 300 kilometers (186 miles) of tunnels.

The tunnels leading to the ossuary pass a representation of a fort, carved out of the rock by an 18thC tunnel worker in his leisure time. Then a chamber with black and white painted pillars leads off to a doorway over which are the words: *Arrête! C'est ici l'empire de la mort.* ("Stop! This is the empire of death.") Beyond it stretches tunnel after tunnel, lined on each side with neatly piled bones, interspersed with rows of grinning skulls, and enlivened by plaques bearing inscriptions of death.

There are 5 to 6 million skeletons here. The whole place is a *memento mori* of the most dramatic kind.

Cernuschi, Musée
7 av. Velasquez, 8ᵉ. ☎ 01-45-63-50-75. Open 10am–5:40pm. Closed Mon, public holidays. Admission charged. Wheelchair access. Métro: Villiers, Monceau.

Paris possesses this interesting museum of Chinese art, situated in a fine house just near the east gate of the **Parc de Monceau,** thanks to a colorful Milanese financier named Cernuschi. A disciple of Garibaldi, Cernuschi was once condemned to death for his revolutionary activities, but was reprieved by Napoléon III and later became a French citizen. Before his death in 1896, he bequeathed his house and magnificent collection of Chinese objects to the city of Paris.

Smaller and less impressive than the collection in the **Musée Guimet,** this exhibition nevertheless gives a very informative picture of the development of Chinese art from prehistoric times. It includes a selection of paintings by modern Chinese artists, but perhaps the most evocative picture is a 13thC ink-and-brush drawing of a bird on a twig, which combines humor and simplicity with sophistication (it is the one on the left as you enter into the museum).

A treasured recent acquisition is a 7thC Tang-epoch wooden funerary statue from northwest China. An imposing Buddha dominates the central hall.

Champ-de-Mars
7ᵉ. Métro: Champ de Mars, Ecole-Militaire.

The Champ-de-Mars is the back garden of the **Tour Eiffel.** It was originally laid out in the 1760s as a parade ground for the **Ecole Militaire,** hence its name, after Mars, the god of war. These days it is anything but martial—just a typically tranquil Parisian park with a symmetrical pattern of tree-lined avenues and numerous pleasant and secluded little corners in which to sit and read or contemplate the wonders of Eiffel's engineering.

A fine new series of statues was erected here in 1989. The composition, created by sculptor Yvan Theimer, commissioned for the bicentenary of the French Revolution, depicts the bronze figures of man, woman, and child, in his **Monument to the Rights of Man.**

If you have children in tow, it is worth making a short detour away from the river to the south, where there are excellent playgrounds, pony rides, and an old-fashioned merry-go-round.

★ Champs-Elysées, avenue des
8ᵉ. Métro: Charles-de-Gaulle-Etoile, George-V, Franklin-D-Roosevelt, Champs-Elysées-Clemenceau, Concorde.

If there is one Parisian street that is known throughout the world it is this one. It forms a great triumphal tree-lined sweep from **Place de la Concorde** to the **Arc de Triomphe.** At its lower end, as far as the intersection known as the Rond-Point, it is bounded by strips of park. Then, along the stretch that climbs in a shallow ramp toward the Arc de Triomphe, it is lined by imposing buildings: offices, auto shops, movie theaters, airline offices, restaurants, and sidewalk cafes. The quality of this part of the avenue has been deteriorating in the past 10 years, and this problem is now being taken in hand. A 5-year 200-million-franc refurbishment plan—with the planting of a second row of trees, clampdowns on parking, and new street lamps and kiosks designed by talented young French architect Jean-Michel Wilmotte—was completed in 1995 and has decidedly improved the tone of the area. One of the positive results of the recent work here is that the Champs-Elysées has been classified as a tourist area, meaning shops can stay open on Sunday.

Chapelle Expiatoire

Square Louis XVI, 29 rue Pasquier, 8ᵉ. ☎ 01-42-65-35-80. Open summer 10am–1pm and 2–5pm; winter: closes 4pm; closed holidays. Admission free. Métro: St-Augustin or Havre Caumartin.

This solidly built chapel, in a little square off boulevard Haussmann, was erected by Louis XVIII, in memory of Louis XVI and Marie Antoinette on the site of a graveyard where 3,000 victims of the Revolution, including the royal couple, were buried. Within the chapel are monuments dedicated to them. The 2-story chapel is surrounded on all sides by a templelike portico and arcade, and overlooks a peaceful little square, which offers a pleasant place to sit down as a respite from shopping on the **Grands Boulevards.**

Chasse et de la Nature, Musée de la (Museum of Hunting and Nature)

60 rue des Archives, 3ᵉ. ☎ 01-42-72-86-43. Guided tours. Open 10am–12:30pm, 1:30–5:30pm. Closed Tues, holidays. Admission charged. Métro: Rambuteau, Hôtel-de-Ville.

Everything you ever needed to know about hunting is assembled in an attractive old **Marais** mansion: hunting weapons of all kinds; stuffed animals; and paintings of famous hunters and huntresses, such as Diana by Breughel and Rubens, and St-Eustache by Cranach.

The building, the Hôtel de Guénégaud des Brosses, with its well-mannered courtyard and dignified design, was built by François Mansart between 1648 and 1651 and was in a dilapidated condition when François Sommer took it over in the early 1960s. His own big-game trophies are among those on display. Now the building stands beautifully restored, to delight architectural as well as hunting enthusiasts.

Cinéma Henri-Langlois, Musée du

Palais de Chaillot, pl. du Trocadéro, 16ᵉ. ☎ 01-45-53-74-39. Guided tours (compulsory, at 10am, 11am, 2pm, 3pm, 4pm).

Admission charged. Closed Mon, Tues, public holidays.
Métro: Trocadéro.

The modest entrance to this museum (allied to the **Cinématheque Française**) at the bottom of a flight of steps in the **Palais de Chaillot** does not prepare the visitor for the riches within. The museum's staff takes visitors first through the early technology of cinematography, dating back to 1895, then through a series of galleries full of the trappings that have enabled moviemakers to create a world of make-believe.

There are sets from famous movies such as *The Cabinet of Doctor Caligari,* costumes such as the tunic worn by Rudolph Valentino in *The Sheik,* Garbo's robes, papier-mâché monsters, a robot from Fritz Lang's *Metropolis* . . . and much more. The conducted visit takes about an hour and a quarter.

Cinémathèque Française

Palais de Chaillot, Jardin du Trocadéro, 7 av. Albert-de-Mun, 16°.
☎ 01-47-04-24-24. Admission charged. Métro: Trocadéro.

The film library in the **Palais de Chaillot** is a national institution for the screening of distinguished films from all periods of cinema history. See also "The Arts."

Cité de la Musique

See Villette, Parc de la.

Cité des Sciences et de l'Industrie (City of Science and Industry)

See Villette, Parc de la.

Clemenceau, Musée

8 rue Franklin, 16°. ☎ 01-45-20-53-41. Guided tours. Open Tues, Thurs, Sat, Sun 2–5pm. Admission charged. Métro: Passy.

The apartment where the statesman Georges Clemenceau lived from 1895 until his death in 1929 is preserved exactly as he left it, down to the quill pen with which he wrote. The environment has the stamp of an exceptionally powerful and many-faceted personality.

★★★ Cluny, Thermes de/Musée National du Moyen Âge

6 pl. Paul-Painlevé, 5°. ☎ 01-43-25-62-00. Open 9:15am–5:45pm. Closed Tues, public holidays. Guided tours (Museum) Wed, Sat, Sun 3:15pm. Guided tours (Thermal Baths) Wed, Sat, Sun 2pm. Admission charged. Métro: Cluny-La-Sorbonne.

This outstanding museum in the **Latin Quarter** is a remarkable archaeological site housing a great collection of ancient and medieval objects. It comprises 2 buildings: the remains of the Gallo-Roman baths or **Thermes de Lutèce** (circa AD 200) and the exquisite

The Thermal Baths of the Hôtel Cluny

Flamboyant Gothic **Hôtel de Cluny**. One of only four such buildings now remaining in Paris, the hotel was constructed at the end of the 15thC as a Parisian residence for the abbot of Cluny, in Burgundy. The U-shaped building incorporated the ruins of the thermal baths and enclosed an inner courtyard. The internal layout has remained remarkably intact; the chapel, on the 1st floor, has an exquisite vaulted Flamboyant Gothic ceiling.

The Gallo-Roman Baths would have consisted of 3 large rooms, the hot steam bath; the tepid bath; and the *frigidarium,* or cold bath. This 15-meter-high (50 ft.) cold-water bath has survived, and is the oldest vaulted room in France. The foundations of the other spaces are still clearly visible, together with the drains and hot-air ducts.

The museum contains one of the richest medieval collections in the world, yet the entire collection can be viewed comfortably in half a day. Many treasures, both ecclesiastical and domestic objects, are arranged to present a picture of everyday life. There is a complete panorama of monumental sculpture, and the recently rediscovered 21 heads of the Kings of Judah, from the cathedral of Notre-Dame, can now be seen. The museum contains a large array of ecclesiastical and votive items, such as reliquary boxes, patens, chalices, and candleholders; a dazzling display of dozens of pieces of stained-glass work spanning the centuries; as well as textiles and tapestries, furniture, metalwork, and paintings.

This is an opportunity to see one of the finest collections of medieval tapestry work in existence. The museum's most famous exhibit, in a special 1st-floor hall, is the set of 6 late 15thC tapestries known as the *Lady with the Unicorn,* woven in lively detail, in beautiful, muted colors. Five of the tapestries symbolically illustrate the 5 senses, and the 6th is thought to illustrate mastery of them. A card explaining what is happening in each tapestry can be found in a box near the door. Look for the little smile on the face of the unicorn as he catches sight of himself in the mirror.

Cognacq-Jay, Musée

8 rue Elzevir, 3ᵉ. ☎ 01-40-27-07-21. Guided tours. Open 10am–5:40pm. Closed Mon, holidays. Admission charged. Métro: St-Paul.

Ernest Cognacq, creator of the Samaritaine chain of shops, and his wife, Louise Jay, opened to the public their collection of 18thC art in the 1920s. Paradoxically, Cognacq was no art-lover—he boasted that he had never entered the Louvre—and he became a collector purely for status reasons. However, with expert advice he succeeded in acquiring many works of the highest rank, such as Boucher's *Le Retour de Chasse de Diane,* Tiepolo's *Le Festin de Cléopatre* and Reynolds' portrait of Lord Northington. Watteau, Fragonard, Rembrandt, and Gainsborough are among other artists represented.

Located in the sumptuous 17thC Hôtel de Donon, the collection also includes a remarkable collection of porcelain ornaments, gold and silver boxes, and other small *objets d'art.*

La Comédie Française

2 rue de Richelieu, 1ᵉʳ. ☎ 01-40-15-00-15. Not open to public except for shows. Wheelchair access. Métro: Palais-Royal/Musée-du-Louvre.

After it was founded in 1680 by Louis XIV, this famous company of actors moved house several times and finally settled on the present site at the end of the 18thC. The theater, which has evolved over the years into the grand colonnaded building that it occupies today, is set in a prime position next to the **Palais–Royal.**

The theater was closed in 1995 for 8 months of work, at a cost of $12 million, to restore and renovate the famous **Salle Richelieu.** The room is now equipped for the hearing- or sight-impaired visitor. Traditionally, the repertoire has emphasized classical French dramatists such as Molière, Corneille, and Racine, but lately it has been widened to include modern and foreign playwrights.

★★ La Conciergerie

1 quai de l'Horloge, 1ᵉʳ. ☎ 01-43-54-30-06. Reduced joint ticket with Sainte-Chapelle. Guided tours. Open June–Aug daily 9:30am–6:30pm; Sept, Apr, May daily 9:30am–6pm; Oct–Mar daily 10am–4:30pm. Closed holidays. Admission charged. Métro: Cité, Châtelet-St-Michel.

The Conciergerie has a gloomy atmosphere that matches its gloomy history as a place of imprisonment, death, and torture. Part of the great palace built on the north side of the **Ile de la Cité** by King Philippe the Fair (1284–1314), it is now incorporated into the **Palais de Justice** complex. The name is derived from the title of the royal officer called the Concierge ("Comte des Cierges," or Count of the Candles). He was superintendent of the palace and was empowered to administer justice in its environs. Increasingly, the Conciergerie took on the functions of a prison, especially after the building became for a time the seat of parliament, which was also the country's supreme court.

It was here that such malefactors as Ravaillac, assassin of Henry IV, and Damiens, who attempted to kill Louis XV, were brought and hideously tortured before being executed. However, it was during the Revolution that the Conciergerie received its real baptism of blood. Its most famous prisoner was Marie-Antoinette, who was kept here before being taken to the guillotine. Her cell is now a chapel to her memory, but her name is only one of a list of many who passed through on their way to execution. The revolutionary leader Danton condemned 22 Girondins, de Robespierre condemned Danton, the Thermidor Convention condemned de Robespierre. In all, nearly 2,600 prisoners were sent for execution from the Conciergerie between the winter of 1793 and summer of 1794. You can still see the grim little room where they were shaved and relieved of their possessions before being taken to the tumbrels. In 1792, 288 prisoners were murdered in the prison itself.

Despite the unpleasant vibrations created by this history, the building does, in fact, possess some beautiful features: the **Salle des Gardes,** the first room you enter, with its elegant vaulting and carved bosses; the magnificent **Salle des Gens d'Armes,** 69 meters (226 ft.) long and 27 meters (89 ft.) wide, with 3 rows of 8 pillars, which is sometimes used as a setting for concerts; and **the kitchen,** with its 4 fireplaces, each big enough to roast an ox, which, in the 14thC, provided food for 5,000.

The chapel, which housed the 22 condemned Girondin deputies, now contains a depressing but intriguing little collection of mementoes, including a guillotine blade, Marie-Antoinette's crucifix, and 2 portraits of her from life.

Concorde, place de la
8e. Métro: Concorde.

The largest square in Paris is also arguably the most striking and beautiful townscape in the world, but to appreciate the square fully, you must brave the whirling blizzard of traffic and cross the road to the center. It is advisable to use the 2 official crossings.

There once stood in the middle of place de la Concorde an equestrian statue of Louis XV, in whose reign the square was laid out. This was removed during the Revolution and replaced briefly by an allegorical statue of Liberty. Now the site is occupied by the 3,300-year-old **obelisk of Luxor,** given to King Louis-Philippe by Mohammed Ali, Viceroy of Egypt, and erected in 1836.

A few yards from this spot stood the guillotine which, during the Revolution, claimed over a thousand victims including Louis XVI and Marie-Antoinette. Two **fountains** resplendent with water nymphs and sea-gods stand to the north and south of the obelisk.

Le Corbusier, Fondation

10 sq. du Docteur-Blanche, 16ᵉ. ☎ 01-42-88-41-53. Open 10am–12:30pm, 1:30–6pm (Fri 5pm); closed Sat, Sun, public holidays. Admission charged. Métro: Jasmin.

The name Le Corbusier is synonymous with modern French architecture. This foundation, the purpose of which is to present Le Corbusier's work to the public, occupies 2 villas designed by the master himself in 1923. It encompasses a library, a photographic archive, and a collection of paintings and sculptures by the architect. Temporary exhibitions are also held on various aspects of his work.

Crypte Archéologique

See Notre-Dame.

Dalí, Espace Salvador

Espace Montmartre, 11 rue Poulbot, 18ᵉ. ☎ 01-42-64-44-80. Open 10am–6pm. Admission charged. Métro: Abbesses.

L'Univers Fantasmagorique de Dalí (the Crazy World of Dalí) is a 1990s re-creation of the life and work of Salvador Dalí (1904–89), the larger-than-life Surrealist artist. Dalí lived and worked in Montmartre in the late 1920s, when he first dabbled with surrealism— a style of interpretation that was to influence him for the remainder of his life.

Some 330 of Dalí's works have been gathered together to make a spectacle that uses all the senses— special, surreal sound-effects and visual tricks set off the extraordinary collection of work.

La Défense

To the northwest of Paris. RER: La Défense.

This vast commercial and residential complex, lying beyond the river to the northwest of Paris, has been nicknamed "Manhattan-sur-Seine." Certainly it has the brutality but arguably less style than "Manhattan-sur-Hudson." Begun in the 1960s, it dominates the western horizon of the city with its growing cluster of skyscrapers.

The main zone of La Défense focuses on a 1.2-kilometer-long ($^3/_4$-mile) podium running approximately west to east and descending toward the Seine in a series of terraces laid out with trees. On the south side, the prospect contains a Joan Miró sculpture, *Les Deux Personnages,* which is painted in primary colors. Opposite stands Calder's giant red mobile.

See the **Grande Arche de la Defense.**

Delacroix, Musée National Eugène

6 rue de Furstemberg, 6ᵉ. ☎ 01-43-54-04-87. Guided tours. Open 9:45am–5pm. Closed Tues. Admission charged. Métro: St-Germain-des-Prés, Mabillon.

Eugène Delacroix (1798–1863) was one of the great romantic painters of the 19thC, a Wagner among artists. His vivid canvases of battle scenes, lion hunts, and other stirring subjects have a controlled fire to them, like Delacroix himself, whom the poet Baudelaire described as "a volcanic crater artistically concealed beneath bouquets of flowers."

In his last years, Delacroix lived a life of almost monastic seclusion in a charming left-bank apartment with a studio overlooking a little garden. This apartment is now preserved as a museum and is full of photographs, letters, portraits, and other mementoes of the artist.

Dôme Church

See Invalides, Hôtel National des.

Egouts (Sewers)

A kiosk marks the entrance at the Pont de l'Alma, facing 93 quai d'Orsay, 7ᵉ. ☎ 01-47-05-10-29. Guided tours obligatory. Open 11am–5pm summer; 11am–4pm winter. Closed Thurs, Fri, also last 3 weeks in Jan. Admission charged. Métro: Alma-Marceau.

"Below Paris," wrote Victor Hugo in *Les Misérables,* "is another city." He was referring to the sewer network, the existence of which is vital to the gracious city above. Created by the engineer Eugène Belgrand in 1850, the sewers have been in need of massive maintenance for some years. A 5-year, $200 million renovation program began in 1991. Laid end-to-end, its tunnels would stretch from Paris to Istanbul, and a small section of this labyrinth just a few steps from the **Tour Eiffel** has been equipped for public viewing.

Visitors are shown an exhibition of documents on the history of the sewers, followed by an audiovisual display about the workings of the system. A guided tour takes visitors through dripping tunnels, past waste-collection pits, and along the edge of a murky gray river. Instructive but smelly. Once you know the odor of the sewers, you will occasionally catch whiffs of it from gratings as you walk through the city.

Ennery, Musée National d'

59 av. Foch, 16ᵉ. ☎ 01-47-23-61-65. Open Thurs and Sun 2–6pm. Closed Mon–Wed, Fri, Sat, Aug. Admission free. Métro: Dauphine.

Ming vases, *netsuke,* images of Buddha, porcelain dogs, Chinese furniture—these and other Oriental objects collected by the 19thC dramatist Adolphe d'Ennery and his wife are displayed in part of their opulent house. He bought indiscriminately, and perhaps 1 in 10 of the objects have any real value. However, the museum has a curious, musty charm; it is actually part of the the **Musée Guimet.**

Flea Market

See Marché aux Puces below, and "Shopping."

Forum des Halles

1ᵉʳ. Métro: Les Halles; RER: Châtelet-Les-Halles

Burdened with an almost insurmountably tacky reputation, the Forum in Les Halles, Paris's one stab at the indoor-shopping-mall concept, has brooked a facelift of sorts recently. The new Gaumont cinema complex—which resembles nothing so much as a sleek airport lounge with its modular bar in the center and interactive video screens stuck about in corners—has a glossy winsomeness, and a new wing of the mall itself dedicated to some younger, trendier designers is shaping up well.

But they're only stabs. For the most part, this remains a loud and dirty mall with one of the most haphazard and mostly unappealing selections of restaurants and stores to be found in Paris. The one real use Parisians make of Les Halles is to stop in at **Au Pied de Cochon** (see "Dining") for a snack in the wee hours of the morning.

The Forum was opened in 1979 in the final stages of the rebuilding of Les Halles, Paris's former whole-sale food market. It was designed by Paul Chemetov, who also designed the new Ministry of Finance building, which juts boldly out into the Seine in the east of Paris.

Located here is an excellent branch of the **Grévin waxworks museum,** which is devoted to the Paris of the Belle Epoque and contains an imaginary reconstruction of a Parisian street of 1885 (Grand Balcon, Forum des Halles, 1ᵉʳ; ☎ 01-40-26-28-50; open Mon–Sat 10:30am–6:45pm, Sun and holidays 1–6:30pm).

The Forum is also home to the **Vidéothèque de Paris,** an archive of film material of all eras relating to Paris. The Vidéothèque has 3 projection rooms where films from a collection of 4,500 titles are shown, with a different theme each week. There are facilities for individual viewing (2 Grande Galerie, porte St-Eustache, 1ᵉʳ, ☎ 01-40-26-34-30; open Sun, Tues–Fri 12:30–8:30pm, Sat 10am–8:30pm, closed Mon).

There is also the **Musée de l'Holographie** (Level 1, 15 Grand Balcon, Forum des Halles, ☎ 01-40-39-96-83; open Mon–Sat 10am–7pm, Sun, holidays 1–7pm; guided tours).

At the north side of the Forum is the **Pavillon des Arts,** a striking steel-and-glass building for temporary exhibitions (101 rue Rambuteau, 1ᵉʳ, ☎ 01-42-33-82-50; open 12:45–7:30pm, closed Mon, holidays).

Gobelins, Manufacture Nationale des (Tapestry Factories)

42 av. des Gobelins, 13ᵉ. ☎ 01-44-08-52-00. Open Tues, Wed, Thurs. Guided tours compulsory, every 15 min. from 2–2:45pm. Admission charged. Métro: Gobelins, Place d'Italie.

If you have ever struggled with a home tapestry kit and found that it tried your patience, you should visit the Gobelins factory to find out what patience really means. Here, skilled weavers, carefully chosen and trained from the age of 16, work their way millimeter by millimeter across huge upright looms at the rate of as little as 1 square meter a year. Thus it can take 3 to 4 years to complete a single tapestry with 2 or 3 people working on it full time.

The techniques used are essentially the same as when the Gobelins was founded as a royal factory under Louis XIV, but the tapestries are now worked in a far wider range of colors (14,920 altogether), and the subjects are no longer scenes of royal occasions and the like, but copies of modern paintings or designs.

The Gobelins is a state enterprise, and its products are never sold. They are either made use of by the government or given as gifts. The atmosphere of the factory complex in the southeast of Paris is rather like an old university college, with a cobbled quadrangle, garden, and apartments for the employees. A guided tour of the factory is given, which incorporates the 2 other state workshops of Savonnerie (carpets) and Beauvais (tapestries made on a horizontal loom). In an era of mass-production, here is craftsmanship of the highest standard.

★★★ Grand Carnavalet, Musée de l'Histoire de la Ville de Paris

23 rue de Sévign, 3º. ☎ 01-42-72-21-13. Guided tours. Open 10am–5:40pm. Closed Mon, holidays. Admission charged. Wheelchair access. Métro: St-Paul, Chemin-Vert.

Newly renamed the Grand Carnavalet, this important museum is still often referred to simply as the Musée Carnavalet. It's impossible to underestimate the kind of surprising treasures you find here. Think of suites full of real Louis XIV, Louis XV, and Louis XVI furniture; a reconstitution of an Art Deco pharmacy; and even a re-creation of Proust's bedroom (cork lined, which he was sure would help his asthma), appointed with his own furniture.

Every phase of Parisian history, from prehistoric times to the present day, is illustrated in painting, sculpture, models, furniture, and decoration—all chronologically ordered in a series of splendid rooms in 2 exquisite mansions of the **Marais,** the Hôtel Carnavalet, and the Hôtel Le Peletier de Saint-Fargeau.

The Hôtel Carnavalet played its own part in the history of the city. Built in the 1540s and later modified by Mansart, it possesses a gracious entrance courtyard with allegorical reliefs of the 4 seasons, and a contemporary statue of Louis XIV by Coysevox, anachronistically dressed as a Roman general wearing a wig. From 1677 to 1696, the house was occupied by Madame de Sévigné, who immortalized herself by a series of lively and witty letters, and who played hostess to distinguished writers and thinkers of her time. Her apartments are on view, and she still seems to cast her benign spell over the building.

Hôtel Carnavalet: Its rooms cover the period from prehistory to 1789. Relics of the Gallo-Roman settlement of Lutetia, the Merovingian and Carolingian periods, and the Paris of the Middle Ages are all laid out, room after fascinating room. Roman finds include coffins, leather shoes, domestic implements, and a room full of old tradesmen's signs, as well as the entire front of a druggist's shop. The contents are absorbing but, importantly, the number of exhibits always seems manageable. By being selective, it is perfectly possible

The Courtyard of the Hôtel Carnavalet

to move through each room and take it in without consuming the entire day.

Many are the insights into domestic life, and one of the highlights of the museum are the many models, most of them old pieces rather than ones commissioned by the management, showing parts of the city. A model of the Ile de la Cité in 1527, made at the beginning of the 20thC using an old engraving, shows houses and other buildings right up close to the front of Notre-Dame. Dozens of paintings and drawings depict the townscape throughout the centuries; and in some instances, remarkably little has changed.

Hôtel le Peletier de Saint-Fargeau: This now contains all the museum's material from the Revolution to the present day. A vast section is dedicated to the Revolution, and here you will find models of the guillotines, portraits of revolutionary leaders, placards, and paintings of the royal family in captivity and even being executed. Other rooms contain relics from the First and Second Empires, including many memorabilia of the Emperor Napoléon. Numerous busts and paint-ings depict politicians and society beauties, in-cluding François Gérard's famous portrait of Madame Récamier.

The 20thC is represented by paintings and in a number of dazzling room settings. Two valuable examples of Art Nouveau are to be seen in the private room designed for the Café de Paris in 1899 by Henri Sauvage, and the interior of Fouquet's jewelry shop, which was totally designed by Alphonse Mucha. The opulent decor of the ballroom of the Hôtel de Wendel, created in 1924, is the climax to the visit.

The Hôtel Le Peletier de Saint-Fargeau was built around 1690 for Michel Le Peletier, a State Councillor and financial administrator. Its style is more sober, as befitted the house of a magistrate, and the main staircase and gilt-paneled room on the 1st floor are the only original items of interior decoration. The 2 buildings have been ingeniously linked together, and it is possible to walk between the two at the 1st-floor level.

★★★ Le Grand Louvre

Palais du Louvre, 1er. ☎ 01-40-20-53-17. Guided tours. General tours for individuals, in English, 3–6 times daily (except Tues) according to season; register 15 min. ahead. Groups must reserve up to 2 months in advance. Museum open 9am–6pm, until 9:45pm Mon and Wed; closed Tues. Admission charged. Métro: Palais-Royal/Musée-du-Louvre.

"I never knew what a palace was until I had a glimpse of the Louvre," wrote the 19thC American author Nathaniel Hawthorne. Today he would be surprised to find the main courtyard, the cour Napoléon, dominated by a crisp glass-walled pyramid, flanked by 3 smaller pyramids and 7 stretches of water, 2 with fountains, which mark the new entrance to the museum. The work of the Chinese-American architect I. M. Pei, this pyramid is only one feature of a vast new development begun in 1981 on the initiative of former President François Mitterrand, and which will be completed by 1997 at a cost of just over $1 billion.

It is easy to forget how stale and unwieldy the Louvre had grown before Pei's redesign. Many Parisians—faced with the crowds, the inconvenience, the labyrinthine difficulty of it all—had simply stopped going to the Louvre, which seemed quaintly out of step in a city as dynamic as Paris.

Today a visit to the new Grand Louvre reveals how much of that has changed. Easily accessible by newly created entrances opening onto the place du Palais-Royal and the Tuileries Gardens, filled with rehung collections basking in new light and space, and conveniently equipped with restaurants, shops, and parking— the Louvre seems literally to have come alive.

The Glass Pyramids of the Louvre

It involved massive underground excavations to create new galleries, a centralized public reception area, and all the facilities that a museum handling 5 million visitors each year could need. The 3 wings of the vast palace now have a much-needed central focal-point, and distances between the many galleries have been considerably shortened. The latest phase of development to be completed was the opening of the Richelieu (north) wing, the former Ministry of Finance, and the opening of the Carrousel du Louvre, an underground shopping mall. The new **Musée de la Mode** was slated to have opened by the end of 1996.

In the process of excavating the cour Napoléon and the cour Carrée, some 20,000 artifacts were found, the relics of a *quartier* that was demolished in 1852. More exciting still was the discovery of the foundations of the original 12thC fortress, built by Philippe Auguste, renovated by Charles V as a residence, and then demolished by François I in the 16thC in order to create a palace that was expanded piecemeal by every major French monarch up to Napoléon III.

Above these foundations is the cour Carrée, which was designed by Pierre Lescot for François I in the Renaissance style. In the 17thC, Louis XIII commissioned Lemercier to extend the west facade of the Cour Carrée in the same style, and the remainder was built by Louis XIV. Particularly noteworthy is the majestic colonnade of 52 Corinthian columns along the outside of the court. This was the work of Claude Perrault and is one of the outstanding examples of the classical style in Paris. From the cour Carrée, the Louvre grew haphazardly westward in 2 gigantic wings as successive monarchs added pavilion after pavilion until it finally linked up with the now vanished Tuileries palace. Today the Louvre is so vast that it can only be encompassed in a single sweep of the eye by observing it from the air or from a high vantage point.

In the Hall Napoléon, under the Pyramid, a bank of video screens offers day-by-day information on all changeable elements; there is a bookshop, restaurants, and audiovisual rooms, as well as a reception staff on call to answer any specific questions about the museum or its exhibits. There are free programs—even themed visits are offered, on such subjects as the birth of Christian art.

The exterior: Large-scale repairs and renovations have been taking place both inside and out, and by 1997, the restoration of the stonework and facades of the Louvre will be completed, after a period of 13 years. The effects of weathering, and, more seriously, of pollution, have taken a serious toll on the 86 statues of great men who line the cour Napoléon at 1st-floor level, and each imperfect piece of stone has been replaced and reworked on site, to a high standard of perfection. A small number, including the statues remade of Poussin, Rabelais, and Colbert, have been totally remade.

Reception area and underground galleries: The main entrance to the museum is through the pyramid. From the spacious underground reception area, the Hall Napoléon, there are striking views of the palace through the glass walls of the pyramid. This is also the gathering point for anyone wishing to take a guided tour. A display of chalcography (copper and brass engravings) is also here, along with temporary exhibition spaces that are well signposted. The huge crypt under the cour Carrée contains the massive, cyclopean remains of the ramparts and keep of the 12thC fortress. Continue via the Gothic Crypt of St-Louis; this area also boasts a display of the wealth of objects found during the excavation.

The museum above ground has 7 departments: Greek, Etruscan and Roman Antiquities, Oriental Antiquities, Egyptian Antiquities, Objets d'Art, Graphic Arts, and Paintings and Sculptures.

Greek, Etruscan, and Roman antiquities: This heading encompasses every chapter in the history of classical art, from early Hellenic times to the end of the Roman Empire. These works are located in the Denon and Sully wings.

The armless ★ *Venus de Milo* was found in 1820 by a peasant on the Greek island of Milos and is one of the museum's most prized items. Dating from the 3rd to 2nd century BC, she embodies all the idealized beauty and dignity invested by the Greeks in their portrayals of the human form. Her face is rather masculine, a reminder that the Greeks of that time particularly exalted male physical beauty.

Another famous exhibit in this section is the headless ★ *Winged Victory of Samothrace* (circa 200 BC). She dominates a grand staircase, which was rebuilt in the 1930s especially for her display. Reconstructed from pieces found in 1863, the left wing was entirely remade using the right wing as a model. The statue commemorates a naval victory and was created in the style of a ship's figurehead, symbolizing victory with far more impact than any triumphal arch.

Belonging to a much earlier period (6thC BC) is the **Hera of Samos.** In this work and the other statues nearby, you can see the stiffness and frontal emphasis often found in ancient Egyptian statues—so different from the Venus de Milo. Hera, in her enclosed roundness, recalls statuary made from tree trunks. Look out, too, for the **Rampin Horseman.** He has an archaic smile, and his beard and hair are stylized, geometrical approximations of reality. The bronze **Apollo of Piombino** (5thC BC) has superb copper inlay.

Oriental antiquities: This section includes artifacts drawn mainly from the civilizations of Mesopotamia, the Far Eastern section of the collection being in the **Musée National d'Arts Asiatiques.** Among the most impressive items here are the black basalt stele bearing the **Code of Law of King Hammurabi of Babylon** (1792–50 BC), the **Stele of the Vultures,** and the **Stele of Naram–Sim.**

Egyptian antiquities: This is one of the finest Egyptian collections in the world, thanks to long-standing French prominence in this field. Founded in 1826, its first curator was the great Egyptologist Champollion, decipherer of the Rosetta stone, which is now in the British Museum in London. Situated in ground- and 1st-floor galleries in the Sully wing, the collection contains such masterpieces as the great sandstone bust of **Amenophis IV** (Akhenaton), which was presented to France by Egypt in 1972. Look, too, for the superb **Gebel-el-Arak knife,** dating from about 3400 BC, the **jewels of Rameses II,** and the **statue of Queen Karomama.**

Sculptures: Housed on the new Richelieu wing, this section encompasses the whole history of French sculpture, from its origins to the 19thC, and includes works by foreign sculptors, such as Michelangelo's **Captives** and Benvenuto Cellini's bronze relief of the **Nymph of Fontainebleau.** The French sculptures range from austere medieval religious images, through Renaissance works such as German Pilon's *Three Graces.*

Objets d'art and furniture: The collection of Objets d'art is located on the 1st floor, primarily in the Richelieu wing. In the Denon wing, **The Galerie d'Apollon,** luxuriously decorated in 1661, has murals by Le Brun featuring a Sun God Apollo, symbolizing the Sun King, Louis XIV. The central ceiling was painted by Delacroix in 1848. This is an appropriate setting for the **Crown Jewels**—gorgeous crowns and regalia used at the coronation of the French kings, as well as priceless jewels such as the 137-carat diamond known as the **Regent,** purchased from England in 1717.

One of the most eagerly awaited features of the new Richelieu wing was the opening of the **Napoléon III apartments.** Left intact, although carefully regilded and restored, these rooms are a rich treasure of the ostentatious Second Empire style, filled with a pompous blend of gilt, velvet, and boiseries. Also on the 1st floor of the new wing is a magnificent collection of objects from the Middle Ages to the 17thC, including the series of 12 tapestries from the 16thC known as the *Chasses de Maximilien.*

Paintings: This department is the museum's greatest pride and constitutes one of the most comprehensive collections of paintings in the world. The redesign of the Louvre has meant that some 2,000 paintings have been added to the 4,000 that were already on view. From the vast Salle Sully, you can catch a marvelous view along one of Paris's great axes: from the pyramid and the **Arc de Triomphe du Carrousel** through to **L'Etoile** and **La Défense.**

The collection was begun by François I, who acquired the Louvre's most famous exhibit, Leonardo da Vinci's ★ *Mona Lisa,* along with other Italian masterpieces. Also called *La Gioconda,* thanks to the most mysterious of smiles, she is now displayed behind bullet-proof glass and is the subject of major security precautions.

The Louvre undoubtedly has the richest collection of Leonardos possessed by any museum in the world, as it also includes *Bacchus,* a *John the Baptist,* the *Virgin of the Rocks,* a small portrait of a lady, *La Belle Ferronnière,* and the *Virgin and Child with Ste-Anne.* In each of Leonardo's paintings, you will see how he has suppressed 2-dimensional line in favor of mass and tone value, creating 3-dimensional illusion. This technique is called *chiaroscuro,* Italian for "light-shadow." Further, by use of very thin coats of glaze, hard outlines are obscured, giving the subject a hazy look. This technique is called *sfumato,* Italian for haze. Leonardo also strove to reveal the intention of the soul through gestures. In the ★ *Virgin of the Rocks,* the group is held together by various significant gestures: pointing, praying, blessing, and protecting. In the ★ *Virgin and the Child with Ste-Anne,* Mary is shown sitting on the lap of her mother Ste-Anne and reaching out toward the baby Jesus, who, in turn, reaches toward his future sacrifice for mankind, which is symbolized by a lamb. The *Mona Lisa* is not the only one smiling. That mysterious smile can be found elsewhere, for instance in the *John the Baptist*.

In addition to the Leonardos, there is a wealth of paintings by Titian, Raphael, Veronese, and other artists of the Italian Renaissance, as well as earlier and later Italian works.

A small but distinguished Spanish collection includes such masterpieces as El Greco's ***Christ Crucified*** and Murillo's ***The Young Beggar,*** as well as works by Goya and Velázquez. English works are also not numerous, but include portraits by Gainsborough and Reynolds.

The Flemish, Dutch, and German masters are well represented, and there is a series of Rembrandts.

French paintings form the bulk of the collection, and range from the 14th through 19th centuries. You will find Poussin's limpid canvases of mythological and allegorical subjects, La Tour's religious paintings with their striking effects of light and shadow, and Watteau's delicate scenes of gaiety touched with a nuance of melancholy.

New spaces in the Richelieu wing are dedicated to the Northern Schools and Early French paintings from the 14th through 17th centuries. If it is size and splendor you want, then move around into the 19thC rooms in the Denon wing, where you will find David's vast painting ***The Coronation of Napoléon*** and works by other 19thC painters such as Delacroix and Corot.

Graphic arts: In the past, the graphic arts (drawings, engravings, pastels) were never on permanent display. They are now found in various locations on the 2nd and 3rd floors.

Grand Palais, Galeries Nationales du
3 av. du Général Eisenhower, 8ᵉ. ☎ 01-44-13-17-17. Open 10am–8pm, Wed 10am–10pm. Closed Tues. Admission charged. Métro: Champs-Elysées-Clémenceau.

The Grand Palais and the **Petit Palais,** built for the Universal Exhibition of 1900, echo each other like 2 thunderous fanfares across avenue Winston-Churchill, which runs from avenue des **Champs-Elysées** to the **Pont Alexandre III.** Some people would call them fussy and pompous, but it would be fairer to call them joyous and exuberant pieces of architectural rhetoric, although the Grand Palais oversteps the mark perhaps with its gargantuan porticoes, its frescoes, and its mass of cartouches and swags of carved stonework.

The western part of the building is now given over to the **Palais de la Découverte,** a science museum. The rest of the Grand Palais is used for temporary art exhibitions and other large-scale trade shows and exhibitions. The interior is as imposing as the exterior, particularly the main hall, with its lavish mosaic frieze and central spiral staircase. The building is dominated by a huge 43-meter (141-ft.) dome and an unmistakeable glass-and-iron vaulted roof.

The Grand Palais has suffered recently from structural defects; a new program aims to restore the foundations as well as the glass roof, though final plans for its renovation haven't yet been decided.

★ Grande Arche de la Défense

Take the Grande Arche exit from RER. ☎ 01-49-07-27-57. Open Mon–Sat 9am–6pm, Sun, holidays 9am–8pm. Last admission 1 hr. earlier.

The newest great arch in a city of arches, the awesome, monolithic Grande Arche focuses all eyes on the western end of **La Défense.** The Danish architect J. O. von Spreckelsen described his winning design as "an open cube—a window on the world." It is certainly that.

From the cavernous space beneath it—as wide as the avenue des Champs-Elysées—can be seen the dramatic west-to-east alignment of the arch with the **Arc de Triomphe,** the obelisk at **Place de la Concorde,** the **Arc de Triomphe du Carrousel,** and the **Grand Louvre.** Above soars the vast marble-covered cube of the arch, 90 meters (295 ft.) high and lined with office windows: a void large enough to shelter Notre-Dame. Through the 2 verticals of the arch, the dramatic west to east alignment of La Défense with the Arc de Triomphe and the Louvre comes into sharp focus.

Below the Grande Arche is the Musée de l'Automobile and the Dôme Imax, a marvelous 180° cinematic dome.

La Grande Arche de la Défense

Grévin, Musée

10 blvd. Montmartre, 9e. ☎ 01-47-70-85-05. Open daily 1–6pm. Admission charged. Métro: Richelieu-Drouot, Rue Montmartre.

Cabinet fantastique is the claim of the words over the entrance, and fantasy is certainly what you experience here. This is the original Grévin waxworks museum, founded in 1882 by designer Alfred Grévin. The involvement of the financier Gabriel Thomas ensured the financial backing, and the building developed as the Belle Epoque became more *belle.*

In 1900, Grévin built the lovely 1st-floor theater, with the assistance of sculptor Antoine Bourdelle, who contributed the sculptures. The stage curtain bears an original painting by Jules Cheret. The whimsical Palais des Mirages was bought after the 1900 World Exposition, and has been operational within the Grévin since 1904.

As you enter, a grotto with distorting mirrors takes you one step away from reality. Then, suddenly, you have arrived in a glorious, domed hall where it is hard to know whether to look up at the gilding or around you at the various witty juxtapositions of famous characters. Some of the waxworks are of contemporary French personalities, but the vast majority are international figures: François Mitterrand, Woody Allen, Michael Jackson.

Even more alluring are the historical tableaux—Napoléon and Josephine surrounded by an entourage, and in a lavish drawing room that is actually furnished with original period pieces. There are the inevitable scenes from the French Revolution, including Louis XVI and Marie Antoinette in prison, and Marat, seen slumped in the actual wooden bathtub in which he died. The figures are so well made that you never doubt they'll all move the second you look away.

A trip to the movies is also part of the fare—a series of movie sets takes you through the age of Gable and Lombard, Hitchcock, Monroe (complete with skirt swirling in the updraft), Chaplin, and Liza Minelli. Even Sylvester Stallone is there, as well as the Invisible Man.

Don't miss the performances of magic and conjuring that take place each afternoon in the lovely 1st-floor theater, where many of today's stars of the world of magic have made their debut over the years.

Another Grévin is located at the **Forum des Halles** (Grand Balcon, Level 1, Forum des Halles, rue Pierre Lescot, 1er; ☎ 01-42-26-28-50; open Mon–Sat 10:30am–6:45pm, Sun, holidays 1–7pm), where the Paris of the

Belle Epoque is re-created in 21 scenes, including an imaginary reconstruction of a Parisian street of 1885 and a *son et lumière* (a sound and light show) of Paris in 1900.

Guimet, Musée

See Arts Asiatiques-Guimet, Musée National des.

Les Halles

In the center, to the northeast of the Louvre, in the 1er.
Métro: Les Halles, Châtelet-Les-Halles.

This area of the city is bounded roughly by **rue Etienne-Marcel** and **rue de Rivoli** to the north and south, with the **Bourse du Commerce** and the **Pompidou Center** marking the west and east boundaries. The Forum des Halles is in the natural center.

During the 12thC, the area became a bustling food market (Zola called it "the belly of Paris") and it remained so until 1979, when the traders all moved to a huge new site at Rungis, near the airport at Orly, taking the atmosphere with them and leaving the city of Paris with the problem of deciding what to do with the area.

The following years saw a total transformation. The graceful old glass-and-iron market hall, built under Napoléon III, was torn down and the ensuing hole in the ground was replaced by a commercial complex, the **Forum des Halles.** Some of the old buildings have been renovated; the 16thC **Fontaine des Innocents** *(pl. Joachim du Bellay)* has been restored, and much of the area has been pedestrianized. There remain a few food merchants and a number of bars and restaurants with a touch of character, including **Pharamond,** a glory of Art Nouveau decorative tiles (see "Dining") and **Au Pied de Cochon** (the haven for lovers of shellfish and pigs' feet).

Hébert, Musée National Ernest

85 rue du Cherche-Midi, 6e. ☎ 01-42-22 23-82. Open 12:30–6pm, Sat, Sun 2–6pm; closed Tues. Admission charged. Métro: St-Placide, Vanneau.

Housed in the Hôtel de Montmorency, a small and gracious 18thC mansion on the Left Bank, this museum is devoted mainly to temporary exhibitions of the works of society painter Ernest Hébert (1817–1908) and his contemporaries.

Henner, Musée National Jean-Jacques

43 av. de Villiers, 17e. ☎ 01-47-63-42-73. Open 10am–noon, 2–5pm. Closed Mon. Admission charged. Métro: Malesherbes, Wagram.

This collection contains about 700 paintings, drawings, and sketches by the Alsatian artist Jean-Jacques Henner (1829–1905), who was one of the great individualists among painters. Following no school, but inspired by the old masters, he created canvases of delicate luminosity and haunting grace.

En Herbe, Musée
See Bois de Boulogne.

Histoire de France, Musée de l'
See Archives Nationales.

★★ Histoire Naturelle, Muséum National d'(National Museum of Natural History)
In the Jardin des Plantes. 57 rue Cuvier, 5e. ☎ 01-40-79-30-00. Guided tours. Gardens and zoo open daily 7:15am (summer) or 8:15am (winter) to dusk. Gallery of Evolution open daily 10am–6pm (Thurs until 10pm). Gallery of Entomology open Mon–Fri 1–5pm; Sat–Sun 10am–6pm. Other galleries open weekdays 10am–5pm, Sat, Sun, 10am–6pm. Greenhouse, open weekdays 1am–5pm; Sat–Sun 10am–6pm. Everything except park and zoo closed Tues and holidays. Admission charged. Métro: Jussieu, Monge.

Born in 1645 as a garden for medicinal plants, and dramatically restored in 1994, this 350-year-old museum has once again found its way into the hearts of Parisians, who queu up long lines on the weekends to take the kids along to see the skeletons.

It includes the following galleries:

Paleontology: Skeletons, bones, and pickled organs, both human and animal; and casts of prehistoric monsters.

Paleobotany: A small collection of plant fossils, petrified tree trunks, and other such recondite objects that will be of interest mainly to specialists.

Mineralogy: Fossils, crystalline growths, and precious stones.

Entomology: Just beyond these buildings, outside the perimeter of the garden proper, is the **Gallery of Entomology,** which claims to display "the most beautiful insects of the world."

Evolution: Extensive renovation of the long-closed Gallery of Zoology at the west end of the garden was completed in June 1994 and it has since been rebaptized the **Gallery of Evolution.** This gallery has become the centerpiece of the museum's permanent exhibitions, including 120 rare or extinct species. In addition to the museum there are temporary exhibition rooms, a learning center, an auditorium, and a multimedia center.

There is also a gallery for interesting temporary exhibitions. Giant indeed is the cross-section of a giant redwood, a gift in 1927 from the American Legion Department of California.

Guided tours: Ornithological walks take place each Wednesday at 9:15am throughout the year—your chance to make better acquaintance with the dozens of bird species that live in the gardens. Free themed walks are given September to June; details can be obtained from the ticket office.

Historique de la Ville de Paris, Musée
See Grand Carnavalet.

Homme, Musée de l' (Museum of Mankind)
Palais de Chaillot, pl. du Trocadéro 16°. ☎ 01-45-05-72-72. Guided tours. Open 9:45am–5:15pm. Closed Tues, public holidays. Admission charged. Métro: Trocadéro.

Occupying the west wing of the **Palais de Chaillot,** this museum contains one of the world's most important collections devoted to anthropology, ethnology, and prehistory. The objects are, for the most part, arranged according to geographical region and include all manner of intriguing objects, from a Navajo sand-painting to Japanese costumes. The excellent South American section includes a shriveled Inca mummy in a fetal position, which inspired Munch's painting *The Scream*.

There is an area devoted to the arts and technologies of different world regions, and another to anthropology, dealing with the biological and physical characteristics of man. The museum also has a fine restaurant with superb views of the **Tour Eiffel.**

Hôtel de Rohan
18thC Marais mansion built for the bishops of Strasbourg. See **Archives Nationales.**

★★ Hôtel des Archevêques de Sens
1 rue du Figuier, 4°. ☎ 01-42-78-14-60. Forney Library open Tues–Fri 1:30–8:30pm, Sat 10am–8:30pm. Closed Sun, Mon. Admission free. Métro: Pont-Marie, St-Paul.

This mansion at the south edge of the Marais is such a perfect specimen of medieval architecture, with its pepper-pot turrets and pointed arches, that if you came upon it without prior knowledge you might think it was 19thC imitation Gothic, or perhaps a stray building from a Hollywood movie set in the Middle Ages.

In fact, it is one of the oldest houses in Paris and was built by Tristan de Salazar, Archbishop of Sens, between 1475 and 1507. It was an anachronism even

L'Hôtel de Sens

in its day, since the archbishop, who came from a military family, could not resist adding a few touches to create the illusion of a fortified castle—a dungeon, watchtower, and watchwalk. The building was a late burst of Gothic feudalism at the dawn of the French Renaissance.

It is now owned by the City of Paris and houses the Forney Library, a library of science, technology, arts, and crafts. Make a point of seeing the jewel-like formal garden fronting the building and wander in to inspect the fine courtyard.

Hôtel de Soubise

18thC Marais mansion with a superb courtyard. See **Archives Nationales.**

Hôtel des Ventes (Auction rooms)

Hôtel Drouot-Richelieu, 9 rue Drouot, 9ᵉ. ☎ 01-48-00-20-20. Open Mon–Sat 11am–6pm. Closed Sun, Aug. Métro: Richelieu-Drouot. Hôtel Drouot-Montaigne, 15 av. Montaigne, 8ᵉ. ☎ 01-48-00-20-80. Hours as above. Admission free. Métro: Alma-Marceau.

The Parisian equivalent of Christie's or Sotheby's or Parke Bernet, the Hôtel des Ventes has, like auction rooms everywhere, an atmosphere of glamor and excitement. In France, auctioneering is a more strictly regulated business than in most countries and is controlled by the Compagnie des Commissaires Priseurs, the auctioneers' professional body, whose members can display a gold plaque outside their door.

The old Hôtel des Ventes, which stood on the site of the Hôtel Drouot-Richelieu, was demolished in the 1970s. However, in 1980 the new Hôtel Drouot was completed—a stylish building of steel, dark-tinted glass, and concrete, with traditional touches such as a steep, vaulted roof, and dormer windows.

In recent years, operations have diversified and the most prestigious sales now take place in the well-heeled avenue Montaigne showroom. Both auction houses have various rooms, where all kinds of objects—French tapestries, Italian drawings, autographed letters, and Chinese vases—change hands under the eye of a *commissaire priseur* perched behind a high desk. A fascinating place to visit even if you are not bidding.

Hôtel de Ville (Town Hall)

Place de l'Hôtel-de-Ville, 4ᵉ. ☎ 01-42-76-40-40. Building open Mon–Fri 9am–6:30pm, Sat 9am–6pm. Guided tours to salons, Mon only 10:30am; for reservations ☎ 01-42-76-50-49. Admission free. Métro: Hôtel-de-Ville.

There has been a town hall on this site since 1357, when one of the earliest mayors of Paris, Etienne Marcel, moved the city council here. His equestrian statue now stands facing toward the Seine by the south side of the building.

The first town hall was replaced by a more imposing one in Renaissance style, which was burned down by the Communards in 1871. The present edifice (1874–82) is a fairly convincing copy of its predecessor, but has a ponderous 19thC touch to the ornate facade—its numerous statues of Parisian dignitaries ensconced in niches.

For many years Paris had no mayor and was governed by a prefect of the city, but in 1977 the office of mayor was re-established, and the Hôtel de Ville became his headquarters. The 109 councilors meet in a spacious, wood-paneled chamber, which can be viewed during sessions, from a public gallery. Other rooms can be visited by conducted tour on Monday mornings.

The City of Paris has its public relations department at the Hôtel de Ville (entrance at 29 rue de Rivoli). Here you can find exhibitions on Paris as well as other information relating to the municipality.

Hugo, Maison de Victor

6 pl. des Vosges, 4ᵉ. ☎ 01-42-72-10-16. Guided tours. Open 10am–5:40pm. Closed Mon and holidays. Admission charged. Métro: St-Paul, Chemin-Vert, Bastille.

This is the house where Victor Hugo, author of *Notre-Dame de Paris* (*The Hunchback of Notre-Dame*), lived from 1832 to 1848. By the time of his death in 1885, Hugo had attained the status of national hero. He was given a spectacular public funeral attended by mourners in their thousands and was buried with the high and mighty few great men, in the **Panthéon.**

Many people do not realize that Hugo, as well as being a great writer and distinguished public figure, was also an artist of genius, and the house is full of hundreds his drawings, paintings, and lithographs— mostly dreamlike or surrealistic works depicting eerie landscapes with curious vegetation and somber castles. There are also many portraits, documents, and other mementoes of his public and private life. One room is devoted to illustrations of Notre-Dame de Paris by various artists and also contains Rodin's powerful bust of Hugo. The novelist was also an accomplished interior decorator, and the mansion contains several replicas of rooms from his other abodes.

Ile de la Cité and Ile St-Louis

1er and 4e. Métro: Cité, Pont Marie.

The Ile de la Cité floats in the Seine like a graceful galleon carrying more than 2,000 years of history as its cargo, for it was here that Paris began, when the tribe known as the Parisii settled on the island in the 3rdC. Trailing behind it is the smaller and less heavily laden Ile St-Louis.

★★ **Ile de la Cité:** A good place to begin is the little garden on a spit of land at the north end of the Ile approached by a stairway from the **Pont Neuf**. On the other side of the bridge, where the island begins to widen out, is a charming little triangular square, **place Dauphine,** which André Breton describes in his novel *Nadja* as "one of the most profoundly secluded places I know." Farther on, straddling the width of the island and bounded by boulevard du Palais, is the vast historic complex containing the **Palais de Justice,** the **Sainte Chapelle,** and the **Conciergerie.** Across the boulevard is the rather forbidding **Préfecture de Police,** headquarters of the immortal Inspector Clouseau, off-set by the **flower market** in place Louis Lépine, which on Sundays becomes a colorful **bird market.**

The focal point of the island is the **place du Parvis-Notre-Dame,** crowned by **Notre-Dame cathedral** and bounded on the north side by the **Hôtel-Dieu hospital,** the foundations of which date from the 7thC. A riverside walk leads around the south side of the cathedral to the garden of **square de l'Ile de France,** at the east tip of the island. At the very end is the **Mémorial de la Déportation,** an underground vault commemorating the French victims of the concentration camps. Its stark simplicity conveys solemnity, dignity, and compassion.

Immediately to the north of the cathedral lies a cluster of streets, including **rue Chanoinesse.** The name of this street derives from the canons of Notre-Dame whose houses used to line the street. Only 2 of these, nos. 22 and 24, remain. They date from the 16thC, but there are many fine facades belonging to later periods.

Off rue Chanoinesse is rue de la Colombe, where the line of the **old Gallo-Roman wall** is traced in the cobblestones. Continue north to **quai aux Fleurs;** there are no flowers here, but of interest are 2 stone heads over the doorways of nos. 9 and 11. These represent the ill-fated lovers Abelard and Héloise, who lived in a house on this spot in the 12thC. The quai aux Fleurs leads east from here to the **pont St-Louis,** linking the 2 islands. From the bridge there is a fine view of the lacework of flying buttresses and spires at the eastern end of Notre-Dame.

Ile St-Louis: The Ile St-Louis, named after Louis IX of France, has a different and quieter atmosphere than its neighbor, being more private and picturesque. Many of the fine houses have remained intact. Two of the finest are the **Hôtel de Lausun** (17 quai d'Anjou)—admire the magnificent drainpipes—and the **Hôtel Lambert** (1-3 quai d'Anjou), both designed by Louis XIV's architect Le Vau.

The island is an architectural feast and also the town's first real-estate development, built as a unit in the 17thC. All along the riverfront are houses with stately porticos and interesting stone carving. Many of them also bear plaques commemorating the distinguished men who lived here—aristocrats, politicians, artists, poets. The poet Baudelaire lived at no. 22 quai de Béthune. The scientist Marie Curie lived at no. 36 quai d'Orléans from 1912 until her death in 1934.

The spine of the island is rue **St-Louis-en-l'Ile,** with its church of the same name, built between 1664 and 1725 and marked by a curious pierced spire and an ornate wrought-iron clock. The street is full of little shops and restaurants, many with old and interesting frontages. At no. 35 is the tiny bookstore **Librairie Ulysse,** which specializes in rare secondhand as well as new travel books. Two doors away, at no. 31, is **Berthillon,** one of the best ice-cream shops in Europe, with a constant line of customers outside to prove it. A newer branch, **La Flore en l'Ile** (2 rue Jean du Bellay), is at the western tip opposite the pont St-Louis.

But the Ile St-Louis is mostly a peaceful place, with its quiet streets and a tree-lined riverside walk around

The Islands of the Seine

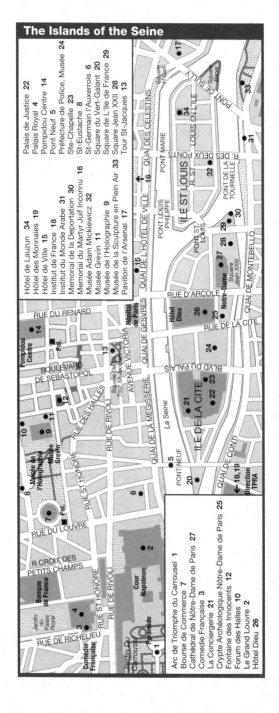

most of the island. Its little park, **square Barye,** at the east end, has a tiny play area for small children where parents can sit and read peacefully.

The **quays** that line the banks of the Seine on either side of the Ile de la Cité and Ile St-Louis afford some superb views of the islands and of Notre-Dame. Particularly magnificent are the riverscape views from pont des Arts, square René Viviani, pont de l'Archevêché, pont de la Tournelle, and pont de Sully on the Left Bank, and quai de la Mégisserie and quai des Célestins on the Right Bank.

The parapets of the quays are lined with stalls—the famous **bouquinistes**—selling secondhand books, especially along the Left Bank (see "Shopping").

Institut de France
21-25 quai de Conti, 6°. ☎ 01-44-41-44-41. Not open to public except cultural groups by arrangement. ☎ 01-43-29-55-10. Admission charged. Métro: Pont-Neuf, Mabillon.

The Institute is a majestic building, with a concave semi-circular facade facing the Seine. It was founded as a college and library with money bequeathed by Cardinal Mazarin, and was built by the prolific architect Le Vau in 1663 to 1664 on the site of the Nêsle gate and tower, which had formed part of the medieval city wall.

The college was suppressed after the Revolution, and in 1805 the building became the seat of the recently created Institut de France, which it remains to this day. Of the 5 learned academies that make up the institute, the best known is the Académie Française.

Invalides, Hôtel National des
Esplanade des Invalides, 7°. ☎ 01-44-42-37-72. Admission charged. Métro: Latour-Maubourg, Varenne. RER: Invalides.

When Louis XIV's architects designed this building in the 1670s as a military hospital and rest home for his wounded, elderly, or infirm soldiers (*invalides*), they poured into it all the architectural rhetoric of the Sun King's era.

Most of the building, whose foundations were finally laid in 1671, is the work of Libéral Bruant, with the esplanade by Robert de Cotte. The 196-meter-long (645 ft.) facade overlooks a wide esplanade that sweeps down to the Seine. The great portico is guarded by statues of Mars and Minerva; the dormer windows in the roof are framed by huge suits of armor crafted in stone. The courtyard, with its double colonnade, is particularly fine. Jules Hardouin-Mansart's Dôme church, which seems to be part of the facade but is, in fact, set well back, dominates the whole edifice, especially now with its regilded roof.

In its heyday, this building housed nearly 6,000 old soldiers. Now the number has dwindled to a handful, and the Hôtel des Invalides has a new but related role as the home of 4 museums and as the resting place of Napoléon Bonaparte.

Musée de l'Armée (Army Museum). ☎ 01-44-42-37-72. Tickets valid for 2 consecutive days; also valid for Napoléon's tomb. Open Apr–Sept 10am–6pm, Oct–Mar 10am–5pm. Closed holidays.

This collection of militaria, one of the largest in the world, is divided into 2 sections, housed on the east and west sides of the courtyard. The east side tells the story of the French Army, illustrated by pictures, models, and military mementoes of all kinds.

Two large rooms on the ground floor, the Salle Turenne and the Salle Vauban, were once refectories for the inmates of the building. Now, the former contains a fine collection of flags and standards, including those from World War I; the latter is devoted mainly to exhibits relating to the cavalry, among them a row of life-sized dummies of dashing uniformed men on horseback.

Upstairs, a series of rooms covers different periods of French military history, dealing, commendably, with defeat as well as victory. Predictably, Napoléon I features prominently. His death mask is here, as is a reconstruction of the room at Longwood House, St. Helena, where he died in 1821.

On the 3rd floor, where there were once craft workshops manned by the *invalides,* there are now exhibits relating to the Second Empire and the Franco-Prussian War.

On the west side of the courtyard are 2 more former refectories, the Salle François I (which is currently being renovated) and the Salle Henri IV, which look back to the days when soldiers went into battle clad in armor.

Two rooms at the rear are filled with 15th- through 17th-century weapons, and there are also displays of prehistoric and Oriental weaponry. Upstairs, the exhibits are from World Wars I and II. There is also a room filled with model artillery guns; look out of the window into the cour de la Victoire and you will see an impressive collection of the real thing.

Musée des Plans-Reliefs (Museum of Relief Maps and Plans). ☎ 01-45-51-95-05. Joint ticket (see Musée de l'Armée, above). Open Apr–Sept 10am–12:30pm, 2–6pm; Oct–Mar 10am–12:30pm, 2–5pm.

Housed on the 4th floor, this museum has finely
detailed miniature versions of many towns, including
Mont St-Michel, Metz, and Strasbourg.

**Musée de l'Ordre de la Libération (Museum of the Order of
Liberation).** 51bis blvd. de La Tour-Maubourg. ☎ 01-47-05-04-10.
Open daily, Apr–Sep 10am–6pm, Oct–Mar 10am–5pm. Ticket to
Musée de l'Armée gives free admission.

The Order of Liberation was created by Général de
Gaulle to honor those who gave outstanding service in
the liberation of France. The museum, not linked with
the Musée de l'Armée, has photographs, documents,
and mementoes of the Free French, the Resistance, the
Deportation, and the Liberation.

St-Louis-des-Invalides. Esplanade des Invalides, 7ᵉ. ☎ 01-44-42-
37-72. Admission charged. Métro: Latour-Maubourg, Varenne. RER:
Invalides.

This church, with its cool, light, barrel-vaulted interior, was where soldiers of the Hôtel des Invalides wor-
shipped. Its main entrance faces the cour d'Honneur.
When the Dôme church was added, the two opened
into one another and shared a common altar. A barrier
in the form of a glass screen now separates them. Berlioz's
Requiem received its 1ˢᵗ public performance here in 1837,
on the superb 17thC organ.

Dôme Church and Tomb of Napoléon. Joint ticket (see Musée de
l'Armée, above).

When the rest of Hôtel des Invalides had been completed, Louis XIV decided that it needed an added touch
of splendor, and he commissioned Hardouin-Mansart
to add the Dôme church to the south side of the building. It was begun in 1677 and completed by Robert de
Cotte after Mansart's death in 1708. With its high,
slender, gilded dome, and its portico with 2 rows of
columns (Doric below, Corinthian above), it is
considered one of the great masterpieces of its era. The
dome itself, regilded in 1989 for the bicentennial, gleams
in a most self-congratulatory way from just about
every vantage point in Paris.

However, the church is less visited for its architecture than for the fact that it contains one of the most
prestigious graves in the world, the **tombeau de
Napoléon I,** whose body was brought to Paris from
St. Helena in 1840, already 19 years after his death. The
elaborate crypt and tomb, designed by Visconti, was
not ready for another 21 years, and the emperor was
finally entombed amid lavish funeral celebrations in
1861.

Les cendres, or, literally, the remains (rather than the
ashes, for Napoléon had been buried conventionally),

Dôme Church of
Les Invalides

had been parted with by the British most reluctantly, and their return was greeted as a national triumph by the French, despite the intervention of the years.

The Emperor now lies encased in 6 coffins, one inside the other, which in turn are enclosed within a beautiful red porphyry sarcophagus on its pedestal of green granite. This rests in an open, circular crypt surrounded by a gallery which houses reliefs commemorating his achievements.

Napoléon's son, the King of Rome, who died in 1832 at the age of 21, also lies here. This was not the young man's original resting place. His remains were brought to Paris in 1940, on the centenary of the return of the emperor's remains. The instigator of this was A. Hitler, Esq.

Pause to appreciate the rest of the interior: the altar with its elaborate baldachin supported on twisted columns; the cupola with its vivid paintings by La Fosse; and the side chapels containing the tombs of Maréchal Foch and other military heroes.

Napoléon would have been pleased with his final resting place. "I wish my remains," he said, "to repose on the banks of the Seine among the people of France whom I have loved so much."

Jacquemart-André, Musée

158 blvd. Haussmann, 8e. ☎ 01-42-89-04-91. Guided tours.
Open 9:30am–12:30pm and 1:30pm–6pm. Closed Mon.
Admission charged. Métro: Miromesnil.

The recently restored, opulent interior of what was once a private house forms a pleasing setting for the 18thC and Italian Renaissance works that were collected voraciously yet discerningly by the banker Edouard André and his wife, the portraitist Nélie Jacquemart. She continued to add to the collection after André's death in 1881, eventually bequeathing it to the **Institut de France,** along with the grand neoclassical house that her husband had built in 1875.

Among the collection you will find sculptures by Donatello and paintings by Botticelli, Titian, and Uccello, including the magnificent *St. George Slaying the Dragon.* There are French 18thC painters galore— Watteau, Fragonard, Greuze, and Boucher—and foreign schools by Rembrandt, Reynolds, Murillo, and others. Frescoes by Tiepolo, a Savonnerie carpet, 4 **Gobelins** tapestries depicting the seasons, and a wealth of furniture and objets d'art are on display. The Boucicault *Book of Hours,* which once belonged to Diane de Poitiers, is also there to be seen.

Jardins des Plantes (Botanical Gardens)

5ᵉ. Admission free to gardens, entrance fee for zoo.

Llamas, pink flamingos, orangoutans, South American eagles, a round animal house built under Napoléon in the shape of a Legion of Honor cross, a reptile house, an open-air cafe, excellent playing facilities for children, and much more—the Jardin des Plantes has many facets. It is a park, botanical garden, and zoo, and also contains the Museum of Natural History.

The menagerie is the oldest public zoo in the country and dates back to the Revolution. Despite some rather antiquated installations (some of which are being improved), it is very popular, particularly with children, who seem to enjoy its small scale. Near the zoo, the botanical garden, established in the 17thC as a medicinal herb garden, contains a wide variety of European and tropical plants. Some of the specialized areas, such as the alpine garden, are open for shorter hours than the main gardens. Tunnel-like avenues of plane trees lead down to the Scine.

★ Jeu de Paume, Galerie Nationale du

1 Pl. de la Concorde, Jardin des Tuileries,1ᵉʳ. ☎ 01-47-03-12-50. Open Tues noon–9:30pm, Wed–Fri noon–7pm, Sat–Sun 10am–7pm; closed Mon. Admission charged. Métro: Concorde, Tuileries.

This Second-Empire pavilion matches its twin, the **Orangerie des Tuileries,** in a corresponding position straight across the **Tuileries** gardens. Originally the tennis court (jeu de paume) of Napoléon III, the building was widely known for many years as the home of one of the world's greatest collections of Impressionist paintings. This entire collection was rehoused in 1986, in the **Musée d'Orsay.**

The almost inevitable substantial refurbishment took place, and the Jeu de Paume has now reopened as a major gallery for contemporary art. Architect Antoine Stinco's stark scheme has stripped the interior bare of all decoration, leaving the large spaces created by the restoration work to speak for themselves when displaying very large and unusual works of art. The grand, clean, classical lines of the exterior have remained unaltered.

The gallery has no permanent collection, but there is a program of exhibitions focusing on little-known contemporary artists, a video-screening room, a good bookstore, and an excellent little designer-cafe, selling designer-snacks at surprisingly un-designer prices.

Latin Quarter
On the Left Bank, between Ile de la Cité and the Jardin du Luxembourg, in the 5e. Métro: St-Michel, Cluny-La-Sorbonne, Maubert-Mutualité, Cardinal-Lemoine.

The name Quartier Latin carries with it the image of a way of life: colorful, vibrant, intellectual, rebellious, bohemian and, above all, cosmopolitan. The Latin Quarter lies at the heart of the Left Bank and comprises most of the 5e and a sliver of the 6e districts, taking in the streets immediately to the west of the boulevard St-Michel.

Its name derives from the presence of the **Sorbonne** university and other colleges in the district, the scholars of which formerly spoke Latin. The area is still full of students, not only from the Sorbonne but also from the neighboring Collègede France, the university of Jussieu a little farther to the east, and the Ecole Normale Supérieure to the south.

The term Latin Quarter is doubly appropriate, for the area now called the **Montagne Ste-Geneviève,** around the **Panthéon,** was once the focal point of the Roman colony. Although the governor had his palace on the Ile de la Cité, it was here that the forum, temple, and baths were built. Virtually the only Roman remains to be seen in Paris are the great thermal baths at the Thermes de Cluny museum and in the Arènes de Lutèce.

The main artery of the Latin Quarter is **boulevard St-Michel.** This busy, tree-lined thoroughfare, full of bookstores and cafes, rises at the south end of the Jardins du Luxembourg and descends south toward the Seine into place St-Michel, which is dominated by the huge **St-Michel fountain.**

The boulevard St-Michel is intersected by the other great artery of the Left Bank, **boulevard St-Germain.** At their junction is the **Musée National du Moyen Age/Thermes de Cluny,** in the Flamboyant Gothic Hôtel de Cluny, one of many architectural riches in the district. Here, too, is the refurbished métro station of Cluny-La-Sorbonne, which at track level boasts the signatures of literary giants from across the centuries spread across its vast mosaic-and-ceramic ceiling.

Turn up rue Soufflot and you will be confronted by the massive facade of the repository of France's greatest men, the Panthéon, standing on the Montagne Ste-Geneviève. Behind it to the left is the exquisite church of **St-Etienne-du-Mont** and to the left is the **Ste-Geneviève library,** built in the mid-19thC on the site of the medieval Montaigu college. Behind it, in rue Clotilde, is the **Lycée Henri IV**, the buildings of which incorporate the refectory and belfry of the old abbey of Ste-Geneviève.

There are 3 other important churches in the area: **St-Séverin, St-Julien-le-Pauvre,** and **St-Nicolas-du-Chardonnet;** the latter is the stronghold of traditional Catholics, and still holds Mass in Latin.

The district's main attraction, however, lies not so much in its monuments as in the tortuous streets that twist around each other along the riverbank. The strongest impression of the cosmopolitan bohemian life comes from the streets around St-Séverin and St-Julien-le-Pauvre. Here are restaurants of many nationalities, small bookstores, intimate little cafes, nightclubs, and experimental cinemas.

The pedestrian zone of rue de la Huchette and its tributaries is particularly full of color and atmosphere. Leading off rue de la Huchette is the amusingly named **rue du Chat-qui-Pêche** (Street of the Fishing Cat), said to be the smallest street in Paris.

A stone's throw to the east (37 rue de la Bûcherie) is one of the most fabled bookstores in the city, **Shakespeare and Co.,** which specializes in English-language books, both new and secondhand. Between the wars, Sylvia Beach owned the original Shakespeare and Co. at 12 rue de l'Odéon, which was the meeting place of expatriate literati such as James Joyce, Ezra Pound, Henry Miller, and Ernest Hemingway. Eventually it was reincarnated in its present location by a genial American, George Whitman, who still runs the place

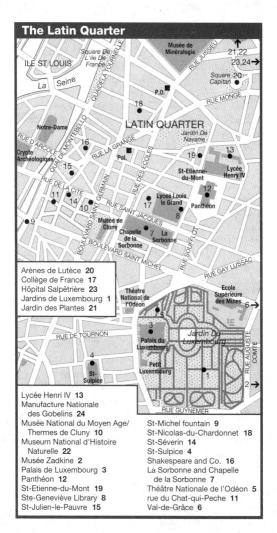

The Latin Quarter

ILE ST LOUIS

La Seine

Square De L'ile De France

QUAI DE LA TOURNELLE

RUE JUSSIEU

Musée de Minéralogie

21,22
23,24 →

Square Capitan 20

RUE MONGE

P.O.

18

Notre-Dame

LATIN QUARTER

Jardin De Navarre

RUE D'ARCOLE

QUAI DE MONTEBELLO

16

RUE LA GRANGE

RUE DES ECOLES

13

19

St-Etienne-du-Mont

Lycée Henry IV

Crypte Archéologique

15

Pol.

RUE DE LA CITE

11   14   10

RUE SAINT JACQUES

RUE SAINT GERMAIN

17

Lycée Louis le Grand

8

12

Panthéon

9

Musée de Cluny

Chapelle de la Sorbonne

7   La Sorbonne

BOULEVARD SAINT MICHEL

BOULEVARD SAINT GERMAIN

RUE SOUFFLOT

RUE GAY LUSSAC

Arènes de Lutèce	**20**
Collège de France	**17**
Hôpital Salpêtrière	**23**
Jardins de Luxembourg	**1**
Jardin des Plantes	**21**

Théâtre National de l'Odéon

Ecole Supérieure des Mines

6 →

RUE DE TOURNON

3

Palais du Luxembourg

Jardin Du Luxembourg

RUE AUGUSTE COMTE

4

St-Sulpice

Petit Luxembourg

1

2 →

RUE GUYNEMER

Lycée Henri IV	**13**
Manufacture Nationale des Gobelins	**24**
Musée National du Moyen Age/ Thermes de Cluny	**10**
Museum National d'Histoire Naturelle	**22**
Musée Zadkine	**2**
Palais de Luxembourg	**3**
Panthéon	**12**
St-Etienne-du-Mont	**19**
Ste-Geneviève Library	**8**
St-Julien-le-Pauvre	**15**

St-Michel fountain	**9**
St-Nicolas-du-Chardonnet	**18**
St-Séverin	**14**
St-Sulpice	**4**
Shakespeare and Co.	**16**
La Sorbonne and Chapelle de la Sorbonne	**7**
Théâtre Nationale de l'Odéon	**5**
rue du Chat-qui-Peche	**11**
Val-de-Grâce	**6**

with great verve, and from time to time accommodates penniless writers in rooms above the shop.

In the Latin Quarter one senses fewer barriers than in many other districts; the area seems to offer an invitation to anyone who comes here to participate in its life. No doubt this is because of the presence of so many nationalities and so many students.

Légion d'Honneur, Musée National de la

2 rue de Bellechasse, 7e. ☎ 01-45-51-87-05. Guided tours by prior arrangement. Open 2–5pm. Closed Mon, public holidays. Admission charged. Métro: Musée d'Orsay, Solférino.

The museum is housed in the Hôtel de Salm, a fine 18thC mansion, built in Palladian style and resembling the White House in Washington, DC. Former occupants have included the writer Madame de Staël and Napoléon Bonaparte. The house was acquired by the Grand Chancellery of the Legion of Honor soon after the Order's creation by Napoléon in 1802. It was burned down during the Commune in 1871 and almost immediately rebuilt in 1878.

The museum's function is devotion to the history of chivalric orders and other awards for distinction. Many such awards from foreign countries are featured, and examples of Britain's Victoria Cross and Order of the Bath are to be seen, as well as a rich selection of French insignia, regalia, and documents. The section on the Legion of Honor itself reveals that Rodin, Utrillo, and Colette were among the recipients.

Louvre, Musée du
See Le Grand Louvre.

Luxembourg, Jardins du
Guided walks once a month, Apr–Oct. Métro: Vavin, Luxembourg, Port-Royal.

The **Palais du Luxembourg,** which houses the French Senate, was built between 1612 and 1624 by Marie de Médicis, the widow of Henry IV. Finding the Louvre boring as a place of residence, she bought the house and grounds of the Duc de Piney-Luxembourg, then standing in a semirural position on the southern edge of the city.

Beside the duke's house (now known as the **Petit Luxembourg),** she built a grandiose mansion designed by Salomon de Brosse in the style of the Pitti Palace in Florence, but keeping the traditional French layout around a grand courtyard. However, her stay was short-lived, for in 1630, only 5 years after she had moved in, she was banished for life to Cologne.

During the Reign of Terror (1793–4), the palace became a prison, but after 1795, it housed the higher parliamentary assemblies, and the building underwent a series of alterations and enlargements. The Petit Luxembourg next door is now the residence of the Senate's president.

The gardens, like the palace, are French, with Italian touches such as the baroque **Medici fountain,** which stands at the end of a long pool filled with goldfish and flanked by shaded walkways. The focal point of the gardens is a large octagonal pool, surrounded by formal terraces and *parterres* and usually filled with a fleet of toy sailboats. The rest is an engaging mixture of formality and intimacy, with plenty of little secret corners as well as broad, straight avenues.

One of the great delights of this park is its statues. Here you will find, among others, Delacroix, Verlaine, George Sand, Stendhal, and Flaubert. You may guess the importance to the French of the various literary names, by comparing the size and complexity of their public tributes. In *avenue de l'Observatoire,* which forms an extension to the gardens, is an exuberant fountain with an armillary sphere held up by female figures representing the 4 quarters of the globe.

The gardens also have tennis courts, an elegant circular pond where you (or your child) can rent boats, donkey rides, a large marionette theater, the **Théâtre du Luxembourg** (☎ 01-43-26-46-47, afternoon shows, admission charged), a school of beekeeping and arbori-culture, and an open-air cafe under the trees—reminiscent of a painting by Renoir.

★★ La Madeleine

Place de la Madeleine, 8ᵉ. ☎ 01-44-51-69-00. Guided tours. Open 7am–7pm, Sun 7:30am–1:30pm, 3:30–7pm. Admission free. Métro: Madeleine.

Built to look like a Roman temple, this grand edifice, with its simple lines and colonnade of soaring Corinthian columns, stands at the hub of one of the most prosperous districts of Paris, confident of its own architectural splendor, yet apparently still uncertain of its role as a Christian church.

Begun as a church in 1763, during the reign of Louis XV (it was designed by Constant d'Ivry as a small-scale version of St-Louis-des-Invalides), it never seems to have quite thrown off the image of the bank that it nearly became in the early 19thC—other ideas included a theater, a banqueting hall, a Temple of Glory to Napoléon's army, and a railway station. After much debate and many changes of design, it was finally inaugurated in 1842, and consecrated as a church in 1845.

Contrasting with the rather austere exterior, the sensual beauty of the interior comes as something of a surprise—a feast of softly colored marble, gilt Corinthian columns, rich murals, and some fine sculpture, including Rude's *Baptism of Christ* and the *Rapture of Saint Mary Magdalene* by Marochetti, which dominates the high altar.

The church possesses a superb organ, and concerts are held here several times a week, including free

Sunday afternoon concerts during the academic year. Visitors are not allowed to tour during concerts. La Madeleine has recently undergone a major program of refurbishments—especially to the west facade, the roof, and the southern steps—including a million-dollar program to restore the front facade and columns. Work will continue on the roof and cornices in 1996.

Le Marais

3ᵉ and 4ᵉ. Métro: Hôtel-de-Ville, St-Paul, Chemin-Vert, Temple, St-Sébastien-Froissart, Filles-du-Calvaire, Arts-et-Métiers, Rambuteau.

This fascinating district has a grave beauty that is haunting and powerful. The stamp of the Middle Ages is still firmly imprinted on the narrow, huddled streets, lined by venerable houses built in the 16th through 18th centuries.

The name means "marshland," and this is what the area was until the 12thC when it was drained by the Knights Templar. It became the site of many other religious communities that have since disappeared but bequeathed their names to certain streets: rue des Blancs-Manteaux, rue des Filles-du-Calvaire, and rue Ste-Croix-de-la-Bretonnerie. The Knights' fortress, the **Temple,** became a prison during the Revolution. It was here that the royal family was held; today nothing remains of this building. The site, lying at the north of the Marais, is now a charming and secluded little park, the **square du Temple.**

By the 15thC, the Marais had begun to be a fashionable residential district for the aristocracy. By the 17thC it had reached its heyday, abounding in gracious mansions of the kind that became the model for the traditional French hotel, with a courtyard at the front and a formal garden at the back. There are more mansions remaining in the Marais than in any other district of Paris. By the early 18thC, the nobility began to move west to the Faubourg-St-Germain. The Marais became less favored and thereby began a gradual decline, which lasted until de Gaulle's Minister of Culture, André Malraux, made it a conservation area in 1962, just in time to save it from wholesale redevelopment. Since that time, a restoration program has uncovered many treasures.

Not surprisingly, the Marais possesses what is claimed to be the oldest house in Paris, 3 rue Volta, built in about 1300, and also the second oldest, 51 rue de Montmorency, built in 1407 as a charitable lodging house. The house is now a restaurant. Near rue Volta is the Quartier du Temple, which includes the **Musée**

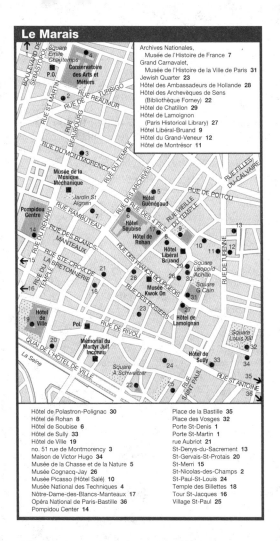

Le Marais

Square Émile Chautemps
P.O.
Conservatoire des Arts et Métiers 4
BOULEVARD DE SEBASTOPOL
RUE ST MARTIN
RUE BEAUBOURG
RUE REAUMUR
RUE DE REAUMUR
RUE DU TEMPLE
RUE TURBIGO
RUE DU MONTMORENCY
Musée de la Musique Méchanique
Jardin St Aignan
Pompidou Centre
RUE RAMBUTEAU
RUE DU RENARD
RUE DES BLANCS-MANTEAUX
RUE STE-CROIX DE LA BRETONNERIE
RUE DU TEMPLE
Hôtel de Ville 19
QUAI DE L'HÔTEL DE VILLE
La Seine
Mémorial du Martyr Juif Inconnu
Square A. Schweitzer
Pol.
RUE DE RIVOLI
Musée de la Musique Méchanique
RUE DES ARCHIVES
RUE DES 4 FILS
Hôtel Guénégaud 5
Hôtel Soubise 6
RUE DE POITOU
RUE VIEILLE DU TEMPLE
RUE DES FILLES-DU-CALVAIRE
Hôtel de Rohan
Hôtel Libéral Bruand
Square Leopold Achille
Square G Cain
Musée Kwok On
RUE DES FRANCS BOURGEOIS
RUE DES ROSIERS
RUE DE TURENNE
Hôtel de Lamoignon
Hôtel de Sully 33
Square Louis XIII
Place des Vosges
RUE ST PAUL
RUE ST ANTOINE
Village St-Paul 25

National des Techniques (Technological Museum) and the church of **St-Nicolas-des-Champs.**

This northern part of the Marais also boasts, to the west, the **Archives Nationales** and **Musée de l'Histoire de France,** housed in the outstanding **Hôtel de Soubise** and **Hôtel de Rohan, and,** to the east, the **Grand Carnavalet** museum, which occupies 2 adjoining mansions, the Hôtel de Carnavalet and the Hôtel Le Peletier St-Fargeau. Just to the north of the Archives Nationales, in rue des Archives, is another notable site, the Hôtel de Guénégaud des Brosses, now

housing the **Musée de la Chasse,** a quietly harmonious Mansart building.

Around the Grand Carnavalet is a wealth of beautiful hotels. Best known are the **Hôtel Libéral-Bruand**
in rue de la Perle, and the **Hôtel Salé** in rue de
Thorigny, which is the home of the **Musée Picasso.**

Also worth a detour in nearby rue de Turenne are
the **Hôtel de Montrésor,** now a school, and the **Hôtel
du Grand-Veneur,** former home of the master of the
royal hunt. The facade is adorned with a boar's head
and other symbols of hunting; inside, the impressive
staircase is decorated with trophies (inquire with the
caretaker, if you wish to visit). Farther along the street
is **St-Denys-du-Sacrement,** built in 1835 in the
Roman style, which contains a Deposition by Delacroix.

An Itinerary: A short walk, beginning at the
Seine, introduces you to some of the highlights in the
southern part of the Marais. Just east of the **Hôtel de
Ville** is the church of **St-Gervais-St-Protais.** A Gothic
building with a superb classical facade, it contains some
fine works of art, including lovely stained glass, and, in
the north transept, a Flemish Passion painted on wood.
Walk down to the river and along to the **Hôtel des
Archevèques de Sens,** one of the oldest mansions in
the city and now in use by the City of Paris as the **Bibliothèque Forney.** Continue east for a short distance,
then turn north up rue des Jardins-St-Paul, off of which
an archway to the right leads into the **Village St-Paul,**
a huddle of tiny craft studios and antique stores.

Twisting north, turn left at rue St-Antoine to visit
the church of **St-Paul-St-Louis,** built in the Jesuit
style in the 17thC. Return down rue St-Antoine to
the 17thC **Hôtel de Sully** (no. 62), which is now the
headquarters of the Administration of National Monuments (check for temporary architectural exhibits).
There's a particularly fine inner courtyard, and the interior contains paneling and painted ceilings. Turn up
rue de Birague into the graceful red-brick expanse of
Place des Vosges. Leave it by the northwest corner
and walk west down rue des Francs-Bourgeois to the
corner of rue Pavée (on the left) and the **Hôtel de
Lamoignon,** now the **Paris Historical Library** (open
Mon–Sat 9:30am–6pm), with its curious little corner
tower jutting out over the sidewalk. The courtyard and
building are of majestic proportions, the facade divided
by tall Corinthian pilasters.

Opposite is the **Carnavalet** museum. Beyond it,
up rue Payenne, is **square Georges-Cain,** a magical

little oasis of a garden, full of intriguing fragments of sculpture. In the same street are 2 interesting buildings, the **Hôtel de Chatillon,** at no. 13, and the **Hôtel de Polastron–Polignac,** next door. At no. 8 rue Elzévir (the next street along, which runs parallel with rue Payenne) is the **Cognacq-Jay museum.**

Retrace your steps to the Hôtel de Lamoignon, walk south down rue Pavée and immediately right into the area which for centuries has been a **Jewish Quarter.** In this street, rue des Rosiers, and in rue des Ecouffes (the second street on the left) and nearby streets, are several synagogues, kosher-food stores, and Hebrew booksellers.

At the end of rue des Rosiers, turn right into rue Vieille-du-Temple. At no. 47 is the **Hôtel des Ambassadeurs de Hollande** (not open to the public), one of the finest mansions in the Marais and once the home of Beaumarchais, who wrote the *Marriage of Figaro* here. On the next street to the left, **Notre-Dame-des Blancs-Manteaux,** is a graceful little church with an ornate Flemish wooden pulpit. Opposite the church is the attractive **rue Aubriot**, dating from the Middle Ages.

Continue past the church to the next intersection and turn left down the rue des Archives. Glimpse, down the first street on the right (the rue du Plâtre), the brilliant primary colors of the Pompidou Center. The **rue des Archives** has the curious nickname of "the street where God was boiled." The name dates from 1290, when a moneylender was said to have cut up a host (communion bread) with a knife. To his surprise the host began to bleed, whereupon he threw it into boiling water which immediately turned red. The unfortunate man was apprehended and burned at the stake, and soon afterward a church was built on the site of his house to commemorate the miracle.

Around this church the **monastery of Carmes-Billettes** grew up in the 14thC. The **Temple des Billettes,** on the left after the next intersection, was rebuilt in the 18thC and is now Lutheran. The charming little cloister survives—the only complete medieval cloister in Paris, with a Gothic vaulted ceiling. It's usually open to wander around: Look for the doorway to the left of the main church door.

Continue a little farther along rue des Archives and take the next turn right along rue de la Verrerie to another interesting church, that of **St-Merri,** completed in 1612, but anachronistically built in the Flamboyant

Gothic style. Its front (west) is richly decorated, and it houses the oldest bell in Paris, made in 1331.

A block to the north of this church, up rue St-Martin, lies the **Pompidou Center,** taking the visitor with a jolt from some of the oldest architecture in Paris to a building that proclaims itself firmly in the 20thC. Alternatively, head in the opposite direction to reach the Hôtel de Ville: Turn left when you reach the rue de Rivoli, from where there is a good view of the **Tour St-Jacques.**

★★ Marché aux Puces (Flea Market)

Rue des Rosiers, St-Ouen. Open Sat, Sun, Mon 7:30am–7pm. Admission free. Métro: Porte-de-Clignancourt.

A sprawling bazaar lying in an otherwise uninteresting area to the north of the boulevard Périphérique, the market, now with more than 2,000 stalls, extends for about 4 miles. It consists of a maze of alleys lined with booths, or more often, small shops, selling an intriguing variety of antiques and bric-a-brac, furniture, and secondhand clothes. An official leaflet, listing stall-holders by type, published in English and Japanese, as well as French, can be obtained from the information booth in the Marché Biron, rue des Rosiers. See also "Markets" in "Shopping."

Marine, Musée de la (Maritime Museum)

Palais de Chaillot, pl. du Trocadéro, 16ᵉ. ☎ 01-45-53-31-70. Open 10am–6pm. Closed Tues. Admission charged. Métro: Trocadéro.

The symbol of Paris is a ship, so it is appropriate that the city should possess a fine maritime museum. There is hardly anything relating to the French Navy and to seafaring in general that you will not find here, from old ships' cannons and figureheads to the bridge of a modern warship, from astrolabes to radar equipment.

The museum is proud of its collection of model ships from the 17thC to the present day. The earliest dates from the creation of the French Navy by Colbert in 1678, and includes warships, merchantmen, fishing craft, and pleasure boats. The mysteries of 18th and 19thC shipbuilding are explained, as well as under water exploration, navigation instruments, the development of the steamship, and the great French explorers and engineers, such as de Lesseps and La Pérouse.

A series of paintings on naval themes includes Vernet's series of 13 images of the ports of France. Another prized possession is a sumptuous barge that was commissioned to be made for Napoléon, decorated in beige, green, and gold, and propelled by 28 oars.

Workshop activities for children ages 8 to 11 are held from time to time. The museum plans to open a new section that will be the first naval collection devoted to yachting and nautical sports.

Marmottan, Musée

2 rue Louis-Boilly, 16ᵉ. ☎ 01-42-24-07-02. Guided tours. Open 10am–5:30pm. Closed Mon. Admission charged. Métro: La Muette, Ranelagh.

This collection was begun by the 19thC industrialist Jules Marmottan and enlarged by his son Paul, who left it, along with his imposing house, to the Académie des Beaux-Arts, which now administers it as a museum. Its appeal lies not so much in the value of the individual works as in the wayward charm of a private collection comprising paintings, furniture, and ornaments, displayed in a series of beautiful rooms, which have all been recently renovated.

Although there are works of many periods, 3 periods deserve special mention: a very fine collection of works of art and Empire-style furniture from the Napoleonic era; a superb little group of medieval (13thC) miniatures (the Wildenstein Bequest); and enough works by Monet and his contemporaries to make this museum second only to the **Musée d'Orsay** for works by the Impressionists. Paintings include Monet's ***Impression, Soleil Levant,*** from which the term Impressionist is derived, and also many of his paintings of water lilies.

Mode et du Costume, Musée de la (Fashion Museum)

Palais Galliéra, 10 av. Pierre 1er-de-Serbie, 16ᵉ. ☎ 01-47-20-85-23. Guided tours. Open 10am–5:40pm. Closed Mon and holidays. Admission charged. Métro: Iéna, Alma-Marceau.

To many people, Paris and fashion are synonymous. Visit this stylish museum and you are sure to learn something new about the art of dressing. The museum plays host to an intermittent series of well-mounted temporary exhibitions on various aspects of clothing and its history.

Even if fashion does not interest you, it is worth taking a look at the building. The Palais Galliéra was built in a striking neoclassical style by the Duchesse de Galliéra in the decade from 1878 to 1888. The south front gives onto a charming public garden with a truly Italian feel, where the sun splashes down onto the colonnaded facade and over the park with its fountains, statues, and shaded benches.

Monceau, Parc de

Entrance in Boulevard de Courcelles, 8ᵉ. Métro: Monceau, Villiers.

This is an unusual, rather poetic place. The entrance, through a gateway in a tall railing along boulevard de Courcelles, reveals a picturesque garden in the English style.

Beside a little lake, there is a semicircular Roman colonnade; dotted about among the chestnuts, acacias, and plane trees are curious objects: a pyramid, a stone archway, and some classical columns. These are all follies remaining from the garden designed for the Duke of Orléans by the writer and painter Carmontel in the late 18thC.

A delightful spot for a shady picnic lunch on warm days, it is characteristically used to full advantage by Parisians.

★★ Monde Arabe, l'Institut du

1 rue des Fossés-St-Bernard, 5ᵉ. ☎ 01-40-51-38-38. Wheelchair access. Guided tours. Open 10am–6pm. Closed Mon. Admission charged. Métro: Jussieu, Cardinal-Lemoine, Sully-Morland.

Islamic architecture for the space age might be an apt description of architect Jean Nouvel's building, which houses this important institute. The south side of the building, for example, is shielded from the sun by windows fitted with metal screens based on Islamic patterns. Its light-sensitive apertures are designed to open and close like the lens of a camera.

The overall effect of the building can seem rather harsh and inhospitable, with its razor-sharp edges, dull gray tones, and windswept plaza. Don't be put off, for the design, as hi-tech inside as it is outside, provides a cool, shady, peaceful environment in which the Arab civilizations are celebrated and explained. Steel, glass, light, and shade are the basic materials not only of the entire building, but of the inspired modes of display of the museum's treasured artworks and artifacts. A real high point is a gallery of modern Arab art, containing a permanent display of work as interesting and adventurous as any to be seen in Paris.

To the Anglo-Saxon eye, Arab culture both secular and religious can seem acutely exotic, even remote. But this institute sits naturally here at the heart of the French capital, which until a generation ago, ruled an empire in North Africa. Even now, France retains many active political and cultural ties with North Africa, and 2 million Arabs live in metropolitan France, forming the largest Arab community outside the Middle East.

The center is the result of a collaboration between France and 20 Arab countries.

Other facilities include a library, an audiovisual center, an excellent shop, and a top-floor restaurant (see "Dining") with a terrace commanding a fine view over Notre-Dame, the Iles de la Cité and St-Louis, and the Right Bank.

Le Monde de l'Art

18 rue de Paradis, 10ᵉ. ☎ 01-42-46-43-44. Open Tues–Sat 11am–7:30pm. Open Mon 2–7:30pm. Closed Sun. Admission charged. Métro: Gare de l'Est.

Housed in what was once the exquisite premises of the Hyppolyte Boulanger ceramic tile manufacturer, is a bold, bold, bold gallery of contemporary art. What is most interesting about the place is the contrast between the old, which has been lovingly preserved in all its turn-of-the-century splendor, and the artwork itself, which is upbeat, modern, and mostly rather experimental.

The leading light behind the organization is Raphaël Doueb, who sees the center developing as an international forum for all the arts. Another center was opened in September 1993 at 33-35 rue Guénégaud, 6ᵉ (☎ 01-43-29-11-71).

Rue de Paradis is rather off the beaten track for most tourists, but you may be in this part of town to see the **Musée Grévin,** the **Portes St-Denis and St-Martin,** or the Baccarat Museum just along the street.

It is worth calling in to look at the building whether or not the exhibits are to your taste. If you like both the architecture and the art displayed, then this is an exhilarating 30 minutes.

Monnaie, Musée de la

11 quai de Conti, 6ᵉ. ☎ 01-40-46-55-33. Guided tours by appointment at least 1 month in advance; call ☎ 01-40-46-55-35. Open 1–6pm, (Wed 1–9pm). Closed Mon, public holidays. Admission charged. Métro: Pont-Neuf, Odéon, St-Michel.

This simple but dignified mansion, which overlooks the Seine, across from the **Grand Louvre,** was once the home of the Princess de Conti, but was taken over by Louis XV in the 18thC and remodeled by Jacques Denis Antoine to serve as the Royal Mint.

It houses a permanent collection of coins and medals and the equipment for making them; the museum brings to life the objects that we take almost for granted, with audiovisual presentations explaining how they are produced and used. Small exhibitions on related subjects are often mounted.

As the making of coins has been transferred elsewhere, the workshops in the building now concentrate on the manufacture of medallions of all kinds. A sales gallery here (accessible from 2 rue Guénégaud) offers a selection of medallions. These are not necessarily solemn objects—one has the cancan as its theme and shows a high-kicking leg. The Mint will even create your own medallion—if you can afford it.

Montagne Ste-Geneviève
See Latin Quarter.

Montmartre
To the north of the city center, in the 18e. Métro: Abbesses, Pigalle, Blanche, Anvers, Barbès-Rochechouart, Château-Rouge, Marcadet-Poissonniers, Jules-Joffrin, Lamarck-Caulaincourt.

In AD 250 the martyred St-Denis is said to have picked up his severed head and walked up and over a hill to the north of the city. Since then millions of people have made the journey in more conventional style up through the winding streets of what is now called Montmartre or simply the **Butte** (hillock). Montmartre is a district full of contrasts. By turn quiet, raucous, quaint, sordid, and hauntingly beautiful, it's a must on the itinerary of anyone wishing to absorb the spirit of Paris.

For centuries Montmartre was a country village, bristling with windmills that supplied flour to the city below. Then in the 19thC, it became part of Paris, and its picturesque charm and atmosphere and low rents attracted painters, sculptors, writers, and musicians. The late 19thC was the heyday of bohemian Montmartre—when Toulouse-Lautrec drew the cancan girls at the Moulin Rouge in place Blanche; when Picasso, Braque, and others created cubism at the Bateau-Lavoir studios (burned down in 1970, but since rebuilt) in place Emile-Goudeau; and when artists' models hung about place Pigalle looking for work. By 1914, most of the artists had migrated to the Left Bank, and the great tourist influx had already begun.

Today, Montmartre has a number of different faces. The garish nightlife that Toulouse-Lautrec loved to portray has now spread all along **boulevard de Clichy** and the surrounding streets. **Pigalle** today has become decidedly sleazy, the artists' models now replaced by numerous members of an older profession. This is the Montmartre of neon lights, strip clubs, and cheap glitter. Farther up the hill in the area around the Sacré-Coeur, the ghost of the old Montmartre still lingers, but strictly for the tourists' benefit. Yet behind the

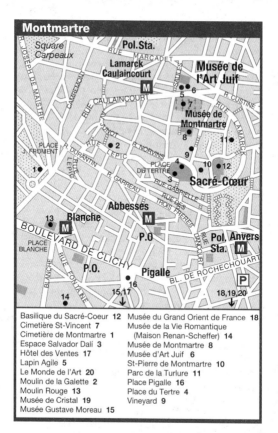

facade of fake bohemianism, Montmartre is still a village, an ordinary community endowed with a strong sense of its own history. This aspect is most evident on the north side, an area of quiet residential streets.

An Itinerary: There are several ways to begin a visit to Montmartre—probably the easiest is to take the Métro to Lamarck-Caulaincourt. Climb the stairs heading south and cross rue Caulaincourt. Look at once for a sign directing you along rue St-Vincent toward the Cimetière St-Vincent, final resting place of Utrillo, and the Musée de Montmartre. At the pretty, countrified intersection with rue des Saules is the cafe **Lapin Agile,** a famous meeting place in the bohemian days. A pretty cottage on a rather dull street, it was saved almost 100 years ago from demolition by speculative builders when it was bought by cabaret singer Aristide Bruant. On the slope to the right is a little **vineyard,** the last survivor within the Parisian boundaries. Every year, on the first Saturday in October, the vintage is celebrated by festivities and a procession.

Head up rue des Saules and turn left into the pretty rue Cortot. Here is the entrance to the **Musée de Montmartre** (12 rue Cortot, ☎ 01-46-06-61-11; open 11–5:30pm, closed Mon and some holidays). A house with a terraced garden, inhabited by many artists in the past, it contains interesting mementoes of the district.

Within a short walk is the Butte's most prominent feature, the magnificent church of the **Sacré-Coeur.** Beside this landmark is the church of **St-Pierre de Montmartre,** a remnant of the great medieval abbey of Montmartre. Downhill to the west lies **place du Tertre** with its cafes and cobbled, leafy square. The artists are still there, selling their pictures, although perhaps their numbers have declined in favor of the charcoal portrait artists and their ilk. Just off the place du Tertre is the **Espace Dalí,** (11 rue Poulbot, ☎ 01-42-64-40-10; open 10–6pm) a humorous and spectacular tribute to the master of the surreal.

Some of the artists who made Montmartre famous are buried in the Butte's 2 cemeteries, the small **Cimetière de St-Vincent** and the much larger **Cimetière de Montmartre.** Beyond the smaller cemetery, to the north of rue Caulaincourt, is a museum of Jewish art, the **Musée d'Art Juif** (42 rue des Saules, ☎ 01-42 57-84-15. Open Sun–Thurs 3–6pm, closed Fri, Sat, Aug, Jewish holidays).

Other ways to the top of Montmartre: An alternative route up the Butte is to leave the métro at place Pigalle and bump and bounce your way on the tourist train with a running commentary in French and English. It takes away the pain of walking, but of course removes most of the pleasure of experiencing Montmartre as well.

The well-loved **funicular** that carried thousands up the south slope of the Butte is no more. Today's gleaming, spacious **carriages,** operating independently of each other, can carry up to 4,500 visitors per hour (a frightening thought). The trip lasts little more than a minute, and for some is a happy alternative to the countless steps to Sacré-Coeur.

Children who tire of the views of Paris, can be turned lose in the quiet and attractive playground in **Parc de la Turlure** (just behind and to the right of Sacré-Coeur) or in square Suzanne Buisson (off avenue Junot).

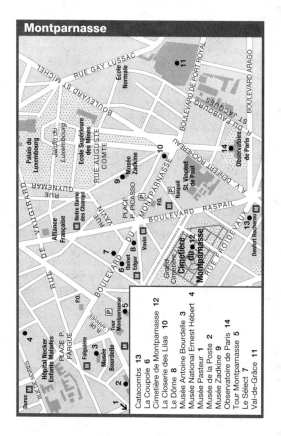

Montparnasse

Montparnasse

To the south of the city, in the 14e. Métro: Montparnasse-Bienvenüe.

Montparnasse, or "Mount Parnassus," was in Greek legend the mountain sacred to Apollo and the Muses. This was the nickname given to a grassy mound, formed from the debris of old quarries, which in the 17thC became a favorite haunt with student versifiers, who would gather to recite their poems. In the 18thC, the mound was leveled off, but the name stuck, and so did the carefree, pleasure-loving image. By the time of the Revolution, cafes and pleasure gardens had sprung up in Montparnasse, and it was here that the cancan was first performed.

In many ways Montparnasse is to the Left Bank what Montmartre is to the Right. Both are situated on hills; both, in their heyday, have been haunts of artists and literati, and both have since undergone a change of image. Montmartre now thrives on its picture-postcard quaintness, whereas Montparnasse became the victim of an uncharacteristically hard-nosed policy of redevelopment, exemplified by the Tour Montparnasse and a crop of mostly indifferent new buildings sur-rounding the redeveloped railway station; an exception is the elegantly modern **Meridien Montparnasse hotel** (see Accommodations). The once charming **rue de la Gaîté,** home of a number of lively little theaters in days gone by, has seen some of those theaters run to seed and the area become swamped by ever more shops selling "marital aids" and girlie magazines.

But don't turn your nose up at the **Tour Mont-parnasse** just because it's ugly. The view from the top is breathtaking—one of the best in Paris, and there's no need to wait in line for the privilege.

There are still glimpses of the old Montparnasse, as it struggles valiantly to survive, along **boulevard du Montparnasse,** which was once the center of flourishing artistic endeavor. Among those drawn to the boulevard and its surrounding streets were artists Rousseau, van Dongen, Modigliani, Chagall, and Whistler; writers Rilke, Apollinaire, Max Jacob, and Cocteau; musicians Satie and Stravinsky; and political exiles including Lenin and Trotsky. Between the wars, the district was popular with American expatriates, most notably Ernest Hemingway.

Artists and intellectuals thronged the new cafes of the boulevard: La Coupole, Le Sélect, Le Dôme, and La Closerie des Lilas, which was one of Hemingway's favorite retreats. Those were the days when Montparnasse was one mad, continuous party—a period that is vividly described by Georges-Michel in his novel *Les Montparnos* (1924). It was this writer who coined the word "Montparno" to refer to an inhabitant of the district.

Today the sparkling cafe life of Montparnasse has declined. Only **La Coupole, Le Sélect,** and **La Closerie des Lilas** (see "Cafes & Tea Salons" in "Dining") keep alive something of the atmosphere. The writers have dispersed, although there are still many artists' studios in the area.

Montparnasse enjoyed a brief moment of glory during the Liberation of Paris in 1944, when the **Gare Montparnasse** was used as the headquarters of General Leclerc. It was here that the German military governor signed his surrender. In 1967, it was demolished to make way for the present station complex, which incorporates huge blocks of offices and apartments. A new wave of modernization began again in the late 1980s, bringing the station into the age of the high-speed TGV train.

The station is the point of arrival from Brittany, so Montparnasse is traditionally a Breton area, especially rue Montparnasse, where there are still excellent restaurants serving crêpes and Breton cider.

The streets to the northwest of the station are relatively unspoiled. Here you will find the **Musée de la Poste** in boulevard de Vaugirard

The tranquil **Cimetière de Montparnasse** contains the graves of writers such as Baudelaire and Maupassant, de Beauvoir and Sartre; composers César Franck and Saint-Saëns; and other distinguished figures. The more recent provocateur Serge Gainsbourg also lies here. One of the graves has a bronze effigy of a couple sitting up in bed—no doubt very daring for its time. Another is decorated with Brancusi's sculpture, *The Kiss,* a tender and moving piece. A map of the cemetery is obtainable from the gatehouse.

One other attraction brings visitors to Montparnasse these days—a visit to the **Catacombs,** where, at **place Denfert-Rochereau,** you can penetrate the peace of thousands of ex-Parisians who have rested here for around 200 years. Unlike the cemetery, this is a less-than-uplifting place, but much visited nevertheless.

Montsouris, Parc de

Blvd. Jourdan, 14e. Métro: Porte d'Orléans. RER: Cité-Universitaire.

The most striking feature of this appealing park, with its hills, lake, and rambling paths, is a Moorish-looking building with onion domes, a replica of the Bey of Tunis's palace, given by the Bey for the Paris Exhibition of 1867.

The nearby Cité Universitaire, a student residential complex, set in grounds just south of the park, is interesting because the buildings date from the 1920s, each building representing the traditional architecture of a different country. The Brazilian and Swiss pavilions were designed by Le Corbusier.

The park also contains the Paris meteorological observatory and a tower marking the south bearing of the former Paris meridian.

Monuments Français, Musée National des

Palais de Chaillot, 1 pl. du Trocadéro, 16e. ☎ 01-44-05-39-10. Guided tours. Wheelchair access. Open 10am–6pm. Closed Tues. Métro: Trocadéro.

Try to imagine part of the facade of Chartres cathedral standing right next door to a tympanum from Reims, a pair of gargoyles from Nantes, and some sculptures from Notre-Dame, and you will get some idea of what to expect when you enter this museum. For the student of sculpture, it is a treasure house; for the lay visitor, an enjoyable feast of make-believe.

You might well wonder whether you had stumbled into the **Cinéma** museum, also housed in the **Palais de Chaillot,** and were looking at relics of a Hollywood movie studio's props department—except that the replicas here are better made than on any movie ... so well made, in fact, that, even close up, it is hard to tell that these are not stone- or wood-carvings but plaster copies. The same skill is seen in the department devoted to mural painting, where you may suddenly find yourself apparently inside a 12thC Romanesque church, painted with biblical scenes in flat ochers, browns, and reds.

The original idea behind the museum was to restore French sculpture to its rightful place among the arts by showing casts of distinguished works. Formerly called the Museum of Comparative Sculpture, it was given its present title in 1937 and widened to include mural paintings and a small amount of stained glass. An important program of renovation will commence in 1997.

Moreau, Musée Nationale Gustave

14 rue de La Rochefoucault, 9e. ☎ 01-48-74-38-50. Guided tours. Open Mon and Wed 11am–5:15pm, Thurs–Sun 10am–12:45pm and 2–5:15pm. Closed Tues and holidays. Admission charged. Métro: Trinité, St Georges.

"His sad and scholarly works breathed a strange magic, an incantatory charm which stirred you to the depths of your being," wrote the novelist J. K. Huysmans of symbolist painter Gustave Moreau (1826–98). The house and studio of the artist, located on the edge of **Montmartre,** where he lived a reclusive life, now hold a collection of the strange, dreamlike works that are filled with mysterious symbolism. Many of these are large canvases, and the studio is all the more charming for having been adapted by the painter himself to the needs of his work.

Moreau left an enormous body of work to the nation; only Picasso and Turner have ever left larger bequests.

Moyen Age, Musée National du

See Cluny, Thermes de.

★★★ Notre-Dame de Paris, Cathédrale de

Place du Parvis-Notre-Dame. ☎ 01-42-34-56-10. Guided tours.
Open 8am–6:45pm; for museum and towers see below.
Métro: Cité, St-Michel.

One of the world's great architectural masterpieces, the cathedral of Notre-Dame dominates the skyline of central Paris with its lacy facade and its 2 solid rectangular towers. It has fascinated artists and writers over the centuries and was the setting for Victor Hugo's famous novel *Notre-Dame de Paris* (*The Hunchback of Notre-Dame*), whose hero, the bell-ringer Quasimodo, has become a figure of legend. "A vast symphony in stone" is how the novelist described it.

For 800 years the history of Paris has unraveled around the cathedral. Its towers have looked down upon wars, revolutions, executions, pilgrimages, and today a virtually unceasing stream of tourists. It is one of the symbols not only of Paris but of France itself, and appropriately, set into the ground just in front of the main doorway, is a brass plaque marking the zero point from which all distances from Paris are measured.

The site of Notre-Dame has been a place of worship since pagan times, when a temple to Jupiter stood there. Later came 2 adjacent Christian churches, one to the Virgin Mary and the other to St. Stephen. These were removed in the 12thC, when the building of Notre-Dame began—a process that was to take nearly 200 years. By 1330 the cathedral stood complete in its essential form, although in the 17th and 18th centuries sweeping internal alterations were carried out. During the Revolution, most of the statues of the portals and choir chapels were destroyed, the bells were melted down, the treasures were plundered, and the cathedral became a Temple of Reason.

In the mid-19thC, a magnificent restoration was carried out by the architect and restorer of ancient

The Cathedral of Notre-Dame

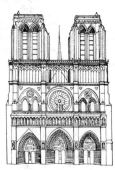

buildings, Viollet-le-Duc, who replaced hundreds of destroyed carvings, as well as building a new spire and creating new vaults and walls. He aspired not only to restoring the existing building but to help it to be what he felt it should have been—Gothic above all things. During the Commune of 1871 the whole cathedral very nearly perished when the Communards made a bonfire of chairs in the choir. Luckily, the building was saved by the lack of air and the dampness of the walls. A spot of "cleaning" was also carried out in the early 1960s, under the de Gaulle administration.

More—and major—renovations are in progress today. In 1991, a 10-year program of works began, and sections of the structure are likely to be shrouded or enveloped in scaffolding for some time. Many of the cathedral's current structural problems are caused by wear and tear and atmospheric pollution. The Ile de la Cité has always suffered badly from exhaust emission from the tourist buses which gather in the vicinity, often keeping their engines running to maintain air-conditioning. Before the restoration program started, a ban on parking in front of the cathedral was imposed.

Eleven million people visit Notre-Dame each year. It is a wonder that it does not feel more like a railway station.

As you enter: An unusual feature of the cathedral is that its floor is absolutely level with the street, so that it seems to welcome passersby to enter without formality.

Before going into the building, spend a while taking in the abundant sculptures on the ★ **facade,** remembering that most are skillful copies or restorations done under the direction of Viollet-le-Duc. It was he who instigated the carving of the 28 kings of Israel who stand in a row known as the **King's Gallery,** across the facade. The heads of the originals of these are now in the **Musée du Moyen Age (Cluny)** museum.

The 3 doorways are known as the **portals of the Virgin Mary, of the Last Judgment,** and **of Ste. Anne,** and the stonework is richly carved with appropriate figures, such as Christ sitting in judgment (over the central doorway) flanked by the Virgin Mary and St. John as intercessors. Look for some of the smaller carvings, such as the zodiacal signs on the left-hand portal, and the curious medallions on the central one, representing virtues and vices: Purity is a salamander, and pride is a man being thrown from a horse (these have also been given an alchemical interpretation).

The other facades also have some fine carving; the most famous sculpture of all is that of the **Virgin,** by the door of the north transept, carved in the 13thC and unscathed in the Revolution, except for the loss of the Child.

Inside the cathedral: Once you are inside the cathedral, before looking at the individual features, take in the majestic construction of the building; its walls rise in the traditional Gothic manner, through 3 tiers of arches to a ribbed, vaulted ceiling that seems infinitely far away. Stand in the center of the transept and you will feel the full impact of the architecture. From here you will also get a good view of the **rose windows**—3 great shimmering pools of light and color to the north, south, and west. Only the north rose, made in 1270, retains most of its original glass. The south window was extensively restored in the 18thC, and the west window in the 19thC. It is partly hidden by the largest organ in France, which has been refurbished as part of the current overall scheme.

Features of the transept that are worth seeing include the lovely 14thC statue of the *Virgin and the Child* against the south pillar flanking the entrance to the chancel, and the 18thC **statue of St-Denis** against the opposite pillar.

Around the nave is a series of chapels containing many fine sculptures and paintings, mostly from the 17thC. In the **St. Peter chapel** on the south side, there is some beautiful 14thC woodwork, carved with representations of saints. In the **ambulatory,** there are more chapels, filled with the mausoleums of various bishops of Paris.

The **high altar** in the chancel was made in the 19thC to a design by Viollet-le-Duc. Behind it is an 18thC **Piéta** and to the right, a statue of Louis XIII, who in 1638 consecrated his kingdom to the Virgin. To the left is a statue of Louis XIV.

On the south side of the ambulatory, a door leads to the **treasury** (open 9:30am–5:45pm, closed Sun), where a collection of plate and other treasures, including a reliquary said to contain a fragment of the Cross, can be inspected.

No visit to Notre-Dame would be complete without climbing the **towers** (☎ 01-43-54-22-63, open Apr–Sept 9:30am–5:30pm, Oct–Mar 10am–5:30pm, closed Sun; hours may vary according to season and weather, admission charged). You ascend 387 steps via the north tower, then cross over to the south tower, passing a

Gargoyle detail from Notre-Dame

series of splendid gargoyles and carved monsters, including the striga (a kind of vampire), who gazes, chin resting on his hands, over the city. In the south tower you can visit, with a guide, the belfry containing the great 13-ton bell that is rung only on special occasions.

The south tower can be climbed to the top, and on the descent you will pass a room containing a museum of the cathedral's history. For a more detailed presentation of the building's history, cross the street to the **cathedral museum** (10 rue du Cloître Notre-Dame, 4ᵉ, ☎ 01-43-25-42-92, open Wed, Sat, Sun 2:30–6pm), which houses a worthwhile and fascinating collection of objects, pictures, and documents that illustrate the cathedral's history.

Notre-Dame de Paris: Crypte Archéologique

Place du Parvis-Notre-Dame, 4ᵉ. ☎ 01-43-29-83-51. Open 10am–6pm Apr–Sept, 10am–5pm Oct–Mar. Closed certain public holidays. Métro: Cité, St-Michel.

This museum resulted from the discovery of an important archaeological site in front of **Notre-Dame,** and it was roofed over after the excavation had finished. The resulting vault is the largest structure of its kind in the world.

Descending a stairway from the square, one literally steps down into the Paris of an earlier age, finding an underground chamber where Gallo-Roman ramparts jostle the cellars of medieval houses. The remains are superbly presented, with information on the early history of Paris, illustrated by detailed models of the city at various stages.

Observatoire de Paris

61 av. de l'Observatoire, 14ᵉ. ☎ 01-40-51-22-21. Guided tours compulsory at 2:30pm on 1st Sat of the month only, by arrangement; apply in writing to the Service des Relations Extérieures at above address. Admission charged. RER: Port-Royal.

This chaste building, with its 2-domed octagonal towers, was built between 1667 and 1672. No iron was used in the construction because it might have affected the instruments, and wood was also avoided for fear of fire. The south wall of the building marks the latitude of Paris.

Today, the Observatory remains a major research center for astronomy and related services. In theory, the building and its small museum can be visited by guided tour on the first Saturday of every month, but there is usually a waiting list, sometimes of 2 to 3 months. However, the charming garden behind the Observatory, entered from boulevard Arago, is open to all, free of charge.

Opéra National de Paris-Bastille

120 rue de Lyon, 12e. ☎ 01-40-01-17-89. Open 11am–6:30pm. Closed Sun. Wheelchair access. Métro: Bastille.

Despite its splendor, the much-loved **Opéra National de Paris-Garnier** had been declared technically inadequate some years earlier when the decision was taken in 1982 to build a new opera house on the site of the Bastille.

Architect Carlos Ott won the commission in the face of competition from 750 contenders, and work began in 1985. The new opera house, its multifaceted glass frontage dominating place de la Bastille, was inaugurated during the bicentenary celebrations in 1989, was formally opened in 1990, and was finally opened in 1991 to reveal to the world a large prestigious opera house in its finished form. The modern glass ceiling echoes the lusters and decorated ceilings of the opera houses of an earlier age, reflecting the gray-blue granite of the walls and the oak block floor, as well as the giddying tiers of balconies that sweep up toward the roof.

As well as the main auditorium (2,700 seats), the Opéra National de Paris-Bastille houses a 500-seat amphitheater and a small studio (see also "The Arts"). Acoustic and other technical problems bedeviled the scheme even after it opened, and perhaps a year elapsed before the difficulties were resolved. Programming of the Opéras Bastille and Garnier is done jointly, under the global promotional title of Opéra National de Paris, and while the full-scale operatic performances now happen exclusively at the Opéra Bastille, the glorious Opéra Garnier now serves as a major venue for both ballet and contemporary dance.

Undoubtedly, the conception and birth of this opera house were troubled. Many are not kind about the building's design. Still, it has moved in and certainly isn't going anywhere, looking a lot like a beached white whale on the vast place de la Bastille.

See also **place de la Bastille.**

★ Opéra National de Paris-Garnier

Place de l'Opéra, 9ᵉ. ☎ 01-47-42-53-71. Guided tours 10am–4:30pm (☎ 01-40-01-17-89 for program details). Closed Sun, Aug, holidays, and during matinee performances. Métro: Opéra.

When Charles Garnier, architect of the Opéra, was asked by the Empress Eugénie whether the building was to be in the Greek or Roman style, he replied indignantly, "It is neither Greek nor Roman. It is in the Napoléon III style, Madame!"

Recently closed for 6 months while it was given a highly needed refurbishing, no building epitomizes more strikingly the heavy opulence of that era. During its construction between 1862 and 1875, the builders encountered an underground lake, which now lies beneath the cellars of the building, and where the "Phantom of the Opéra" had his dwelling. Above, however, all is brightness and gaiety.

The ornate facade, with its multitude of columns, friezes, winged figures, and busts of famous composers, is the architectural equivalent of Offenbach's music: lighthearted and irresistible. Inside, the tone changes. The richly colored marble staircase, where caryatids hold elaborate candelabra, evokes the setting for Belshazzar's Feast.

As for the auditorium, it has all the right ingredients: red velvet, gold leaf, and an abundance of plaster nymphs and cherubs. The only discordant element is the domed ceiling painted by Chagall—exquisite but out of place.

During the day you can walk around the building in exchange of a small fee, but the only way to really see the Opéra is to attend a performance there. The

L'Opéra
Garnier

removal of the major operatic performances to the **Opéra Bastille** in 1990 has permitted the Opéra Garnier to establish a fine, varied program of international ballet and contemporary dance. See also "The Arts."

Opéra Quarter

In the center, to the north of the Louvre, in the 9e and 2e. Métro: Opéra, Madeleine, Havre-Caumartin, Chaussée d'Antin Lafayette, Richelieu-Drouot, Quatre-Septembre, Pyramides, Tuileries, Palais-Royal/Musée-du-Louvre.

This distinctive area surrounding the magnificent old Opéra building falls roughly between boulevard Haussmann and rue de Rivoli to the north and south, and rue de Richelieu and the Madeleine to the east and west. More than any other district of Paris, it bears the stamp of Baron Haussmann, Napoléon III's energetic Prefect of the Seine, who replanned much of central Paris in the years 1853 to 1870 and whose signature was the wide boulevard and spacious townscape. It was he who carved out **place de l'Opéra,** which many considered unnecessarily large at the time, as well as avenue de l'Opéra, rue Auber, and rue Halévy, which clasp the ornate Opéra buildings as in a forked stick.

Boulevard des Italiens and its extensions were already a fashionable area for rich pleasure-seekers, but with Haussmann's developments and the Gare St-Lazare near at hand, the quarter also became a thriving commercial and financial center. This transformation was accelerated by the building of the métro at the beginning of the century.

The district today preserves both of these aspects. Everywhere you look there seem to be palatial banks, such as the frothy pile of the **Crédit Lyonnais** in boulevard des Italiens, and huge shops—the renovated **Trois Quartiers** in boulevard de la Madeleine, **Au Printemps,** and **Galeries Lafayette** in boulevard Haussmann. There are also many smaller but often more expensive shops, some bearing anglophile names like "Old England," others inimitably French, like the designers in the elegant rue **St-Honoré,** which becomes the even more elegant **rue du Faubourg-St Honoré.**

The most luxurious street of all, however, is **rue de la Paix,** leading from the Opéra to place Vendôme and lined with sumptuous jewelers, including Cartier.

Theaters in the district, apart from the Opéra itself, include the highly-regarded **Salle Favart** (Opéra

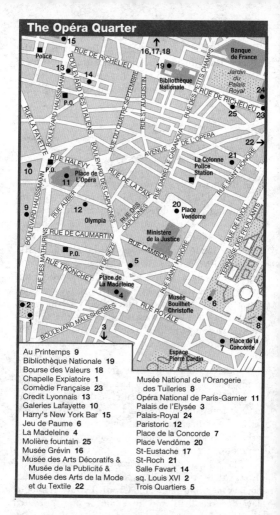

The Opéra Quarter

Police
RUE DE RICHELIEU 15
16,17,18
13 14 19
BOULEVARD DES ITALIENS
Banque de France
P.O. Bibliothèque Nationale
Jardin du Palais Royal 24
RUE DES PETITS CHAMPS
RUE DE RICHELIEU
25 23
RUE LA FAYETTE
RUE DU QUATRE SEPTEMBRE
RUE ST-AUGUSTIN
RUE HALEVY
22
AVENUE DE L'OPÉRA
BOULEVARD HAUSSMANN
10 P.O. La Colonne Police Station
21
Place de L'Opéra 11
RUE DE LA PAIX
RUE DANIELLE CASANOVA
RUE AUBER
RUE DES CAPUCINES
RUE SAINT-HONORÉ
9 12
20 Place Vendôme
Olympia
BOULEVARD HAUSSMANN
RUE DE CAUMARTIN
P.O.
Ministère de la Justice
RUE DES CAPUCINES
RUE CAMBON
RUE DE SÈZE
RUE DES MATHURINS
RUE TRONCHET
5
RUE DE RIVOLI
RUE SAINT-HONORÉ
TERRASSE DES FEUILLANTS
Place de La Madeleine
4
Musée Bouilhet-Christofle 6
RUE ROYALE
8
2
1
BOULEVARD MALESHERBES
3
Place de la Concorde 7
Espace Pierre Cardin

Au Printemps **9**
Bibliothèque Nationale **19**
Bourse des Valeurs **18**
Chapelle Expiatoire **1**
Comédie Française **23**
Credit Lyonnais **13**
Galeries Lafayette **10**
Harry's New York Bar **15**
Jeu de Paume **6**
La Madeleine **4**
Molière fountain **25**
Musée Grévin **16**
Musée des Arts Décoratifs &
  Musée de la Publicité &
  Musée des Arts de la Mode
  et du Textile **17**

Musée National de l'Orangerie
  des Tuileries **8**
Opéra National de Paris-Garnier **11**
Palais de l'Elysée **3**
Palais-Royal **24**
Paristoric **12**
Place de la Concorde **7**
Place Vendôme **20**
St-Eustache **17**
St-Roch **21**
Salle Favart **14**
sq. Louis XVI **2**
Trois Quartiers **5**

Comique) and the **Comédie Française,** the seat of classical French drama. One of the Comédie's greatest (and funniest) dramatists, Molière (1622–73), is commemorated by the **Molière fountain,** near the site of his house in rue de Richelieu. The fountain is a grand affair with a bronze statue of the playwright sitting on a pedestal supported by 2 languid female figures—a somewhat solemn monument for so humorous a writer.

Another appealing fountain lies a short distance farther up rue de Richelieu in **square Louvois,** a small park beside the Bibliothèque Nationale. Pudgy cherubs on dolphins support a great bowl decorated with the signs of the zodiac, surmounted by 4 buxom women representing France's great rivers, the Seine, Saône, Loire, and Garonne. The park, with its chestnut trees, is one of the few intimate little retreats in the district.

In the search for imposing architectural riches, you need only cross the road to the **Bibliothèque Nationale** or go west to **place Vendôme** and the **Madeleine,** or south to the **Palais-Royal** or the church of **St-Roch.** One rather curious monument lies on the north fringes of the quarter. This is the **Chapelle Expiatoire,** built by order of Louis XVIII to the memory of his brother and sister-in-law, Louis XVI and Marie-Antoinette. It stands in **square Louis XVI,** now another tranquil little garden off boulevard Haussmann, but formerly a cemetery where lie victims of the guillotine. Louis XVI and Marie-Antoinette were also buried here, until Louis XVIII had their bodies removed to St-Denis. Inside, the chapel is a classical mausoleum, like a miniature Panthéon, with statues of the unfortunate couple and a gloomy crypt.

At no. 5 rue Daunou is the famous American watering-hole, **Harry's New York Bar.** On the night before a US presidential election, a mock poll is held among the clientele. More often than not it predicts the winner.

Orangerie des Tuileries, Musée National de l'

Pl. de la Concorde, Jardin des Tuileries, 1er. ☎ 01-42-97-48-16. Open 9:45am–5:15pm (ticket office closes at 4:30pm). Closed Tues and holidays. Admission charged. Métro: Concorde.

Across the Tuileries from the **Jeu de Paume** is this matching pavilion housing the Walter-Guillaume collection of paintings. Exhibits cover the period from the end of the Impressionist era to 1930, and include works by Renoir, Cézanne, Matisse, Derain, Soutine, and Picasso.

The gallery's other major possession is a collection of 8 huge *Grandes Nymphéas* (*Waterlilies*) canvases by Claude Monet, painted at Giverny between 1915 and the artist's death in 1926. These complement the collection on view in the **Musée Marmottan.**

★★★ Orsay, Musée d'

1 rue de Bellechasse, 7e. ☎ 01-40-49-48-14. General recorded information ☎ 01-45-49-11-11. Open Tues, Wed, Fri, Sat 10am–6pm, Thurs 10am–9:45pm, Sun 9am–6pm (June 20–Sept 20 opens daily at 9am). Closed Mon. Admission charged. Wheelchair access. Métro: Solférino. RER: Musée d'Orsay.

What better place for a major museum of the 19thC than the former Gare d'Orsay, a splendid example of *fin-de-siècle* grandeur, which has been beautifully restored and skillfully converted for museum use?

The Building: The site of the former Palais d'Orsay—occupied only by the strangely romantic ruins of the cour des Comptes since the razing of the palace in the Commune of 1871—was bought by the Paris-Orléans railway company, which felt itself to be disadvantaged by the remoteness of its Gare d'Austerlitz. This became the location of a monumental yet modern new station, designed by Victor Laloux, which opened 2 months after the World Fair, in July 1900. Built around metal structures, the edifice was meant to be decorative as well as functional. In response to criticisms of the construction of such a large metal structure just across the river from the **Tuileries,** Laloux masked it with a stone facade along the quay and the front of the hotel on rue de Bellechasse.

With its single hall, 32 meters (105 ft.) in height, 16 underground railway tracks and vast reception areas, the station was, for close to 40 years, the terminus of the main line to the southwest with about 200 departures each day.

The challenge of turning a space that had been designed for people to pass through into one where people would be encouraged to linger, and of mastering the immense volume of space without breaking or enclosing it, was met in a concise and imaginative way by the female Italian architect Gae Aulenti. The existing glass panes, metal structures, and decorative moldings might have provoked imitation—yet the reshaping was done through contrast and simplicity, concentrating uniquely on the solid medium of stone.

The Collections: The entire collection now comprises 2,500 paintings and 250 pastel drawings, 1,500 sculptures, 1,100 objets d'art, and 13,000 photographs, to which works are constantly being added.

An Itinerary: No floor plan need be given here— the Musée d'Orsay is laid out in such a way that the visitor can follow the clear signs and gauge the scale of the exhibition areas so easily that a diagram would be superfluous.

Ground Floor: Begin by passing through the Second Empire collection. Here is the cool, formal classicism of Ingres, the fluid, romantic canvases from Delacroix's later period, the calm, pastoral scenes of Millet and Corot, and the early work of the

Impressionists-to-be: Manet, Monet, and Renoir. There are also some striking sculptures in the center aisle, as well as a broad-ranging architecture section and a large area devoted to the **Opéra National de Paris-Garnier,** with a model of the **Opéra Quarter** under a glass floor and a cutaway model of the Opéra building itself.

Top Floor: If you follow the recommended route, you then go straight to the upper level, where you find the great Impressionist collection, shown to best advantage in the natural light. Here you will see classics such as Monet's *Rouen Cathedral,* van Gogh's *Self-Portrait,* Renoir's joyful *Moulin de la Galette,* and many more. Other works on this floor include the eerie scenes of Henri "Le Douanier" Rousseau, and the paintings of the Pont-Aven school: Gauguin, Bernard, and Sérusier.

While on the top floor, you might wish to visit the cafe located behind the face of the enormous station clock—you can watch the hands moving as you sip your coffee.

Middle Floor: Finally, descend to the middle level, to the glass-domed rooms overlooking the Seine. Among the paintings exhibited here are the uncanny visions of the symbolists and, as a total contrast, the vivid canvases of Bonnard. The decorative arts are well represented on this floor. There is a series of rooms with superb Art Nouveau objects gathered from France and beyond (Charles Rennie Mackintosh, William Morris, and Frank Lloyd Wright are to be found in company with Hector Guimard and René Lalique), and a section devoted to the decorative arts of the Third Republic is appropriately housed in one of the ornate public rooms of the old station hotel.

The elegant former restaurant of the hotel has sprung to life again as the **Restaurant du Musée d'Orsay** (1 rue de Bellechasse, 7ᵉ. ☎ 01-45-49-42-33, open daily for lunch, Thurs evenings only for dinner, closed Mon; credit cards: V, MC), a large, bright room, all white-and-gold, with chandeliers and an exquisitely painted ceiling.

Palais de Chaillot

Place du Trocadéro, 16ᵉ. Métro: Trocadéro.

The commanding height on the Right Bank of the Seine, known as the Chaillot, has been occupied by a series of buildings. It began as a country house built by Catherine de Médicis in the 1580s. After the Restoration, Charles X wanted to build a monument

The Palais de Chaillot

to commemorate the French capture of the Trocadéro fort near Cadiz in Spain. This was never built, but the name stuck and was given to an elaborate palace created there for the Paris Exhibition of 1878. Its successor, built for the Exhibition of 1937, was called the Palais de Chaillot, and the name Trocadéro was kept for the square onto which the north side of the building faces. The whole complex is aligned with the **Tour Eiffel** and the **Champ-de-Mars** across the river, creating a dramatic townscape.

With its simple lines, neoclassical colonnades, and heroic sculptures, the palace is reminiscent of the monumental Fascist and Soviet architecture of the period. But it has aged well, and its sandstone facade has a crisp elegance. From a spacious piazza with a magnificent view of the Eiffel Tower, 2 curving wings reach out, embracing a garden that slopes down toward the Seine, the central axis of which is laid out in a descending series of fountains and pools.

The Palais de Chaillot now houses the following museums: **Du Cinéma Henri Langlois, de l'homme, de la Marine,** and **des Monuments Français.** Also housed here are the film library of the **Cinémathèque Française** and the Théâtre National de Chaillot, with its 2 auditoriums.

Palais des Congrès: Centre International de Paris
Place de la Porte-Maillot, 17e. Métro: Porte-Maillot.

A streamlined, multipurpose building, opened in 1974, dominates the chaotic spaghetti intersection by the northeast corner of the **Bois de Boulogne.** It comprises the Palais des Congrès and a vast hotel. The palais itself is a low-rise block, housing exhibition halls, shops, restaurants, movie theaters, conference rooms, a discotheque, an air terminal, and the huge and impressive Main Conference Hall, home of the Paris Symphony Orchestra and also used for conferences, concerts, and shows (no admittance unless attending an event).

Palais de la Découverte (Palace of Discovery)

Avenue Franklin-D-Roosevelt, 8ᵉ. ☎ 01-40-74-80-00; ☎ 01-43-59-18-21 (recorded message). Open Tues–Sat 9:30am–6pm, Sun, holidays 10am–7pm. Closed Mon. Planetarium lectures 4 or 5 times a day; for information call ☎ 01-40-74-81-73. Admission charged. Métro: Champs-Elysées-Clemenceau, Franklin-D-Roosevelt.

The imposing west wing of the Grand Palais, with its huge domed entrance hall, is a place in which to wonder at the properties of the mathematical entity pi, the structure of the atom, the nature of laser beams, or the fundamentals of genetics. These and many other branches of discovery are imaginatively presented and kept up to date. What makes the Palais de la Découverte attractive is that attendants are present in every room to explain and demonstrate the exhibits.

The museum has a **planetarium** where different aspects of the universe are projected onto a hemispherical dome. There are regular temporary exhibitions, film shows, and lectures.

Palais de l'Elysée

55 rue du Faubourg-St-Honoré, 8ᵉ. Métro: St-Philippe-du-Roule, Champs-Elysées-Clemenceau, Miromesnil.

Built in 1718 for the Comte d'Evreux and later lived in by Madame de Pompadour and Napoleons I and III (Napoléon I signed his abdication here), this palace, with its extensive garden, has since 1873 been the official residence of the French president and the meeting place of the Council of Ministers. The public is not allowed in, but you can glimpse the elegant facade and courtyard beyond a heavily guarded gateway.

Palais Galliéra

See Mode et du Costume, Musée de la.

Palais de Justice de Paris (Law Courts)

2 blvd. du Palais, 1ᵉʳ. ☎ 01-44-32-54-54. Open Mon–Fri 9am–6pm. Closed Sat, Sun, holidays. Métro: Cité, St-Michel; RER: Châtelet-Les Halles.

Together with **Sainte-Chapelle** and the **Conciergerie,** the Palais de Justice forms a vast complex of buildings running the whole width of the **Ile de la Cité,** with an imposing courtyard and entrance on boulevard du Palais. There was a palace here in Roman times, and later the site was occupied by a magnificent royal residence, which in the 14thC became the seat of parliament. It was here that Louis XIV proclaimed to parliament *"L'Etat, c'est moi!"* Since the Revolution, the buildings have been occupied by civil and criminal law courts.

The most impressive room in the complex of courts and galleries is the **Lobby** (Salle de Pas-Perdus), formerly the great hall of the palace, which was twice destroyed by fire, the second time during the Commune of 1871. It was rebuilt in its present form in the 1870s. The royal courtiers are now replaced by lawyers and litigants scurrying about the "cathedral of chicanery" as Balzac called it. If you want to see them in action, you can visit any except the juvenile court.

★★★ Palais-Royal

Place du Palais-Royal, 1ᵉʳ. Métro: Palais-Royal/Musée-du-Louvre.

Few buildings in Paris have played as many different roles as the Palais-Royal. Built by Cardinal Richelieu in the 17thC as his private palace, it later came into the hands of the Orléans family—one of whom was the dissolute regent Philippe II of Orléans, who turned the palace into a scene of frenzied orgies.

His descendant, the so-called "Philippe Egalité," needing to raise money, built matching terraces of apartment houses around the garden, with an arcade at ground level in which there were premises for tradesmen. These buildings form the splendid quadrangle, the **cour d'Honneur,** that one can enter to the north of the palace.

This much-prized courtyard has been the subject of government expenditure since 1992, and a reworking has taken shape, under the guidance of an American landscape architect residing in France, Mark Rudkin. Statues in need of repair have been taken away for surgery and others have taken their place. He has met the challenge of navigating around the much-criticized sculpture, which consists of a series of black-and-white columns of unequal height, created by the artist Buren. More pleasing are 2 great bowls of water upon which oscillate large stainless-steel spheres. A number of new and elegant shops have recently opened under the graceful arcades rimming the courtyards, making this an interesting spot to pass an afternoon cut off from the noise of the city center.

In the heated period before the Revolution, this quadrangle was the scene of rallies and demonstrations; Marat called it the "nucleus of the Revolution." Then, after the execution of Philippe Egalité, the palace, its gardens, and cafes, became a center of gambling and prostitution. Returned to the Orléans family at the Restoration, the palace was sacked during the Revolution of 1848 and set on fire by the mob during the Commune of 1871. Now the offices of the Council of

State, the Constitutional Council, and the Ministry of Culture are all headquartered here.

Palais de Tokyo

Palais de Tokyo, 11 av. du Président-Wilson, Paris 16ᵉ. ☎ 01-45-53-54-36. Open Tues, Thurs–Sun 10am–5:30pm, Wed 10am–8:30pm. Closed Mon. Subject to change once building conversion begins. Wheelchair access. Métro: Iéna, Alma-Marceau.

This elegant building is a typical example of the Art Deco architecture of the 1930s. It has housed several museums, including the **Musée d'Art Moderne de la Ville de Paris** in the left wing.

The transformation of the right wing of the Palais de Tokyo into the Palais du Cinéma is currently taking place. The Palace will be equipped with every piece of new technology to enable it to become the focal point of cinematic and photographic knowledge. The halls and monumental staircases are being sensitively refurbished and the building is being given a general *grands travaux* treatment. Its reopening is planned for 1997.

★★★ Panthéon

Place du Panthéon, 5ᵉ. ☎ 01-43-54-34-51. Guided tours. Open Apr–Sept 9:30am–6:30pm, Oct–Mar 10am–5:30pm. Closed holidays. Admission charged. Métro: Cardinal-Lemoine. RER: Luxembourg.

The nave of the Panthéon, closed since 1989 due to falling masonry, was opened again in 1995—though there are still protection nets up there. They'll stay there until 2000, when the ambitious $6.2 million restoration of the frail building begun in 1986 is completed.

Meantime, you can once again see for yourself the 19thC paintings (still under restoration) by Puvis de Chavannes recounting the story of Ste. Geneviève. And there's a smart new reception area designed by architect Sylvain Dubuisson.

History—Church or Mausoleum? For nearly half its existence, this building has led a schizophrenic existence. It was initiated by Louis XV in thanksgiving for his recovery from an illness, and was intended as a more magnificent shrine to Paris's patroness Ste. Geneviève than the old abbey church of that name that stood on the site. Situated in a commanding position on the Montagne Ste-Geneviève, this panthéon was built in the form of a Greek cross, with a dome at the intersection and a massive portico with Corinthian columns.

Hardly had it been completed than the new revolutionary government decided to change it from a church into a mausoleum for the remains of great Frenchmen. For this purpose, many of the windows were blocked

The Panthéon

up, hence its rather bald and forbidding appearance. Twice it was to revert to its role as a church and then back again to a secular mausoleum. It was permanently secularized in 1885 to provide a suitable resting place for Victor Hugo.

In March 1851, Léon Foucault performed his famous experiment here to prove that the earth rotates: He assembled the great scientists of the day and hung a 28-kilogram (62 lb.) pendulum inside. Since then, the pendulum has been in the Musée des Arts et Métiers—in April 1996 it was brought back to the Panthéon to repeat Foucault's famous experiment.

The Present: Plans for restoration include work on the north and south facades and the stained glass. They are also releading the dome. The recent discovery of Soufflot's first building plans are making the task of restoration much easier, for much of the iron structure was undetectable.

The Dome: The dome gives access to one of the most rewarding views, and is one of the easiest of Paris's tall buildings to climb. There are 250 steps, but after only 100, you reach the main gallery, where it is impossible not to stop and look down into the main body of the former church. Curiously devoid of all ecclesiastical trappings and with a great empty expanse of floor, it still feels like a church despite its many years of deconsecration. The famous canvases by Puvis de Chavannes (on the ground floor) are visible, and being in the gallery allows you to see at close quarters into the triple cupolas of the dome, with its frescoes depicting *Justice* and *Glory*.

Another stair leads to a higher vantage point within the cupola. Then, after a thrilling (but safely enclosed) walk out across the roof, you reach the circular colonnaded viewing platform; from where, because of its wide construction, you feel relatively well supported. A panorama of 360° can be viewed, and there are useful boards indicating the many buildings to be seen.

The Crypt: In a series of vaulted corridors beneath the building lie the remains of a number of illustrious Frenchmen. Voltaire and Rousseau take pride of place; their tombs are much larger and grander than any others, and they effectively greet visitors upon arrival. Rousseau's tomb seems to reflect his continual search for truth—for through a door, at one end of the plinth, reaches a hand holding a torch. Hugo shares his compartment with Zola—a curious pair of cell-mates, each probably outscribbling the other to this day. Others buried here include the building's architect, Soufflot; the chemist Berthelot; and the wartime Resistance leader Jean Moulin.

Paristoric

11bis rue Scribe, 9ᵉ. ☎ 01-42-66-62-06. Open Mar–Sept 9am–9pm, Oct–Apr 9am–6pm (9pm on Sat and Sun). Admission charged. Métro: Opéra. RER: Auber.

Paristoric is a 40-minute cinematic experience that brings the city of Paris to life in a devastatingly beautiful sweep through the 2,000 years of her history from Roman Lutèce to the Grande Arche. Image pours into image on the giant screen as each era of history is unfolded through its personalities, its buildings, and its monuments. The images are accompanied by a fine soundtrack, and simultaneous translation is available in 8 languages. Recommended as an introduction to Paris or as a quick refresher for nostalgic visitors at the end of their stay.

"Passages"

Of interest as much for their architectural qualities as for the shopping opportunities, Paris's many arcades (*passages*) merit exploration.

Long before pedestrian zones came into vogue, Paris had many arcades, covered walkways, and colonnades where the elegant *flâneur* could stroll or window-shop, unhampered by traffic and sheltered from the rain. At the beginning of the 19thC, there were about 140 arcades in Paris. Haussmann and later developers reduced the number to a couple of dozen, and some are now rather down-at-heel, although they are gradually acquiring a new lease on life with the increase in pedestrianization schemes around the city.

The 1^e and 2^e arrondissements are particularly rich in arcades and passages, and to link them up creates a charming, offbeat walk.

Begin at the **Palais-Royal** by entering at the southeast end of the garden and going counterclockwise around the colonnade, with its stamp and medal dealers, booksellers, and pipe store. Then double back down rue de Montpensier, exploring the 4 covered passages (de Richelieu, Potier, Hulot, and de Beaujolais) that link this street with rue de Richelieu. Then turn right along rue de Beaujolais and go through passage des Deux Pavillons.

Across rue des Petits-Champs are the entrances to the beautiful Galerie Colbert and Galerie Vivienne. Return to rue des Petits-Champs and turn right, walking past rue Ste-Anne and turning right up passage Choiseul, full of smart boutiques, leading to rue St-Augustin.

Another little foray into the arcades will take you north along rue de Choiseul to boulevard des Italiens. Turn toward boulevard Montmartre and continue traveling east past rue Vivienne to the point, next to the **Musée Grévin,** where the 2 arcades lead off the boulevard. To the north, passage Jouffroy extends into passage Verdeau.

To the south, passage des Panoramas links up with a small rabbit warren of arcades, with a curious mixture of shops and restaurants. Here you are no longer in the land of the very wealthy. These pretty arcades retain their 150-year-old feel, but their shops sell everything from walking canes, antiques, and secondhand books, to imported artifacts from the Third World, sarees, and silk stationery.

One gallery that is apart from the others still merits a visit if you are near the **Forum des Halles.** Emerge into rue Montmartre and skirt round **Les Halles** by **St-Eustache.** Walk through the colonnade surrounding the **Bourse du Commerce,** then cross rue du Louvre and turn left down rue Jean-Jacques Rousseau to the lovely Galerie Véro-Dodat. This arcade, with its gracefully proportioned shopfronts and carved mahogany paneling, is bathed in a gentle, warm, brown light. There are 2 new decorative-arts galleries here, the shoe shop of Christian Louboutin, an attractive restaurant, and a cafe serving delicious Tarte Tatin.

Pasteur, Musée

25 rue du Dr-Roux, 15ᵉ. ☎ 01-45-68-82-82. Guided tours by prior arrangement. Open 2–5:30pm. Closed Sat, Sun, Aug, public holidays.Admission charged. Métro: Pasteur.

The name of Louis Pasteur (1822–95) has been immortalized in the word *pasteurization*. His development of immunization and other disease-controlling methods is legendary and has saved innumerable lives. Pasteur's house, now surrounded by the buildings of the Pasteur Institute, is a museum affording an interesting glimpse of both the scientific and private life of this great man. His remains rest in a magnificent tomb in the basement, built in the form of a small Byzantine chapel, with rich mosaics illustrating different aspects of his work.

Pavillon de l'Arsenal

21 blvd. Morland, 4ᵉ. ☎ 01-42-76-33-97. For guided tours, call ☎ 01-42-76-33-97. Open Tues–Sat 10:30am–6:30pm, Sun 11am–7pm; Closed Mon. Admission free. Métro: Sully-Morland.

This beautiful 19thC pavillon was originally designed to house a painting collection, though it later served various commercial purposes. In 1954, the fine building was bought by the city to conserve it's archives and was opened to the public as a museum in 1988— its intention, to keep the public aware of its city, both old and new.

All manner of information and exhibitions relating to the architecture and urban development of Paris are housed here. Plans and models of projected redevelopments can be inspected here, and the pavilion also serves as a venue for information on all kinds of schemes for public debate.

★ Père Lachaise, Cimetière du

20ᵉ. Open daily. Métro: Père-Lachaise.

Like many old cemeteries, this one, the largest in Paris, has a powerfully romantic appeal. Named after Louis XIV's confessor, this cemetery was originally the site of a Jesuit house of retreat, and its hilly ground was laid out in 1804. The closely huddled graves encompass a wide variety of sepulchral art.

It is easy to lose your way among the twisting, tree-lined lanes, but at the newsstand across from the main entrance you can purchase a map that marks the graves of the many celebrities buried here. These include Molière, Balzac, de Musset, Chopin, Rossini, Colette, Edith Piaf, Oscar Wilde, Modigliani, Maria Callas, and Jim Morrison. The monument to Wilde is a massive block by Jacob Epstein, adorned with a winged Egyptian figure. The tomb of Abelard and Héloise, erected in 1779, has been thoroughly restored.

One of the most visited graves is that of the spiritualist Allan Kardec, whose followers can sometimes be seen communing with his spirit by passing their hands over his statue.

Petit Palais, Musée du

Avenue Winston-Churchill, 8e. ☎ 01-42-65-12-73. Guided tours by prior arrangement. Open 10am–5:40pm (hours of temporary exhibitions vary). Closed Mon, holidays. Admission charged. Métro: Champs-Elysées-Clemenceau.

Completed in 1900 along with the neighboring **Grand Palais,** in time for the World Exhibition, the Petit Palais has rather more harmonious proportions and a less obtrusive personality than the other. It lies a stone's throw from the **avenue des Champs-Elysées.**

In the galleries facing the outside of the building, you will pass from ancient Egyptian and classical sculptures, through medieval and Renaissance art, to paintings, furniture, and porcelain of the 18thC. The inner galleries are devoted to French art of the 19th- and early 20thC. This is a wonderfully rich collection including works by Delacroix, Courbet, Corot, Manet, Monet, Cézanne, Pissarro, Sisley, Redon, and Bonnard. Among famous individual works are Courbet's painting of 2 sleeping women, *Le Sommeil,* and Bonnard's vibrant *Nu dans le Bain.* Bonnard's palette is here on display as well—a riot of color like his paintings. The museum also offers a program of changing exhibitions.

The galleries are surrounded by a courtyard, which—with its Roman-style colonnade, pool, and garden—is a charming place for a short break.

Photographie, Centre National de la

Hôtel Salomon de Rothschild, 11 rue Berryer, 8e. ☎ 01-53-76-12-32, ☎ 01-53-76-12-31 (recorded information). Open daily noon–7pm. Closed Tues. Admission charged. Métro: George V.

In 1993 the Centre National de la Photographie moved from the Palais de Tokyo to this splendid building, which houses the Fondation Nationale des Arts Graphiques et Plastiques. A site for retrospective exhibitions dedicated to artists such as Henri-Cartier-Bresson, Irving Penn, or William Klein, as well as thematic shows tracing such subjects as fashion photography, panormaic photography, and more.

Piaf, Musée Edith

5 rue Crespin du Gast, 11ᵉ. ☎ 01-43-55-52-72. Open 1–6pm, by appointment only. Closed Fri–Sun, Sept, holidays. Métro: Ménilmontant.

Piaf—a name that rings out the word *Paris* whenever it is spoken. Her generation, and her time, are long gone, yet her memory lives on in the heart of every Frenchman, and her songs—*Non, je ne regrette rien; La Vie en Rose; Milord*—are unforgettable far beyond the boundaries of France.

The daughter of an acrobat, she started her career in music hall, where she acquired the name *Piaf* (Parisian argot for little sparrow). This perfectly suited the waiflike little woman and the street-life subject matter of her songs. Her unhappy life revolved around marred marital relationships, sex, drugs, illness, and personal tragedy, and her resonant voice overflowed with the emotions of her circumstances. This small, privately run museum of Piaf memorabilia is open to visitors by appointment only.

★★★ Picasso, Musée

Hôtel Salé, 5 rue de Thorigny, 3ᵉ. ☎ 01-42-71-25-21. Guided tours. Open 9:30am–5:30pm. Closed Tues. Admission charged. Wheelchair access. Métro: St-Paul, Filles du Calvaire.

Picasso was rare among major artists in that all his life he kept a significant proportion of his own paintings and sculpture for his personal collection. Much of this collection passed to the French government in lieu of tax after Picasso's death, and it was decided that a new museum would be created to house it. The Hôtel Salé, a gracious 17thC **Marais** mansion, both emphasizes and complements the modernity of Picasso's work.

Although many of his famous paintings are already in other museums, this collection gives a unique personal view of the whole span of Picasso's long, creative life. The works range from his astonishing childhood creations such as *Girl with Bare Feet,* painted when he was only 14, through his blue, rose, and cubist periods, to the inimitable style of his later years. The joy, anguish, and turbulence of his private life are brought out in these works, for Picasso was an extraordinarily self-revelatory artist.

The museum contains works by other artists from Picasso's collection, including paintings by Cézanne, Renoir, Matisse, and Rousseau. This gem of a museum is both satisfying and yet small enough in scale to be perfectly manageable for a short visit—an excellent stop for those easily fatigued by big museums.

★★★ Pompidou Center (Centre National d'Art et de Culture Georges-Pompidou)

Plateau Beaubourg, 4ᵉ. ☎ 01-44-78-12-33. Day-passes available. Guided tours daily at 3:30pm with English-speaking guides. Open Mon, Wed, Thurs, Fri noon–10pm; Sat, Sun, holidays 10am–10pm. Closed Tues. Métro: Hôtel-de-Ville, Rambuteau, Châtelet.

The surprising popularity of the Pompidou Center since it's opening in 1977—more people come through its doors each year than visit the Louvre—is both a testament to the success of its mission and, unfortunately, has led to a certain wear and tear both inside and out. To rectify that, the museum is currently in the process of $140 million renovation program slated to be finished in the year 2000.

Like the Eiffel Tower nearly a century ago, the Centre Georges-Pompidou (or Centre Beaubourg, as it is often called) has aroused both shock and admiration. It houses one of the world's largest collections of contemporary art, as well as a dynamic program of dance, music, and cinema, and now attracts 8 million visitors a year. Shaped like a giant matchbox on its side, brightly painted as though in a child's coloring book, and enveloped in a cat's cradle of gleaming steel girders, it looks like a crazy oil refinery designed by a child.

It is one of the most revolutionary buildings of its age. Built on the initiative of President Georges Pompidou as part of the redevelopment of Les Halles, it was designed by the British architect Richard Rogers and the Italian Renzo Piano. The building is turned inside-out, with its intestines—pipes, shafts, escalators, etc.—festooned around the outside, thus liberating large areas of space within. The main escalator runs in a transparent tube up the front of the building, so that the visitor can see a changing panorama of the city while ascending the 5 stories for the superb view at the top.

The Pompidou Center

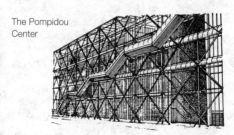

The Beaubourg radiates a sense of celebration that spills over into the surrounding area. A never-ending succession of street entertainers, everything from poets to jugglers and fire-eaters, can be encountered on the vast, sloping piazza.

By 1997, the exterior of the building as well as the plaza will be refurbished, including repaving the area, planting trees, and renovating the studio of the sculptor Brancusi, located outside in the plaza. Then the work inside will begin. While the museum will not be closed at any time during it's renovation, it will reduce programming and export many of its shows to sites both around the city and abroad.

The **Bibliothèque Publique d'Information** (Public Information Library) is essentially a library of the 20thC; it has some half a million books, and plans to reach a million. It also has a research center devoted to the periodical press. This much-used facet of the museum will have its own entrance on rue Rambuteau when the renovation is finished.

All the audiovisual programs, colloquiums, and cinemas will be grouped together in one underground area. The ground floor is slated to house the restaurant and bookshop.

The Beaubourg also comprises the **Musée National d'Art Moderne.** When the renovations are complete, this department will almost double in size and be located on the 4th and 5th floors. The 3rd floor will be devoted to frequently changing exhibitions of contemporary works, that is, from about 1965 to the present. The permanent exhibition contains works from 1905 onward, starting with Fauvism (from the French *fauve,* meaning "wild beast") and progressing through cubism, abstract expressionism, Dadaism, surrealism, and other movements right up to the present day.

Under cubism, for example, you will find a number of painters who, in their different ways, shared the same tendencies: an interest in elementary forms, such as the cube and the cylinder, and a renunciation of color in favor of light and shape. The works represented include Georges Braque's *Young Girl with a Guitar,* Picasso's *Seated Woman,* and Fernand Léger's *La Noce,* which also anticipates futurism in its suggestion of movement through repetition of shapes in a sequence. In a similar way, surrealism is represented by artists as diverse as Salvador Dalí, Max Ernst, and Joan Miró, all of whom developed in very different directions.

Certain artists reappear as they pass through different phases. Picasso crops up here and there as his style and subject matter change. We see him pass through a period of interest in classical antiquity, exemplified by his *Minotaur;* then his work becomes increasingly abstract. Other painters—Kandinsky, Matisse, Braque, Léger—also manifest changing styles. Thus, one perceives the dynamic way in which 20thC art has developed, with schools merging, overlapping, and breaking away.

The works also include many sculptures, such as Constantin Brancusi's deliciously simple *Seal* in gray-and-white marble, and Raoul Haussmann's Dadaist work *The Spirit of our Times,* showing a dummy-like head with a purse, watch, and other oddments stuck to the skull.

★★ Pont Alexandre III

7ᵉ and 8ᵉ. Métro: Champs-Elysées-Clemenceau. RER: Invalides.

The broadest bridge in Paris and also one of the most beautiful, Pont Alexandre III forms part of a great triumphal way leading down avenue Winston-Churchill, past the **Grand Palais** and **Petit Palais,** across the Seine and down the esplanade to **Hotel des Invalides.** Built for the 1900 World Exhibition, it was named after Czar Alexander III of Russia (1845–94).

The bridge is flanked by 2 massive pillars at each end, whose recently regilded decorations represent, on the Right Bank, medieval and modern France, and, on the Left, Renaissance France and the era of Louis XIV. All along the bridge are cast-iron lamp standards with the ornate, prosperous look that characterized the Belle Epoque.

★★★ Pont-Neuf

1ᵉʳ. Métro: Pont-Neuf.

"Of all the bridges which were ever built, the whole world who have passed over the Pont-Neuf must own that it is the noblest, the finest, the grandest, the lightest, the longest, the broadest that ever conjoined land and land together upon the face of the tremendous globe."

Thus wrote the 18thC English novelist Laurence Sterne of the bridge that spans the **Seine** in 2 sections, divided by the west spike of the **Ile de la Cité.** He might have added that, despite its name meaning "new," it is also the oldest. Work started in 1578 on what was the 1st bridge to have no houses or shops on it.

Completed in 1604 and inaugurated in 1607 by Henry IV, whose equestrian statue stands at the center, it has 12 arches, all of slightly different sizes. The bridge, the 2 halves of which are not quite in line, was designed by Androuet du Cerceau. The cornices overlooking the river are carved with a row of amusing faces caricaturing Henry IV's ministers and courtiers, and there are comic carvings of stall-holders, pickpockets, and tooth-drawers. The semicircular niches along its length would have served the array of stall-holders who plied their trade there despite the ban on shops.

Porte St-Denis and Porte St-Martin

Boulevard de Bonne Nouvelle and blvd. St-Martin, 10e. Métro: Strasbourg-St-Denis.

These 2 triumphal arches, situated close to one another on the **Grands Boulevards,** were built in the 1670s to commemorate Louis XIV's military victories. They replaced 2 fortified gates that had disappeared along with the old perimeter wall. Both bear reliefs glorifying the Sun King, but the porte St-Denis is the grander and more elaborate of the two.

The immediate area holds little interest, and the presence of these 2 fine arches is uplifting. This stretch of the **Grands Boulevards** is past the pale for quality stores. Its main attractions are the big cinemas, particularly the Art Deco Grand Rex, the **rue de Paradis** with its crystal and glassware emporia, the little theaters on the boulevards, and the **Musée Grévin.**

Poste, Musée de la

34 blvd. de Vaugirard, 15e. ☎ 01-42-79-23-45. Guided tours on request. Open 10am–6pm, Sun noon–7pm. Closed public holidays. Admission charged. Métro: Montparnasse-Bienvenüe, Pasteur, Falguière.

Did you know that in 1870, during the Siege of Paris, microfilm messages were carried out of the city by pigeons whose wings were stamped with a postmark? This is one of many snippets of information to be gleaned here on 4 floors of imaginative displays on philately and the history of worldwide postal communication—everything relating to the subject, from postmen's uniforms and mailboxes to modern sorting machines and stamp-making equipment. There are stamps galore and a ground-floor gallery showing postage-stamp art.

The museum was closed for major renovation recently, during which a new section for children and a display area for pen collection were built.

Préfecture de Police, Musée des Collections Historiques de la

4 rue de la Montagne-Ste-Geneviève, 5e. ☎ 01-44-41-52-50. Open Mon–Fri 9am–5pm, Sat 10am–5pm. Closed Sun. Admission free. Métro: Maubert-Mutualité, St-Michel.

A sober but fascinating collection of documents and objects is housed in this little museum in the heart of the **Latin Quarter.** It presents a panorama of police and criminal activity in Paris from the *ancien régime* to the 20thC. On display are frightening criminal tools and weapons, and documents such as the orders for the arrest of such prominent figures as Danton and Marat's assassin, Charlotte Corday.

Publicité, Musée de la

107 rue de Rivoli, 1er. ☎ 01-44-55-57-50. Joint admission if required, with Musée des Arts Décoratifs and Musée des Arts de la Mode et du Textile. Open Wed–Fri 2–5:30pm, by appointment. Closed Sat–Tues, public holidays. Wheelchair access. Métro: Tuileries, Palais-Royal/ Musée-du-Louvre.

Posters and other forms of publicity material from France and beyond are organized into first-rate temporary themed exhibitions in this new museum, which relocated from cramped quarters in rue de Paradis only recently. Exhibits are drawn from an archive of more than 120,000 items, some dating as far back as the end of the 18thC. There is also a video and reference library.

Quatre-Saisons, Fontaine des (Four Seasons Fountain)

57-59 rue de Grenelle, 7e. Métro: rue du Bac.

When this fountain was built by Bouchardon in the 1730s, to supply water to the district, Voltaire complained that such a splendid monument should not have been erected in so narrow a street. He had a point, for the 2-tiered facade cannot be seen to best effect unless you are standing immediately in front of it. A central portico with a seated figure representing Paris is flanked by elegant, reclining personifications of the Seine and Marne, and on either side are curved walls adorned with statues of the 4 seasons.

Radio-France, Musée de

116 av. du Président Kennedy, 16e. ☎ 01-42-30-21-80. Guided tours (compulsory) at 10:30am, 11:30am, 2:30pm, 3:30pm, 4:30pm. Closed Sun, public holidays. Wheelchair access. Métro: Mirabeau. RER: Maison de Radio France.

This huge glass-and-aluminum edifice, shaped like a giant cylinder, is the nerve center of French radio. Built between 1953 and 1963, it is a statistician's delight—500 meters (800 yd.) in circumference, with 3,500 personnel, 58 studios, and 1,000 offices. Architecturally, though, it may leave the visitor cold. Its main attractions are the extensive **museum of the history of radio and television** and the concerts and shows held there on a regular basis.

Immediately outside, midstream and keeping company with the pont de Grenelle, is a surprising replica of the **Statue of Liberty.**

Renan-Scheffer Maison
See Vie Romantique, Musée de la.

Rodin, Musée
Hôtel Biron, 77 rue de Varenne, 7ᵉ. ☎ 01-47-05-01-34. Guided tours. Open 9:30am–5:45pm (4:45pm in winter). Closed Mon and holidays. Admission charged. Wheelchair access. Métro: Varenne.

Auguste Rodin (1840–1917) is widely considered to be the greatest sculptor of the 19thC. You will see why when you visit this museum, housed in a splendid 18thC mansion near **Les Invalides.** It is impossible not to marvel at the way in which Rodin magically transformed stone, clay, or bronze into the living tissue of human emotion and experience. Take, for example, his famous work, *Le Baiser* (*The Kiss*), which powerfully evokes in white marble the tenderness of love between man and woman; or his ***Homme qui Marche*** (*Walking Man*), which embodies all the urgency and thrust of human aspiration; or *La Cathédrale,* where a pair of hands speaks of piety and contemplation.

The delightful garden surrounding the museum makes an ideal setting for many of Rodin's works. Here we find, among others, casts of his ***Balzac, Le Penseur*** (*The Thinker*), **La Porte de l'Enfer** (*The Gates of Hell*), and **Les Bourgeois de Calais** (*The Burghers of Calais*). Temporary exhibitions of works by other artists are held in a building near the entrance.

Musée Rodin (Hôtel Biron)

The lovely **Hôtel Biron** was built by Gabriel the Elder for a rich wig-maker in 1728 and was subsequently lived in by, among others, Marshal Biron, who was beheaded in 1793. Later, the building became a convent, and much of the painted and gilt paneling was ripped out, although some has been restored. At the beginning of this century the building was bought by the State and was made available for artists. Rodin himself occupied a ground-floor studio from 1907 until his death. The gardens have recently been redesigned and restoration work has also been carried out to the rooms in the interior of the museum, in particular the 18thC *boiseries*.

★ Sacré-Coeur, Basilique du

Place du Parvis-du-Sacré-Coeur, 18ᵉ. ☎ 01-42-51-17-02. Church open 6:45am–11pm. Dome and crypt open Apr–Sept 9am–7pm; Oct–Mar 9am–6pm. Wheelchair access. Métro: Abbesses, Anvers, Château-Rouge, Lamarck-Caulaincourt.

Subject of countless travel posters and paintings, the Sacré-Coeur has acquired the status of a visual cliché. However, seen afresh, in its superb setting on Montmartre's hill, the Butte, it has stunning impact and beauty, whether glimpsed from a train as it draws into one of the northern stations or revealed suddenly as you turn a corner on one of the old streets nearby. (See also **Montmartre**.)

The church rose, phoenixlike, from the ashes of the Franco-Prussian War of 1870. As a reaction to the despair aroused by France's defeat, parliament vowed, in 1873, to erect a church in Paris as a symbol of contrition and a manifestation of hope. For its design, a competition was held and there were 78 entries. The winner was an architect named Abadie, with a Romano-Byzantine plan. The first stone was laid in 1875 and the cathedral was completed by 1914, but World War I delayed its consecration until 1919. Since 1885, wor-shipers have kept up perpetual adoration before the high altar, continuing even through the German occupation.

The material used for the church was Château-Landon stone, which hardens and whitens with age—you can see how much grayer the stonework of the interior is, compared with the gleaming exterior. The design is not to everyone's taste, but many find the outline of its 5 beehivelike domes pleasing.

Approach the church by the long flight of steps from the south (or you can go part of the way by funicular, or the whole way up, from Place Blanche, on the little

Sacré-Coeur

tourist train). This way you get the full impact of the main facade, with its great portico surmounted on each side by equestrian statues of St-Louis and Joan of Arc. The bell tower to the north, which is higher than the rest of the church, contains one of the largest bells in the world, weighing nearly 19 tons.

The interior is light and elegantly proportioned. The eye follows the great rounded arching sweeps of stonework up to the cupola, with its clerestory and its 2 encircling balconies, and down again to the nave, coming to rest on the natural focal point, the great **mosaic** in the alcove above the high altar. This mosaic, one of the largest in the world, depicts Christ with outstretched arms, exposing a golden heart. Grouped around him are worshipers, including the Virgin, St. Michael, and Joan of Arc.

The **crypt,** entered by a stairway from the west aisle, is somewhat gloomy and severe. It contains the church treasury and a number of chapels, the central one possessing a **Pièta** on the altar.

By the same stairway, one ascends a narrow and twisting staircase to the **dome.** The 360° panorama is breathtaking, but the views out over Paris are vertiginous.

St-Augustin

46 blvd. Malesherbes, 8ᵉ. Open daily. Closed Sun afternoons, holidays, school holidays, and first 2 weeks of July. Métro: St-Augustin.

Surprisingly little fuss is made of this Second Empire church on the intersection of boulevards Haussmann and Malesherbes, considering that its architect was Victor Baltard, architect of Les Halles. It has the distinction of being the first truly large building in which a cast-iron frame and supporting pillars were used, for Baltard was a master at new construction techniques.

A member of the Reformed Church, like Haussmann, Baltard chose Roman and Byzantine forms for his inspiration. The constraint on him was the site itself—a narrow space between two great avenues. When you look at the building from the vast place St-Augustin, the frontage does indeed seem small—almost weighed down by the weight of the recently renovated dome. His only option for the building to make its presence felt was to go for height. The church measures almost 100 meters (109 yd.) in length and the dome is some 80 meters (87 yd.) high and spreads out from 22 meters at the portals to 40 meters at the transept.

Yet the individual features of the facade are pleasing. The rose window measures some 24 feet (7m) across. The main doors are of oak covered with figured bronze bearing some lovely low-reliefs by Mathurin Moreau.

★★★ Sainte-Chapelle

4 blvd. du Palais, 1er. ☎ 01-43-54-30-09. Reduced joint ticket with Conciergerie. Guided tours. Open Apr–Sept 9:30am–6pm, Oct–Mar 10am–4:30pm. Closed holidays. Admission charged. Métro: Châtelet, St-Michel, Cité. RER: St-Michel.

It is hard to describe the beauty of this church without hyperbole; its interior is one of the most thrilling visual experiences that Paris affords. Formerly adjacent to a palace of the medieval kings, it now stands hidden away in a side courtyard of the **Palais de Justice** on the **Ile de la Cité.** It was built by Louis IX (St-Louis) in the 1240s, to house relics believed to be the Crown of Thorns and a portion of the True Cross (which cost the king more than the church itself). They were kept in a tabernacle on a platform over the high altar, and on feast days the king would take out the Crown of Thorns and hold it up before his courtiers and the public. The relics are now kept in **Notre-Dame.**

When the Revolution came, the church suffered the indignity of being turned into a flour shop, then a club, and finally a storage place for archives. Under the Commune in 1871, it narrowly escaped destruction by fire.

The building has an unusual double-decker construction with 2 chapels, one above the other. The upper one, dedicated to the Holy Crown and the Holy Cross, was intended only for the king and his

Sainte-Chapelle

retinue. The lower one, dedicated to the Virgin Mary, was for the staff of the chapel and certain officials of the court.

Entering by the rather dark **lower chapel,** you will see the low ceiling supported by columns painted in the 19thC. From here, mount a spiral staircase to the ★ **upper chapel** and emerge into a soaring chamber to be dazzled by the jeweled light that pours through the enormous ★ **stained-glass windows** on every side. The remarkable effect of lightness was achieved by what was then the revolutionary technique of supporting the roof on buttresses.

The window to the left of the entrance depicts scenes from Genesis. The remainder, taken clockwise, show more Old Testament events, as well as the story of Christ. The next-to-last window is devoted to Ste-Hélène and the True Cross, together with St-Louis and the relics of the Crucifixion. The **rose window** to the west shows scenes from the Apocalypse.

The Sainte-Chapelle and its neighbor, the **Conciergerie,** present a striking contrast. The latter represents the baseness and cruelty of the Middle Ages; the former embodies all that was God-seeking in the medieval world.

St-Denis, Basilique

Place de l'Hôtel-de-Ville, 2 rue de Strasbourg, St-Denis. ☎ 01-48-09-83-54. Open Apr–Sept Mon–Sat 10am–7pm, Sun noon–5pm; Oct–Mar, Mon–Sat 10am–5pm, Sun noon–5pm. Métro: St-Denis-Basilique.

Visitors on their way to Paris from Roissy/Charles-de-Gaulle Airport are often surprised to see an imposing cathedral rising out of grim industrial surroundings. It is the Basilique St-Denis, necropolis of the kings of France and precursor of the Gothic style of architecture that swept over Europe.

The Crypt
of St-Denis

It was in the 12thC that the learned Abbot Suger,
friend of Louis VII, decided to rebuild his church dedicated to the Apostle of France, St-Denis. Having
been beheaded in Montmartre by the ungrateful
Gallo-Romans for trying to show them Christianity,
St-Denis walked northward with his head tucked
under his arm until he fell down, on the spot where his
church was later founded. The prestige of being buried
near the relics of a saint made the church a natural choice
for a royal necropolis for all but a handful of French
kings and their queens, starting with Dagobert in the
7thC.

The **tombs and statuary** of the kings are as good
a reason for visiting St-Denis as the church itself. The
tombs are empty, however. During the Revolution, 800
royal bodies were pitched into a communal grave in
the crypt under the north transept. Luckily, the tombs
were saved from destruction—the archaeologist Lenoir
having had the foresight to remove them to safety some
time earlier.

In the late 13thC, Louis IX (St-Louis) ordered purely
symbolic effigies of all his ancestors back to the 7thC;
but, from the death of Philippe the Bold in 1285, like-
nesses were taken from real portraits. Particularly notable are the **Renaissance mausoleums** of François I
and Henry II. Unfortunately, all the tombs are chained
off, and close inspection is difficult.

The beginnings of lightness, harmony, and rational
disposition of the elements in the church itself, pro-
claim the spirit of a new age and the close of the Dark
Ages. Elements that had been developed separately were
now combined for the first time: the Latin cross plan
with radiating pilgrimage chapels, the pointed arch, and
the ribbed groin vault. You can see these facets of Suger's
original plan in the ambulatory, apse, and facade. The
latter has an air of dissymmetry, with its pointed Gothic
and rounded Romanesque arches and its missing north

tower. The facade boasts the first-ever **rose window,** a feature that was soon to become standard.

Within the church, a further progress toward lightness was made in the next century, when the architect Pierre de Montreuil gave the nave, side aisles, and chancel an architectural lift that recalls his masterwork, the **Sainte-Chapelle.**

St-Etienne-du-Mont

Place Ste-Geneviève, 5°. ☎ 01-43-54-11-79. Open daily 8am–noon, 2–7pm. Closed Mon in July, Aug. Admission free. Métro: Cardinal-Lemoine.

Built between 1492 and 1626, the church is a mixture of styles that defy all the rules of architectural purity. The result is rather like a crazy composite photograph, amalgamating elements from contrasting buildings. Take the main facade, with its 3 pediments piled one on top of the other, combining classical motifs with a Gothic rose window stuck in the middle. The belfry is similarly eclectic, begun in the medieval style and topped with a little Renaissance dome. Nevertheless, the whole effect is pleasing.

The interior, which preserves greater consistency of style, has some remarkable features, notably the 16thC **rood screen,** with its delicately pierced stonework and its 2 flanking spiral stairways. This is the only surviving rood screen in Paris and is worth going a long way to see. The interior of the church is exquisitely light and airy, and the sight of it comes as a welcome relief if your spirit is subdued after visiting the **Panthéon** nearby.

There is also the Flamboyant vaulting over the transept, the 5.5-meter (18-ft.) hanging keystone,

St-Etienne-du-Mont

the splendidly ornate organ loft (1630), and the richly carved wooden pulpit (1650). At the west end of the nave is a slab indicating where the Archbishop of Paris was assassinated by an unfrocked priest in 1857. Those buried in the church include the writers Pascal and Racine, both commemorated by plaques on either side of the entrance to the Lady Chapel.

The chapel to Ste-Geneviève, created in 1803, contains the stone on which her body had rested in the former abbey church of Ste-Geneviève before her remains were destroyed during the Revolution. All that is left of her body is a bone or two, now preserved in an elaborate reliquary.

Although the church was badly plundered and damaged during the Revolution, it was later skillfully restored and today contains some valuable works of art. A medium-term restoration program to the facade was completed in 1993.

The cloister of the 2 charnel houses, at the far end of the church, is easily missed, yet it contains a series of **stained-glass panels** that is considered to be second only to the windows at the **Sainte-Chapelle.** The cloister once looked out over a small charnel house, which in turn opened out onto a larger cemetery, hence its name. Its main interest lies in the 12 stained-glass panels, put together in 1734 from the remains of 22 original windows. These panels infill the arches of the cloister, so the brilliantly colored glass can be seen at eye level. Like all domestic glass of the time, the colors were embedded into the glass with enamel. An inexpensive booklet is available, which explains the content of each panel of glass, as well as the history of the church.

St-Eustache

2 rue du Jour, 1ᵉʳ. Open daily. Admission free. Métro: Les Halles.

This lovely church, the largest in Paris after **Notre-Dame,** deserves to be better known than it is. For centuries it has stood at the focal point of Parisian history and, until recently, was the local church of Les Halles market. Now it surveys the **Forum des Halles** with the solid equanimity of the Middle Ages confronting the transience of the present day.

The site was originally occupied by a small 13thC chapel to Ste-Agnes, later rededicated to St-Eustache, the 2ndC Roman who, like St-Hubert later on, is said to have seen a vision of the Cross between the antlers of a stag. The building, with its elegant flying buttresses, took shape between 1532 and 1640. It is a curious mixture, the form being Gothic, the details classical.

Many famous names crop up in the history of the church. Cardinal Richelieu, Madame de Pompadour, and Molière were baptized in it, and Louis XIV celebrated his first communion here. During the Revolution, the church was pillaged, then made a Temple of Agriculture. In 1844, it suffered a worse fate when it was devastated by a fire. It was completely restored by Baltard, the architect of Les Halles market, and today stands as one of the finest of Paris's architectural monuments.

The interior is thrilling, with its exhilarating vertical emphasis. Everything thrusts upward to the ceiling with its delicate network of ribbed vaulting and elaborately carved bosses. The stained glass is luxurious, and there are some important works of art here, including an early Rubens, *Pilgrims at Emmaus,* and Pigalle's sculpture of the Virgin, on the altar of the Lady Chapel.

One of the church's proudest possessions is its organ. After a thorough restoration, it is now one of the finest in the city. Concerts are held here periodically, carrying on a well-established musical tradition. It was here in 1855 that Berlioz conducted the first performance of his *Te Deum.*

St-Germain l'Auxerrois

2 pl. du Louvre, 1ᵉʳ. Open daily. Admission free. Métro: Louvre Rivoli, Pont-Neuf.

Opposite the east end of the **Grand Louvre** stands a church that embodies a fascinating resumé of medieval architecture. There has been a church on this site since the 6thC, when an oratory dedicated to St-Germanus was built. The present building is the fourth on the spot and is a combination of 500 years of architectural design.

The oldest part of the building is the 12thC Romanesque belfry behind the transept crossing. It played a somber role during the Wars of Religion when, in 1572, Catherine de Médicis ordered the bells to ring out to signal the start of the Massacre of St-Bartholomew. Three thousand Huguenots, in town to celebrate the marriage of Henri de Navarre to his cousin Marguerite de Valois, were slaughtered in their beds and thrown from the windows.

In the 13thC, the Gothic ambulatory and chancel, the Lady Chapel on the right, and the central portal were all added. St-Germain l'Auxerrois became the royal parish church in the 14thC when Charles V transformed the Louvre from fortress to medieval palace. The nave dates from this century. During the 15thC, the unusual and Flamboyant Gothic porch was built, with its lovely multiribbed vaulting. Then in the 16thC, the Renaissance came, leaving its mark on the doorway north of the choir, and the late Gothic transept portals were added.

In the 17thC, Versailles was built, the court abandoned the Louvre to the court artists, who made their studios there, and St-Germain became their parish church. Many artists, sculptors, and poets are buried here. Even today artists and show people come here on Ash Wednesday to celebrate a special mass. Royalists have not been forgotten: Every year on January 21, the anniversary of his execution in 1793, a Mass is said for Louis XVI.

★★ St-Germain-des-Prés

Place St-Germain-des-Prés, 6ᵉ. Open daily. Admission free. Métro: St-Germain-des-Prés, Mabillon.

The oldest church in Paris stands passively at the hub of the lively **St-Germain Quarter.** Its origin dates back to AD 542, when the Merovingian King Childebert I, son of Clovis, brought back from Spain the tunic of St-Vincent, and a golden cross said to have been made by Solomon. To receive these relics, he built a monastery and church, which was at first called the Basilica of St-Vincent and St-Croix, but later came to be named after St-Germanus, the Bishop of Paris, who consecrated the church in AD 558 and was buried there.

As the burial place of the Merovingian kings and a seat of the great Benedictine order, it became virtually a miniature state in its own right, possessing 17,000 hectares (42,000 acres) of land, its buildings fortified by towers and a moat fed from the Seine. For centuries, it stood in meadows called the Pré aux Clercs (a curious thought, this, as you survey the contemporary citycenter scene).

The church was destroyed twice by the Normans, and its present form dates from the 11thC. During the Revolution, the abbey was dissolved and the property subjected to an orgy of vandalism in which the royal tombs and most of the buildings were destroyed, the church itself being turned into a saltpeter factory. Of the once-splendid complex, only the church, minus its transepts, and the abbot's palace on the northeast side remain.

Except for a few capitals and columns, nothing that can be seen in the church is earlier than 11thC. The interior is an interesting mixture of different periods, with its Romanesque arches, Gothic vaulting, and polychrome wall painting by the 19thC artist Hippolyte Flandrin. The works of art in the church include a 14thC Virgin and Child known as Notre-Dame de Consolation, and a number of fine tombs, including that of John Casimir, a 17thC Polish king who became abbot of St-Germain. There are also tombs of 2 Scottish noblemen, William and James Douglas, courtiers of Henry IV, and Louis XIII respectively.

Beside the church, facing south, a little garden shaded by chestnut trees is a tranquil and secluded refuge from the busy boulevard St-Germain.

St-Germain Quarter

On the Left Bank, in the 6ᵉ and 7ᵉ. Métro: Mabillon, Odéon, St-Germain-des-Prés, rue du Bac, Solférino.

The St-Germain district is really made up of 2 adjacent quarters: **St-Germain-des-Prés,** consisting roughly of the northern half of the 6ᵉ; and the **Faubourg-St-Germain,** comprising the northeast section of the 7ᵉ. These 2 areas have their own distinct personalities, complementing each other well.

The former community first grew up around the great medieval monastery and **church of St-Germain-des-Prés,** but for centuries it lay outside the Paris boundaries and remained cut off from the life of the city. Its only link with the Right Bank was a ferry (*bac*), which was reached by rue du Bac. This remained the case until the 17thC, when Louis XIV began to extend the Louvre, for which purpose stone had to be brought from the quarries at Denfert-Rochereau in the south. The ferry was too slow a means of bringing it across the river, and so the **pont-Royal** was built, ending the isolation of St-Germain.

It was also Louis XIV who established the **Ecole des Beaux-Arts,** across the river from the Louvre. Later, after the Louvre had become a museum, the narrow footbridge known as the Passerelle des Arts (now **pont des Arts)** was built, to allow the students to cross the river to look at the works of art. The construction of the pont-Royal turned St-Germain-des-Prés into a thriving community, and it soon became a favorite haunt of writers and intellectuals.

The **Faubourg-St-Germain** is—faubourg meaning "suburb"—as the name implies, of more recent origin. During the reign of Louis XIV, the aristocracy had been concentrated around the court at Versailles, but under the more relaxed regime of Louis XV, they felt able to take up residence in Paris again and chose the plain to the east of the Hôtel des Invalides as the place to build their homes.

The result can be seen today in the gracious houses that line such streets as rue de Lille, rue de l'Université, rue de Grenelle, and rue de Varenne. In recent years the majority of the larger ones have become government buildings or embassies. The **Hôtel de Matignon** (57 rue de Varenne) is now the residence of the Prime Minister, while the **Hôtel de Courteilles** (110 rue de Grenelle) has become the Ministry of Education. Rue de Grenelle is also the site of the lovely **Quatre-Saisons** fountain. A few well-heeled families still live in the area, and the atmosphere retains the privileged, inward-looking quality that it has always possessed, whether dominated by aristocrats or civil servants.

The buildings belong to a felicitous period when French architecture had thrown off the Italian influence and blossomed into a light but restrained elegance. This was typified by the **Hôtel Biron** at the western end of rue de Varenne. Now the **Musée Rodin,** this is one of the few houses in the area that you can enter easily.

The link between these 2 areas is **boulevard St-Germain,** a great bow-shaped thoroughfare that touches the Seine at each end. Begin a stroll down the boulevard perhaps somewhere near the secluded little church of St-Thomas d'Aquin, which lies just off the route to the north. This is still the Faubourg-St-Germain, but, approaching the church of St-Germain des-Prés itself, everything becomes busier, more colorful, and more cosmopolitan. Turn right opposite the church into rue des Ciseaux, a little Italian enclave with many pizzerias. This spills over into the rue des Canettes (Duckling St.), which runs up to St-Sulpice— see the little ducklings over the doorway of no. 18.

Farther east, rue Grégoire de Tours is full of Greek restaurants. This street leads into rue de Buci. Here and in the neighboring rue de Seine is one of the best **outdoor food markets** in the city of Paris.

The church of St-Germain-des-Prés dominates the intersection of boulevard St-Germain, rue de Rennes, and rue Bonaparte. This is the heart of the district that has come to be known as the *Capitale des Lettres* (Literary Capital), a role that it began to take on in the 17thC

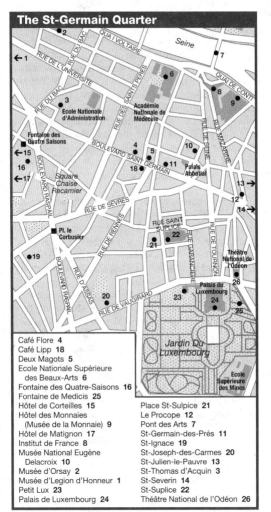

The St-Germain Quarter

when the Comédie Française played in what is now
rue de l'Ancienne Comédie. **Le Procope** (see "Dining"), at no. 13, was the haunt of Molière, Corneille,
Racine, and, in later centuries, Voltaire, Balzac, Verlaine,
and Anatole France.

Between the wars, the quarter was fueled by an influx of writers from Montmartre and Montparnasse,
who met habitually in the 3 great cafes in front of
St-Germain-des-Prés: **Flore, Lipp,** and **Les Deux
Magots** (see "Cafes & Tea Salons" in "Dining"). Pub-
lishers, booksellers, painters, and art dealers also set up
shop there in increasing numbers.

After World War II, St-Germain became the headquarters of a new generation of intelligentsia, revolving around Jean-Paul Sartre and the existentialists. In those days they crowded into jazz cellars such as the Tabou in rue Dauphine and small bars such as the Bar Vert in rue Jacob. The atmosphere of the district has inevitably changed since then, but the "Germanopratins," as the inhabitants are called, are friendly and bubbling, and there is always a lively atmosphere, especially around place St-Germain-des-Prés by the church, where most evenings you will find street performers at work.

A gentler atmosphere of festivity is often to be found nearby in the quaint little tree-lined rue de Furstemberg, where the glow of the old-fashioned street lamps attracts singers, guitarists, and harpists. The great 19thC artist Delacroix had his studio here (it is now the **Musée Delacroix)** and the Romantic spirit is still strongly felt, especially at night.

Apart from the Delacroix, there are few museums in this part of Paris. As well as the **Musée d'Orsay** and the Rodin, there is the **Musée de la Monnaie** and the **Légion d'Honneur.** However, the district makes up for this deficiency in the density of its **small art galleries** (mostly around rue de Seine and rue Mazarine) and its secondhand bookstores.

There are many little pockets in St-Germain where history can be found. One of them is **cour du Commerce-St-André,** an ancient alley off rue St-André-des-Arts. If you look through the windows of no. 4, you will see part of one of the **towers of the medieval city wall.** At no. 9 was the site of the workshop of a German carpenter called Schmidt, who built the first guillotine and tested it out on unfortunate sheep.

St-Joseph-des-Carmes

70 rue de Vaugirard, 6ᵉ. Guided tours at 3pm on Sat (except July), call ☎ 01-42-22-41 80. Admission charged. Métro: Rennes, St-Placide.

This elegant little church forms part of the **Institut Catholique de Paris** complex, which stands on the site once occupied by a great Carmelite monastery with vast gardens, many treasures, and a priceless library.

During the Revolution, the monastery was closed, its treasures confiscated, and the buildings turned into a prison where, in September 1792, 115 priests and 3 bishops were massacred. Their bones are buried in the crypt of the church, which today possesses a gloomy atmosphere despite its fine works of art. These include, to the left of the transept, a marble *Virgin and Child* after a model by Bernini.

St-Julien-le-Pauvre

1 rue St-Julien-le-Pauvre, 5ᵉ. Open daily. Admission free. Métro: St-Michel, Maubert Mutualité.

This enchanting little building set in a charming garden, square René Viviani, and facing **Notre-Dame** from the Left Bank, is the oldest complete church in Paris, built between 1165 and 1220. Only parts of **St-Germain-des-Prés** are older. The beauty of the interior, with its elegantly foliated capitals, is all the more potent for its modesty. The wooden screen (iconostasis) across the choir is a reminder that this is now a church of the Melchite (Greek Catholic) rite. From the square there is also an attractive view across rue St-Jacques to **St-Séverin.**

St-Michel, boulevard

Called the Boul 'Mich, this is the main artery of the Left Bank. See **Latin Quarter,** above.

St-Nicolas-des-Champs

254 rue St-Martin, 3ᵉ. Open daily. Closed Sun afternoons. Admission free. Métro: Arts-et-Métiers, Réaumur-Sébastopol.

Begun in the 12thC, this church boasts distinguished features from different periods: a Flamboyant Gothic facade and belfry, a fine Renaissance doorway on the south side, and many paintings from the 17th through 19th centuries. In the St-Michel chapel, a pudgy archangel steps daintily on a pitiful bald-headed devil. The high altar is curiously like a stone bath complete with lion's feet. In short, the church is a mixture of beauty and bathos.

St-Roch

296 rue St-Honoré, 1ᵉʳ. Open daily. Admission free. Métro: Pyramides, Tuileries.

As Paris grew westward in the 17thC, the need arose for a new parish church in the vicinity of the **Palais-Royal.** St-Roch was created, and the author of the Grand Siècle, Louis XIV himself, laid the first stone in 1653. The interior is marked by some of the great creative personalities that make the 17thC alive to us today.

There is the tomb of André Le Nôtre, a kind old man, friend to Louis XIV, and the first gardener to make history, with the park of Versailles. He also created the nearby **Tuileries.** Other tombs include those of the playwright Corneille and the philosopher Diderot.

The church itself was designed by some of the most important architects of the 17thC, notably Jacques Lemercier, and work was prolonged into the 18thC, making for a combination of classical and baroque elements, with a Jesuit-style facade designed by de Cotte in 1736.

Unlike the Gothic churches of Paris, the church is not oriented east-to-west but north-to-south because of the terrain. It is also unusually long, with one chapel following another, beyond the chancel.

In the nave, one can admire the vaulting, which has penetrating arches. This part of the building was financed in 1719 by John Law, the Scottish wheeler-dealer of the Mississippi Bubble. The pulpit is in the highly theatrical baroque style by Challe (1755).

The round-domed room beyond the chancel, the Lady Chapel, was designed by Jules Hardouin-Mansart. Its ceiling portrays the cloudscape of the *Triumph of the Virgin* by J. B. Pierre (1750), and above the altar, with its nativity group, is a mass of clouds in gilded stucco. Behind the Lady Chapel is the small Holy Communion Chapel, and behind this a Calvary Chapel. The church has 3 organs and excellent acoustics, making it a fine musical auditorium, and concerts take place regularly.

As you leave, pause by the bullet-riddled facade. These marks are a reminder of a terrible battle that took place in front of the church in 1795. The Republican Convention was under attack by royalists and anarchists, but thanks to the technical skill of the leader of the Republican forces, the Revolution was saved. The leader: a 27-year-old general, Napoléon Bonaparte.

St-Séverin

Rue des Prêtres St-Séverin, 5e. Open daily. Métro: St-Michel, Cluny-La-Sorbonne.

Tucked away among the labyrinth of narrow streets in the **Latin Quarter** to the east of boulevard St-Michel, St-Séverin is one of the most cherished medieval churches in the city, possessing a quiet magic all of its own. The church is named after 2 saints named Séverin: a hermit who once lived on the site in an oratory dedicated to St-Martin, and a namesake of the same era who was Abbot of Agaune.

The present building was begun in the early 13thC and was much altered and enlarged in the 15thC, when it was stamped with the so-called Flamboyant (or flamelike) style to be seen in the shape of the stonework in which the stained-glass windows are set. The double ambulatory, with its forest of columns, one of them with twisted veins, is particularly fine.

What the church lacks in size it makes up for in the perfection of its proportions and the delicacy of its decoration. Every arch, column, piece of ribbed vaulting, and lozenge of stained glass sings out in joyful harmony. Perhaps this is why it is such a wonderful place for listening to music—don't miss a concert here if you get the chance. The only discordant note is the ungainly baroque touch given to the chancel in the 18thC when part of the arcade was rounded and faced with false marble—the effect is comparable to that of a nun wearing an ostrich-feather hat.

Adjoining the church to the south is a little garden shaded by trees and bordered on 2 sides by the arcades of the former charnel house. Standing in the garden (possible during concerts), you may feel yourself to be in a time-warp, for beyond the cloistered calm stands the neon-lit front of a restaurant.

St-Sulpice

Place St-Sulpice, 6e. Open Mon–Sat. Closed Sun, except services. Métro: St-Sulpice, Mabillon.

Unlike many of the other great churches of Paris, this one does not form part of an imposing townscape. It looms unexpectedly out of the maze of narrow streets to the north of the **Palais de Luxembourg.**

Starting life as a modest medieval church dedicated to St. Sulpicius, the 16thC Archbishop of Bourges, it was reconstructed in a piecemeal fashion between the years 1655 and 1788 by 6 different architects, the essential classical form being the work of the Florentine Giovanni Servandoni. The result is not the hodgepodge that one might expect, but a grand and harmonious whole, apart from the nonmatching towers over the portico with its 2 tiers of columns.

During the revolutionary period, the church became a Temple of Reason, then of Victory. In November 1799, it was the scene of a sumptuous banquet in honor of Napoléon Bonaparte.

The interior houses vast recesses of space, and the stillness seems trapped beneath a great weight of stone. There are many interesting objects in the church, including 2 enormous shells serving as holy-water stoups, with rocklike bases sculpted by Pigalle.

Another feature worth noticing is the **bronze meridian line** running from a plaque set into the floor of the south transept to a marble obelisk in the north transept. The sunlight, passing through a window in

the south transept, strikes the line at different points to
mark the equinoxes and solstices.

The Lady Chapel, at the east end of the church, is
heavily ornate, with Pigalle's *Virgin and Child* floating
above a cascade of plaster clouds. Don't miss the
Delacroix murals in the side chapel immediately to
the right of the main door. The one depicting Jacob
struggling with the Angel is particularly compelling.
The splendid organ, with its 6,588 pipes, is one of the
largest in the world, and organ recitals are given here
frequently.

Sciences et de l'Industrie, Cité des
(City of Science and Industry)
See Villette, Parc de la.

Sculpture en Plein Air de la Ville de Paris,
Musée de la (Open Air Sculpture Museum)
Quai St-Bernard, 5ᵉ. ☎ 01-43-26-91-90. Open 7am–7pm.
Admission charged. Métro: Jussieu, Gare d'Austerlitz, Sully-Morland.

Only a city as basically civilized as Paris would dedicate
500 meters (547 yd.) of prime riverside (between the
Ile St-Louis and the **Jardin des Plantes**) for use as an
open-air park for postwar sculpture. Established in 1980,
beautifully planted with mature bushes and shrubs, with
terraces, elevated plazas and cul-de-sacs, it makes a spectacular environment for a medium whose profile in the
late 20thC remains curiously bland.

Not many of the several dozen pieces on show here
raise the spirit (Ossip Zadkine's prehensile *Naissance des
Formes* stands out), but the location and ambiance of
this 24-hour vantage point are something else. Watch
the riverboats and pleasure boats U-turn at this point,
around the Île St-Louis.

Sewers
See Egouts.

La Sorbonne
Rue de la Sorbonne, 5ᵉ. Visits by arrangement only in writing to the
Rectorat de Paris, Services des Affaires Culturelles, 45 rue des Ecoles,
5ᵉ. Admission free. Métro: Cluny-La Sorbonne, Maubert-Mutualité,
Luxembourg.

The imposing buildings of the Sorbonne, which domi-
nate the center of the **Latin Quarter,** testify to the
long and distinguished history of this world-famous
university. Founded in 1253 by Robert de Sorbon,
confessor to Louis IX, it began life as a college for 16
poor theological students but grew rapidly into a powerful body which had its own government, laws, and
jurisdiction—virtually a state-within-a-state.

In the 17thC, its chancellor, Cardinal Richelieu, commissioned the architect Jacques Lemercier to reconstruct the college buildings and added the magnificent domed Jesuit-style church, the interior of which can, unfortunately, be seen only during temporary exhibitions.

The university was closed during the Revolution, then reopened by Napoléon as the premier university of France. Alas, it no longer exists as a university in its own right. After the student riots of 1968, in which it played a key role, the Sorbonne became merely part of the University of Paris, with its multitude of buildings scattered across the city.

However, the glory of the past still clings to the buildings: the great courtyard with its superb sundial, surmounted by a relief of Apollo in his chariot; the baroque library possessing more than 1.5 million volumes; and the ornate lecture rooms, with their numerous murals.

It is amusing to walk around and rub shoulders with the students. They no longer talk Latin, as they did in the days when the name—Latin Quarter—was born, but they are heirs to an illustrious tradition.

Techniques, Musée National des (formerly Conservatoire des Arts et Métiers)

292 rue St-Martin, Paris 3ᵉ. ☎ 01-40-27-23-31. Open 10am–5:30pm. Closed Mon, public holidays. Métro: Réaumur-Sébastopol, Arts-et-Métiers.

This large technical museum and a college of technology are housed in the former **priory of St-Martin-des-Champs** in the northwest corner of the **Marais.** The two most distinguished elements that remain from the medieval priory are the beautifully proportioned and vaulted refectory, now a library (visits by prior arrangement only), and the church of St-Martin-des-Champs, which is now part of the museum. The collection of more than 80,000 items, of which not more than one-tenth is on display, records developments in the engineering sciences over the last half-millennium.

If archaeologists of the future ever discover this chapel and its contents, they might think that they have stumbled upon a bizarre temple of the 20thC dedicated to the worship of machinery. In the Gothic ambulatory, where the shrines of saints should be, there are engine components, car and airplane motors, and similar objects, some of them placed in glass cases like holy relics, suggesting perhaps the cult of "Our Ford" in Huxley's *Brave New World*.

For the technically minded, the museum is fascinating. Here you can see models and displays demonstrating the technical progress of water power, the automobile, photography, television, musical instruments, printing, clockmaking, railways, and aviation—and more—all examples of man's inventiveness and skill.

The museum is closed for renovation work until 1998. The Lavotsier laboratory and museum shop will remain open daily, 10am to 5:30pm (closed Sun, Mon and holidays). Admission is free.

Tombeau de Napoléon 1er (Napoléon's Tomb)

The Emperor lies in state in the **Dome Church.** See **Invalides, Hotel National des.**

★★★ Tour Eiffel (Eiffel Tower)

Champ-de-Mars, 7e. ☎ 01-44-11-23-45. ☎ 01-44-11-23-23 for recorded information. Guided tours for groups. Open 9:30am–11pm (July, Aug, holidays, open 9am–midnight). Admission charged. Wheelchair access. Métro: Bir-Hakeim, Ecole Militaire. RER: Champ-de-Mars/Tour-Eiffel.

The controversy that once raged over this world-famous tower has long since died down, and it has become universally accepted as the unofficial symbol of Paris. The reason for its construction in 1889 has been almost forgotten: to commemorate the centenary of the French Revolution. Those who think that Gustave Eiffel's design is bad enough should remember that it was one of 700 submitted for a competition in which rival proposals included a gigantic lighthouse capable of illuminating the entire city and a tower shaped like a guillotine to honor the victims of the Reign of Terror. Fortunately, Gustave Eiffel's design was unanimously accepted, and the iron tower was completed in time for the centenary and the World Exhibition. It rose 300 meters (984 ft.) and was a miracle of engineering, comprising 9,547 tons of material. Today its height, including aerials, is 320.75 meters (1,052 ft.), and its weight is 10,100 tons. It was repainted for the 17th time in 1995.

At first, the Eiffel Tower was widely reviled. The writer J. K. Huysmans scornfully called it a "hollow candlestick," and a group of distinguished Parisians published a manifesto declaring it a "dishonor to Paris." Many advocated its demolition, but it was saved by World War I, when it became an important military center for radio and telegraphic transmission. In 1964, it was classified as a national monument.

The journey to the summit is made in 3 stages. The 1st and 2nd platforms of the tower, which can be reached

La Tour Eiffel

by elevator or stairs, support restaurants and souvenir shops. The first-class restaurant, the Jules Verne (see "Dining"), offers panoramic dining. In April 1995, a second restaurant, Altitude 95, was opened on the 1st floor. The 3rd and top platforms, which can be reached only by elevator, have a bar, souvenir shops, and the office, now restored, in which Eiffel worked. The superb panorama over the city can be viewed from behind glass or from a balcony. On a clear day, you can see up to 70 kilometers (44 miles) in any direction.

The tower has witnessed some strange scenes in its history. One man died trying to fly from it with artificial wings; in 1923 a daredevil journalist succeeded in riding a bicycle down from the first platform; and in 1954 it was scaled by 2 mountaineers. However, most people climb it for the view, or simply to be able to say that they have been to the top of the famous Eiffel Tower.

Tour Montparnasse (Montparnasse Tower)

Rue de l'Arrivée, 15ᵉ. ☎ 01-45-38-52-56. Open Apr–Sept 9:30am–11:30pm, Oct–Mar 9:30am–10:30pm (Fri, Sat 11pm). Admission charged. Métro: Montparnasse-Bienvenüe.

Opened in 1973, this 209-meter-high (690-ft.) tower, with its adjacent shopping center, dominates the whole quarter. Many regard it as one of the worst atrocities ever inflicted on Paris, a sad relic of Georges Pompidou's misguided attempts to modernize the French capital. It rises, like a vast black tombstone, from the center of **Montparnasse,** dominating the skyline from almost every part of the city and introducing a discordant element into the otherwise human scale of central Paris. This trend has since been halted.

It must be admitted, however, that the view from the top of the tower is spectacular, and interestingly different from the one afforded by the **Tour Eiffel.** The 56th floor has a viewing gallery with a bar and a good restaurant. You can also go right up onto the 59th-floor flat roof of the building via a very plain staircase.

★★★ Tuileries, Jardin des
1er. Métro: Tuileries.

French formal gardening at its most elegant is exemplified in the Jardin des Tuileries. Laid out by Le Nôtre, gardener to Louis XIV, the gardens occupy a splendid site bounded by the **Grand Louvre, place de la Concorde,** and **rue de Rivoli,** with the twin **Jeu de Paume** and **Orangerie** pavilions on raised terraces at the west end. The central avenue, with its 2 ponds, is dramatically aligned with **avenue des Champs-Elysées** and the Louvre.

There seem to be almost as many statues in the gardens as there are trees: Dotting the walkways are some 150 ancient gods and goddesses, allegorical figures of rivers and the seasons, and, near the Concorde entrance, a bust of Le Nôtre himself. The gardens have many modern sculptures, too, forming a sort of extension of the reorganized Louvre.

Although it is quite plainly popular with Parisians, the peacefulness of the Tuileries, given its location smack in the middle of the city, is striking. Birdsong stills the roar of traffic, which is muffled by massed trees. Children can pass the time happily in their own special play areas, and there is a pond where toy wooden sailboats can be rented.

The spacious Jardins du Carrousel are situated between the place du Carrousel and the actual start of the Tuileries. These are formal, hedge- and tree-lined gardens dotted by 18 statues by Maillol and provide a suitably noble front yard for the Louvre itself.

After the spectacular completion of the Richelieu wing and the underground shopping arcade the Carrousel du Louvre, work now continues on the Jardins des Tuileries, which is being completely redesigned by a team headed up by the young French landscape gardeners Pascal Cribier, Louis Benech, and François Roubaud. The project, begun in 1991, is not expected to be completely finished until 1996. The idea is to restore rather than re-create the gardens, and much attention is being paid to creating both carefully landscaped areas and areas where nature is allowed to bloom somewhat more freely. When it is finished, some 800 trees—notably chestnut trees—will have been planted, bringing the total number of trees in the gardens to 3,000. Some of the existing trees in the Tuileries are 200 years old; unfortunately, neglect and pollution mean that some 20% of them will be eliminated during the restoration—though new plantings will keep the final number of trees the same. At the same time, the installations in the garden—from kiosks to cafes, pony-rides to marionettes—are all being overhauled as well.

However, contrasted with the gaiety of the gardens and the dust of the excavations, is the tragic specter of the vanished Tuileries palace, which once ran north-to-south between the 2 projecting western pavilions of the Louvre, with the **Arc de Triomphe du Carrousel** forming the entrance to its courtyard.

Queen Catherine de Médicis built the palace in the 16thC but never lived there because her astrologer warned her against it, and subsequently an evil spell seemed to afflict the building. It witnessed violent and dramatic events, such as the escape of Louis XVI and his family across the gardens in 1792, the massacre of the Swiss Guards at the same date, and the riots that led to the departure of Charles X in 1830 and of Louis-Philippe in 1848. Finally, the palace was sacked and burned by the Communards in 1871.

Val-de-Grâce.

1 pl. Alphonse-Laveran, 5ᵉ. ☎ 01-40-51-51-92. Open daily.
Métro: Port-Royal.

One of the great architectural treasures of Paris, the Val-de-Grâce hides its light under a bushel, tucked away as it is down rue St-Jacques. In 1622, Anne of Austria, wife of Louis XIII, installed a Benedictine convent here, for use as a retreat. The buildings still remain, including the superbly proportioned cloister. Later she added the church, in thanksgiving for the birth of a son (the future Louis XIV) in 1638, after 23 childless years of marriage; the young king himself laid the first stone of the building in 1645.

The church, in the Jesuit style, has many beautiful features including a cupola, painted with frescoes by Mignand; an unusual 6-columned baldachin over the altar; and an attractive sculpted ceiling, whose pattern is reproduced in the floor tiles.

During the Revolution, the convent was turned into a military hospital, which it remains to this day. It houses a museum relating to the history of military medicine, but this is closed for alterations and is due to reopen in 1997. The Val-de-Grâce stands in an area devoted to medicine, with its large hospital and various medical institutions.

★ Vendome, place

1er. Métro: Tuileries, Madeleine, Opéra.

Few squares in the world convey such an impression of effortless opulence and wealth as this one, now home to the Ritz Hotel, Cartier's, and a handful of other glitzy boutiques. Built under Louis XIV to a design by Jules Hardouin-Mansart (1645–1708), it presents a uniform facade of the utmost beauty of proportion: an arcade at ground level, then Corinthian pilasters rising through 2 stories, topped by a roof with dormer windows. The keystones of the arches are carved with Bacchanalian faces, each with a different expression, like a ring of revelers at some expensive feast. This jolly throng has witnessed many dramatic events in the square. The statue of Louis XIV, which stood in the center, was destroyed during the Revolution and later replaced by a bronze column constructed by Denon, Gondouin, and Lepère from 1806 to 1810, commemorating Napoléon's victories in Germany and modeled on Trajan's column in Rome. This monument was pulled down during the Commune but later re-erected. It is surmounted by a statue of Napoléon.

Besides numerous financiers and aristocrats, the square housed such colorful characters as the Austrian F. A. Mesmer, inventor of mesmerism, who held sessions of "animal magnetism" at no. 16, and Chopin, who died at no. 12.

The place was renovated in 1992, and one can no longer park here, but the strange little bollards that separate the walkways from the traffic lane are awfully hard to spot—and more than one well-heeled shopper has been sent sprawling after colliding with one.

Versailles

See "Excursions."

Viaduc des Arts

9-129 av. Daumesnil, 12e. ☎ 01-40-02-09-07. Open daily 10am–7pm. Admission free. Métro: Gare de Lyon. RER: Gare de Lyon.

As part of its program to revitalize the eastern part of the city, Paris recently refurbished the former raised railway viaduct that crosses the 12e arrondissement and used to carry a train line from the place de la Bastille to the Bois de Vincennes. The railway was closed in 1969, and for a while the vaults housed everything from tramps to fortunetellers to auto shops.

Now completely restored, the 60 dramatic, high-ceilinged vaults have been converted into attractive artist's ateliers, while the top of the massive brick viaduct, where the railroad tracks used to be, is now a flower- and tree-lined walkway.

The city has so far selected 30 contemporary "artisans" to rent these soaring spaces, now baptised the Viaduc des Arts, and it has become a showcase for French crafts and handwork. The Copper and Silver Atelier (nos. 109–113) includes a showroom and a museum. At Marie Lavande (no. 83), artisans repair and restore antique lace and give courses in embroidery. At no. 81, Muriel Guigue Locca shows off her trompe l'oeil technique, including painted boxes and furniture.

Vie Romantique, Musée de la (Maison Renan-Scheffer)

16 rue Chaptal, 9e. ☎ 01-48-74-95-38. Guided tours. Open 10am–5:30pm. Closed Mon, public holidays. Admission charged. Métro: St-Georges, Blanche, Pigalle.

From 1830 this secluded house in Montmartre was the home of the painter Ary Scheffer and the scene of Friday-evening salons attended by such celebrities as Delacroix, Liszt, George Sand, and Chopin. Another guest was the writer Ernest Renan, who married Scheffer's niece. Their daughter later took over the house and continued to hold salons there.

The ground floor houses a permanent exhibition of portraits and memorabilia connected with George Sand. Scheffer's studio has also been reconstructed, and the exhibit relates to many aspects of the literary and artistic life of the 19thC. There is a wonderfully romantic garden with many unusual flowering bushes and plants.

★★★ Villette, Parc de la (Cité des Sciences et de l'Industrie)

30 av. Corentin Cariou, 19e. ☎ 01-36-68-29-30. Open 10am–6pm. Closed Mon. Admission charged. Wheelchair access. Métro: Porte-de-la-Villette, Corentin-Cariou.

A former cattle market and abattoir district at the intersection of the Canal de l'Ourcq and the Canal St-Denis, at the extreme northeast corner of Paris, La Villette is the largest science-and-industry museum in Europe and has recently completed some major projects.

La Villette

The area, including the Villette Basin, has now emerged as a futuristic park and museum complex covering 55 hectares (136 acres). The steel-and-glass frontage of the Cité is 3 times the size of the **Pompidou Center.** Established in the late 1980s, it now includes 3 aquariums, a jazz club, La Géode (a 1,000 sq. meter, 180° cinema), a planetarium, a special-effects cinema, a submarine, a science and technology museum, a museum for children (Cité des Enfants), the Cité de la Musique, and plently of trees and grassy areas. At the 1,000-seat Aquarium restaurant, you can eat and watch fish at the same time.

La Cité de la Musique (City of Music): The Cité de la Musique, designed by Christian de Portzamparc, took 11 years to finish and cost almost $200 million. It includes the Conservatoire National de Musique, which relocated here from cramped surroundings in the 8ᵉ, and its museum, with its impressive collection of instruments, including some exquisite harpsichords and spinets. There are also a library, a music school, and concert halls with a regular music program.

La Cité des Enfants (Children's Museum): This is quite simply the most exciting museum for children of all ages in the city of Paris. Opened in 1992, there are 2 spaces—one for ages 3 to 5, and another for ages 6 to 12. Included here are a 20-square-meter (24-sq.-yd.) ant farm, a butterfly greenhouse, robots, interactive televisions, waterplay areas (kids are provided with aprons), and the Techno Cité, where children are given a chance to understand the workings of machines and computers. Visits are 1½ hours.

Vincennes, Bois de

To the east edge of Paris, beyond the Périphérique.

This great open space of woodland lies to the southeast of Paris at the opposite pole to the **Bois de Boulogne.**

It is a little larger (995ha) and a little less fashionable than its counterpart and yet in no way inferior. See **Château de Vincennes** below.

Vincennes, Château de

Avenue de Paris, 94300 Vincennes. ☎ 01-43-28-15-48. Guided tours compulsory for both keep and chapel. Open Oct–Mar 10am–5pm, Apr–Sept 10am–6pm. Métro: Château-de-Vincennes. RER: Vincennes.

The Château de Vincennes is made up of a series of buildings of different periods, parts of which have served at various times as royal residence, prison, porcelain factory, and arsenal. The main entrance is approached across a vast moat, and the whole place has a rather forbidding aspect that mirrors its grim history. Henry V of England died in the keep in 1422, and in 1944 the Germans executed 26 members of the Resistance, who had blown up part of the castle and set fire to one of the pavilions. The **keep** (*donjon*)—the only medieval example near Paris—houses a small museum of the castle's history. However, it will be closed for restoration work for approximately 5 years.

Opposite the keep is a Gothic chapel, the **Sainte-Chapelle,** which was founded by Charles V in 1379, and modeled on the one of the same name on the **Ile de la Cité.** It has some fine stonework and magnificent stained-glass windows. Both chapel and keep can only be seen with a guide. To the south of the keep and chapel are 2 17thC **pavilions** facing each other across a courtyard. Louis XIV spent his honeymoon in one of these buildings in 1660.

The restoration of the château was begun on the order of Napoléon III and continued spasmodically for a century. It is still not complete.

Bois de Vincennes: Enclosed by Philippe Auguste in the 12thC as a royal hunting ground, the Bois de Vincennes was made into a park for the citizens of Paris by Louis XV and was given to the city by Napoléon III in 1860. Since then, many inroads have been made into it, and much of the greenery has been lost. In recent years, however, the city of Paris has started to reclaim some of the lost parkland; thousands of trees have been planted and new avenues laid out.

Starting at the château and traveling clockwise, you come first to an attractive floral garden, the **parc floral** (Esplanade du Château de Vincennes, ☎ 01-43-43-92-95; open daily from 9:30am, closes Apr–Sept 8pm, Oct and Mar 6pm, Nov–Feb 5pm; admission charged). An important visitor attraction these days, this garden—as well as being planted with an interesting variety of flora—has a lake, an excellent children's play area, a butterfly farm, a restaurant, and riding stables. Flower shows are held regularly, and there is a busy program of entertainment for children (clowns, puppets, magic) and adults (jazz, choral singers, popular events).

Beyond the theater to the east is the **Lac des Minimes,** which has 3 islands, a restaurant, boating facilities, and the garden of the **School of Tropical Agronomy,** with its Oriental touches and its temple commemor-ating the Indo-Chinese killed in World War I.

Turning south you come to the **Ecole du Breuil** (a school of horticulture), with more lovely gardens and an arboretum. Close by is the **Hippodrome de Vincennes,** a racecourse where you are more likely to find trotting races than the flat-racing and steeplechases of the Bois de Boulogne.

A walk east through the woods will bring you to **Lac Daumesnil,** a popular boating place with a plush cafe-restaurant on one of its two islands. On the south bank is the **Temple Bouddhique** (Buddhist temple), which contains the largest effigy of Buddha in Europe, made of glass fiber and covered with gold leaf.

On the north side of the lake is the largest of the Paris zoos, the **Parc Zoologique de Paris** (53 av. St-Maurice, ☎ 01-44-75-20-10; open 9am–6pm; métro: Porte Dorée, St-Mandé-de-Tourelles). Here you can see elephants, bison, kangaroos, peacocks, and many other animals and birds roaming in natural-looking sur-roundings. There are 2 cafes and a huge artificial rock from the top of which you have an excellent view over the Bois to the east and Paris to the west.

See also the **Musée des Arts d'Afrique et d'Océanie,** which is close by and merits a detour, especially for the aquarium.

★★★ Vosges, place des
4ᵉ. Métro: St Paul, Chemin-Vert.

The oldest square in Paris is also arguably the most beau-tiful. It was built on the orders of Henry IV, who wished to create a square suitable for ceremonial occasions, but it was not finished until 1612, 2 years after his death. Planned as a single unit of matching facades, it was begun with the King's Pavilion on the south side, which is counterbalanced to the north by the Queen's Pavilion. The buildings are constructed of red brick and pale gold stone, with an arcade at ground level in which are a number of shops and cafes—try Ma Bourgogne (no. 19) at the northwest corner.

In its solid, quiet elegance, place des Vosges, like the rest of the **Marais** in which it is situated, is rather uncharacteristic of the city of Paris.

The square had many distinguished residents. Madame de Sévigné was born at no. 1bis, Richelieu lived at no. 21, and Victor Hugo at no. 6, which is now a museum (see **Hugo, Maison de Victor**).

In the recently renovated garden enclosed by the square, where summer *fêtes* and duels once took place, children now play and lovers stroll. Fashionable Paris has long since moved westward, but place des Vosges retains an aristocratic patina.

Zadkine, Musée

100bis rue d'Assas, 6ᵉ. ☎ 01-43-26-91-90. Guided tour, by appointment, Tues 2:30pm. Open 10am–5:30pm. Closed Mon, holidays. Admission charged. Métro: Vavin, Notre-Dame-des-Champs.

Here is a collection of works by the Russian-born painter Ossip Zadkine, assembled in the home where he lived and worked from 1928 until his death in 1967. The house, studio, and garden are all crammed with Zadkine's creations, which display a remarkable range of styles, from his early primitive and cubist sculptures to the monumental work of later years. A second studio has been opened at the bottom of the garden and contains works by the artist's contemporaries.

PARIS FOR KIDS

IN THE CITY THAT IS REPUTED TO HAVE MORE GREEN space than London, an astonishing amount is in the form of small, well-tailored public gardens bristling with signs marked *Pelouse Interdite* (Keep off the grass). On the positive side, the larger parks offer pony and donkey rides and miniature farms, and Paris has many fun places for young visitors: zoos, museums, theaters, and circuses. A good way to find out what's on is to consult the weekly guides *l'Officiel des Spectacles* and *Pariscope*.

Best Bets for Kids

The single best place to take children is **La Cité des Sciences et de l'Industrie,** otherwise known as **La Villette.** This museum complex has different activities and spaces for children under 5 and for 7- to 11-year-olds, and many attractions—a submarine, a 180° cinema—guaranteed to thrill older children. Older children especially like the **Musée Grévin** (in Montmartre), the wax museum that now has effigies of Claudia Schiffer and Michael Jackson, among others. On the weekend try taking your children to the **Musée des Arts Forains,** where the replicas of old merry-go-rounds are enlivened by jugglers and musicians. And children—from toddlers to adolescents—are enraptured by the crocodile pit in the aquarium in the **Musée National des Arts d'Afrique et d'Océanie.**

Parks & Zoos

Kid-friendly parks include the charming **Jardin de Babylone** (rue de Babylone between rue Vaneau and rue du Bac), whose beautiful lawns, belonging to a nearby convent, are hidden behind a stone wall; the **Pré Catelan** in the **Bois de Boulogne;** and the grassy area close to the fountains in front of the **Palais de Chaillot.**

For parks with activities, the top of the list is the **Jardin d'Acclimatation** (open daily 10am–6pm, admission charged), which is a veritable children's paradise on the edge of the Bois de Boulogne (☎ 01-40-67-90-82). It offers enough distractions to please the most demanding youngster, including a puppet show, distorting mirrors, an archery range, miniature golf, and a small zoo. Kids will enjoy riding to it on a miniature train from Porte-Maillot (afternoons in July and Aug; Wed, Sat, and Sun afternoons in winter).

The **Bois de Vincennes** has boating lakes and the **best zoo** in Paris, with lots of wild animals (open daily 9am–6pm, admission charged). Its **Parc Floral** (☎ 01-43-43-92-95; open daily 9:30am–5pm winter, to 6pm in spring and fall, to 8pm in summer; admission charged) has an excellent range of play facilities—including a terrific, sculptural slide worthy of Disney—and a delightful butterfly farm.

Founded in 1794, and one of the oldest zoos in the world, the **zoo** in the **Jardin des Plantes** (☎ 01-40-79-30-00) boasts a prettily landscaped terrain and a collection of snakes, wild felines, and various other wildlife (open daily 9am–6pm admission charged). You can go through the whole zoo in about an hour. It has a good crêperie, too.

The **Buttes-Chaumont** (☎ 01-42-40-88-66) has dramatic scenery, grass you can walk on, roller-skating, and donkey rides. Although a little off the beaten track, this park is worth a detour. It's a bit hilly and hard to negotiate with a stroller, but it's full of nice areas to sit and picnic. It also has an artificial mountain and lake, a waterfall cave, and a mini ferryboat.

The **Champ-de-Mars** has a playground for roller-skating and skate-boarding. There are also pony rides and puppet shows, and a lovely old-fashioned merry-go-round. This is worth a detour when you're visiting the nearby Tour Eiffel.

The excellent **Luxembourg** gardens are ideally located for a respite from your visit to the **Latin Quarter.** It has donkey rides, a pond to sail rented toy boats, old-fashioned swings, and a large marionette theater. An enclosed play area reserved for parents and children under 6 has a paying entrance, but wonderful things to ride on and climb. And once you're in, your children are in relative security. It's a spacious park, but very crowded on sunny weekends.

The **Parc Montsouris** is another elegant park to the south of the city. Somewhat hilly, it boasts the best layout for children on the Left Bank. Unlike the Luxembourg gardens, the closed-off play areas are free and arranged by age; they are nestled near the lake. A duck-filled artificial lake is here, too, so bring along the leftover rolls from your breakfast tray.

The small but imaginative **Jardin des Enfants aux Halles** (105 rue Rambuteau, 1ᵉʳ, ☎ 01-45-08-07-18; métro: Les Halles) has tunnels and mountains as well as slides in the area in front of the church of St-Eustache near the Forum des Halles. For 7- to 11-year-olds, it's open Tuesday, Thursday, and Friday 9am to noon, and 2pm to 6pm; Wednesday and Saturday 10am to 6pm; Sunday 1pm to 6pm. For younger children and parents, it's open Saturday morning. The park is closed in bad weather. Minimal admission is charged, and reservation can be made on site. Its staff speaks English. It's a great place to go before taking the family for a pizza lunch across the way at the very kid-friendly **Chicago Meatpackers** (8 rue Coquillière, 1ᵉʳ, ☎ 01-40-28-02-33; métro: Les Halles), where a toy train runs overhead and magicians give shows in a special roped-off kids-play area.

Also in the center of Paris is the **Tuileries,** which has small play areas, donkey rides, puppet shows, and a lovely model-boat pond. Some of the children's activities are occasionally closed as the park is undergoing extensive remodeling through 1996. In summer, a full-sized fairground moves in.

Whether or not you plan to go into the **Cité des Sciences** (see below), the **Parc de la Villette** is a truly fascinating place to visit, with 10 thematic gardens— Garden of Mirrors, Bamboo, Wind, etc.—running from the Cité de la Musique at one end (Métro: Porte de Pantin) to La Grande Halle de la Villette at the other. There are indoor activities at the **Cité des Enfants** (see below), so plan your visit here with plenty of time to see everything.

Special Museums, Attractions & Workshops for Kids

The **Pompidou Center** (rue Rambuteau, 4ᵉ; métro: Rambuteau) has the advantage of combining plenty to interest adults and kids. Inside, there's a **vidéothèque** and a **children's workshop** (L'Atelier des Enfants. ☎ 01-44-78-49-17; open for children 6–12, Wed, Sat, and school holidays, 1:30–5:30pm; admission charged). Just outside the center, in the pedestrianized Place Kandinsky, is a decorative (that is, not for wading) pool that contains a number of larger-than-life, brightly-colored sculptures. This is a good place for a brief rest.

For a creepy kind of old-fashioned fun, especially for preteens and teens, no place beats the **Musée Grévin** (10 blvd. Montmartre, 9ᵉ, ☎ 01-42-46-13-26; métro: rue Montmartre; open daily 1–7pm, 10am–7pm during school holidays; admission charged). Its very convincing waxworks—everyone from Napoléon to Michael Jackson—will fascinate older children. There's also a 1900s "spectacle of illusion" and a conjuring show in the theater, all within a glorious building. Very good value.

For teenagers, there's a smaller but equally fascinating **branch of the Grévin** at the **Forum des Halles** (Musée du Forum des Halles, Grand Balcon, 1ᵉʳ, ☎ 01-40-26-28-50; métro: Les Halles; open Mon–Sat 2–6pm, closed Sun and public holidays; admission charged), which concentrates on scenes from Belle Epoque Paris.

Other museums that children would especially enjoy include the following:

The **Musée National des Arts et Traditions Populaires** (☎ 01-44-17-60-70) displays everyday French objects, including toys, from past centuries. Admission charged.

The **Palais de la Découverte** (☎ 01-40-74-80-00) is a science museum with a planetarium. Admission charged.

The **Musée de l'Armée** (Army Museum) at **Les Invalides** (☎ 01-45-55-37-70). Admission charged.

The **Musée des Techniques** (Technical museum ☎ 01-40-27-23-31) has push-button working models of machines. Admission charged. The museum is closed for renovation until 1997.

The **Musée de la Marine** has attractions for children 8 to 11 (☎ 01-45-53-31-70). Admission charged.

The museum not to miss is the **Parc de la Villette**, where the Cité des Sciences et de l'Industrie is based. Don't be put off by the rather dry-sounding name: La Villette includes the new **Techno Cité,** for children 11 and older, which is a kind of hands-on initiation to technology, as well as a **planetarium** and a real **submarine** inside which kids can walk around. The **Géode** offers a panoramic cinematic experience for children 3 to 12; the new **multimedia film** is full of wonderful special effects, projected inside a space-age dome (open 10am–6pm daily, except Mon; admission charged). The **Cité des Enfants** features floors you can bounce on, sound waves you can see on a screen, a whole room of water-play (they hand out plastic aprons), and a 180-square-foot **ant farm** (☎ 01-40-05-72-23 or 01-36-68-29-30 for recorded information).

Theaters, Movies, Circuses & Other Events

A list of movies and circuses can be found in the **"Pour les Jeunes"** section of *l'Officiel des Spectacles.*

There's more than a good chance of catching a favorite movie while in Paris, as there are more than 200 movie theaters; many of them screen films in English (advertised as V.O.—*version originale*).

"Experiences" & Thrills

Most older children enjoy climbing the **Tour Eiffel, Tour Montparnasse, Arc de Triomphe, Notre-Dame, Sacré-Coeur, Panthéon,** and **Arche de la Défense** (see "Sights & Attractions") or, by contrast, plunging underground into the **Egouts** (sewers) or the **Catacombs**—but the latter, with its thousands of skulls, is not for the young or squeamish.

Disneyland Paris

Boîte Postale 100, F-77777 Marne-La-Vallée CEDEX 4. Hotel reservations from the USA: 407-W-DISNEY. Reservations in Paris: ☎ 01-60-30-60-30. Tickets on sale at the Bureau de Tourisme; 1 admission price gives access to everything within the park except for the shooting gallery; free for children under 3. Open summer 9am–11pm; winter 10am–6pm. Times and dates of parades and fireworks displays will also vary according to season. Check with Paris Bureau de Tourisme or by calling the reservations number.

The experience to cap it all, if time allows, is of course Disneyland Paris. The RER takes you all the way there in 40 minutes. If you've never been to a Disneyland before, don't miss it. The cost of staying at a hotel here is high, so if you're comfortable with your Paris accommodations, keep them, and use the RER to get to the park. It's cheap and fast. Either way, get through those gates very early or plan to stay until 11pm (in summer); the lines will be shorter then.

The spectacular **Disney parade** brings the streets almost to a standstill each afternoon as a hundred costumed characters pass down **Main Street USA** on carnival floats like you've never seen before.

Some Hints: Avoid admission lines by buying your tickets in advance, either from the Disney Store (44 ave des Champs-Élysées, 8ᵉ, ☎ 01-45-61-45-25), RER stations and other outlets, or from the Office du Tourisme. Two- or three-day tickets are cheaper.

There are some decent meals to be had here, but you can spend up to 2 hours eating them. This is one time when fast food may make more sense.

At **City Hall,** the first large building on the left of Main Street USA, is the **visitor information center.** Here you can pick up a free copy of a **detailed site guide and map,** which is exactly what you need to find your way around.

The parades are worth taking time out to see—but while these are going on, it's a good time to get onto some of the rides without waiting too long. Each day, a **massive afternoon parade** gets under way, and thousands of people stop to wave at the larger-than-life colorful characters as they roll past. A **fireworks display** precedes a **night-time parade** of floats lit with thousands of tiny lights.

Getting There

By Train: RER trains (line A4) stop at Marne LaVallée/Chessy, outside the main gates, and delivers visitors from Paris in 40 minutes. The same station will be served by the TGV (*train grande vitesse*), providing fast links to and from Brussels, London, Lille, and other main cities in France.

By Car: From Paris, take Route A4 (the road to Reims), due east from the city; take exit 14 and follow the signs to the resort.

From the Airports: There are direct shuttle buses from both Orly and Roissy-Charles-de-Gaulle (the latter also a 15-minute TVG link).

Parking: Disneyland has visitor parking for 11,500 cars, and the charge is not expensive. A moving walkway will sweep you from the parking lot along toward the main gates.

Where to Stay

If you're planning to do the park from dawn to dusk, then stay in one of the Disneyland hotels, if you can—it's part of the fun. All are very close, and the farther ones are served by a never-ending stream of complimentary buses. Each hotel is designed around a different, quintessentially American theme—from the luxury of the **Disneyland Hotel** to the ruggedness of the

Hotel Cheyenne to the pioneering log cabins of **Camp Davy Crockett.** Reservation inquiries: in the United States, call ☎ 407/W-DISNEY; from other countries, call Disneyland Paris at ☎ 33/01-60-30-60-30.

Planning Your Trip

If you're staying at one of the hotels, check in around midday, and spend the afternoon enjoying the resort. The hotels have various attractions, from kids' play areas to shops, bars, tennis courts, and skating rinks. There's a golf course, and four of the six hotels have indoor pools (one of the best—with water slides and more—is in the hotel called the **Davy Crocket Ranch,** which also has pony and horseback riding). Have dinner at **"Buffalo Bill's Wild West Show"**—take in the early show, at 6:30pm, and don't forget to reserve ahead (see Festival Disney, below). Spend the rest of the evening taking in **Festival Disney,** with it's music, shops, and street entertainers (see below). Then use the whole next day to see the park.

Mammals, Birds & Fish . . .

At the **Musée National des Arts Africains et Océaniens** at the **Bois de Vincennes,** there's a splendid aquarium and some crocodiles, too.

Ferme Georges-Ville is a 12-acre farm where you can watch the cows, goats, and donkeys graze—though you can't pet them—at Bois de Vincennes (Route du Pesage, 12ᵉ; open Mar–Oct, Sat–Sun 10am–7pm; Nov–Feb, Sat–Sun 10am–5pm; admission charged).

Rides

River trips are also popular with the young (see "Useful Telephone Numbers & Addresses" in "The Basics"). The canal trip organizers, however, will often not accept young children.

The **Centre International de l'Automobile,** in Pantin to the east of Paris, is well worth a trip for any child old enough to handle a simulator (☎ 01-48-10-80-00).

Sports

For information about sports, including roller-skating and cycling, see "Staying Active," particularly for details of the gigantic **Aquaboulevard leisure center** (4 rue Louis-Armand, 15ᵉ, ☎ 01-40-60-10-00; métro: Balard, Porte de Versailles), where you might easily spend a whole day.

STAYING ACTIVE

For details on all aspects of sports, including major spectator events, contact **Allô Sports** (☎ 01-42-76-54-54; Mon–Fri 9am to 7:30pm). Some facilities are also listed in the weekly magazines *L'Officiel des Spectacles* and *Pariscope*. See also "Spectator Sports," in this chapter.

Sports A to Z

Aerobics

Aerobics—including high/low impact, body sculpting, cardio-funk, and step—are offered at the **American Church,** 65 quai d'Orsay, 7°étro: Invalides, ☎ 01-47-53-04-56). Classes are in English and cost 40F a class.

Biking

Paris has a love/hate affair with biking. Though cycle-racing is a French passion—culminating in the annual **Tour de France,** which finishes in Paris in July—and in spite of the fact that an estimated 100,000 2-wheelers take to the streets of the city daily, the city has a rough time accommodating cyclists. The last official bike route that ran through the city streets siphoned bikers precariously between the bus and car lanes—guaranteeing a hair-raising ride—and was almost immediately abandoned by mutual consent.

For visitors interested in renting a bike for a day, contact **La Maison du Vélo** (11 rue Fénélon, 10°, ☎ 01-42-81-24-72; métro: Gare du Nord, Poissonière; cost Mon–Fri 150F, Sat–Sun 260F. A deposit of 1,500F is charged). For general inquiries, get in touch with the **Fédération Française du Cyclisme** (5 rue de Rome, Bâtiment Jean Monnet, 93561 Rosny-sous-Bois Cedex, ☎ 01-49-35-69-00).

If you want to peddle around on your own, your best bet is to stay off the streets and hit one of the city's

2 main parks—the **Bois de Boulogne** on the west and the **Bois de Vincennes** on the east. Both of them offer some 4-star attractions: boating lakes, places to dine, spectacular woodlands—and a zillion vendors selling balloons and whirligigs. The Bois de Vincennes is somewhat less hectic and also has France's largest zoo, a 14thC château, a magnificent floral park, and a nifty children's playground that includes a truly spectacular multislide.

For the Bois de Vincennes, rent a bike near the entrance of the Parc Floral (no phone; July–Sept, daily 9am–7pm; Oct–June, Mon–Fri 9am–7pm, Sat 9am–1pm and 2pm–7pm). Rates start at 28F per hour. Scores of dirt trails crisscross the 2,300 acre park, none of it particularly hilly. There are 2 lakes you can aim for—Lac Daumensnil and Lac des Minimes; the latter is more secluded. Many bikers stick to the shaded paths that run along the canals. A cycling track (6.6km/4 miles around) invites more serious cyclists. You can follow the paths to the château, but the traffic gets fairly heavy and you'll have trouble avoiding it.

Bikes can also be rented in the Bois de Boulogne, behind the Relais du Bois, route de Suresnes. For times and rates, see above information on the Bois de Vincennes.

Interested in taking a biking tour through the city? **Paris à Velo, C'est Sympa!** offers 5-speed Arrow bikes and an unhurried, 3-hour, 10- to 15- mile tour of some of the city's safer thoroughways. Tours include sites of historical or architectural interest—a Salvation Army building designed by Corbusier, the Canal St-Martin, or Chinatown, for example. Tours are conducted in English. Contact this touring company at 9 rue Jacques Coeur, 4e (☎ 01-48-87-60-01, métro: Bastille). Three-hour daytime tours: 150F; 130F for under age 26. Evening tours: 170F; 150F for under age 26. Membership fee: 20F. Prices include bike rental.

The SNCF Train Plus Vélo scheme (☎ 01-30-41-84-32) allows you to make a train journey and then have the use of a waiting bicycle on arrival, from one of a number of centers including those as far afield as Fontainebleau and Rambouillet. Bicycles can also be rented from Paris-Vélo (Rent-A-Bike), 2 rue Fer-á-Moulin, 5e (☎ 01-43-37-59-22)

Health Clubs

Although there are many health clubs in Paris, most are open to members only—and day fees can run upwards of 150F. Many larger hotels now have saunas, pools, and fitness facilities for guests.

If you're serious about working out, it's worth the trip to the the 11ᵉ arrondissement to check out the 6,000-square-foot **Weider Gym.** Built along the lines of high-tech US gyms—most Parisian gyms are more geared for beginners and intermediates—Weider features 180 Gerva Sport Weight lifting stations, as well as an advanced selection of stationary bikes, stair machines, rowing machines, and cardiovascular fitness machines. It's located at 49bis rue Sedaine, 11ᵉ (☎ 01-47-00-66-88; métro:Voltaire or Breguet-Sabin).The fee is 70F a day. Open Monday through Friday, 7:30am to 10pm; Saturday 8am to 7pm; Sunday 8am to 5pm.

Roller-Skating

With their caps turned backwards and their pants big enough to accommodate a couple of friends, Parisian teenagers have taken to roller-skating, Rollerblading, and skateboarding with the same enthusiasm as their American counterparts. There are a number of outdoor roller-skating and skateboarding *pistes;* good spots include the place des Invalides, the shaded walkways of the Bois de Boulogne, and the big esplanade flanking the Palais de Chaillot. Of all of these, the Palais de Chaillot is the place to watch hardline inliners put on a show. You can rent Rollerblades and the protective equipment that goes along with them at **La Maison du Patin,** 21 rue des Quatres Cheminées, Boulogne (☎ 01-46-08-29-27; métro: Marcel Sembat; Mon–Fri 30F per day, Sat–Sun 80F per day. Closed all day Sun and Mon morning. Deposit: 1,300F).

Swimming

Paris has a number of excellent municipal pools, details of which can be obtained from **Allô Sports** (☎ 01-42-76-54-54) or by looking in the telephone directory under *Piscines.* Not all pools are open all day. Public schools are closed on Wednesday, so pools are often busiest then.

The massive if somewhat raucous leisure center **Aquaboulevard** (4 rue Louis Armand, 15ᵉ, ☎ 01-40-60-10-00; métro: Balard; open Mon–Thurs 9am–11pm, Fri 9am–midnight, Sat 8am–midnight, Sun 8am–11pm) offers much more than just swimming: Imagine a sprawling acquatic park with a wave machine, a water cannon, giant slides, and special water games for children, as well as aerobics, bowling, billiards, golf, a gymnasium, a health club, massage, a solarium, squash, tennis, and yoga.

One of the city's better pools is the **Piscine des Halles** (10 pl. Rotonde, 1ᵉʳ, ☎ 01-42-36-98-44; métro: Les Halles; open Mon 11:30am–8pm, Tues, Thurs, Fri 11:30am–10pm, Wed 10am–7pm, Sat–Sun 9am–5pm). The racing lanes here are a full 2 meters wide, making passing easier and attracting some of the city's most serious lap clockers. Not a place to splash around in, but if getting a good workout in a huge (50m by 20m) pool of power swimmers is your idea of an afternoon, this is the place to come.

The **Piscine Reuilly** (13 rue de Hénard, 12ᵉ, ☎ 01-40-02-08-08; métro: Montgallet; open Mon 11:30am–1pm, Tues and Fri 7–8am and 11:30am–1pm, Wed 7–8am and 11:30am–5:30pm, Thurs 11:30am–1pm and 4:30–10pm, Sat 10:30am–5pm, Sun 8am–5:30pm) is a bit off the beaten track, but modern and clean, with windows on 3 sides and a view over the park.

While it's not municipal, the skylit pool on the top floor of the Japanese-owned **Hôtel Nikko de Paris** (61 quai Grenelle, 15ᵉ, ☎ 01-40-58-20-00; métro: Charles Michels) offers a fairly luxurious but not particularly spacious place to swim while watching the sun go down on an early evening. Open to all, it's located along the Seine behind the Eiffel Tower. The fees (40F) are a bit higher than at your average pool, but it's usually empty.

Tennis

Municipal courts (for example in the Luxembourg gardens) and many private ones are available. To play in the Luxembourg Gardens, obtain a free **Paris Tennis card** from **Allô Sports** (☎ 01-42-76-54-54), and make reservations through minitel. Rates are 34F per hour, 50F for a floodlit court, and 72F for a covered court.

General information on tennis is available from Allô Sports (☎ 01-42-76-54-54), **Fédération Française de Tennis** (☎ 01-47-43-48-00), or the **Ligue de Tennis de Paris** (☎ 01-44-14-67-89). The **Stade Français** club (Porte de St-Cloud, 2 rue du Cdt. Guilbaud, 16ᵉ, ☎ 01-46-51-66-53) is open to visitors, although you have to be a member to play. Courts can also be rented from **Gymnase Club, Tennis Flandrin** (92 blvd. Flandrin, 16ᵉ, ☎ 01-47-55-89-70; métro: Porte Dauphine). Rates are 70F for morning and afternoon sessions, 140F from noon–2pm and 5–10pm. Membership is not required.

Walking & Rambling

Historical and cultural guided walks around Paris take place year-round. See **Randonnées Pédestres** in *L'Officiel des Spectacles* or *Pariscope*. For general information, contact the **Fédération Française de la Randonnée Pédestre** (64 rue de Gergovie, 14ᵉ, ☎ 01-45-45-31-02).

Spectator Sports

Conveniently, the 16ᵉ contains the major tennis and soccer/rugby stadiums: **Roland-Garros** (2 av. Gordon Bennett, 16ᵉ, ☎ 01-47-43-48-00) and **Parc des Princes** (24 rue du Cdt. Guilbaud, 16ᵉ, ☎ 01-42-88-02-76), where such events as the French Open Tennis Championships (either May or June) take place. (See "Calendar of Events" in "The Basics.")

The main arena for spectator sport is the **Palais Omnisports de Paris-Bercy** (2 blvd. de Bercy, 12ᵉ, ☎ 01/43-42-01-23) near the Gare de Lyon, where you can see anything from basketball and judo to motorcycle racing and show jumping.

The principal racecourses (hippodromes) are at **Longchamp** (Bois de Boulogne) and **St-Cloud** (12km/8 miles west of Paris) for flat-racing, and **Auteuil** (Bois de Boulogne; métro: Porte d'Auteuil; Mon, Thurs) for steeple-chasing.

Other courses in or comfortably near Paris are found at **Chantilly, Evry, Enghien, Maisons-Laffitte,** and **Vincennes.** Check details in the sports section of the Wednesday edition of *Le Figaro* newspaper.

See the "Calendar of Events" in "The Basics" for the most important of the annual meetings.

SHOPPING

P ARIS GAVE THE WORLD THE BOUTIQUE, THE SMALL
specialty shop that still embodies the intimate character of Parisian shopping. Entire *quartiers* are blanketed
with boutiques, specializing in everything from antiques
to zippers. There are some very good department stores,
but boutiques exhibit the individuality, variety, and
flair that makes Paris Europe's most seductive city for
shopping.

What to Buy

Impeccable tailoring, luxurious fabrics, and a chic that
all the world looks to for direction are epitomized in
the haute couture collections created by a handful of
Parisian designers. But haute couture in Paris is like a
diesel engine pulling a long train of fashion offshoots
from designer ready-to-wear to knock-offs in the
sentier (the garment district, mostly located in the 3rd
arrondissement).

Children's clothing in Paris is dominated by an
upmarket group of chain stores (**Jacadi, Prénatal,
Sergent Major**), which offer sturdy, well-designed
clothes, with a few luxury children's brands (**Bonpoint,
Tartine et Chocolat**) as the icing on the cake.

Aided by a rich tradition of decorative arts and culinary history, the French have picked up on the art of
staying home, eating in, and feathering their nests with
a vengeance. Next to women's fashions, accessories for
the home—everything from exquisite professional
cookware to antique linens, Provençal pottery, scented
candles, and engraved stationery—are especially close
to the French heart. Over the past decade, a bumper
crop of new boutiques catering to cooking and deco-
rating needs has emerged, and many of them are as
cutting-edge as the city's fashions.

Where to Go

Shops are woven into the fabric of Paris, so going shopping often requires a good deal of walking. Nonetheless, there are areas specializing in certain products: the open-air bookstalls on the Left Bank, for example; the designer-clothing shops lining the avenue Montaigne; or the art galleries tucked away in the Marais.

Shopping Districts & Streets

While the densest concentration of stores and boutiques can be found in the following areas, don't forget to explore others. Try wandering among the fabric shops, discount boutiques, and resale shops near the Abbesses métro stop up to Montmartre. Or, at the opposite extreme, stroll among the designer boutiques tucked under the colonnaded arcade of the Palais Royal.

Boulevard Haussman   This busy avenue behind the Opéra is where you'll find, cheek by jowl, the city's 2 largest department stores, **Galeries Lafayette** and **Au Printemps.** This whole area is full of big stores: **Prisunic** is here, and **Marks and Spencer** is across the street. Hence this is a good place for one-stop shopping. Down the rue de la Paix is the **place Vendôme,** where all of the city's mega-priced fine jewelers are concentrated. In between are many shops that are either overpriced or truly designed for tourists. There are some duty-free shops, however, like **Raoul et Curly,** that have good bargains on perfumes and beauty products.

Avenue Montaigne   As real estate goes, this is right up there with Madison Avenue and Milan's Via Montenapoleone. Avenue Montaigne is high-fashion heaven, though sometimes it looks more like a mausoleum: one giant empty marble palace after another. Couture was born in this part of town—in the so-called golden triangle—and this is where the **top designer houses** still are, sided by stores full of pricey women's shoes, handbags, and accessories. If you're particularly well dressed, a visit here can be soothing in an elaborately pantomimed way.

Place des Victoires   This wide, circular place is a mecca for a variety of **cutting-edge designs,** from clothes to shoes to decorative objects for the home. Every other person you run into is a magazine editor scouting finds. The best shops crowd the square, running over into the nearby **Gallery Vivienne,** and the adjacent **rue Etienne Marcel.**

Rue Faubourg St-Honoré Start at **rue Cambon,** where the Laura Ashley shop is, and stroll straight down the length of this street. When you reach the guards surrounding the Elysée Palace, the ride's almost over. On the way are a wealth of **upscale Parisian fashions, stationery stores,** and **leather-goods shops.**

Les Halles The glassed-in, multistory **Forum** that sits in the middle of this pedestrians-only shopping area is Paris's version of an indoor shopping mall, with none of the *faux* cheer. Just masses of kids from the *banlieu* (suburbs) who get squeezed out of the RER train 3 floors below you with astonishing alacrity. Les Halles (pronounced *Lay Al*) is full of untempting stores selling jeans, cheapo gadjets, and not much else. On the outskirts of Les Halles, clustered around the nearby **Etienne Marcel métro stop,** are a trove of internationally **famous kitchenware shops.**

Rue de Passy Home to a crowd of up-market and **astronomically priced shops** catering to residents of one of Paris's most expensive neighborhoods, this 16th arrondissement locale is becoming more and more frequented by tourists and wealthy shoppers from all over the city.

Left Bank The tight crochet of streets hugging the river offers everything from **fine bookstores** to **designer shops** to **discount shopping.** The **rue du Pré-aux-Clercs** is especially good for **younger designer fashions;** look for more **elegant lingerie** and **leather goods** on the **rue des Sts-Pères.** This part of town is a pleasure to shop in not only because of the variety of stores and prices, but also because you have so many landmark cafes—the Flore and Deux Magots among them—to rest your feet when you're tired.

The Marais Here, tiny boutiques are scattered through some of the oldest streets in Paris. The main aorta is **rue des Francs Bourgeois,** which runs into the **Place des Vosges** and is sprinkled with an eclectic mix of boutiques selling **antique silver, jewelry,** and **sporty fashions** for men and women. Nothing brilliantly innovative, and a real dearth of designer wear, but some nice places for **gifts** and—and this is a real boon—most of these shops are **open on Sundays,** when the rest of the city is closed.

Auctions

Whether you're interested in browsing or actually buying, it's worth a trip to **Drouot** (9 rue Drouot, 9ᵉ. ☎ 01-48-00-20-20), Paris's most prestigious auction house. Items to be auctioned—from humble bargains to rare works of art—are on view the day before a sale in the auction house's 16 rooms. If you can't stick around for the auction itself (which usually takes place around 2pm), you can leave a sealed bid. Experts are always on hand and are for the most part extremely helpful. There are numerous catalogues on sale as well. A more than pleasant place to pass an afternoon and, surprisingly, not at all intimidating.

Fast Facts

Hours   Stores are open in general from Monday to Saturday, with the occasional smaller shops observing a traditional day of rest on Mondays. In general, store hours are from 9:30/10am to 6:30/7pm, though some department stores (Monoprix, for example) stay open later or are open at night once a week (often Thursday). Paris is far from shut down in August, though most boutiques stagger vacation periods sometime in late summer. Stores are virtually all closed on January 1, May 1, July 14, August 15th, and December 25.

"Duty Free"   You're better off buying certain products in the airport. In the duty-free shops at Orly and Charles-de-Gaulle airports, you will get a minimum discount of 20% on all items and up to 50% on liquor, cigarettes, and watches. Among the items on sale are crystal, cutlery, chocolates, luggage, wine, whisky, pipes and lighters, lingerie, silk scarves, perfume, knitwear, jewelry, cameras and equipment, cheeses, and antiques.

The drawbacks of airport shopping are that the selections are limited and, of course, you must carry your purchase with you onto the plane.

Sales   Look for the word *soldes* pasted in the windows. Traditionally, the big sale periods are January and July, when stores often knock 30% to 50% or more off prices.

Shipping   Many stores will ship for you, at a price; inquire about fees, duties, and insurance. The post office will, too—but remember that duties can be applicable on all sorts of items; and if you're doing the shipping yourself, you had best learn the regulations by calling the US customs office first. Your hotel concierge will usually be able to turn up the name of reliable shippers for you, too. If you're shipping a large piece of furniture from a dealer or the flea market, they'll find the shipper and take care of the paperwork.

Clothing Sizes   Clothing sizes vary in the U.S., the UK, and even between mainland European countries. When you can, try the clothes on.

Tax Refunds   If you've been in the country less than 3 months, you're entitled to a refund on the value-added tax (VAT) on purchases made in France to take home—under certain conditions.

These export discounts average 13%. You must spend at least 1200F in the same store, but food, wine, and tobacco don't count, and the refund is granted only on purchases you carry home with you. The big department stores have détaxe departments: make all your purchases in the store, then bring your sales receipts to the détaxe office and they will prepare one détaxe form for you.

Here's what you must do:

Show the clerk your passport to prove you're eligible for the refund. You will then be given an **export document in triplicate** (2 pink sheets and a green one), which you must sign. You'll also be given an **envelope addressed to the store.** Go early to your departure point, as there are often lines waiting at the booth marked **détaxe at French customs.** If you're traveling by train, go to the détaxe area in the station before boarding. You can't get your refund documents processed on the train. The refund booths are outside the passport checkpoints.

Only the person who signed the documents at the store can present them for refund. Give the 3 sheets to the **customs official,** who will countersign and hand you back the green copy. Save this in case problems arise about the refund. Give the official the envelope addressed to the store (be sure to put a stamp on the envelope). One of the processed pink copies will be mailed to the store for you. Remember, you must have the merchandise with you—keep it in an accessible place in your luggage as you will often be asked by the customs official to produce it. Usually you will be reimbursed by check in convertible French francs sent by mail to your home; sometimes the credit is made directly to a credit card account. If you don't receive your tax refund in 4 months, write to the store, giving the date of the purchase and the location where the sheets were given to the customs officials. Include a photo-copy of your green refund sheet.

U.S. Customs   You're allowed to bring back into the United States overseas purchases with a retail value up to $400, providing you have been out of the country at least 48 hours and you have not claimed similar exemptions within 30 days. After your duty-free $400 is reached, a tax of 10% is levied on the next $1,000 worth of items purchased abroad.

You pay no duties on antiques or art if they're at least 100 years old, even if they cost $4 million. In addition, you're allowed to send 1 gift a day to family or friends back home, so long as it's value doesn't exceed $50. Perfumes costing more than $5, liquor, cigarettes, and cigars can't be sent duty-free.

Shopping A to Z
Antiques

Whether you're a browser or intent on purchasing, Paris is one of the greatest antiques capitals of the world. Many dealers have stands at the **flea market at Clignancourt** (see "Flea Markets" on page 245). A number of small shops specializing in everything f rom archaeological finds to Art Deco furnishings are located in the **St-Germain Quarter,** especially around **rue Bonaparte** and **rue Jacob.** Antiques shops are also gathered at the following addresses:

Village Saint Paul
23-27 rue St-Paul, 4e. Métro St-Paul.
A collection of secondhand shops and less expensive antiques shops gathered in a hidden jumble of tiny streets and courtyards.

Le Louvre des Antiquaires
2 pl. du Palais-Royal, 1er. Métro: Palais-Royal.
A covered market housing 3 floors and some 250 dealers of fine antiques—very hushed and chichi.

Village Suisse
54 av. de la Motte-Picquet (at av. de Suffren), 15e. Métro: La Motte-Picquet-Grenelle.
More than 150 shops in a tiny village dotted with tiny landscaped squares. A wonderful place for weekend strolls.

Bookshops

Booklovers—whether fluent in French or not—will want to stroll the stalls of the *bouquinistes* that line the

river from the **Pont Royal** to the **Hôtel de Ville,**
open whenever the weather is nice. The Left Bank has
a number of beautiful bookshops—a few notable ones
even make strolling the boulevard St-Germain bear-
able. A few good addresses:

Gibert Jeune
5 pl. St-Michel, 5ᵉ. Métro: St-Michel.

A big general French bookstore that's an institution,
especially for French students. All kinds of everything.
If Woody Allen lived in Paris, he'd make a movie about
people meeting here.

W. H. Smith
248 rue de Rivoli, 1ᵉʳ. Métro: Concorde.

A general interest English-language store with a comprehensive selection of magazines and newspapers. Good
selection of recent paperbacks, and you can get the
Sunday *New York Times* here (which you cannot buy
on newsstands in Paris because of a deal they have with
the *Herald Tribune,* which they partly own), albeit days
late.

China, Glass & Silver

Au Bain Marie
10 rue Boissy d'Anglas 8ᵉ. Métro: Concorde.

Two floors of everything for the kitchen and table, from
silver coffee pots to Limoges porcelains to charmingly
embroidered linens.

Baccarat
30bis rue de Paradis, 10ᵉ. Métro: Château-d'Eau. Also at 11 pl. de la
Madeleine, 8ᵉ. Métro: Madeleine.

Makers of blown and engraved crystal for more than
200 years, Baccarat carries everything from tableware
to decorative glass objects to a new collection of glass-
and-metal furniture by Andrée Putman. The rue de
Paradis store is also the home of the firm's **museum,**
where the history of the decorative arts can be traced
through the displayed glassware, in chronological order. It's located on a street full of glassware and china
shops, but this same shop is where Baccarat has been
selling to France's finest homes since the 18thC. A
tonier store, recently refurbished by architect Yves
Taralon, is located on the place de la Madeleine. Baccarat
has dusted itself off in recent years—look at some of
the contemporary decorative items, such as the fat,
colorful little glass hearts, designed by Thomas Bastide.

Christofle
9 rue Royale, 8ᵉ. Métro: Madeleine.

Magnificent silver and silver-plated flatware and serving pieces in modern and retro patterns. Also decorative objects and gifts, including silver jewelry. Excellent tarnish-free silver-plated picture frames.

Dîners en Ville
27 rue de Varenne, 7ᵉ. Métro: Sèvres-Babylone.

A stylish boutique carrying everything from traditional faience to ultramodern colored glass to antique silver pieces—with old and new designs stunningly styled together throughout the shop.

Lalique
11 rue Royale, 8ᵉ. Métro: Madeleine.

Jeweler René Lalique founded this firm in the early part of the century, when it became synonymous with the Art Nouveau style. Today, the firm manufacturers some of the world's finest glassware, for the home and table, as well as a small collection of crystal jewelry, including the cabochon ring, originally designed by René Lalique in 1914, and now available in 14 colors.

Limoges-Unic
12 and 58 rue de Paradis, 10ᵉ. Métro: Château-d'Eau.

A one-stop shop for France's famed porcelain, glass, and silver—Limoges, Meissen, Baccarat, Daum, Christofle. They'll deliver anywhere.

Puiforcat
2 av. Matignon, 8ᵉ. Métro: Franklin-D-Roosevelt.

Founded in 1820, Puiforcat is one of Paris's oldest silversmiths, supplying monarchs and noble families for years. Early Puiforcat models—such as the egg cup designed for Napoléon—are in the Louvre. The company reached its zenith in the 1920s, when owner Jean Puiforcat created tea sets and cutlery today considered masterpieces of the Art Deco style. As exclusive as they come, Puiforcat is noted for its solid-silver flatware, in literally hundreds of patterns.

Cooking Supplies

Paris is a cook's heaven; no other city can compete with the array of food-related products for sale here. Department stores all have large cookware departments, but it's more fun to go directly to the major specialists. Be prepared to pay cash and ask for **shipping** and *détaxe* **information.**

Dehillerin

18 rue Coquillière, 1er. Métro: Etienne-Marcel.

It's perhaps the best restaurant supply house in the world, but also sells mostly—happily, sometimes grumpily—on a smaller scale. Look for copper casseroles and saucepans—without which any *batterie de cuisine* is incomplete—individual Le Creuset gratin dishes, and stainless-steel fish poachers. Excellent shipping service.

Kitchen Bazaar

11 av. du Maine, 15e. Métro: Gare-Montparnasse.

High design meets everything you could want in the way of high-tech kitchen equipment and accessories, from traditional jacquard dish towels to the latest in tableware. English stoneware teapots, great wall racks for pots, and state-of-the-art Marlux nutmeg grinders.

A. Simon

36 rue Etienne-Marcel, 2e. Métro: Etienne-Marcel, Les Halles.

Divided into 2 shops: one with metalware, knives, and electrical appliances; the other devoted to pottery, glassware, and a reasonable selection of porcelain. Individual butter ramekins, wooden honey dippers, traditional wide-mouthed Lyonnais salad bowls, as well as brasserie- and cafe-issue ceramic dishes, wine pitchers, water carafes, and cutlery.

Department Stores

Paris has a number of excellent department stores (**grands magasins**) where you can spend the day doing some one-stop shopping. Many offer special discounts for tourists and have staff geared to handling export documentation.

BHV

52-56 rue de Rivoli, 4e. Métro: Hôtel-de-Ville.

Excellent sporting goods, garden tools, books, music, and a dazzling array of hardware. A very good place to pick up that transformer you forgot to bring.

Le Bon Marché

5 rue de Babylone, 7e. Métro: Sèvres-Babylone.

Paris's tony left-bank department store—with a gourmet food store, a slew of eateries on the top floor, and everything else in between. The private-label women's collection is one of the smartest buys in Paris. The selection here isn't as vast as over at the majors—Galeries Lafayette and Au Printemps—but the looks are more fashionable. The closest thing to Barneys in Paris.

Galeries Lafayette

40 blvd. Haussmann, 9ᵉ. Métro: Chaussée-d'Antin. Also:
Montparnasse Centre, 14ᵉ. Métro: Montparnasse-Bienvenue.

A serious attempt to update its fashion image has succeeded in turning both branches of this store into trendy
fashion spots, with vast home furnishings departments
and a wide selection of porcelain, glassware, and cookware. A variety of good, slick ideas, and an abundance
of color. Fashion shows are held twice weekly from
April to October (obtain information and reservations
from hotel concierges or ☎ 01-48-74-02-30). Gener-
ous visitor discounts are available from time to time.
Call at the ground floor **Welcome Desk** to see what's
on offer.

Au Printemps

64 blvd. Haussmann, 9ᵉ. Métro: Havre-Caumartin, Auber.

Bigger than Galeries Lafayette by a smidge, with
women's ready-to-wear in one store and men's in
another. The magnificent stained-glass cupola is a historical monument. Wide range of lingerie, gourmet
boutiques, and a top-floor restaurant, the **Brasserie
Flo** (see "Dining"), renowned for its Art Nouveau
decor. Weekly fashion shows. A **free daycare center**
from 2pm to 7pm (2 hr. maximum) on Wednesday and
Saturday for children ages 2 to 9.

Samaritaine

19 rue du Pont Neuf, 1ᵉʳ. Métro: Pont-Neuf.

The original building along the Seine is classified a historical monument—but by now Samaritaine sprawls
all over the neighborhood: One of the problems with
shopping here is that whatever you are looking for is
inevitably across the street. A huge children's toy department has a **merry-go-round** your kids can enjoy,
while you struggle to find Batman. Samaritaine boasts
the best department store restaurant in the city—the
Toupary, with an unparalleled panoramic view over
the city. Have coffee and gaze.

Fashion

Children's Clothing

Exquisite layettes and hand-embroidered gowns can still
be found in Paris, but good children's fashions are
extremely expensive. The underwear in even the most
basic department stores—such as Monoprix—is very
good and well-priced for the quality.

Agnès B (Children's)
2 rue du Jour, 1er. Métro: Les Halles.

Designer basics for babies and kids to 14. The snap-front cardigans—mini versions of her adult staple—are practical and smart-looking.

Baby Dior
28 av. Montaigne, 8e. Métro: Franklin-D-Roosevelt.

Luxurious and pricey christening outfits, as well as beautifully elegant baby clothes for special occasions—they even have made-to-measure clothes for children under 8. The blue or pink terry baby robes aren't too expensive and make good gifts.

Bonpoint
65 rue de l'Université, 7e. Métro: Solférino.

The Rolls Royce of childrenswear—*tres comme il faut*. Beautiful and classic velvet Christmas outfits, as well as layettes, christening gowns, and preppy looks for future Ralph Lauren customers.

Petit Bateau
13 rue Tronchet, 8e. Métro: Madeleine.

Great underclothing and pajamas for babies and tod-dlers—including good cotton snap-crotch undershirts in a nice collection of solids and prints. A nice selection of affordable basics—pants, T-shirts—too.

Petit Faune
33 rue Jacob, 6e. Métro: St-Germain-des-Prés.

Lovely coordinated knit ensembles for babies, toddlers, and young children. Classic cableknit and other sweat-ers, both solid and patterned, in various styles. Prices are high. If you are looking for a reasonably-priced baby gift, ask to see the pajamas—they're in a drawer and cost less than much of what is displayed.

Men's Clothing

Parisians consider Italian clothing too fussy and English tailoring lacking a certain polish. French suits boast something in between—impeccable tailoring and a low-key chic. Nothing you'll find at stores in Paris is too original, and prices are rarely attractive, so this is a less fruitful vein to mine than women's clothing.

Agnès B Hommes
22 rue St-Sulpice, 6e. Métro: St-Sulpice.

The shirts here are interesting, with a number of attractive patterns in the weave. The leather jackets are gorgeous and priced accordingly.

APC
4 rue de Fleurus, 6ᵉ. Métro: St-Placide.

Using mostly British fabrics, Jean Touitou creates a trendy left-bank look that appeals to the capital's young media crowd.

Cerruti 1881
27 rue Royale, 8ᵉ. Métro: Madeleine.

Low-key, top-quality suits, and luxurious separates with exquisite tailoring and gorgeous Italian fabrics, many designed by designer Nino Cerruti himself.

Charvet
28 pl. Vendôme, 1ᵉʳ. Métro: Opéra.

A real old-fashioned gentleman's tailor, all wood paneling interior and soft-spoken sales help. Everybody from French presidents to Michael Jackson have been to this beautiful, 5-floor shop, which also carries some women's and children's clothes. Ready- and custom-made shirts and suits. The ribbon cufflinks set out in baskets on the main floor are a good inexpensive gift. The pajamas are as beautiful as the shirts.

Kenzo
3 pl. des Victoires, 1ᵉʳ. Métro: Sentier.

Good menswear that's more classic looking than Kenzo's reputation would suggest. A notable choice of large and tall sizes.

Lanvin
15 rue du Faubourg St-Honoré, 8ᵉ. Métro: Madeleine.

Classic elegance in a spacious, 5-floor store designed by Terence Conran. A little of everything, and one of the best-reputed made-to-measure suit departments in France. The women's shop is across the street.

Rykiel Homme
194 blvd St-Germain, 7ᵉ. Métro: St-Germain-des-Prés.

Young, trendy, and, oddly, very New York. From the ultrasimple, ultraluxurious black leather jacket to a good selection of sweaters.

Victoire Hommes
15 rue du Vieux Columbier, 6ᵉ. Métro: St-Sulpice.

The men's annex of the famous women's boutique, this small but well-stocked shop specializes in fine cotton shirtings by Hartford, sportswear, and some suits. A good spot for men looking for classical clothing with a subtle something more.

Women's Clothing
Designer Shops

Agnès B

6 rue du Jour, 1ᵉʳ. Métro: Les Halles.

The young French woman's concept of basics. Two floors of unfrilly separates, including leggings, trenches, and the famous snap-front tops at affordable prices.

A.P.C.

3 rue de Fleurus, 6ᵉ. Métro: St-Placide.

A color palette that ranges from black to tan and back again. Basics with a cutting edge, and some accessories, well priced, given where you are.

Azzedine Alaïa

7 rue du Moussy, 4ᵉ. Métro: Hôtel-de-Ville.

Women revere Alaia like they revere Yves St. Laurent, though probably not the same women. Skin-tight dresses in stretch fabrics exquisitely cut. The same address houses Alaia's lower-priced shop, where he sells collections that are at least a year old at 30% to 50% off.

Chanel

31 rue Cambon, 1ᵉʳ. Métro: Concorde.

The suit. The handbag. The perfume. The epitome of chic. Designer Karl Lagerfeld introduced everything from jeans to homeboy looks to the Chanel runways. Are you ready to pay $200 for a stretch headband? If you are, fight the busloads of Japanese tourists having their picture taken on the sidewalk outside and go for it.

Christian Dior

30 av. Montaigne, 8ᵉ. Métro: Franklin-D-Roosevelt.

This is really a humongous designer department store, all dove-grey velvet and glass. Knitwear, furs, linens, hats, menswear, handbags, childrenswear, and more—all under one roof. Great for gifts: head downstairs where there are a lot of surprisingly inexpensive silver-plated and ceramic items; the store will gift wrap your purchase and everyone will think you spent a fortune. Italian Gianfranco Ferre has been designing the women's line here since the late 1980s; his soigné suits and big evening dresses have put the home of the New Look back on the fashion map.

Christian Lacroix

73 rue du Faubourg St-Honoré, 8ᵉ. Métro: Concorde.

Lacroix unveiled the first new couture house in 20 years in Paris in the mid-1980s, revitalizing the industry. His ready-to-wear line is wildly inventive, and his wacky colors and fabric mixes, often bordering on kitsch, bring an upbeat punch to fashion.

Claude Montana
31 rue de Grenelle, 7e. Métro: Sèvres-Babylone.

Colors like boiled sweets and a cut that would have warmed Jane Jetson's heart. His short trench is a classic, likewise the A-line skirts.

Comme des Garçons
42 rue Etienne Marcel, 2e. Métro: Etienne Marcel.

Japanese designer Rei Kawakuba pioneered apocalyptic chic, and her designs still have a gloomy, fashion priestess air that not everyone is going to go for. Still, her work with fabric and her recent move into color and decoration have attracted new fans each season. Men's store at no. 40.

Gianni Versace
62 rue du Faubourg St-Honoré, 8e. Métro: Concorde.

A multistory palace with the whole Versace universe— the crazy patterns, sky-high skirts, the safety-pin skirts. Under all the show, there's fabulous craftsmanship and some of the best fabrics in the world. You can also find menswear and even housewares (towels, china) here.

Givenchy
8 av. George-V, 8e. Métro: Alma-Marceau.

Hip retro-master John Galliano just signed to design for this house, following the retirement of Hubert Givenchy.

Inès de la Fressange
14 av. Montaigne, 8e. Métro: Franklin-D-Roosevelt.

The aristocratic former Chanel model struck gold when she turned her hand to designing. The clothing here is around 30% cheaper than her top-price neighbors on the avenue Montaigne. Well-constructed basics, from colorful suits to pajamas to loafers, though the best of her collection is dressy weekend wear—tweed jackets, velvet jeans, snakeskin loafers. The store looks like a child's paintbox, with friendlier sales help than Paris usually boasts. Some good gifts among the small selection of linens and painted ceramics.

Irié
8 rue du Pré-aux-Clercs, 7e. Métro: St-Germain-des-Prés.

Surprisingly affordable prices for a smorgasbord of young fashion that runs the gamut from fur-trimmed suits to iridescent cocktail dresses. On a good street to browse for unusual fashion finds.

Haute Couture

If you're interested in buying a couture dress, get ready to spend $20,000. In addition, you'll almost surely have to spend a couple of weeks in town being fitted. You can't walk into the couture showings held twice-yearly in Paris: These are mainly for the press and valued clients. Start by contacting the couture house directly for an appointment. You can get the list of couturiers from the **Chambre Syndicale de la Haute Couture Parisienne** (☎ 01-42-66-64-44).

Around the world, *couture* has eased into the vernacular as a shorthand adjective to describe anything "ruinously luxurious"—from jeans to sunglasses to the priciest lines of ready-to-wear designers. In France, couture means none of these things. The Parisian *haute couture* is a precise body of roughly 20 fashion houses, vigilantly watchdogged by the 125-year-old Chambre Syndicale de la Haute Couture Parisienne. Chanel, Dior, and Givenchy are haute couture houses; Azzedine Alaïa isn't—any more than Giorgio Armani or Jean Paul Gaultier.

For years, Paris couture houses have straddled a never-never land between being a real business—selling handsewn creations to approximately 1,500 international clients who can afford them—and an artistic escape valve, through which designers unleash their imaginations. The business part is least important; as the apex of the fashion world's creativity, couture is the jewel in the crown—a talisman as potent to the French as the Royal Family is to the English.

Couture houses almost all lose money in themselves—but exist thanks to a trickle-down effect. They are the diesel engines pulling a profitable train of ready-to-wear, accessories, and perfumes.

What elevates couture to the ranks of art? As opposed to ready-to-wear, which is factory-made, couture outfits are created inside the 4 walls of a fashion house, in the *ateliers,* or workrooms, where seamstresses, led by the designer, build each dress by hand. Decoration is at a premium. For a couture collection, there are specialists in handmade fake jewels, shoemakers, feather makers, and dyers capable of getting 1 yard of fabric the precise shade of fuchsia for 1 pair of gloves. For one recent dress for the House of Christian Dior, François Lesage's fabled embroiderers put in 1,000 hours festooning the dress with bugle-beaded starfish, mother-of-pearl flowers, and rose-colored rhinestones.

Today, Paris's couture houses are all undergoing changes. Hubert Givenchy retired in 1995—though the cutting-edge British designer John Galliano has been hired to take his place. A few years ago, Yves St. Laurent sold his entire firm, lock, stock, and sewing machines, to the French state oil and gas concern Elf Sanofi—for nearly a quarter of a billion dollars. The French and everyone else are continually readying eulogies for the haute couture. But as Jacques Mouclier, president of the Chambre Syndicale de la Couture Parisienne, pointed out, "Thirty years ago the *L.A. Times* announced that couture was dead. People always ask, 'What's the point?' Personally, I have never understood why people are so eager for the couture to die."

Jean-Paul Gaultier

30 Faubourg St-Antoine, 12e. Métro: Bastille.

Fashion's *enfant terrible,* always breaking new ground. The sailor-striped knit tops (for men and women) are a classic that never go on sale. This is Gaultier's newly opened flagship store and carries his perfume, his furniture on wheels, his well-priced jeans line, and more.

Jil Sander

52 av. Montaigne, 8e. Métro: Franklin-D-Roosevelt.

Massive, marble, and cold, this is the Parisian flagship of the German designer. Working-women cotton to Sander's low-key, classic stylings, fabulous materials, and meticulous workmanship. The 1890 townhouse used to house the atelier for one of France's first women couturières, Madeleine Vionnet, so there's some metaphysical torch passing (woman designer to woman designer) going on here.

Kenzo

3 pl. des Victoires, 2e. Métro: Bourse.

A Japanese designer who has made his home in Paris for more than 30 years, Kenzo is a hipster at heart, with a keen fondness for floral cotton separates, circus colors, and bankable gabardine and corduroy jackets and pants. Kenzo Jungle, the second line, is a hot seller.

Discount Fashions

Many stores in Paris sell last year's designer clothing at reduced prices. Look for signs that say *dégriffé*. Many such stores are in the area around **rue St-Placide** (6ᵉ, Métro: Sèvres-Babylone). Also, stores with **stock** in the title often sell one label's surplus at reduced prices. The **rue d'Alésia** (14ᵉ, métro: Alésia) is lined with such stores for men, women, and children—including **Dorotennis Stock** (74 rue d'Alésia) for Dorothée Bis and the **SR store** (64 rue d'Alésia) for Sonia Rykiel.

Azzedine Alaia (18 rue de la Verrerie, 4ᵉ. Métro: Hôtel-de-Ville)   Last year's collection (and some before that) at half price.

Le Mouton à Cinq Pattes (8-10 and 48 rue St-Placide, 6ᵉ. Métro: St-Placide)   All sorts of bargains for men, women, girls, and younger children are to be found in this shop, which sells everything from last year's shoes and boots to imperceptibly flawed suits and dresses, including designer names.

Réciproque (89-123 rue de la Pompe, 16ᵉ. Métro: Victor-Hugo)   A Parisian institution, this resale shop is where chic women come to drop off designer clothing they've worn once, or sometimes not at all—you can usually find some clothes here with the tags still on them. Everything is immaculately cleaned before going on the racks, and the lucky few have turned up goodies like Hermès bags and Chanel suits. Furs, jewelry, household gifts, and more, all divvied up between the various shops that stretch along the street.

Raoul et Curly (47 av. de l'Opéra, 2ᵉ. Métro: Opéra)   Paris's most famous duty-free shop. Everything from handbags to scarves, but everyone comes here for the perfume and the make-up. It's tiny, crowded, and bustling, so know what lipstick shade you're looking for before you step foot inside. Prices here are good—around 20% to 30% off—whether you are buying détaxe or not. With the détaxe: non-EC residents with a passport and spending moe than 2860 F get the tax taken off, too.

Lolita Lempicka

13bis rue Pavée, 4ᵉ. Métro: St-Paul.

Well-dressed young Parisians go mad for Lolita's little suits.

Romeo Gigli
46 rue de Sévigné, 3e. Métro: St-Paul.

Is it art or is it clothing? This Italian designer put everyone into eggplant in the late 1980s, and the international downtown art crowd still can't get enough.

Sonia Rykiel
175 blvd. St-Germain, 6e. Métro: St-Germain des Prés.

A classic of sorts by now, Rykiel has made a career selling sleek, unlined knits—mainly black—and big accessories stamped with her name to busy professional women like herself. This is her rather recently opened flagship boutique, a handsome affair that carries the whole Rykiel universe.

St-Laurent Rive Gauche
6 pl. St-Sulpice, 6e. Métro: St-Sulpice.

It doesn't matter what he does anymore, he's fashion's Matisse—probably the greatest colorist the design world ever had. Look for elegant, classic jackets and the most perfectly cut pair of pants in the world. A mushroom-and-black boutique that's the home of good taste.

Thierry Mugler
10 pl. des Victoires, 2e. Métro: Bourse.

Clothing for the divas among us: lethal shoulder pads, hourglass cuts, and tough-girl leathers, all masterly crafted. Beautiful fabrics and workmanship, but make sure you can carry it off before you chunk down the change.

Ventilo
27bis rue du Louvre, 2e. Métro: Sentier.

Citified country clothing on 3 floors, including leather jackets and long fluid dresses. There's a cafe on the top floor where the editors from the nearby newspaper offices of *Le Figaro* like to have a light lunch—you can reserve a table by the window (☎ 01-42-33-18-67).

Yohji Yamamoto
3 rue de Grenelle, 7e. Métro: Sèvres-Babylone.

The maestro of Japanese fashion, Yamamoto dazzles with his inventive cuts and textile wizardry—though the clothes of tomorrow aren't everybody's cup of tea for today. His simpler, more wearable and somewhat lower-priced line, Y's, is at 25 rue du Louvre, Métro: Louvre.

Gifts

Casa Lopez
32-36 galerie Vivienne, 2e. Métro: Bourse.

A large selection of petit-point canvases—flowers, flower wreaths, and baskets of fruit—ready to embroider. Tapestry rugs, sold by the square meter, and cotton area rugs.

Catherine Memmi
32-34, rue St-Sulpice, 6ᵉ. Métro: St-Sulpice.

An elegant temple of white, cream, and ecru. French sheets and towels, in cotton and linen, plain or embroidered. The bestsellers are the taupe waffled-cotton guest towels. Wooden bath brushes, herbal bath oils, and gift soaps individually wrapped in tissue paper.

Diptyque
34 blvd. St-Germain, 5ᵉ. Métro: Maubert-Mutualité.

The home of the world's most famous candles.

En Attendant les Barbares
50 rue Étienne Marcel, 2ᵉ. Métro: Etienne Marcel.

The boutique that launched a style-shot—neobaroque—heard round the world in the late eighties. Though it carries mostly furniture, there are a lot of nice collectibles and gifts for the home, like the bestselling colorful paste glass candlesticks from Migeon & Migeon, as well as the latest in recycled and papier mâché designs.

Jules des Prés
19 rue du Cherche Midi, 6ᵉ. Métro: Sèvres-Babylone.

Decorative, tightly regimented dried-flower creations, plus an excellent choice of spices and individual potpourri.

Hilton McConnico
28 rue Madame 6ᵉ. Métro: St-Sulpice.

The design world of the transplanted Atlantan who shot to fame art-directing the cult film *Diva*. A spacious, gilt-trimmed shop showing off McConnico's sprightly and colorful designs (especially cacti) on decorative porcelains, home linens, and furniture.

Muriel Grateau
29/31 rue de Valois, Palais Royal, 1ᵉʳ. Métro: Louvre-Palais Royal

A charming boutique with many objects for the home, though there is a good selection of Grateau's pared-down women's fashion basics—sweaters and shirts—as well. Most of the ojects here combine French taste with Italian manufacturing—such as the Venetian linen napkins in 36 colors and the Murano mouth-blown glassware.

Multibrand Shops Specializing in Designer Clothing

No city gives birth to cutting-edge fashions quicker than Paris. The following are the city's style dials—where up-and-coming designers are showcased alongside cutting-edge fashions by the world's top designers.

Absinthe (74 rue Jean-Jacques-Rousseau, 1er. Métro: Louvre)   A bit precious and hushed, but a good window on avant-garde European design. Handbags by Jamin Puech.

Bonnie Cox (38 rue des Abbesses, 18e. Métro: Abbesses)   Staking out a narrow fashion territory up at the foot of Montmartre, Bonnie Cox is a small but good shop for the latest looks that won't break your purse. Carries Xüly Bet and Lolita-style knits by Aridza Bross.

Details (15 rue du Jour, 1er. Métro: Les Halles)   The grandma of Paris's alternative boutiques, with 2 floors of everything from children's clothes to Dider Lavilla pocketbooks to clothes by GR 816, Marcel Marongiu, and other cutting-edge designers.

Kashiyama (147 blvd. St-Germain, 7e. Métro: St-Germain-des-Prés)   A good-sized store with comprehensive selections from Gaultier, Dolce & Gabbana, Jean Colonna, Martin Margiela, Dries Van Noten, and other high priests of fashion. Some designer wedding dresses are found downstairs.

Maria Luisa (2 rue Cambon, 1er. Métro: Concorde. ☎ 01-47-03-96-15)   The latest fashions from cutting-edge designers including John Galliano and Rifat Ozbek, as well as a good window on younger designers who are often priced to sell.

Victoire (10–12 pl. des Victoires, 2e. Métro: Bourse)   The grande dame of trendy Parisian boutiques, this small but tony shop has an expertly chosen selection of cutting-edge designer clothing, including Prada, DKNY, and Dolce & Gabbana. Don't touch the pile of sweaters without asking for help.

Papier Plus

9 rue du Pont Louis Philippe, 4e. Métro: Pont-Marie.

Beautiful colored writing paper by the sheet, blank or lined notebooks, photograph albums, all of them exquisite.

Soleïado

78 rue de Seine, 6ᵉ. Métro: Odéon.

Gaily printed cotton fabrics that spell Provence. Savvy Parisians buy it by the meter and make their own table-cloths for a lot less than the ready-made ones, which are also on sale here. All sorts of household linens, as well as some clothes, including sturdy cotton men's shirts.

Swarovski

7 rue Royale, 1ᵉʳ. Métro: Concorde.

An Austrian firm that has been making some of the finest crystal in the world since the 1800s, Swarovski carries a collection of colored and baroque jewelry, handbags dripping icicles, and decorative objects for the home. These are rare gift items with price tags to match.

Gourmet Foods & Wines

Parisians still buy their bread in one store, charcuterie in another, and cheeses in yet another. No matter in which part of the city you find yourself, every neighborhood will offer up a good selection of preserves, wines, mustards, herbs, cheeses, pastries, and more. For the smartest food shops, hit the streets around the Madeleine. And, if you're looking for a last-minute gift, remember that every neighborhood will have either a market or grocer's open even on a Sunday morning. Mustard from Dijon or a bottle of olive oil from Provence are a lot cheaper bought in the city's shops than they are in the duty-free boutiques at the airport.

Bakeries

À La Flûte Gana

226 rue des Pyrénées, 20ᵉ. Métro: Gambetta.

Devotees claim its the best bread in Paris by a great French baking family. Specializes in *flûtes* (a thin baguette) and brown bread with wheat germ. The little pizzas to take out are great as are the caramelized all-butter pinwheel pastries. Also sells a good range of cakes and *petits fours*.

Lionel Poilâne

8 rue du Cherche Midi, 6ᵉ. Métro: St-Sulpice. Also at 49 blvd. de Grenelle, 15ᵉ; Métro: Bir-Hakeim.

People have a fetishist attachment to Lionel Poilâne's crusty loaves—baked in wood-fueled ovens and containing no preservatives. Almost as famous as the bread are Poilane's cinnamon-dusted apple tarts, which everyone tries to imitate and which you should try to catch warm. Delicious, buttery shortbread cookies called "les punitions" are sold in handsome wooden boxes.

Cheese

Androuet

41 rue d'Amsterdam, 8ᵉ. Métro: St-Lazare.

A temple to cheese. The best Munster from Alsace brought to the perfect stage of maturity here in the shop. Special boxes for traveling.

Barthélémy

51 rue de Grenelle, 7ᵉ. Métro: rue-du-Bac.

Roland Barthélémy is probably Paris's most famous cheese specialist, who has supplied everyone from left-bank aristocrats to the kitchens of the Elysée Palace. Practical paper-carton gift boxes.

Chocolates

Jadis et Gourmande

27 rue Boissy d'Anglas, 8ᵉ. Métro: Concorde.

A chocolate specialist with a knack for inventive creations—the best are the chocolate animals filled with delicious coffee beans. You can order inscriptions on chocolate creations as well.

Maison du Chocolat

255 rue du Faubourg St-Honoré, 8ᵉ. Métro: Ternes.

Maybe the best chocolate in the city, with many a devotee around the globe. Dark truffles, liqueur-filled chocolates, bricks of chocolate, and more. They even sell jars of liquid chocolate for desserts. The coffee-cream-filled éclair is worth the stratospheric price.

Gourmet Boutiques

Fauchon

26, 28, 30 pl. de la Madeleine, 8ᵉ. Métro: Madeleine.

One of the world's most celebrated food stores, with 3 large boutiques, including one with a restaurant—Fauchon carries more than 20,000 products, like all-butter Madeleines in attractive balsa-wood boxes. Many of the spices are good, including first-quality saffron threads that are worth the money. Wonderful gift service; will ship anywhere.

Fouquet

22 rue François 1ᵉʳ, 8ᵉ. Métro: Franklin-D-Roosevelt.

A wide range of teas and jellies and an exceptionally pretty array of traditional French candies—including caramels and berlingots sold by weight. Lovely old-world atmosphere.

Hédiard

21 pl. de la Madeleine, 8e. Métro: Madeleine.

A more manageable, more human Fauchon, with exotic products and spices (the peppercorn mixture is very nice), rare fruits, and an outstanding wine selection.

Mariages Frères

30 rue du Bourg-Tibourg, 4e. Métro: Hôtel-de-Ville.

Founded in 1854, this is the only French tea stockist that can compete with the London outlets. Some 400 varieties of tea originating from 30 countries, plus a range of their own marmalades, shortbread cookies, and lovely enameled teapots.

Look for the "birthday tea," launched in 1995, that comes in a lovely little urn-shaped tin for around $25. A tea salon is also found here: see "Dining."

A L'Olivier

23 rue de Rivoli, 4e. Métro: St-Paul.

Famous for their own olive oil, sold in 3 varieties, by the liter or carafe, and for a number of esoteric oils including hazelnut, walnut, and almond. Also a wide choice of vinegars, mustards, and a tempting selection of olives set forth in great open trays.

Pétrossian

18 blvd. de La Tour-Maubourg, 7e. Métro: La Tour-Maubourg.

The finest caviars and smoked fish—also a relatively new selection of foie gras. Their other specialty is *poutargue* (dried and salted mullet roe). Tasty.

Ice Cream

Berthillon

31 rue St-Louis-en-l'Ile, 4e. Métro: Pont-Marie.

Superb ice cream and sorbets, made from the freshest fruits. Try the coconut.

Pastries

Dalloyau

101 rue du Faubourg St-Honoré, 8e. Métro: Madeleine.

Founded in 1802, this is where the famous layered chocolate cake called the "Opéra" was invented. For fabulously rich cakes and pastries, also terrific sorbet sold in individual cups.

Lenôtre

44 rue d'Auteuil, 16e. Métro: Michel-Ange-Auteuil.

Gaston Lenôtre is one of the city's outstanding pâtissiers who has built a veritable empire around his cooking. Excellent chocolates, ice cream, and prepared foods. Heaven is in his St-Honorés and charlottes.

Wines

Legrand
1 rue de la Banque, 2e. Métro: Bourse.

One of the city's most spectacular turn-of-the-century boutiques, carrying a vast selection of little-known burgundies, great Bordeaux, and all those regional wines the owners ferret out.

La Cave aux Champagnes
15 rue des Grands Augustins, 6e. Métro: Odéon.

A stylish-looking new shop with cut-stone walls, wine racks, and huge baskets—all brimming with champage. Owner Sylvie Caillotin stocks more than a hundred types of bubbly, from steals to the most expensive, like Bollinger's Vielle Vigne Française.

Les Caves Taillevent
199 rue du Faubourg St-Honoré, 8e. Métro: St-Philippe-du-Roule.

Taillevent-owner Jean-Claude Vrinat owns this ultra-tony wine shop, which is run by his daughter Valérie and overseen by wine expert Didier Bordas. The Tiffany's of wine boutiques, the shop looks small but there are some 5,000 bottles in the back. A surprisingly good selection of inexpensive wines.

Hats

Elvis Pompilio
62 rue des Sts-Pères, 7e. Métro: St-Germain-des-Prés.

A young Belgian designer whose mad sky-pieces are all the rage with models and movie celebrities. His bestsellers include little *bibis* (caps) decorated with mushrooms, herbs, and flowers.

Jean Barthet
5 rue de Surène, 8e. Métro: Madeleine.

Milliner to the stars and supplier of headwear to the international jet-set. Custom-made and ready-made, with the accent on elegance.

Marie Mercié
23 rue St-Sulpice, 6e. Métro: St-Sulpice.

Marie Mercié brought hatmaking out of the 19thC and into the new. Her creations are hailed for their wit—and her fashion shows are some of the wildest in the city.

Philippe Model

33 pl. du Marché-St-Honoré, 1ᵉʳ. Métro: Pyramides.

Paris's mad hatter. Switched-on headwear fashions and growing collections of shoes (his stretch grosgrain slippers are an avant-garde classic by now), gloves, and bags.

Jewelry

In Paris, jewelry, like fashion, is rated: ***Haute joaillerie*** means the top firms, working with precious and unusual gems; under them fall the ready-to-wear lines. Both offer extremely inventive creations; their difference is mostly in the costliness of the gems and materials used.

Haute Joaillerie

The *haute joaillerie* firms are mostly clustered around place Vendôme. Prices for the top jewelry lines usually begin at 4 or 5 thousand dollars—and quickly reach the millions of dollars. However, faced with the recent recession, most top jewelers have recently launched budget lines or a line of watches—along the lines of the Cartier "Must" collection—to augment their client list. So if you are looking to spend closer to a grand than a mill, it's still worth your while to pop in and have a look around.

Boucheron

26 pl. Vendôme, 1ᵉʳ. Métro: Opéra.

The house that surprisingly launched one of the world's bestselling perfumes a few years ago.

Cartier

13 rue de la Paix, 1ᵉʳ. Métro: Opéra.

Precious jewelry is still on sale here, but the success of their second line—the watch! the watch!—has almost made everyone forget that. Their signature 3-ring band in 3 different golds costs under a thousand dollars.

Chanel

7 pl. Vendôme, 1ᵉʳ. Métro: Opéra.

Coco herself called diamonds "the most value in the smallest package." A few years ago, the firm that practically invented costume jewelry with all those ropes of fake pearls opened their first-ever store dedicated to precious jewelry, i.e., diamonds, pearls, and rubies, et al. Mademoiselle herself designed a collection of "real" jewelry in 1932, and the current pieces repeat many of those designs.

Van Cleef et Arpels
22 pl. Vendôme, 1ᵉʳ. Métro: Opéra.

Alongside those big, big diamonds, a new line of more affordable items ($1,000 dollars and up).

Young Designers

Many young and talented jewelry designers are working in Paris today. Their works—often one-of-a-kind pieces—make wonderful gifts and are widely collected as they are, in many cases, still very affordable. Look for names such as Hervé Van Der Straetan, Stefano Poletti, and Sophie Levy.

Cécile et Jeanne
12 rue des Francs-Bourgeois, 3ᵉ. Métro: Bastille.

A creation of contemporary jewelry that has the look of archaeological finds. The young designer here, Jeanne, also creates jewelry for French museum shops. Resins, bronze, glass, amethyst, etc., with each piece made by hand. Prices start at $20.

Naïla de Monbrison
6 rue de Bourgogne, 7ᵉ. Métro: Solférino.

The Leo Castelli of contemporary jewelry design, Monbrison has an international clientele for the top jewelry designers she features—including Juliette Polac and Geraldine Grinda. Running her tiny jewel-like shop like an art gallery, she stages regular exhibitions of various designers—but ask to see things that aren't exhibited; she has plenty of stock.

Sic Amor
20 rue du pont Louis Philippe, 4ᵉ. Métro: Pont-Marie.

A sunny, pocket-sized accessories boutique selling jewelry, shoes, handbags, and furniture. In addition to the designs on display, you can order custom wedding rings and more. Look for Stefano Poletti's silver bracelets with sea themes and glass brooches filled with real ivy; and the baroque, gilded creations of Hervé Van Der Straeten, who has worked for Lacroix and Claude Montana.

Leather Goods & Accessories

La Bagagerie
41 rue du Four, 6ᵉ. Métro: St-Germain-des-Prés. 12 rue Tronchet, 8ᵉ. Métro: Madeleine. 74 rue de Passy, 16ᵉ. Métro: Muette

Reasonable prices for a you-want-it-we-got-it selection of well-made bags in everything from patent leather to suede and calfskin, in lots of colors. The 2-handled shopping "sacs" are the house specialty. An excellent place to get a bag that looks distinctly French and won't ruin you.

Céline

24 rue Françcois-1ᵉʳ, 8ᵉ. Métro: Franklin-D-Roosevelt. Also at 3 av. Victor-Hugo, 16ᵉ. Métro: Charles-de-Gaulle-Etoile.

For years a staid standby for conservative French women, Céline has dusted itself off in recent years—with a fresh-looking, never-too-outré line of handbags, clothing, and leather accessories. While still seen as a less gla-morous cousin to Vuitton or Hermès, Celine is worth taking a new look at: The design and quality of their leather handbags is topnotch, with prices to match.

Didier Lavilla

38 rue de Sévigné, 4ᵉ. ☎ 01-42-74-48-40. Métro: St-Paul.

Lavilla's nylon tote bag with the gold rings and shoul-der strap became a fashion classic a few years ago when fashion editors began carrying them around to the runway shows. Terrific prices for handbags that are fashionable and truly practical, made mostly of nylon or sueded pigskin.

Hermès

24 rue du Faubourg St-Honoré, 1ᵉʳ. Métro: Madeleine.

They used to make saddles, now they're the depart-ment store to end all department stores—carrying everything from leather cases for Post-it Notes to the world's most famous pocketbook, the Kelly bag, to crystal stemware. On opening day of their yearly sale in June, the line to enter starts forming at 5am. Recently, the ready-to-wear here has been getting better look-ing—and not just the jodhpurs. This is where the French buy their agendas: Choose from a gorgeous range of colors, leathers, and formats, and if you don't see what you want, you can design your own from their components.

Hervé Chapelier

13 rue Gustave Courbet, 16ᵉ. Métro: Victor-Hugo.

The best—and bestselling—little nylon backpack in Paris, in a rainbow of colors. Also a good selection of other totes and carryalls.

Lancel

43 rue de Rennes, 6ᵉ. Métro: St-Germain-des-Prés.

Grainy leather handbags in a broad selection of bright colors like yellow and green. Less expensive than the new Vuitton colored handbags but with the same look to them. A good selection of small leather gift items—from key chains to agendas.

Louis Vuitton

54 av. Montaigne, 8ᵉ. Métro: Franklin-D-Roosevelt.

The familiar patented initials and a new line of colored leathers—green, yellow, and red—that update the line. A massive marble shop that's always full.

Prada

5 rue de Grenelle, 6ᵉ. Métro: Sèvres-Babylone.

This dusty old Milanese leather-goods company shot up out of nowhere in the late 1980s, when they introduced their black vinyl handbag with the chain handle that instantly became a fashion classic. Nylon and leather bags that are the height of chic. Also, sleek Audrey-Hepburn-in-the-1950s-style clothing and shoes next door.

Lingerie

Almost everyone over the age of 15 is interested in buying French lingerie, whether it's for yourself, a wife, or a girlfriend. Most women know that the indefinable notion of French fashion starts with lingerie.

Sabbia Rosa

73 rue des Sts-Pères, 7ᵉ. Métro: Sèvres-Babylone.

The most famous women's lingerie store in the city and supposedly where Frenchmen go to buy underwear for their mistresses. Owner Moana Moati has been steering pampered wives, executives, models, and their paramours to the right silk pastel undies in various degrees of naughtiness for the past 18 years. An almost invisible string bikini costs more than $100—now you get the picture.

Chantall Thomass

1 rue Vivienne, 1ᵉʳ. Métro: Bourse.

This firm sells so much lingerie that even the clothes are beginning to look like underwear. This is a store-as-private-house concept, and the slips and thigh-high hosiery are well set-off by the baroque furnishings.

Markets

Flea Markets

Each weekend flea markets come to life around the peripheries of Paris, selling furniture and antiques of varying quality, old clothes, china, books, linens, and just plain junk. Open Saturday, Sunday, and sometimes Monday, they invite bargaining. Never hesitate to offer a solid 10% to 15% less than the quoted price—and possibly more if you're paying cash or buying more than one thing from the same vendor. Sad to say, but you'll almost always get a better price if you bring along French friends and let them do the talking. If you do want to negotiate, just politely state your counteroffer, and don't expect miracles—the merchants in the Parisian flea markets are not terribly concerned about your walking away empty-handed. Most vendors will not accept credit cards, but many will gladly ship their merchandise worldwide. There are several places to change money in Clignancourt, and, surprisingly, they offer a very competitive rate.

Marché aux Puces de St-Ouen

Familiarly called Clignancourt. Porte De Clignancourt, 18e. ☎ 01-40-11-54-14. Métro: Porte de Clignancourt. Open: Sat 9am–6pm, Sun 10am–6pm, Mon 10am–6pm.

This is reputedly the largest flea market in Europe—and it will take you a good 2 hours to browse your way through most of it. All of Paris seems to get up Saturday and Sunday morning for a trip here—the ambitious try to arrive at the crack of dawn to begin haggling the minute the vendors start unloading their trucks. When you get off the métro, you're in a sort of second-hand-clothes hell—keep walking, the real market begins further on.

A large part of the Clignancourt flea market isn't that at all: It's an antiques fair, where furniture costing a small fortune is displayed next to precious paintings. But there are also alleyways full of junk piled in boxes, so snoop around. Not only furniture, but antique jewelry, rare books, china, glassware, and more are to be found here. If you're interested in serious shopping, buy a copy of the official guide, which lists stallholders according to type. It's published in English, Japanese, and French, and can be found at the larger stands.

Marché aux Puces de Montreuil

20e. Métro: Porte de Montreuil.

If you have a car, you can also try the flea market here, where the bargains—especially furniture, china, and old silverplate—are often bigger. Lots of old toys, books, and appliances are spread out on the pavement on blankets. It's just outside the métro stop.

Marché aux Puces de Vanves

14e. Métro: Porte de Vanves.

Even better bargains or bric-a-brac. Open Saturday, Sunday, Monday, but primarily Saturday morning.

Food Markets

Every neighborhood in Paris has an outdoor food market at least several days a week. If you're staying in a hotel, these probably won't interest you that much, though fruit, cheeses, and olives are often sold at them. One of the most famous and cheapest food markets in Paris is the **Marché d'Aligre** on **place d'Aligre** (12e; métro: Ledru-Rollin), mornings from Tuesday to Sunday. As you wend your way down the stall-lined streets, you'll notice the market taking on a distinctly North African accent.

The most upscale food market in the city is the **Marché Biologique** on **boulevard Raspail,** between the rue de Rennes and the rue du Cherche Midi, which is open on Sunday mornings only. This is where chic housewives and conscientious students come to buy organically grown fruits and vegetables—and even breads.

If all you want is to stroll through a market, picking up flavors, flowers, and maybe a bit of chèvre, probably the prettiest place to go is the market on the **rue de Buci** in **St-Germain-des-Prés** (Métro: Mabillon). Crowded and cheerful, the market runs from the boulevard St-Germain down the rue de Seine and then onto rue de Buci. Open Tuesday through Sat-urday 8am to 1pm and 4pm to 7pm; and Sunday mornings.

Flower Markets

The best flower market is at the **place Louis-Lépine** on **quai de la Corse** (4e; métro: Cité), open until 4pm every day, and Sunday mornings. Cabbage roses, lilies, paper whites, freesia, and more arrive daily from Holland and the South of France. Keep an eye peeled for seasonal varieties and rarities such as black roses—which are actually very dark purple. On Sunday, there's also a bird market here.

Booksellers

When the weather is nice, Paris's famed *bouquinistes* open up their stalls along the Seine. Prices aren't always cheap, but you might be astounded by the quality of the books.

- **Quais des Grands-Augustins,** Conti, and Malaquais, 6e. Métro: St-Michel.

- **Quai du Louvre** and **quai de la Mégisserie,** 1er. Métro: Pont-Neuf.

- **Quai Voltaire,** 6e. Métro: Musée d'Orsay.

Museum Shops

A cottage industry capitalizing on the city's artistic treasures has burgeoned in Paris in recent years. Don't think strips of tacky postcards and the like: Today's museum shops are the nec plus ultra in designer shopping. Generally, museum shops are just inside the entrance to the museum, before you reach the ticket desk, so you can visit without paying the entrance fee. Seriously worth a detour.

Try the **Musées des Arts Decoratifs** for elegant crystal stemware; the boutique **Musées et Creations** in the **Louvre Carrousel** for plates and linens designed by contemporary artists; **Paris Musées** (which groups together gifts from all Paris's national museums, including the Louvre and the Musée d'Orsay; 37 rue des Francs Bourgeois, 4ᵉ) for linen Louis XIV dishtowels designed by Robert Le Heros; the **Musée d'Orsay** for reproductions of objects (a pitcher, a bowl) copied from famous Impressionist paintings; the **Musée de la Marine** for a beautiful black-and-red felt table throw with a maritime motif or Haviland china decorated with anchors; the **Musée de la Poste** for writing paper, stamps, and pens; the **Boutique du Musée du Louvre** for plaster reproductions of statues in the Louvre— from Degas' *Les danseuses* to a life-sized *Victory at Samothrace*—now there's a gift.

Perfume & Cosmetics

The main department stores carry the most complete selections. Dozens of shops surround the Opéra, but prices can vary by quite a bit (see **Raoul et Curly** in "Discount Fashions," above). Many *parfumeurs* offer fixed discounts of 30% and say so in the window—they generally offer good value.

Annick Goutal
14 rue de Castiglione, 1ᵉʳ. Métro: Tuileries.

A gilt and mirrored shop reminiscent of a boudoir. Goutal develops her scents herself. Pretty bottles and gold, ribbon-tied packaging.

Caron
34 av. Montaigne, 8ᵉ. Métro: Franklin-D-Roosevelt.

Perfumes and powders. Beautiful swansdown puffs in bonbon colors. Big Baccarat decanters filled with the house perfumes. A small shop—and the only place that sells Black Narcissus.

Comptoir Sud Pacifique
17 rue de la Paix, 2ᵉ. Métro: Opéra.

A tony if low-key establishment where French movie stars come to concoct their own personalized scents, sold in aluminum bottles. A lot of travel accessories. It doesn't look like a perfume shop from the outside—more a boutique on board the *QE2*.

Guerlain
68 av. des Champs-Elysées, 8ᵉ. Métro: George-V.

Shalimar, Jicky—perfumes for *perfumeurs,* and simply the best. Very attractive old-fashioned bottles of *eaux de toilette*—the most famous being Eau de Guerlain. They carry a scent for the home that's only sold in Paris; they'll try to sell it to you with the (costly) diffuser, but just explain you already have one and only need the scent refill—any old pottery diffuser will do the same job.

Shoes

Christian Louboutin
19 rue Jean-Jacques Rousseau, 1ᵉʳ. Métro: Louvre.

Already a cult figure among fashion conscious Parisians, Louboutin—a former assistant to the legendary Roger Vivier—is a young designer whose specialities include heels plated in 24-carat gold, hand-carved woods, and hand-painted *peau-de-soie.*

Robert Clergerie
5 rue du Cherche Midi, 6ᵉ. Métro: St-Sulpice.

A mix of trendy and classic styles. Very good boots and some assorted handbags. His second line is carried at **Espace,** located at 22, rue de Grenelle, 7ᵉ. (Métro: rue du Bac.)

Patrick Cox
62 rue Tiquetonne, 2ᵉ. Métro: Etienne-Marcel.

Cox, a London-based designer, has designed shoes for Vivienne Westwood and John Galliano. Kicky patent leather mules and babydolls, also some lower-priced moccasins.

Stephane Kélian
6 pl. des Victoires, 1ᵉʳ. Métro: Sentier.

The master of wovens, braids, sculptural heels, bow ties and more. The cutting edge of footwear fashions. Some handbags, too.

Textiles

Whether for fashion or home, French textiles—especially the world-famous silks from Lyons—are certainly one of the country's finest arts.

Le Marché St. Pierre
Place St-Pierre, 18ᵉ. Métro: Anvers.

For the best prices in Paris for all fabrics, housewives and fashion designers alike crawl through the bins at the Marché St. Pierre. The most famous of the many textile firms crowding the square and adjoining streets is **Dreyfus**, at 2 rue Charles-Nodier (Métro: Anvers). Established in 1918, this warehouse has 5 floors of fabric, with the real cheap stuff—remnants and discounted bolts—stuffed into bins on the ground floor. Prepare to elbow.

Rodin
36 av. des Champs-Elysées, 8ᵉ. Métro: Franklin-D-Roosevelt.

For haute couture fabrics and more at top prices. Good twice-yearly sales.

Toys

French toys can be sophisticated—and very expensive. Foreign-made toys, like Lego or Tinker Toys, cost considerably more than at home.

Le Ciel Est à Tout le Monde
10 rue Gay-Lussac, 5ᵉ. Métro: Luxembourg.

A kite store with 100 varieties; they'll even make kites to order.

Au Nain Bleu
406 rue St-Honoré, 8ᵉ. Métro: Madeleine.

F. Scott Fitzgerald supposedly came here to buy toys for Scottie. Rocking horses, huge plush animals, old-fashioned wooden toys, dollhouses, marionettes, and toy soldiers—the whole French childhood thing, very smart, and every saleswoman here has an attitude.

Si Tu Veux
68 galerie Vivienne, 2ᵉ. Métro: Bourse.

Traditional toys and games, many in wood. Miniature furniture, jointed wooden puppets and animals, and a most appealing section devoted to parties, including clown costumes, and face make-up.

Le Train Bleu
55 rue St-Placide, 6ᵉ. Métro: St-Placide.

Specialist in trains, electric cars, and model cars and airplanes. Also toys for girls and smaller children.

THE ARTS

Opera, Ballet & Dance

The most opulent of the performing arts has a new setting in the **Opéra Bastille.** The old and new opera houses have complementary programs, offered under the joint promotional title of **Opéra National de Paris.** The old **Opéra Garnier** houses classical ballet and contemporary dance, while full-scale operatic productions now benefit from the advanced technical facilities at the Opéra Bastille. Both opera houses have the deepest stages in existence. See the entries on both in "Sights & Attractions."

Opéra Bastille, 120 rue de Lyon, 12ᵉ, ☎ 01-44-73-13-00. Telephone reservations Monday to Saturday 11am to 6pm. Métro: Bastille. The new Opéra has superior facilities but lacks the splendor of the Opéra Garnier. Reservations can also be made by mail.

Opéra-Garnier, Place de l'Opéra, 9ᵉ, ☎ 01-47-42-53-71. Métro: Opéra. Magnificent opulent setting and recently restored. Garnier has the largest corps de ballet in the world. International touring contemporary dance companies perform here regularly. Reservations can also be made by mail.

La Salle Favart or **Opéra Comique,** 5 rue Favart, 2ᵉ, ☎ 01-42-44-45-46. Telephone reservations Monday to Friday 10am to 6pm. Métro: Richelieu-Drouot. A superb 19thC setting for the music of that epoch. Since it reopened in 1990, the Salle Favart has offered a varied program, with 19thC French operas and operettas as well as the classic operatic repertoire.

Theater

There are some 100 theaters in Paris, offering everything from plays in the classic repertoire to vaudeville. Commercial theaters offer the requisite international

Reservations & Publications

Reservations: If you're visiting in summer, remember that many theaters and performance centers close for a month or more. Many theaters take reservations only a few weeks in advance. **SOS Théâtres** (☎ 01-44-77-88-55) or **Chèque-Théâtre** (☎ 01-42-46-72-40) will tell you what tickets are available and will sell you tickets; they are open 10am to 7pm.

You can also purchase tickets by visiting one of the 5 branches of **FNAC**, including those at 136 rue de Rennes, 6e (☎ 01-49-54-30-00), and 71 boulevard St-Germain, 5e (☎ 01-44-41-31-50). To reserve and buy tickets by phone, call their central telephone number 01-49-87-50-50. FNAC offers tickets to theater, rock, and sporting events.

You can also purchase tickets directly from each theater box office, either by phone or in person. They're generally open from 11am to 6pm, closed Sunday. At **Virgin Megastore**, 52-60 avenue des Champs-Élysées, 8e, the ticket office is situated on the level between the ground and 1st floors (☎ 01-49-53-50-50; open daily 10am–midnight, Fri and Sat until 1am, Sun noon–midnight). There's another Virgin Megastore branch in the Carrousel du Louvre, 1er (☎ 01-49-53-50-50; open Wed–Mon 10am–10pm).

You can purchase half-price day-of-the-performance tickets at **Le Kiosque-Théâtre ticket booths** at place de la Madeleine or on the concourse of the Montparnasse train station. The booths are open Tuesday through Saturday 12:30pm to 8pm, Sunday 12:30pm to 4pm.

Publications: *Pariscope* and *l'Officiel des Spectacles*, published every Wednesday, are indispensible. They give performance times, telephone numbers, and more.

---

hits, such as *Cats* or *Les Misérables;* others stage concerts, ballet, and even small-scale operas.

Reservations can often be made only 2 weeks ahead, and seats may be available on short notice. In the spring, the city underwrites special 2-for-1 ticket promotions; check with individual box offices for details.

Théâtre des Champs-Elysées, 15 avenue Montaigne, 8e. ☎ 01-49-52-50-50. Métro: Alma Marceau. Remains faithful to its tradition of offering all types of music, symphony, and chamber concerts, as well as dance and opera.

Théâtre Mogador, 25 rue de Mogador, 9ᵉ, ☎ 01-53-32-32-00. Métro: Chausée d'Antin. Superb classic productions and musicals.

Théâtre National de Chaillot, 1 place du Trocadéro, 16ᵉ, ☎ 01-47-27-81-15. Reservations Monday through Saturday 11am to 7pm, Sunday 11am to 5pm. Métro: Trocadéro. Large-scale new interpretations of classical works, from Molière to Shakespeare, as well as modern pieces. Apéritif-concerts for jazz lovers from 7:30 to 8:15pm.

Théâtre du Rond-Point Compagnie Marcel Maréchal, 2bis avenue Franklin-D-Roosevelt, 8ᵉ, ☎ 01-44-95-98-00. Reservations Tuesday through Saturday 11am to 7pm, Sunday noon to 5pm. Métro: Champs-Elysées-Clemenceau. Founded by the legendary couple of French theater, Jean-Louis Barrault and Madeleine Renaud and once a forerunner of powerful 20thC drama. In 1995, acclaimed theater director Marcel Maréchal arrived to put the place back on the theatrical map. The theater has been extensively renovated.

International Stage Productions

International dance companies and singers with a worldwide reputation usually appear at the **Palais Omnisports de Paris-Bercy** (8 blvd. de Bercy, 12ᵉ, ☎ 01-44-68-44-68; métro: Bercy.) or the **Palais des Congrès** (2 pl. de la Porte Maillot, 17ᵉ, ☎ 01-40-68-22-22; métro: Porte-Maillot). Big productions such as *Cats* or *Les Misérables* appear at the **Palais des Congrès** or the **Palais des Sports** (1 pl. de la Porte de Versailles, 15ᵉ, ☎ 01-48-28-40-10; métro: Porte de Versailles).

Traditional Plays

Les Bouffes du Nord, 209 rue du Faubourg-St-Denis, 10ᵉ, ☎ 01-46-07-34-50. Métro: La Chapelle (*Note:* Not Métro Porte de la Chapelle). Home to English director Peter Brook's French company, and a receiving house for international contemporary theater.

Les Bouffes Parisiens, 4 rue Monsigny, 2ᵉ, ☎ 01-42-96-60-24. Reservations from 11am to 7pm. Métro: Quatre Septembre. Capacious (700 seats), famous, and well-respected theater.

La Comédie Française, Salle Richelieu, 2 rue de Richelieu, 1ᵉʳ, ☎ 01-40-15-00-15. Métro: Palais-Royal. French classical dramatic repertoire of the 17thC was born during the reign of Louis XIV. Molière died on stage here, playing the role of *Le Malade Imaginaire.* The Comédie still presents the works of Molière, Racine, Corneille, and Shakespeare, among others, but also 19th- and 20thC playwrights the likes of Anouilh, Pirandello, and Brecht.

Théâtre Marigny, Carré Marigny, 8ᵉ, ☎ 01-42-56-04-41. Métro: Champs-Elysées-Clemenceau. A large, very beautiful commercial theater with a preference for well-known French literary works.

Théâtre National de l'Odéon or **Théâtre de l'Europe,** 1 place de l'Odéon, 6ᵉ, ☎ 01-44-41-36-36. Métro: Odéon. Tickets on sale at box-office from 11am to 6:30pm (half an hour before performance starts). One of the high spots for contemporary plays.

Classical Concerts

The range of music offered in Paris is matched by the variety of its venues; conventional *salles* vie with theaters, museums, gardens, grand houses, and, best of all, the old churches of Paris.

Churches, some of which have superb acoustics, regularly present concerts by chamber, baroque, and symphony orchestras. The best-known and most popular are: **La Sainte Chapelle** (blvd. du Palais, 1ᵉʳ, ☎ 01-48-01-91-35; métro: Cité); **La Madeleine** (pl. de la Madeleine, 8ᵉ, ☎ 01-42-77-65-65; métro: Madeleine); **St-Germain-des-Prés,** one of the loveliest churches in Paris (pl. St-Germain-des-Prés, 6ᵉ, ☎ 01-43-25-41-71; métro: St-Germain-des Prés); and **St-Roch** (24 rue St-Roch, 1ᵉʳ, ☎ 01-42-44-13-20; métro: Pyramides, Tuileries).

The venue for true music-lovers is **La Salle Pleyel,** 252 rue du Faubourg-St-Honoré, 8ᵉ, ☎ 01-45-61-53-00. Reservations 11am to 6pm, closed Sunday and holidays. Métro: Ternes. Good acoustics and atmosphere combine to make this the high-spot of the capital's music venues. Other concert halls include:

Cité de la Musique, 221 avenue Jean Jaurès 19ᵉ, ☎ 01-44-84-44-84 for information and reservations. Métro: Porte de Pantin. Paris's brand new music center, with concert halls, exhibition spaces, and more, designed by Christian de Portzamparc. The plans for this extension of **La Villette,** the science and industry museum, took over 10 years to complete, and it was finally opened in 1995. Regular classical, contemporary, and world music concerts are presented. Tickets can be purchased at the box office.

Maison de Radio-France, 116 avenue du Président-Kennedy, 16ᵉ, ☎ 01-42-30-15-16 for information and reservations. Métro: Ranelagh. This concert hall is right in the center of the recording studios at the Maison de la Radio. Tickets may be purchased at the box office. Free concerts about twice a month.

La Salle Gaveau, 45 rue de la Boétie, 8ᵉ, ☎ 01-49-53-05-07 for information and reservations. Métro: Miromesnil. Classic and chamber music.

Théâtre des Champs-Elysées. See "Theater" above in this chapter.

Théâtre Musical de Paris (Théâtre du Châtelet), 1 place du Châtelet, 1ᵉʳ, ☎ 01-40-28-28-40 or 01-42-33-00-00 (recorded info). Reservations 11am to 7pm, closed Sunday. Métro: Châtelet. This large venue presents contemporary music as well as chamber music, opera, and symphonies. Dance and theater productions, too.

Variety & Popular Concerts

Big-name French and foreign stars perform at the **Palais Omnisports de Paris-Bercy**, **Le Zénith** at LaVillette, or at **La Cigale** (12 blvd. Rochechouart, 18ᵉ, ☎ 01-42-23-15-15; métro: Pigalle). That bastion of French variety, **L'Olympia** (28 blvd. des Capucines, 9ᵉ, ☎ 01-47-42-82-45 or 1/47-42-25-49 for reservations; métro: Opéra, Madeleine) may soon have to relocate.

Cinema

All of the week's movie listings are published every Wednesday in both the *Pariscope* and the *l'Officiel des Spectacles.* For late-show moviegoers, a word of caution: The métros in Paris stop running at 12:45am.

UGC Ciné Cité les Halles, Parvis de St-Eustache, Level 3 (access Porte du Jour) Forum des Halles 1ᵉʳ, ☎ 01-36-68-68-58. Métro: Les Halles. RER: Châtelet-les Halles. Newly opened in the summer of 1995, this complex offers 80 screenings daily, in 15 different screening rooms, all with giant screens and digital sound. At the cafe inside, you can cruise the Internet while waiting for your film to start. Films are often screened in their original language (VO), with French subtitles.

Le Mac-Mahon, 5 avenue Mac-Mahon, 17ᵉ, ☎ 01-43-29-79-89 and 01-36-65-70-48 (recorded info). Métro: Etoile. Lovely prewar movie theater with star-spangled ceiling. Shows the great American classic movies, in *version original* (VO), of course.

PARIS AFTER DARK

T HERE'S SOMETHING INDEFINABLY SENSUAL ABOUT
Paris in the evening. While it isn't the visibly wild
or naughty place that foreigners used to flock to, there's
a langourous, seductive quality to the city after dark
that's inescapable. You feel it in a walk across a softly lit
bridge, at a cafe surrounded by students and lovers, in
the darkened velvety banquettes of a late-night club, in
the rustle of silk in the seat next to yours at the theater.

At the most expensive—and hopelessly dated—end
of the scale, the spectacular revues with feathered and
sequined scantily-clad beauties continue to flourish,
albeit more geared to busloads of foreign tourists than
the chic locals they once entertained.

Parisians have always loved dancing, so clubs and
discos are crowded and colorful. While admission fees
can be steep, they often include the price of a drink.
Note that prices, especially for drinks, can be vastly
expensive at the most lavish nightclubs—and we are
talking $30 for a beer. If you're in a group of 4 or more
and everyone is drinking, consider buying an entire
bottle of vodka or other hard liquor; though the price
will be high, it comes with a table, as well as free mix-
ers: When you calculate the cost of mixed drinks at the
bar, you might come out ahead. Barhopping is not
really a Parisian diversion, although many good bars
welcome customers for the aperitif hour, or for a late-
night drink. Wine bars are also very popular, especially
with the under-35 crowd.

Dance Clubs
Discothèques

The very word *discothèque* is, of course, French. Paris's
discos tend to be wonderfully flashy affairs, with glittery decor and glittery people, throbbing lights, and

pulsating music. Fashions change, but there are some places, given below, that are at the fore from one generation to the next. See also "Private Clubs," below.

L'Arc, 12 rue de Presbourg, 16ᵉ, ☎ 01-45-00-45-00. Métro: Charles-de-Gaulle-Etoile. Coming up as the rival to Les Bains as the watering hole for this week's celebrities. A tough door policy, and an expensive, if unremarkable, restaurant.

Les Bains, 7 rue du Bourg l'Abbé, 3ᵉ, ☎ 01-48-87-01-80. Métro: Rambuteau, Etienne-Marcel. Located in a converted bathhouse, this has been the number-one spot in town for years. Getting by the doorwoman is the problem here—it helps if you eat dinner in the restaurant upstairs, but even that, according to the owners, isn't a guarantee of entry to the downstairs *boîte*. Still, the upstairs bar is sometimes more fun than the disco below.

Le Balajo, 9 rue de Lappe, 11ᵉ, ☎ 01-47-00-07-87. Métro: Bastille. Captures memories of postwar Paris, wholeheartedly embraced by younger generations. Authentic retro dancing for young and old on Saturdays and Sundays from 3pm to 6:30pm. Disco at night.

Le Bataclan, 50 boulevard Voltaire, 11ᵉ, ☎ 01-47-00-30-12. Métro: Oberkampf. A theater with winning thematic evenings—drag queens of London, etc. Also concerts and variety shows.

Le Bus Palladium, 6 rue Fontaine, 9ᵉ, ☎ 01-53-21-07-33. Métro: Pigalle. A recently reopened mecca for seventies and eighties music, great for those who remember the tunes firsthand. If you like to get down with the Doobie's, here's the place.

La Casbah, 20 rue de la Forge-Royale, 11ᵉ, ☎ 01-43-71-71-89. Métro: Ledru-Rollin. A spacious and stylish India-under-the-Raj–style bar upstairs and a disco downstairs. The door policy here was so severe that people stopped coming; now they've loosened-up, making it pleasant again.

Folies Pigalle, 11 place Pigalle 9ᵉ, ☎ 01-48-78-25-56 or 01-42-49-69-17. Métro: Pigalle. The hottest club currently on the scene, with a strong gay contingent. Absolutely mobbed on weekends.

La Java, 105, rue du Faubourg du Temple, 10ᵉ, ☎ 01-42-02-20-52. Métro: Belleville, Goncourt. An old and somewhat faded stomping ground. Big and earthy, with one of the more relaxed door policies and a solidly unpretentious outlook. The Cuban and Salsa evenings on Thursday and Friday are when it all comes together.

Le Palace, 8 rue du Faubourg Montmartre, 9ᵉ, ☎ 01-42-46-10-87. Métro: rue Montmartre. Cabaret and clubwoman magnate Regine took it over, and now it isn't as popular—apart from occasional theme nights and the famous gay tea dances on Sundays from 5pm to 11pm. **Le Privilège/KitKat,** the afterhours club downstairs, is still packed, though—with lesbian nights on Friday and Saturday.

Le Queen, 102 avenue des Champs-Elysées, 8ᵉ, ☎ 01-42-89-31-32. Métro: George V. Predominantly gay and the liveliest scene in town.

La Scala, 188 rue de Rivoli, 1ᵉʳ, ☎ 01-42-60-45-64. Métro: Palais-Royal. Spacious disco with all the latest electronic gadgetry and stunning lighting. Young atmosphere and absolutely full of tourists, so no one ever knows anyone—which can be great.

Le Tango, 11, rue au Maire 3ᵉ, ☎ 01-42-72-17-78. Métro: Arts et Métiers. The longest-running African and Latin dance club in town. Door policy is easy, drinks cheap. The casual, friendly (and we mean hip contact) atmosphere can be a bit too much for the ladies who don't want to dance with strangers.

Only in Paris—Guingette Music Halls

For a really fun, typically Parisian evening, try one of the **Guingette music halls** out along the Marne—think Arletty and "La Vie en Rose." You'll need a car to take you there, but the walk along the river is fun and nostalgic—and where else you can you tango to accordion music?

Chez Gégène, 162 quai de Polangis, 94 Joinville-le-Pont, ☎ 01-48-83-29-43. RER: Joinville. An old, traditional guingette. Dancing on Friday and Saturday nights from 9pm to 2am and Sunday from 3pm to midnight. Can dine here, too.

La Guinguette de l'Ile de Martin-Pêcheur, 41 quai Victor-Hugo, 94 Champigny-sur-Marne, ☎ 01-49-83-03 02. RER: Champigny. Attracts a young, lively crowd.

Cabarets & Revues

Revues and cabarets can be typically French or have an American flavor. You'll find humorous drag stars or imitators of the singers of yesteryear. At the best-known establishments, the prices are commensurately high, but you get a whole lot of spectacle for your money. In most places, 2 combinations are available: show and dinner or show and a half-bottle of champagne.

Special Moments

Paris by night is breathtaking. Fountains, squares, and monuments are brilliantly lit, cafes and restaurants softly glow, and a dusky sort of halo seems to settle over the city.

At sunset, savor the rooftops of Paris slowly turning to desert rose. The most magical site for this is on the steps of the Sacré-Coeur—though watch out for Euro-hippies fielding dubious verses to old Bob Dylan songs. Also, try the Pont des Arts to catch the last rays of light falling on the Seine, or by the Obelisk in the Place de la Concorde, preferably at the very moment when the lights come on around the square and up the Champs Elysées.

If you've got a head for heights, go for a ride on the big wheel in the funfair in the Tuileries (summer only, open until 12:45am), where you will have a dizzying view of the city twirling below you. Or better still, brave a late-night ride up the Eiffel Tower (open year-round to 11pm, to midnight July–Sept) where the city twinkles below you and the illuminated girders shine like gold filigree. For a more romantic sky-view, have a late-night drink at the **Concorde-Lafayette** at Porte Maillot, where couples snuggle into banquettes, sipping cocktails and staring at the rows of headlights coursing through the city's major throughfares.

To cap a late night out, stroll across one of Paris's most romantic bridges—Pont Neuf, Pont des Arts, or Pont Alexandre III—and watch the sun rise over the Seine. Give the riverbanks a rather wide berth, as they are frequented by some more dubious goings-on late at night. Wander through the Marais or the Latin Quarter and discover the Paris of early morning—pavements being sluiced down, street markets coming to life, and the intoxicating smells of freshly ground coffee and just-baked *pains chocolats* wafting out of the cafes and boulangeries.

Crazy Horse Saloon, 12 avenue George-V, 8e, ☎ 01-47-23-32-32. Métro: George-V. A strip show without the strip—dancers are already *déshabillée* in what they call "the art of nudity." Artistic lighting and risqué costumes. Excellent magicians, too. Crowded and very expensive.

Folies Bergère, 32 rue Richer, 9e, ☎ 01-44-79-98-98. Métro: Cadet, rue Montmartre. It was here that

Maurice Chevalier and Mistinguett sang in the old days. The 1930s decor is magnificent.

Au Lapin Agile, 22 rue des Saules, 18ᵉ, ☎ 01-46-06-85-87. Métro: Lamarck-Caulaincourt. Old haunt of Renoir and Picasso, now devoted to tourists and offering song, humor, and poetry in a small-scale Montmartre atmosphere. Good value for the money.

Lido, 116bis avenue des Champs-Elysées, 8ᵉ, ☎ 01-40-76-56-10. Métro: George-V. (Next door to the Normandie cinema.) Paris's most lavish revue—the famous Bluebell girls, lasers, a skating rink, underwater ballet, and several dozen sets. Seventy million francs were spent to renovate the theater: Imagine 3,000 square meters of red velvet, cut-crystal candelabras, and sequins galore. American Bob Turk, formerly with the Ice Capades, directs.

Michou, 80 rue des Martyrs, 18ᵉ, ☎ 01-46-06-16- 04. Métro: Pigalle. Burlesque-style impressions of the great stars of stage and showbiz. Marvelous drag performances—very funny.

Moulin Rouge (Bal du Moulin Rouge), Place Blanche, 82 boulevard de Clichy, 18ᵉ, ☎ 01-46-06-00-19. Métro: Blanche. Immortalized by Toulouse-Lautrec, this was the birthplace of the cancan. The show is much the same as at the Lido (60 girls! 1,000 costumes!), but less Las Vegas–style and more Parisian. Glitzy ballroom decor with Chinese lanterns. Edith Piaf, Yves Montand, Charles Aznavour, and other luminaries of the Paris stage all stepped into the Moulin Rouge footlights. Today, the cancan is still going strong and 800 fans pour out of the buses to applaud.

Paradis Latin, 28 rue du Cardinal-Lemoine, 5ᵉ, ☎ 01-43-25-28-28. Métro: Cardinal-Lemoine. Wonderful theater, built by Eiffel and restored to glory in the 1980s. Showgirls, showgirls, showgirls—and the feathers fly.

Jazz Clubs

Jazz clubs, with their echoes of the postwar era, have remained largely unchanged since the 1950s, and they consequently offer both nostalgia and entertainment. Paris has always been an international jazz capital, and a number of excellent clubs host performers from all over the world.

The "Musts"

Le Bilboquet, 13 rue St Benoît, 6ᵉ, ☎ 01-45-48-81-84. Métro: St-Germain-des-Prés. A jazz hot-spot and an institution, first opened in 1947. You can have dinner here, too.

Jazz-Club Lionel Hampton, Hôtel Méridien, 81 boulevard Gouvion-St-Cyr, 17ᵉ, ☎ 01-40-68-30-42. Métro: Porte-Maillot. Top New Orleans jazz and blues musicians perform in this chic hotel setting from 10:30pm to 2am. Sunday jazz-brunch, too.

New Morning, 7-9 rue des Petites-Écuries, 10ᵉ, ☎ 01-45-23-56-39. Métro: Château d'Eau. This hangarlike venue features concerts with all the top jazz names.

Le Petit Journal St-Michel, 71 boulevard St-Michel, 5ᵉ, ☎ 01-43-26-28-59. Métro: Luxembourg. A very well-respected jazz venue with a distinctly relaxed atmosphere. A special package includes 8:30pm dinner and the show.

Bars

Some of the most sophisticated bars are found in the smart hotels, where the atmosphere is truly international. Some suggestions: **the Plaza-Athénée, the Crillon, the Ritz, the George-V, the Raphaël,** and **the Bristol.** See "Accommodations" for details.

Prices are generally high, especially for aperitifs or champagne. No harm done in asking for something that is more Parisian and cheaper too, such as Kir (white wine and black-currant sirop), a pastis, or a nonalcoholic drink such as a Perrier.

Bars are almost always crowded before dinner, and then again very late, after everything else has closed. They tend to open around 5pm, and some stay open until dawn. Unlike many other cities, Paris has no legal closing hours.

Some suggested addresses:

La Closerie des Lilas, 171 boulevard du Montparnasse, 6ᵉ, ☎ 01-43-26-70-50. Métro: Vavin. RER: Port Royal. The haunt of Hemingway still attracts assorted artists and literati, in a truly Parisian atmosphere. Good brasserie. See "Restaurants A to Z" in "Dining."

Le Café du Passage, 12, rue de Charonne, 11ᵉ. ☎ 01-49-29-97-64. Métro: Bastille. A trendy late-night wine bar, not far from the Bastille, it attracts a young, fashionable crowd to sip *grands crus* served by the glass.

China Club, 50 rue de Charenton, 12ᵉ, ☎ 01-43-43-82-02. Métro: Bastille. Trendy crowd, elegant bar. Chinese cuisine.

Concorde-Lafayette Hotel, 3 place Général Koenig, 17ᵉ, ☎ 01-40-68-50-68. Métro: Porte-Maillot. Panoramic bar on the 33rd floor of this hotel. Drinks are all the same price and not cheap, but it's worth it for the excellent views of Paris and the Eiffel Tower.

La Coupole, 102 boulevard du Montparnasse, 14ᵉ, ☎ 01-43-20-14-20. Métro: Vavin. Cultural landmark for generations of artists. See "Dining." Basement bar/disco where they have "Mambomania" and salsa on Tuesday nights at 9:30pm. (Wed Caribbean, Thurs Brazilian).

Le Divan du Monde, 75, rue des Martyrs, 18ᵉ, ☎ 01-44-92-77-66. Métro: Pigalle. Serving up theater, music, whatever, on a rotating basis, it's located between Montmartre, Barbès, and Pigalle. The point here is generally multicultural, with Cuban, rap, jungle, techno, and house music. Le Divan is big and loud, but the drinks are cheap for Paris, and the atmosphere is lively.

Le Forum, 4 boulevard Malesherbes, 8ᵉ. ☎ 01-42-65-37-86. Métro: Madeleine. Rather British in style and very relaxed. More than 100 cocktails and 85 whiskies.

Le Fouquet's, 99 avenue des Champs-Elysées, 8ᵉ, ☎ 01-47-23-70-60. Métro: George-V. An old haunt of actors in the days of black-and-white movies. Mix of regulars and tourists, with a very occasional famous face. See also "Cafes & Tea Salons" in "Dining."

Le Hard Rock Café, 14 boulevard Montmartre, 9ᵉ, ☎ 01-42-46-31-32. Métro: Richelieu-Drouot, rue Montmartre. The Paris branch of this worldwide chain.

Harry's New York Bar, 5 rue Daunou, 2ᵉ, ☎ 01-42-61-71-14. Métro: Opéra. *Sank Roo Doe Noo*—an all-American institution. Popular with Parisians, too. Stocks 160 kinds of whisky. Good piano bar in the basement. Closes only on Christmas Day.

Kitty O'Shea's, 10 rue des Capucines, 2ᵉ, ☎ 01-40-15-08-08. Métro: Opéra. Parisian sister of Dublin's famous pub.

Lili La Tigresse, 98, rue Blanche. 9ᵉ. ☎ 01-48-74-08-25. Métro: Pigalle, Blanche. A trendy Pigalle watering-hole for the young and fashionably outrageous. The dancers occasionally get up on the tables and perform a (mild) striptease, but only go if you are under 25 or very in the mood.

Mayflower, 49 rue Descartes, 5ᵉ, ☎ 01-43-54-56-47. Métro: Cardinal-Lemoine. Irish bar with cocktails.

Majestic Café, 34 rue Vielle du Temple, 4ᵉ, ☎ 01-42-74-61-61. Métro: Hôtel-de-Ville, St-Paul. The crowd spills out of the faded but elegant interior and onto the sidewalks. A lively favorite for stylish about-towners.

Pacific Palissades, 51 rue Quincampoix, 3ᵉ, ☎ 01-42-74-01-17. Métro: Les Halles, Rambuteau. The same pianist and singer has entertained here, Thursday through Saturday, for years, with great success.

La Palette, 43 rue de Seine, 6ᵉ, ☎ 01-43-26-68-15. Métro: Mabillon. The eternal St-Germain-des-Prés day or night rendezvous for young and old students. Now that the Flore and Deux Magots are overpriced tourist hangouts, this is the authentic left-bank cafe experience.

Chez Richard, 37 rue Vielle du Temple, 4ᵉ, ☎ 01-42-74-31-65. Métro: Hôtel-de-Ville, St-Paul. Across the street from the Majestic, and generally less crowded, though watch out for weekends around 1am. Two floors of stone walls and floors and plenty of little tables in the back to get cozy over.

Rosebud, 11bis rue Delambre, 14ᵉ. ☎ 01-43-35-38-54. Métro: Vavin. Former rendezvous for the likes of Sartre and de Beauvoir—a classic Montparnasse meeting-place. Still holds good.

SansZ SansS, 49 rue du Faubourg St-Antoine, 11ᵉ, ☎ 01-44-75-78-78. Métro: Bastille. Open daily 9am to 2am. With a bar full of nightcrawlers, faded baroque-style furnishings, and a huge video screen relaying the scene on the street just outside, this cafe looks and feels more like an after-hours club than a place for a coffee. But it's open all day and even serves lunch and dinner. Actually, late mornings and lunchtime are the best times to come. After 9pm, a young, punky-looking crowd spills three-deep out onto the sidewalk.

La Villa, 29 rue Jacob, 6ᵉ, ☎ 01-43-26-60-00. Métro: St-Germain-des-Prés. Ultradesigner flair in this daringly modern hotel (see "Accommodations"). Split-level salons, cocktails. Has jazz performances every night but Sunday.

What's Up Bar, 15, rue Daval, 11ᵉ, ☎ 01-48-05-88-33. Métro: Bastille. A brand new Bastille hot spot designed by a former Philippe Starck assistant, Christophe Pillet. The high-tech sound system, including 2 dozen speakers, means that you can actually talk in a regular voice in spite of the loud music all around you. Open until 2am.

Nightclubs

In Paris as elsewhere, a nightclub is normally "private," although there are varying degrees of privacy, particularly for visitors. However, if you are young or pretty or well-dressed (or ideally all three), the chances increase of being given entry. Hotel concierges are often knowledgeable about what is "in" for foreign visitors.

Le Niel's, 27 avenue des Ternes, 17ᵉ, ☎ 01-47-66-45-00. Métro: Ternes. See "Discothèques" above. Niel's is not as frightfully exacting as some clubs, although how you look is still important.

Private Clubs

The private clubs of Paris are ultrafamous and ultra-expensive. They tend to cater to a more middle-aged crowd, though there is always a crowd of young boys and girls to keep 'em feeling is young. If you gain entry, you can expect to encounter screen stars, top models, and a lot of aging playboys in too-tight blue blazers. For men, ties or bow ties are expected; women, however, can be as outrageous as they like.

If you must go and want to spend a fortune on a drink, ask about: **Castel's** (15 rue Princesse, 6ᵉ, ☎ 01-43-26-90-22; métro: Mabillon), and, of course, **Régine's** (49-51 rue de Ponthieu, 8ᵉ, ☎ 01-43-59-21-60; métro: George V). These are the big names on today's club scene, as they have been for years.

EXCURSIONS

Paris has always been the center of power, politics, and the arts in France, and over the centuries, great châteaux have grown up within easy striking distance of the city. Several important cathedral towns are also close at hand, as well as pretty villages and many magnificent forests, a famous feature of the Ile de France. All these sights make easy 1-day excursions from Paris by car or by public transport.

★★★ Fontainebleau

40 miles (65km) southeast of Paris. By train: from Gare de Lyon to Fontainebleau station, then bus to the palace; by car: on A6 to Fontainebleau exit, then N7; by bus: tours with Cityrama, 4 pl. des Pyramides, 1ᵉʳ, ☎ 01-44-55-61-00, or Paris-Vision, 214 rue de Rivoli, 1ᵉʳ, ☎ 01-42-60-31-25. Tourist office: 31 pl. Napoléon Bonaparte, ☎ 01-64-22-25-68.

Ideally, your visit to Fontainebleau would be a 2-day affair, one to visit the **palace and town,** another to explore the **forest.** This great (25,000ha) expanse of woodland is a remarkable natural phenomenon. Over the millennia, a strange alchemy of glacial action and erosion has produced a surreal terrain of hills, ravines, and extraordinary rock formations. (The sidewalks of Paris are paved with rock from Fontainebleau.) Giant boulders with organic-looking contours lie everywhere, some resembling stranded whales, others sculptures by Henry Moore. Twelve million people a year visit the forest—more than the Eiffel Tower or Disneyland Paris. Little wonder that the forest has been used as a setting for more than 100 movies, in which it has served to represent, among other things, the terrain of the Holy Land, the Wild West, and the Switzerland of William Tell.

The Château of Fontainebleau

☎ 01-60-71-50-70. Guided tours by appointment (choice of theme); special visits for the blind. Open Nov–May 9:30am–12:30pm, 2–5pm;

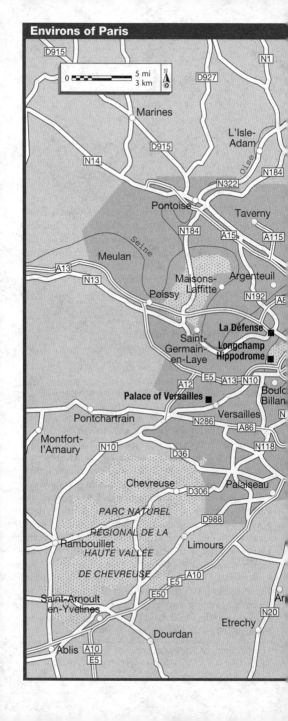

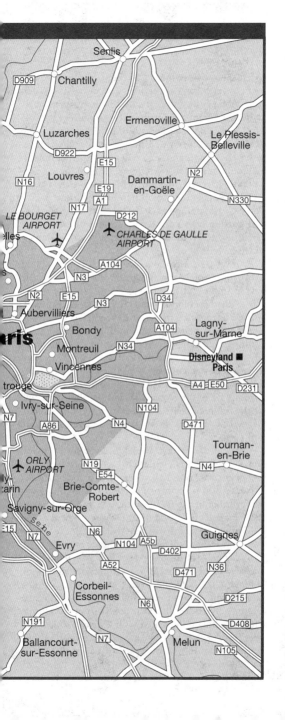

June–Oct 9:30am–5pm (until 6pm in July and Aug). Closed Tues. Admission charged. Wheelchair access.

As a former royal residence, the Fontainebleau château is just as interesting as Versailles and possesses a much more subtle beauty; even the name has a magical quality, deriving from a fountain in the grounds of the palace, *fontaine belle eau* (fountain of beautiful water). The charming town has a well-heeled grace and elegance, with leafy avenues and large, quietly prosperous houses. All around it lies the lovely Fontainebleau forest.

If you have time to spare before visiting the palace, take a walk (allow 45 to 50 min.) through the thickly wooded park, and approach the palace through the **formal garden** with its carp pond, its great parterres designed by Le Nôtre in 1664, and its curious statues, which include a pair of sphinxes.

A royal residence from the 12thC, Fontainebleau saw the birth of 2 French Kings, Philippe The Fair (le Bel) and Louis XIII. But the palace is linked particularly with the colorful François I (1494–1547), rake, military adventurer, friend of Leonardo da Vinci, and one of the greatest royal patrons of the arts in French history. In 1528, he knocked down most of the existing medieval edifice and began to build a new château according to the Renaissance principles that had influenced him during his Italian campaigns. All over the building, carved in stonework and paneling, you will see the fire-breathing salamander that was his emblem. Henry II, Catherine de Medicis, and Henry IV added to the palace.

Most of the French sovereigns lived for a time at Fontainebleau, and the palace has witnessed a rich pageant of history: Louis XIV's decision to revoke the Edict of Nantes was made here; Pope Pius VII lived as a virtual prisoner in the palace from June 1812 to January 1814; Napoléon I made it his favorite residence after the **Tuileries,** and it was here that he came when he abdicated in 1814, before departing for St. Helena.

Fontainebleau has been described as a "rendezvous of châteaux," for it is really a sprawling conglomeration of buildings of different periods, built around 5 courtyards. Before entering, take a walk around the palace. On the north side is the charming **Garden of Diana,** with its fountain decorated with a statue of the goddess. Traveling counter-clockwise, pass into the White Horse Courtyard, or **Courtyard of Farewells,** which was the scene of Napoléon's farewell to his guard. Note the graceful double-horseshoe staircase with its hermetic caduceuses carved in the stonework of the balustrade.

To the right of the stairway is an arch leading into the **Fountain Courtyard,** looking onto the carp pond. On the right, the 2 stone statues of fierce-looking Fô dogs guard the entrance to the **Empress Eugénie's Chinese salons.**

Through another archway to the west is the **gilded door** that is one of the most famous features of the palace. This huge gateway, with its 3 superimposed loggias, was the first structure to be completed when rebuilding began in 1528.

From here, the way leads northeast along the facade of the ballroom. Turn left to stand between the **Oval Courtyard** to the southwest, with its domed gateway, and the **Courtyard of the Kitchens** to the northeast. The gateway to the latter is decorated by 2 huge **Hermes heads** in stone.

Arguably the most remarkable room in the palace is the **François I Gallery,** which was decorated in the years 1534 to 1537 by a team of Italian artists and craftsmen. The walls are adorned with 14 frescoes surrounded by rich decorative stucco work illustrating events or allegorical subjects connected with the reign of François I. One shows an elephant decorated with the fleur-de-lys—an allegory of the king's wisdom; another, symbolizing the unity of the state, depicts François I presenting a pomegranate, symbol of concord, to representatives of different classes.

Another splendid Renaissance-style room is the vast **ballroom,** which was designed by Philibert Delorme under Henry II. It has deep, arched bays, frescoes of mythological scenes, and a coffered ceiling, the design of which is reflected in the woodwork of the floor.

The rooms known as the **apartments of the King and Queen** are a rich confection of different periods, much of the decoration being in the overblown 19thC-style of King Louis-Philippe.

Equally ornate is the series of **Napoleonic rooms**, including the Emperor's Throne Room, bedroom, and council chamber. The Napoleonic bee emblem of industry and discipline figures prominently in the decoration.

Those interested in Napoléon and in militaria should visit the **Musée Napoléonien d'Art et d'Histoire Militaires** (88 rue St-Honoré; open Tues–Sat 2–5pm), which has a splendid collection of military paraphernalia.

Restaurants

Aigle Noir (also a hotel; 27, pl. Napoléon-Bonaparte, 77300 Fontainebleau, ☎ 01-64-22-32-65; **$$$/$$$$**).

François I (3 rue Royale, ☎ 01-64-22-24-68; **$$/ $$$**).

★★ Le Château de Versailles

Château open May 2–Sept 30, 9am–6:30pm. Grand Trianon (separate admission charged) and Petit Trianon (separate admission charged, or cheaper if combined with Grand Trianon) open 10am–6:30pm. Oct 1–Apr 30: château open 9am–5:30pm, Grand Trianon and Petit Trianon open Tues–Fri 10am–12:30pm and 2–5:30pm; Sat and Sun 10am–5:30pm. Gardens open daily dawn to dusk. Château closed Mon, public holidays. For information on opening times, programs, group visits, call ☎ 01-30-84-74-00. Admission charged, but various discounts for children, students, and seniors over 60, depending on day of week and type of entry. (e.g., if not taking guided tour, those under 18 always admitted free. Over 18 and under 26, or over 60 receive reduced rate Tues–Sat. Everyone admitted at a reduced rate on Sun). Guided tours: Compulsory in some parts of building; tours available in English. For guided tours, go to entrance 1; for nonguided tours, go to entrance 2. Audio-guides available. Wheelchair access.

The palace of Versailles is perhaps the greatest monument to absolute monarchy ever built. It is overwhelming, fascinating, unforgettable, but to many people not exactly beautiful. Louis XIV, the Sun King, who built it, was extremely vain, and his palace is an expression of egomania in stone, plaster, and gold leaf.

The site was first occupied by a hunting lodge and then by a small brick-and-stone château, built by Louis XIII and enlarged by his son Louis XIV, the work continuing from 1661 for about 50 years. The architects were first Le Vau, then Jules Hardouin-Mansart. The decoration was supervised by Le Brun, and the gardens were planned by Le Nôtre, creator of the **Tuileries** gardens. At the height of the construction work, 36,000 men and 6,000 horses were employed.

In 1682, Louis decided to make Versailles the court residence and seat of government, and it retained this function until the Revolution. Thus Versailles was the capital of France for more than 100 years. It was the scene of a glittering court, which in its heyday included a thousand nobles, who lived in the palace along with a vast retinue of servants.

Approaching the palace from the station and avenue de Paris, the **stables** (Grandes and Petites Ecuries) are to the right and left of the vast **place d'Armes** in front of the palace. Passing through the great wrought-iron gates, the visitor enters the enormous courtyard,

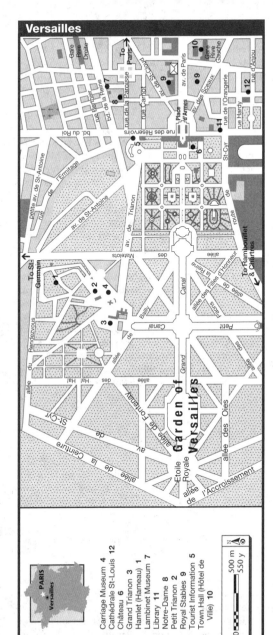

Versailles

To Paris

To St. Germain

To Rambouillet & Chartres

Gare Rive Droite
Gare Rive Gauche
av. de Paris
rue des Chantiers
rue de la Paroisse
rue Carnot
bd. de la Reine
rue Berthier
bd. du Roi
Place d'Armes
rue des Réservoirs
av. de St-Antoine
Petite av. de St-Antoine
rue de l'Ermitage
av. de Trianon
av. des Matelots
allée des
Bailly
allée Bailly
allée du Rendezvous
allée du Hal
Hal des
allée de Fontenay
av. de la Ceinture
St-Cyr
av. de St-Cyr
route
St-Cyr
av. de Paris
av. de Sceaux
rue de l'Orangerie
rue Hardy
rue d'Anjou

Garden of Versailles

Grand Canal
Petit Canal
allée de la Reine
allée des Filles d'Honneur
allée de Paris
Etoile Royale
allée des Oies
allée Royale
av. de l'Accroissement

PARIS
Versailles

Carriage Museum 4
Cathédrale St-Louis 12
Château 6
Grand Trianon 3
Hamlet (Hameau) 1
Lambinet Museum 7
Library 11
Notre-Dame 8
Petit Trianon 2
Royal Stables 9
Tourist Information 5
Town Hall (Hôtel de Ville) 10

0   500 m
0   550 y

N

with its equestrian statue of Louis XIV, erected by King Louis-Philippe, in the middle. Enter by the doorway on the right of the courtyard, and follow the stairway to the upper chapel vestibule, from where the ★ **chapel** can be seen. Dedicated to St-Louis (King Louis IX of France), it is a frothy confection in white and gold, with a sumptuously painted ceiling.

From here you pass into the series of **State apartments,** leading into the astonishing **Hall of Mirrors,** where the 17 windows that overlook the gardens are matched on the opposite wall by a row of arches filled with reflecting glass.

Beside the Hall of Mirrors are the sumptuous **King's apartments,** with the bed where each morning and night the monarch's *levée* and *couchée* took place in front of the assembled courtiers. Louis XIV died of gangrene on this bed on September 1, 1715.

At the opposite end of the Hall of Mirrors are the **Queen's apartments,** followed by the **Coronation Room** and then the south wing. Its 1st floor is taken up almost entirely by the **Hall of Battles,** built by Louis-Philippe, which contains 33 paintings of war scenes. Also on the 1st floor are several rooms, including the **private apartments of the King and Queen.**

The **Royal Opera,** which occupies the end of the north wing, can also be visited only on a guided tour. Its interior is entirely of wood, ornately carved, and painted in gold, blue, and pink.

The Gardens

Admission free. Open daily dawn–dusk.

To understand Versailles fully, it is necessary to appreciate that the whole complex, palace and gardens, is a kind of symbolic Utopia in which one theme is constantly emphasized: that of a solar deity around which everything revolves, just as the state revolves around the king.

This comes across particularly clearly in the gardens, which were laid out by Le Nôtre in a series of highly formal terraces adorned with *parterres,* statues, vases, and fountains. Nature is subdued, as a demonstration of the power of the Sun King, who is represented here as Apollo.

Bear this in mind as you approach the main focus of the garden, the **fountain of Apollo,** down a long avenue flanked by statues and with a carpet of lawn stretching away into the distance. The figure of Apollo in his chariot emerges out of the water, just as in legend the sun rose out of the sea at daybreak. You can also witness the amazing spectacle of the **illuminated fountains,** by night, and the **Grandes Eaux Musicales,** by day, generally Sundays only, from May to October (call the Office de Tourisme ☎ 01-39-50-36-22 for exact details of times and tickets). The **Grande Fête de Nuit,** a fireworks spectacular on the Bassin de Neptune, takes place for a few nights only in July and September.

Beyond the fountain of Apollo stretches the **Grand Canal,** on which there once sailed a flotilla of small-scale ships and gondolas. Today you can rent a boat to row on the canal, in more modest style. The waterway forms a cross, the northern arm of which leads to the **Grand Trianon** and **Petit Trianon.** These are well worth a visit, the former with its pink marble colonnade and lavish interior, the latter more elegant and restrained, with its exquisite theater in which Marie-Antoinette used to act.

Close by is the **Hameau de la Reine** (Queen's hamlet), a collection of mock-rustic buildings where the same queen used to play at leading the simple life.

Recognizing that some of these points of interest are a 15- to 20-minute walk from the château, the management has introduced glass-sided trains (Admission charged; ☎ 01-39-54-22-00 for information and reservations), which offer a running commentary in several languages, and interludes of classical music. These either make a driving circuit, slowing down but not stopping, or allow passengers to descend and be collected again $1^{1}/_{2}$ hours later.

Restaurants

Les Trois Marches–Trianon Palace (1, blvd de la Reine, ☎ 01-39-50-34-12; **$$$$/$$$$$**; closed Sun–Mon.) offers a formidable gastronomic experience in cooly elegant surroundings, overlooking the grounds of the palace. **La Flotille** (Parc du Château, ☎ 01-39-51-41-58; **$$**) is a delightful little restaurant near the east end of the canal, in the palace gardens.

THE BASICS

Before You Go

Tourist Offices

Useful free information on visiting Paris or France can be obtained from the **French Government Tourist Offices** in the United States: 628 Fifth Avenue, New York, NY 10020; 676 North Michigan Avenue, Chicago, IL 60611; 2305 Cedar Springs Road, Dallas, TX 75201; 9454 Wilshire Boulevard, Beverly Hills, CA 90212. For information by phone, call the **France on Call Hot Line** at ☎ 900/990-0040 (50¢ per minute). Isn't it just like the French, charging visitors for the privilege of learning about their country!

Documents

Visitors to France, if they are US, Swiss, Canadian, or Japanese citizens, or are residents in the European Community (EC), do not need a visa—a **passport** or **identity card** is sufficient.

For stays of longer than 3 months, you need to apply for a *carte de séjour,* from the French Embassy in Washington, DC, or from the nearest French consulate.

If you plan to drive, you need a valid **driver's license,** and you must be age 18 or older. An **international driver's license** is not needed. If you're bringing a car into the country, you also need the **vehicle registration certificate,** a **national identity plate** or **sticker** displayed at the rear of the vehicle, and a **certificate of insurance** or **international insurance certificate,** called a **green card,** proving that you have third-party insurance. If you rent a car, the rental company will provide this.

Money

Currency   The unit of currency is the **franc** (**F**), which consists of 100 **centimes** (**c**). There are coins for 5c, 10c, 20c, 50c, 1F, 2F, 5F, 10F, and 20F; notes come in the following amounts: 20F, 50F, 100F, 200F, and 500F.

Exchanging Money   Be sure to bring with you at least 300F before you arrive to cover taxi fare into the city and any sundries—the lines to change money at the airport are long and you won't be in the mood for this the minute you arrive. **Hotels** usually give you the worst rate; try to change money at a **bank** (there will be a sign reading *Change* somewhere outside if it does this) or at an **exchange office.** Almost all banks and exchange offices charge some commission, so you may want to shop around for a good rate, as they vary substantially. Banks are usually open from 9am to 5pm, though hours for individual banks vary. On days preceding public holidays, banks are open only in the morning, although exchange bureaus are open longer. **The Exchange Corporation,** at 140 avenue des Champs-Elysées, 8ᵉ (☎ 01-42-89-35-40) is open everyday from 8:30am to midnight. For more information regarding exchange rates, contact **Thomas Cook currency exchange** at ☎ 800-CURRENCY.

Travelers Checks   Those issued by **American Express, Thomas Cook, Barclays,** and **Citibank** are widely recognized. It's important to note separately the serial numbers of your checks and the telephone number to call in case of loss. American Express issues checks that can be signed by either of 2 parties. They also offer extensive local refund facilities for lost checks through their own offices or agents.

ATMs   Approximately 250,000 Automated Teller Machines (ATMs) in 100 countries are tied to international networks like **Cirrus** and **Plus.** By using your bank card to withdraw money, you will debit the amount from your account. When using an ATM abroad, the money will be in local currency; the rate of exchange tends to be as good, if not better, than what you would receive at an airport money counter or a hotel. Note that international withdrawal fees will be higher than domestic— ask your bank for specifics. To use your bank card at an ATM you will need a **Personal Identification Number** (**PIN**). Contact your bank to program your PIN for the area you will be visiting. Most ATMs outside the United States require a 4-digit PIN.

To receive a **directory for Cirrus ATMs'** exact locations, call 800/424-7787; for **Plus's locations** call 800/336-8472. You can also access the **Visa/PLUS International ATM Locator Guide** through **Internet:** http://www.visa.com/visa.

Also: There is a **Citibank office** at 30 avenue des Champs-Elysées (☎ 01-40-76-33-00) that will allow you to draw money from your **Citibank** or **Cirrus account** as well as on credit cards if you have a **PIN;** the machines are open 24 hours. There is also an **exchange office** at the same address, open during office hours.

Getting Money from Home   Located in more than 70 countries, agents at **American Express MoneyGram** (800/543-4080 in the U.S.) can wire money around the world. Senders must go to an agent in person. Up to $1,000 can be charged on a credit card (only Discover, MasterCard, or Visa—you can't use American Express). Amounts over $1,000 must be paid in cash; the maximum amount for a single transaction is $10,000. Recipients must present a reference number (phoned in from sender) and identification to pick up the cash.

Western Union works in a similar fashion, except that they also allow customers to wire money over the phone by using their credit cards (MasterCard and Visa only). Call 800/325-6000 for its worldwide locations.

Fees for both of the above companies range from 5% to 10%, depending on the amount sent, and method of payment.

Customs & Duties

Customs restrictions differ for citizens of the European Community and for citizens of non-EC countries. Non-EC nationals can bring in, duty-free, 200 cigarettes or 100 cigarillos or 50 cigars or 250 grams of smoking tobacco. This amount is doubled if you live outside of Europe. You can also bring in 2 liters of wine and either 1 liter of alcohol over 38.80 proof or 2 liters of wine under 38.80 proof. In addition, you can bring in 50 grams (1.75 oz.) of perfume, $1/4$ liter of eau de toilette, 500 grams (1 lb.) of coffee, and 200 grams ($1/2$ lb.) of tea. Visitors 15 years of age and over may also bring in other goods totaling 300F, while the allowance for those 14 and under is 150F. (Customs officials tend to be lenient about general merchandise, realizing that the limits are unrealistically low.)

If you're arriving from an EC country, there is no longer a customs tariff or limit placed on goods carried within countries of the union.

When to Go

Parisians tend to leave town in August, which means many of the city's restaurants and entertainments are closed for at least part of the month. September and October are very busy seasons, when trade shows pack the city's hotels and getting reservations at your favorite restaurants—even finding a taxi—is likely to be very hard. Especially avoid the city during the first 3 weeks in October, when textile and fashion shows so choke the city that many hotels, even moderate ones, are booked a year in advance. The same is true, though to a lesser degree, in March. Tourists swamp the city from May through the summer. The best time to come is probably November or April, when the tourist trade is at a manageable flow and the heat is off. Christmas is also a nice time, and many hotels offer their best promotions at this time of the year—be sure to ask about special packages when you reserve. If you're coming to shop, aim for January or June when twice-yearly sales reduce shop prices throughout the city.

The best kept secret about Paris is how dreary the climate is. Most of the year, from September to June, Paris weather is remarkably the same: a lot of gray skies, chilly temperatures, and regular drizzles. In August—and occasionally, July too—Paris can be unpleasantly and surprisingly hot: temperatures average 23°C (75°F), and you might think you were much farther south. The heat is compounded by the fact that, as it is cool most of the year in Paris, very few venues are air-conditioned. Fall and spring are usually chilly, with temperatures falling to the low 50s Farenheit immediately after Labor Day, and it drizzles quite a bit—which is why the odd sunny day brings such exultant cheer all around you. It rarely snows in Paris, and though winter is cold, it's rarely freezing cold.

Call **900-WEATHER** (95¢ per minute) for up-to-the-minute weather forecasts.

Calendar of Events

January
"The City of Paris Invites You to a Concert": Buy one concert ticket and receive two; see the tourist office for information. Twice-yearly **couture shows** are held for the press and are by invitation only.

March
The loud and lively **Foire du Trone,** a giant amusement park, sets up in the Bois de Vincennes and runs

until early June on the weekends, from 2pm until midnight.

April
The **Paris marathon:** Call 01-53-17-03-10 for information.

May
"The City of Paris Invites you to the Theater": Buy one ticket and receive another one free; see the tourist office for information. The **French Open Tennis Championships,** at Stade Rolland Garros, runs late May to early June, though tickets are scarcer than hen's teeth; call 01-47-43-48-00.

June
The **Fête de la Musique** is held every year in Paris on June 21st, the longest day of the year. Musicians set up on every street corner and play all night, to the delight of the city, which turns out in droves for a big citywide street party. Also, there are big open-air concerts at places like the Bastille and the Trocadéro. The **Festival Chopin** takes place in June at the Orangerie in the Parc de Bagatelle (Bois de Boulogne); call 01-45-00-22-19 for information. Also at the end of June, the **Tuileries Gardens amusement park** sets up and stays there until the end of August.

July
Bastille Day celebrates the birth of modern-day France with fireworks, parades, and street fairs, dominating the city on the 13th and the 14th of the month. Also, the **Open-Air Cinema Festival** runs from mid-July to mid-August at the Parc de la Villette (☎ 01-40-03-75-00); buy a ticket and receive a blanket and a deck chair and see a film in the open air. And the **Musique en L'Ile** festival (☎ 01-44-62-70-90) begins in July and ends in September, this is a cycle of concerts held at 3 of the city's most beautiful churches: St. Louis-en-l'Ile, Saint-Germain-des-Prés, and Sainte Chapelle.

September
The **Festival d'Automn** is an annual festival of contemporary music, dance, and concerts—often featuring a solid array of international talent—throughout the city. It runs through December; for information call 01-42-96-96-94. This is also the month for the **Journées du Patrimoine,** when many of the city's public and private monuments—usually closed to the public—are open; for information call 01-44-61-21-50.

October

The **opera season** opens at the Bastille Opera House. For information, call 01-44-73-13-00, but remember tickets need to be purchased weeks ahead of time by phone; months by mail. **Designer ready-to-wear shows** choke the city with retailers and fashion editors, dressed head to toe in black. Also, **FIAC,** the **International Salon of Contemporary Art,** is usually held in October; call 01-49-53-27-00. The **Prix de l'Arc de Triomph,** one of horse racing's big events, is held in early October at the Hippodrome de Longchamp; call 01-49-10-20-30 for information. Also, the **Paris Auto Show (Mondial de l'Automobile),** a showcase for international auto design, is held in early October at the Parc des Expositions at the Porte de Versailles; call 01-43-95-10-10.

November

The **Festival d'Art Sacré de la Ville de Paris** features a series of Christmas concerts held in the city's churches; call 01-45-61-54-99. Also, the **Mois de la Photo** takes place in Paris every other year (with the next in 1998), with nearly 100 photo exhibitions held throughout the city's galleries, museums, and exhibition spaces.

December

The annual **Crêche** goes on view at the Hôtel de Ville; the major **boulevards light up** for Christmas. The **Braderie de Paris** also takes place in the first few weeks—this is a **big sale** where everything from clothes to books to appliances are all up for sale at the Parc des Expositions de Paris at the Porte de Versailles, 15ᵉ, ☎ 01-42-97-52-10.

Mail

Post office buildings are marked by the letters **PTT.** Normal opening hours are Monday to Friday 8am to 7pm, Saturday 8am to noon. Open 24 hours, the **main post office** is at 52 rue du Louvre, 1ᵉʳ (☎ 01-40-28-20-00).

Stamps (*timbres*) can be bought from tobacconists (in *tabacs*), hotels, and post offices. For a 1-ounce (40g) letter, postage to the United States costs 7.90F; a postcard costs 4.30F. **Mailboxes** are yellow and are marked *boîte aux lettres;* they are usually found outside tabacs selling stamps. Allow 7 to 10 days for mail to reach France and for your letters to reach the United States.

Addresses in Paris must all include the **postal zip code,** which combines 750 with the numbers of the *arrondissements.* Thus, the zip code in the 1er arrondissement is 75001, and so on up to the 20^e, where the zip code is 75020. Usefully, the zip code thus shows at once the arrondissement in which any address is to be found.

Electric Current

The electric current is **220V** (50 cycles AC). **Plugs** (*prise de courant*) are standard European, with 2 round prongs. **Adapters** (*transformateurs*) can be bought at any good electrical store in Paris. If you're at a loss, they're on sale in the basement at BHV, the department store at 52 rue Rivoli, 4^e.

What to Pack

Paris is not such a dressy city as it is a sophisticated city, and nothing is appreciated as much as appropriate dress. Except in mid-winter or mid-summer, the most important outerwear item is a raincoat, preferably lined, and a folding umbrella. Paris is a walking city, so bring comfortable shoes. You can't wear sneakers into discotheques, though jeans are ubiquitous, and men should wear jackets—and occasionally ties—to the more expensive restaurants. Outside of the really special restaurants (and, oddly enough, when dining on the Bateaux Mouches), men don't have to wear jackets or ties. Only opening night at the Opera is truly formal, otherwise you wear what you would wear to an expensive restaurant, and even then, don't be surprised to find the people next to you in corduroy pants.

Parisians generally don't wear shorts, though every other tourist does, so take your choice. Bring all your pharmaceuticals with you, if only because contact-lens solution in France runs around $20 a bottle, and things like shampoo and toothpaste are equally costly. Bring the pharmaceutical names of your medicines with you in case you need to replace them.

For Travelers with Disabilities

Though Paris has made a lot of progress over the past 10 years, the city is still not an easy place for travelers with disabilities. Many avenues are broad, and curbs are gently sloped toward the streets at intersections, but public transportation is largely inaccessible to the wheelchair-bound. The métros—with their notorious labyrinth of stairs and escalators—are virtually impossible to negotiate.

La Foundation de France, for its 25th anniversary, has raised 1.2 million francs to create and develop easily accessible buses—but so far the plan is only in development in 7 cities in France (Versailles being one of them). Few public toilets have wheelchair access. Also, a frustrating number of the city's hotels and restaurants are still not accessible. For a list of hotels in Paris offering facilities for disabled travelers, contact the **Association des Paralysées de France,** 17 bd. Auguste Blanqui, 75013 Paris (☎ 01-40-78-69-00), for their guide (100F).

A glossy color guidebook published by the French Tourist Office, *Paris/Ile de France, Pour Tous* is available free and provides valuable information concerning the relative accessibility of **cinemas, swimming pools, pharmacies, parks, restaurants,** and of **public toilets.** Unfortunately, it's available only in French. Get it even if you can't read French—the logos are fairly clear.

Car Rentals

Car-rental agencies are easily found at both airports and in the city, though it's less expensive to rent a car from the United States before you leave and have it waiting for you. If you want an automatic car, be prepared to pay in the higher-priced categories, and be sure to reserve ahead if you need seats for children.

Among the major car-rental companies are: **Avis** (☎ 800/331-1084); **Budget Rent-a-Car** (☎ 800/527-0700); **Hertz** (☎ 800/654-3001); **Kemwell** (☎ 800/678-0678); and **National Car Rental** (☎ 800/227-3876).

Arriving by Plane

There are daily flights to Paris direct from Boston, Chicago, Houston, Miami, New York, and Washington, DC. Flying time is about 7 hours for the East Coast, 11 hours from the West. Almost all US flights to Paris arrive early in the morning, so you may want to find a hotel that lets you check in early, or pay for the night before.

The following airlines have daily nonstop flights to Paris from the United States: **Air France** (☎ 800/237-2747); **American Airlines** (☎ 800/433-7300); **Continental Airlines** (☎ 800/231-0856); **Delta Airlines** (☎ 800/241-4141); **TWA** (☎ 800/221-2000); **United Airlines** (☎ 800/538-2929); and **USAir** (☎ 800/428-4322).

Paris has 2 passenger airports, both within easy reach of the city. **Roissy/Charles de Gaulle,** or **CDG,**

(☎ 01-48-62-22-80) is 14^1/$_2$ miles (23km) to the north of the city. Slightly closer to Paris and somewhat less hectic than CDG is **Orly** airport (☎ 01-49-75-15-15), 8^1/$_2$ miles (14km) to the south. A **shuttle** operates between the 2 airports about every 30 minutes and takes a little over an hour.

At CDG, foreign carriers use Aerogare 1 and Air France uses Aerogare 2. From Aerogare 1, travelers take a moving stairway to reach the customs and baggage claim area.

At Orly, international flights arrive at Orly Sud (south), and domestic flights at Orly Ouest (west). The two are linked by a free shuttle bus.

Getting to Paris from the Airports

By Taxi   There are **taxis** at each airport, but they're expensive and won't necessarily be any quicker than public transportation (see below). Taxi lines are often long; if you have small children, you can usually go to the front. To beat the line you can also hire a porter, who will usually drop you off at the head of the line. From Charles-de-Gaulle/Roissy Airport allow at least 45 minutes in rush hour. Orly Airport is a cheaper, shorter journey, and should take only 30 minutes.

By Car   From Charles-de-Gaulle/Roissy: Take the A1, direction Paris. From Orly: Take the A6, direction Paris. Exits for Paris are marked by various **"Portes"** that take you onto the périphérique (or ring road)—for example, Porte de Bagnolet.

From CDG by Public Transportation   The **RER B** runs every 15 minutes between 5am and 11:59pm to the Gare du Nord from Charles-de-Gaulle/Roissy; the journey takes 35 minutes, but remember you're on a regular commuter train once you leave the airport, so beware of big luggage and tons of commuters. There are **Air France buses** (☎ 01-49-38-57-57; recorded message in French and English) that take 40 minutes when traffic is clear, but over an hour in rush hours. They leave every 12 minutes, between 5:40am and 11pm, to deposit passengers at the Porte Maillot, place Charles-de-Gaulle/Etoile, and the Gare Montparnasse. There is also a **Roissy bus** that leaves every 15 minutes from 6am to 11pm and goes to the Opéra, right in front of the American Express building.

From Orly by Public Transportation   RER C trains take about 35 minutes and leave every 15 minutes for the Gare d'Austerlitz. **Air France buses**

(☎ 01-49-38-57-57; recorded message in French and English) leave every 12 minutes between 5:40am and 11pm and deliver passengers to the Air France station at Les Invalides and Montparnasse in about 30 minutes—this is a convenient option only if you're staying on the Left Bank near either of these sites. The **Orlybus** service operates to and from Denfert-Rochereau, opposite the RER station. The bus leaves from both Orly-Sud and Orly-Ouest every 12 minutes and the journey takes about 25 minutes. There is also something called **Orlyval,** a train that connects the Orly airport to the RER B line outside of Paris. The problem here is that, halfway through your trip, you'll find yourself having to change to a busy commuter train. And this is not very easy if the train is crowded and you have a lot of luggage.

Arriving by Train

The easiest way to connect to Paris from London is the **Eurostar,** which takes 3 hours—a great improvement over even the shortest rail/ferry trip, which takes around 7 hours. The Eurostar to London leaves from and arrives at **Paris-Nord,** 18 rue Dunkerque, 10ᵉ.

Though a plane ride from London to Paris is only an hour, the entire travel time by air usually takes 4 hours—factoring in getting to or from the airport at both ends and arriving 1 hour ahead of time for the flight. So the train ride is actually shorter, and costs less.

High-speed trains connect Paris with other major French cities, and numerous rail possibilities link the French capital with the European continent. For train information, call the **SNCF Grandes Lignes** (☎ 01-45-82-50-50). For trains serving the Ile de France region, call (☎ 01-45-65-60-60).

Staying in Paris
Getting Around

Paris is a wonderful city for walking. Most major attractions are in an easily walked zone that doesn't take more than a few hours to cross (except if you're interested, say, in walking from the Bois de Boulogne in the west to the Bois de Vincennes in the east).

Public Transportation

Paris has one of the best public transport systems in the world, run by the **RATP (Réseau Autonome du Transport Parisien)**. It's safe, clean, notoriously easy

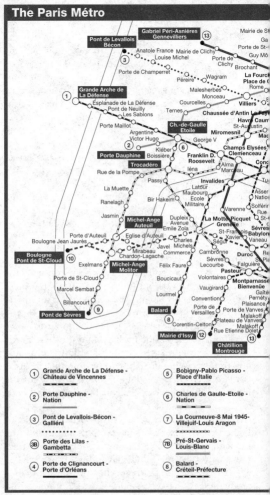

The Paris Métro

① **Grande Arche de La Défense -** **Château de Vincennes**

② **Porte Dauphine -** **Nation**

③ **Pont de Levallois-Bécon -** **Galliéni**

③B **Porte des Lilas -** **Gambetta**

④ **Porte de Clignancourt -** **Porte d'Orléans**

⑤ **Bobigny-Pablo Picasso -** **Place d'Italie**

⑥ **Charles de Gaulle-Etoile -** **Nation**

⑦ **La Courneuve-8 Mai 1945-** **Villejuif-Louis Aragon**

⑦B **Pré-St-Gervais -** **Louis-Blanc**

⑧ **Balard -** **Créteil-Préfecture**

to decipher, and covers virtually every inch of the city—so don't hesitate to use it. Métro, bus, and innercity RER systems use the same tickets. If you buy a 10-pack of tickets (*carnet*), you'll save around 40% over buying them individually. They're for sale in métro stations, at newsstands and other shops with an **RATP sign** out front, and on buses—though here you are only allowed to buy 1 full-priced ticket at a time. At métro stations, you can also buy different tourist passes, such as the **Formula 1,** with unlimited access to métros and buses for 1 day; or one of the **Paris Visite** cards that are available for 2, 3, or 5 days—some passes cover transportation to the airports, too.

Métro lines are numbered and named for their **end stations.** Once you know your direction of travel, simply follow the signs for the name and number you need. On platforms, the other directions are marked with orange *correspondance* signs. Smoking is prohibited.

Inside Paris, 1 ticket is valid no matter how far you go or how many changes you make, and you should retain your ticket until you reach your destination, as you may occasionally come across a ticket-operated barrier when you leave. The métro runs from 5:30am to 12:15am; these times are from the termini.

Métro stations are a popular haunt for musicians of all kinds; the larger, busier stations also have a number of vendors on the concourses selling fruit, jewelry, luggage, etc. As in many great cities, you will also come across beggars, some of whom have taken to addressing a half-full carriage with an apology for their need to ask for money before doing the rounds. The public response, these days, is not necessarily unfavorable. Pickpockets exist, here as everywhere.

Some **buses** are not only handy but offer attractive rides—like the **86** that runs from Nation across the Seine to the Eglise Saint Germain des Prés, or the **29,** which is one of the last lines running buses with open platforms in the rear. **Bus routes** are clearly marked on maps posted on almost all **bus stops.** (These are also good places to go to get your bearings if you're lost and mapless.) The route and all stops are posted inside the bus.

The **RER** (**Réseau Express Régional**) is a fast suburban service that consists of 4 lines, A, B, C, and D. You can use them to travel within the Paris city limits (for which the standard bus/métro ticket is good) or outlying areas, such as Disneyland Paris (which requires a supplementary ticket, the cost of which varies with the distance). RER platforms are separate from the métro platforms and somewhat more difficult to decipher. The service runs from 5:30am to 12:30am.

Taxis

In general, taxis are expensive—most rides cost around $7 or $8, and going from the Invalides to the Bastille, say, can run you $20. You can get a taxi at a taxi stand or by flagging one on a street—though not within 50 yards of a stand. You can telephone for one by ringing **Taxi Bleue** (☎ 01-49-36-10-10). Cabs have a light on the roof: If the white light is on, the cab is free; a smaller orange light means the cab is occupied; no light means the driver is off-duty.

All registered cabs are equipped with meters, and the metered time and distance will be charged according to the time of day and the zones of travel. You will also pay a *supplement* for each item of baggage, for a 4th person (though taxi drivers often refuse a 4 passenger categorically), or if you are picked up at a station. You can tip the taxi driver a few francs if you wish; the French usually just round up the fare to the next 5 or 10 figure (if you owe 32F, for example, give the driver 35F).

Driving Around Paris

If you value your fender, it's wise to avoid driving in Paris—the Parisian drives as if he were competing in the Indy 500 and parks as though he were shoving a book into a tight shelf. The **parking problem** is severe. **Meters** run from 9am to 7pm and are watched over by a blue-uniformed force. There are also a number of expensive **underground garages.**

You should be aware of the following laws: **Speed limits** are 31 mph (50 kmph) in the city; 50 mph (80 kmph) on the périphérique; 56 mph (90 kmph) on main roads; and 80 mph (130 kmph) on autoroutes, but 68 mph (110 kmph) when it's raining.

Cars coming from the right usually have priority—watch out for this in the big traffic circles such as Bastille, where incoming cars from the right will wheel into the circle with terrifying fearlessness. Look for the signs *priorité à droite* (warning that cars on the right take priority over you) or *vous avez priorité* (you have right of way). You will see signs saying simply *rappel* (reminder). This is a reminder that a previous command, such as priority, still applies. All you have to do is remember which. Seat belts are compulsory.

Children under 10 must not travel in the front seat. In the city, honk your horn only to avoid an accident. If you have an accident, don't admit liability or incriminate yourself. Ask any witnesses to stay and give a statement. Contact the police. Exchange names, addresses, car details, and insurance company details with any other drivers involved. In serious accidents, ask the police to contact the *huissier* (sheriff's clerk) to make out a legally acceptable account of the incident. In a dispute, his report will be considered authoritative.

Opening & Closing Hours

Banks have different hours, but their change offices are usually open from 9am to 4pm. Shops open between 9 and 10am and close around 7pm. Most stores do not observe noonday breaks. Museums and galleries tend to be closed on Monday. The Louvre is closed Tuesday. Many restaurants are closed on Sunday or Monday or both.

Public Holidays

New Year's Day, January 1; Easter Monday; Labor Day, May 1; VE Day, May 8; Ascension Day (6th Thursday after Easter); Whitsun Monday (2nd Monday after Ascension); Bastille Day, July 14; Feast of the Assumption, August 15; All Saints' Day, November 1; Armistice Day, November 11; Christmas Day,

December 25. Most museums close on these days, but some stores and restaurants remain open.

Rest Rooms

Public street lavatories of the self-cleaning kind (**sanisettes**) are to be found in abundance and are clean and well looked after. You will find lavatories in many métro stations and the big department stores. If you wish to use a lavatory in a cafe, avoid an argument and order a café at the bar, pay for it, then ask for the toilette. Often you'll find a lady presiding, who will expect a nominal sum (1 or 2F).

Rush Hours

Between 7:30am and 9am, and 5pm to 7pm, the métro is packed with workers going to and from their offices. On Friday afternoon and evening, the weekend traffic out of Paris is very heavy. Try very hard to avoid leaving Paris on the first and last days of July or August, when the entire population of Paris is either leaving for or returning from vacation. If you're traveling to either airport during rush hours, allow plenty of extra time.

Safety

Paris is a big city and though it is largely safe, there is crime here as everywhere. Avoid withdrawing money from cash machines late at night on quiet streets. Women alone can ride the métro in the evening, but it's a good idea not to do this after 11pm. Women alone should especially watch out for riding the métro in certain areas, such as Les Halles, at night, where gangs of kids from the suburbs are charging into Paris for a night out—it may not be life threatening, but it won't be pleasant. Strasbourg St-Denis is a dodgy métro station in the evening. Unless you know what you're looking for, don't go strolling the quais down by the water along the Seine at night.

Smoking

Paris passed a smoking law 3 years ago prohibiting smoking in train and métro stations and airports, and restricting it in cafes and restaurants. In theory, both smokers and proprietors can be fined for noncompliance, but the French haven't taken to the law with much enthusiasm. People don't smoke in the métros or airports anymore, but in cafes and many restaurants, the law goes largely ignored. Many establishments, however, now have smoking sections, and if this is a concern for you, call ahead. Beware, though, that restaurants tend to put the nonsmokers in unattractive corners, and smoking areas aren't usually well-separated: You're likely to have a table of smokers next to you anyway.

Telephones

Almost all telephones now accept cards, not cash, and it can be quite difficult to find coin-operated telephones in stations and at airports. When you find one, it will take 50c, 1F, 2F, and 5F coins. In bars, cafes, and restaurants, you will still find coin-operated phones. Public telephones are also found in post offices and on streets. Phones differ, and you will find instructions clearly indicated on the phones themselves, but in general, you pick up the receiver, then insert your card or money, and wait for the dial tone. If you are using money, insert at least 1F for a local call. The number for information anywhere in France is 12; in coin-operated phones, this is a free call: Insert 1F, and then at the end of your call, it will be returned to you. A busy tone sounds like a fast beep. **Phonecards** (*télécartes*) can be bought at post offices and at shops displaying the sign *Télécarte en vente ici* ("phonecards sold here").

To obtain directory service for the United States, dial 19-33-12-11. Otherwise, to call the **US direct,** dial 19-1 and then the area code.

The **AT&T USA Direct number** is 19-00-11; **MCI** is 19-00-19, and **Sprint** is 19-00-87.

Making calls within France: In the fall of 1996, all phone numbers in France went from 8 to 10 digits. In Paris and the rest of the Ile de France, all numbers now begin with 01. To dial cities outside of the Ile de France, use all 10 digits; you no longer dial 16.

You can make long-distance calls from the Central Post office at 52 rue du Louvre, 1er (☎ 01-40-28-20-00). Open daily 24 hours.

Time Zones

Paris is 6 hours ahead of Eastern Standard Time, and 7 to 9 hours ahead of the other US time zones. It is 1 hour ahead of Greenwich Mean Time (British time) in the winter and 2 hours ahead in summer— that is, 1 hour ahead of Great Britain most of the year.

Tipping

Tipping is less widely practiced in France today, as bars, restaurants, and hotels all include a 15% service and tax charge in their prices (***service compris,*** which can also be indicated by ***s.c.***). If the service has been particularly good, you can show your appreciation by leaving a small extra tip for the waiter. Small tips of only a few francs should be given to cloakroom attendants, tour guides, doormen, hairdressers, taxi drivers, and cinema usherettes. Airport and railway porters have a fixed charge per item.

Useful Telephone Numbers & Addresses

Paris Tourist Offices The **central tourist office** is located at 127 avenue des Champs-Elysées, 8ᵉ, ☎ 01-49-52-53-54. It's open 9am to 8pm year-round except May 1st. Métro: Charles-de-Gaulle-Etoile.

Other offices are at the following locations: **Gare du Nord,** métro: Gare du Nord, ☎ 01-45-26-94-82; **Gare d'Austerlitz,** métro: Gare d'Austerlitz, ☎ 01-45-84-91-70; **Gare de L'Est,** métro: Gare de L'Est, ☎ 01-46-07-17-73; **Gare de Lyon,** métro: Gare de Lyon, ☎ 01-43-43-33-24; **Gare Montparnasse,** métro: Montparnasse-Bienvenue, ☎ 01-43-22-19-19; **Tour Eiffel,** métro: Bir-Hakeim, ☎ 01-45-51-22-15; **Mairie de Paris,** 29 rue de Rivoli, 4ᵉ, métro: Hôtel-de-Ville, ☎ 01-42-76-43-43.

Another office that can be useful is the **Regional Tourism Bureau of Ile-de-France,** which is conveniently located in the underground shopping gallery of the Louvre, the **Galerie du Carousel du Louvre,** 99 rue de Rivoli, 1ᵉʳ; métro: Palais-Royal.

Also, make use of a **telephone help line** that the city of Paris has made available for all tourist information—from finding a wine bar near the Bastille, to where to go horseback riding in Paris, to locating a hotel near the Eiffel Tower—simply by calling the bilingual operators at ☎ 01-44-29-12-12. They're friendly and will go out of their way to help, whatever your question. You can call them between 8am and 8pm, Monday through Friday.

Hot Lines **SOS Help** is an English-speaking crisis line that can be reached by calling ☎ 01-47-23-80-80, daily between 3 and 11pm.

Train Information For train inquiries, call the **SNCF** at ☎ 01-45-82-50-50.

American Express There's an office at 11 rue Scribe, Paris 9ᵉ. ☎ 01-47-77-70-77; métro: Opéra; open Monday through Friday 9am to 6:30pm.

Baby-sitters Baby-sitters of various nationalities can be hired for reasonable prices through **Kid Services** (☎ 01-42-76-54-54, Mon–Fri daytime only).

Embassies and Consulates Unless stated, both the embassy and consulate are at the same address. **Australia,** 4 rue Jean-Rey, 15ᵉ, ☎ 01-40-59-33-00. **Canada,** 35 avenue Montaigne, 8ᵉ, ☎ 01-44-43-29-00. **Ireland,** 4 rue Rude, 16ᵉ, ☎ 01-45-00-20-87. **New Zealand,** 7ter rue Léonard-de-Vinci, 16ᵉ, ☎ 01-45-00-24-11. **United Kingdom,** Embassy 35 rue du Faubourg-St-Honoré, 8ᵉ, ☎ 01-42-66-91-42. **United States of America,** Embassy 2 avenue Gabriel, 8ᵉ, ☎ 01-42-96-12-02; recorded information, in English ☎ 01-40-39-84-11. Consulate 2 rue St-Florentin, 1ᵉʳ. Telephone numbers same as embassy above.

Emergency Numbers **Ambulance,** 24-hour (SAMU) (☎ 15). **Dental Emergencies** (SOS Dentaires) (☎ 01-43-37-51-00). **Fire department** (☎ 18). **Medical emergencies,** doctors making 24-hour house calls (SOS Medecins) (☎ 01-47-07-77-77). **Poison Center** (Centre anti-poison) (☎ 01-40-37-04-04). **Police** (☎ 17).

Late-Night Pharmacy Open 24-hours is **Pharmacie Dhéry,** 84 avenue des Champs-Elysées, 8ᵉ, ☎ 01-45-62-02-41, Métro: George V.

Lost Passport Contact the local **commissariat de police** and your **consulate** immediately. Commissariat numbers are listed in the front pages of any telephone directory. See above in this section for your consulate's address and telephone number. See also "Lost Property," directly below.

Lost Property If you have lost something on the street or on public transportation, go to the **Bureau des Objets Trouvés,** 36 rue des Morillons, 15ᵉ; open Monday through Friday 9am to 6pm; métro: Convention. You can call them to see if they have your passport or driver's license (☎ 01-55-76-20-00). For all other objects you must go there.

PORTRAITS

Paris Architecture

Virtually every great European style is represented in Paris, from Roman to the most contemporary flights of fancy. Let's take a brief look at them.

Roman (1stC to 4thC AD)   The only examples of the Roman era still visible are the Thermal Baths in the **Thermes de Cluny** and the restored **Arènes de Lutèce.** Massive walls, barrel vaults, and heavy rounded arches are typical features of Roman architecture. France has comparatively few Gallo-Roman remains, although some traces are evident in the foundations of the **St-Denis basilica** in Paris.

Romanesque (11thC & 12thC)   The style is characterized by rounded arches, heavy stone walls with small windows, and monumental simplicity. Columns tend to be smooth except perhaps for a flourish at the top. Among the few examples of the Romanesque in Paris are the bell tower and small chancel columns of **St-Germain-des-Prés,** the capitals in **St-Pierre, Montmartre,** the belfry abutting the apse in **St-Germain l'Auxerrois**, and part of the crypt of the **St-Denis** basilica.

Early Gothic (12thC & 13thC)   In place of the rounded arches and plainness of the Romanesque style, the Gothic builders used pointed arches and made great play with stained glass, sculptural decoration, and vertical emphasis. It was preeminently an ecclesiastical style, with the ideal of liberating space, and forcing the eyes upward to God. Walls, supported by buttresses, became thinner and taller.

The forerunner of Gothic architecture in Europe was the **St-Denis** basilica, designed by architect Abbot Suger, on the outskirts of Paris. In the Early Gothic churches, windows were small and decoration comparatively restrained. The outstanding example in Paris is the magnificent cathedral of **Notre-Dame.** Construction began in 1163 and was completed in 1330.

Mid- & High-Gothic (13thC & 14thC)   As the Gothic builders became more skillful at distributing weight through the use of buttresses, they were able to liberate larger areas of wall for stained-glass windows. The **Ste-Chapelle** is one of the finest examples of this period to be found anywhere. The chapel, designed by Pierre de Montreuil, is on 2 stories, with the walls of the upper story completely filled by stained-glass windows. The cathedral of **Notre-Dame at Chartres** is one of the most renowned examples of the High Gothic architectural style, and opened the way for later, even more spectacular architectural developments.

Late or Flamboyant Gothic (15thC)   In the late phase of the Gothic period, builders abandoned themselves to exuberant decoration, characterized by Flamboyant (literally "flamelike") window tracery and columns rising into elaborate fan-vaulting. The best examples are to be seen in the ambulatory of **St-Séverin** and the outstanding facade at **St-Germain l'Auxerrois.** Other Parisian buildings that illustrate this exotic style are the **Hôtel de Sens** (now the **Bibliothèque Forney),** with its highly decorated turrets and battlements; the **Hôtel de Cluny** (now the **Musée National du Moyen Age**); the **Tour St-Jacques;** and the little cloister at the **Temple des Billettes,** in the Marais. The church of **St-Maclou at Rouen** is another outstanding example.

Renaissance (16thC)   Military campaigns in Italy led the French to a gradual understanding of the Renaissance. In architecture, it was marked by a return to Greek and Roman forms and motifs: allegorical sculptures, classical columns, balustrades, pediments, and rounded arches. François I (1515–47) was a patron of the arts who did much to introduce Renaissance architecture to France. One of its leading exponents was Pierre Lescot, who designed part of the **Cour Carrée** at the Louvre. Other examples are the courtyard of the **Hôtel Carnavalet;** the **Porte Dorée** (golden gate) at Fontainebleau, built by Gilles Le Breton; the **Fontaine des Innocents** near the Forum des Halles; and, in interior decoration, the beautiful rood-screen at **St-Etienne-du-Mont.**

French Baroque & Renaissance Classicism (17thC)   In essence, the baroque style is a more ornate version of Renaissance classicism. **Versailles** is a striking example; another is the **east wing of the Louvre.** In ecclesiastical architecture, baroque includes the so-called Jesuit style (based on the church of Gésu in Rome). Paris has many churches of this kind. The **Sorbonne church** (by Jacques Lemercier), **Val-de-Grâce** and **St-Paul-St-Louis** all show the baroque fondness for domes.

One of the outstanding architects of this period was François Mansart, who gave his name to the high-pitched Mansard roof, seen, for example, on the **Val-de-Grâce cloister.** His great-nephew, Jules Hardouin-Mansart, merged baroque with the simple lines of classicism in many superb secular buildings, notably the **mansions in place Vendôme,** and the **Dôme church** at Les Invalides.

Rococo (18thC)   After the death of Louis XIV, and with a child king on the throne, a new, lighter style made its appearance, which was characterized by elaborate but graceful ornamentation. This was **rococo** (*rocaille*), which in Paris was mainly used as a feature of interior decoration—for example, in Germain Boffrand's **Oval Salon of the Hôtel de Soubise.** The **Hôtel Biron** (now the **Musée Rodin**) is an example of the refined elegance of the rococo age.

The 18thC classical, monumental architecture reached its peak in Paris with such structures as the **Louvre colonnade,** the **Ecole Militaire,** and **place de la Concorde.**

Neoclassicism (late 18thC to early 19thC) Between the 1780s and 1830s there was a revival of interest in antiquity, in marked contrast to the ornate rococo style. Once again, order, balance, and clarity became the keynotes. **La Madeleine** illustrates the style. Paris's supreme examples of neoclassicism are the **Panthéon** and the **chapel at Versailles.**

Consulate, Empire & Restoration (early 19thC) Buildings of this period tend to be heavier, less imaginative versions of the classical style, as in the **Arc de Triomphe** and **La Madeleine.**

Second Empire/Early Third Republic (mid-19thC to early 20thC) Uniformity went by the board and was replaced by a great mixture of styles, drawing on many periods. Advanced engineering, exemplified by the **Tour Eiffel,** was often combined with great extravagance of decoration, at least partly because the structural problems solved by the use of iron allowed great decorative freedom. A typical Second-Empire building is Charles Garnier's spectacular **Opéra** which opened in 1875 and is one of the largest theaters in the world.

This extravagant architectural rhetoric was carried into the Third Republic period with such edifices as the **Sacré-Coeur,** the **Grand Palais** and **Petit Palais,** and **Pont Alexandre III.** The Grand Palais interior illustrates particularly well the combination of practicality and decorativeness.

Art Nouveau (late 19thC to early 20thC) Here the mood changes markedly. Art Nouveau decorations on buildings are fluid in appearance, characterized by many elongated loops, and an almost baroque elaborateness of form. It's most obvious in the flowing and sinuous cast-iron entrances to some **métro stations,** designed by Hector Guimard between 1898 and 1904.

Guimard was an important architect in the Art Nouveau style in Paris. He was greatly influenced by the leading Northern European exponent of Art Nouveau, the Belgian architect Victor Horta.

Art Nouveau forms can be seen readily around Paris, particularly in restaurants; there are a number of superb examples, including **Julien,** with its murals by Alphonse Mucha, and **La Fermette Marbeuf 1900.**

Interwar (1918–39) Modernity and functionalism were the keynotes, as elsewhere, during this period, but echoes of tradition were sometimes retained. The combination is seen in the vast **Palais de Chaillot**. A full-blown example of Art Deco is the **Palais de Tokyo,** where good use was made of reinforced stone and concrete to achieve the clean, straight building lines. Both owe their existence to the Paris Exhibition of 1937.

Postwar (from 1945) The 1950s were relatively stagnant as the nation recovered from World War II. Some bleak expanses of glass, steel, and concrete arose in the 1960s, particularly the **Tour Montparnasse** and the **Palais des Congrès** at **Porte-Maillot.**

The **Forum des Halles,** a shopping, leisure, and entertainment complex completed in 1979, replaced Baltard's 19thC market hall, a move that was much regretted once the hall was lost forever.

Rogers and Piano's **Centre Pompidou** was praised and criticized for its innovative design; you'll want to walk around it and make up your own mind.

New Paris (1975–present) Planning policies for Paris changed with the arrival of Jacques Chirac, elected mayor in the mid-1970s. Skyscraper developments were no longer permitted, and the city committed itself once more to retaining its glorious and much-admired unity while allowing a growing dialogue with the world's leading architects.

The product of this policy has been two-pronged. A massive restoration and cleaning program has transformed buildings in many parts of the city, and the boulevards and squares now shine with a fresh gleam— an impression enhanced by the regilding of statues and monuments for the 1989 French Revolution bicentenary celebrations.

The wealth of significant new and newly-converted buildings seems never-ending, each project more impressive than the last. Italian architect Gae Aulenti converted the disused **Gare d'Orsay** into a thrilling exhibition space, while Ieoh Ming Pei's **glass-and-steel pyramid** has merged the late 20thC with the stately buildings of the Louvre in a way that will surely still take one's breath away in the years to come.

Another landmark has been added onto the precise axes laid out 200 years earlier, with the completion in 1989 of the marble-clad **Grande Arche at La Défense,** by von Spreckelsen. Jean Nouvel's innovative **Institut du Monde Arabe,** with its light-sensitive window apertures, has enlivened spirits since it opened in 1987. Carlos Ott's new **Opéra Bastille** has met with a more muted response despite its transformation of the place de la Bastille.

The public debate on architectural projects is a lively one. The fashion for building underground—below the pyramid at the Grand Louvre, for example—has been followed across the street in the Jardins du Carrousel, where the subterranean **Carrousel du Louvre** is a busy, gleaming, underground arcade of boutiques and restaurants. Less enthusiastically greeted so far, is Dominique Perrault's **TGB-Bibliothèque de France,** already underway at Tolbiac, where 4 glass towers, L-shaped like open volumes, belie a vast underground complex of reading rooms and archives. Objections seem to lie less with the design itself than with its suitability for the storage of the precious books from the National Archive.

Customs & Etiquette

To foreigners, Parisians often seem chilly, even snobbish. The fact is the French are not a particularly casual people.

Americans are forever trying to prove themselves good-natured, down-to-earth types, ready to chat with waiters and sales help, friendly to the core. But casual affability in Paris is often met with icy stares and monosyllabic replies. What Parisians—especially in service industries—are generally looking for from non-Parisians are politeness and respect, not gregariousness. In other words, what Americans are busy trying to pull down, the French are just as furiously trying to put up. The French hate false expressions of intimacy—though to the visitor they may not seem false—and they'll often make you pay for them. One of the things I was most often asked when I first moved to Paris (other than whether Americans ate hamburgers for dinner every night) was why we all say "have a nice day" to each other all day long.

The first and last thing to remember is: Take a deep breath when dealing with the French. Be patient. Don't rush them. And mind the following:

1. Paris must have more cats and dogs per person than any other city. There's nothing you can say if the table next to you is occupied by a woman and her poodle eating out of a plate. If that really bothers you, don't take the table.

2. Once you sit down at a table in a restaurant, you really can't get up and ask for another one.

3. Unless you're still in college, don't bring flowers to a dinner party. If you absolutely must say it with roses, then send them; before or after, it won't matter. In general, don't have a hissy about arriving empty-handed; the French do it all the time. For business meetings, never bring wine or a bottle of anything. And if dinner is over and you happen to see a tray full of orange juice and champagne winging by, down one: It means it's time to go.

4. Don't raise your hand across the restaurant, and don't raise your voice. Order your food before you order your wine. The French have made the leap and now acknowledge that you can drink red wine with fish and white wine with cheese—so have what you want.

5. Take an ambassadorial approach. You'll be rewarded with more information and taken better care of—from dry cleaners to waiters. Your goal should be to have every person you

encounter thinking well of you when you're
finished.

6. Don't ever allow yourself to be rushed, especially in a restaurant—even if you're struggling
with an incomprehensible menu where every
dish is named after a medieval French province.
Take your time and don't let anyone intimidate
you—but, again, don't shout when you're ready.

7. The French don't consider it proper to drink
anything with your meal except water or wine,
but go ahead and have what you want. And remember that no matter how many times you
ask for your coffee with dessert it will inevitably come after.

8. In restaurants with a cheese plate, you're
entitled to have a bit of all of them—though it's
not considered correct to chop off enormous
hunks of any one of them. And remember that
the French lie in wait for Americans who cut
the nose off the Brie: Slice everything from the
side.

9. Be prepared to spend more time at meals than
you would in the States; meals are an all-night
affair in French restaurants. And though you may
want to call your waiter over 2 minutes after
you get in to order, it's customary to wait until
he approaches the table.

10. You're never required to pay more than the
total on the bill. By law, service charges are fac-
tored into every restaurant and cafe bill. You
never leave centimes for a tip, no matter how
many.

11. The French don't usually butter their bread at
dinner. If you would like some, feel free to ask
for it—just remember that you'll be breaking a
culinary cannon. However, some dishes call for
buttered bread, such as certain shellfish and
saucisson. It's worth noting that the butter you
will be served is unsalted.

INDEX

PARIS

1-12 Paris Street Atlas
13-14 Montmarte Area
15 Montparnasse Area

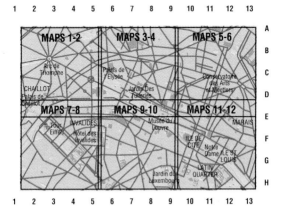

KEY TO MAP SYMBOLS

City Maps

▨	Major Place of Interest	P	Parking
▨	Park	Ⓜ	Metro
▨	Built-up Area	—	Railroad
═══	Divided highway	◄—	One way street
═══	Primary road	🛈	Information
═══	Secondary road	**8**	Adjoining Page No.
═══	Other road		

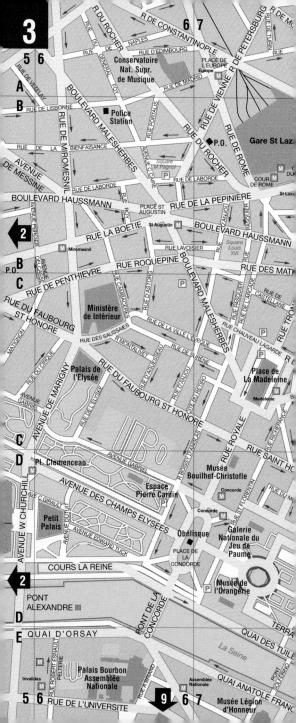

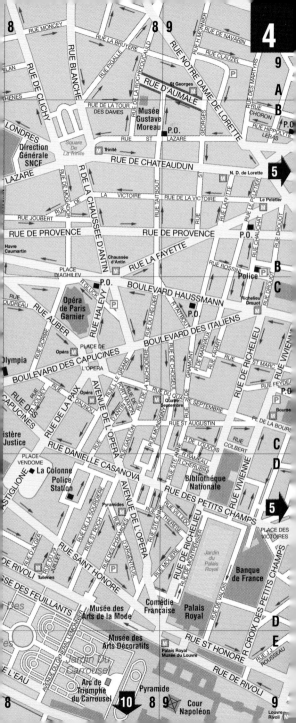

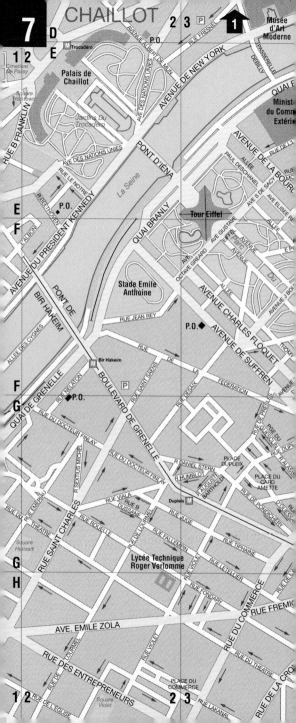

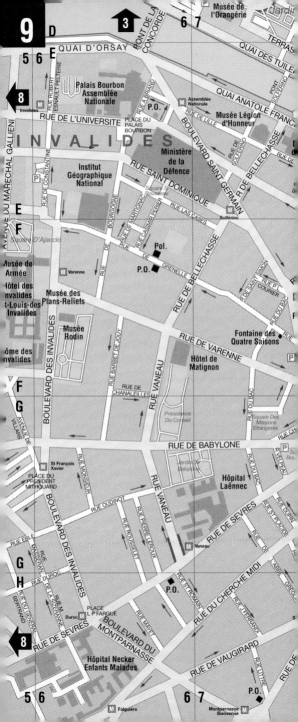

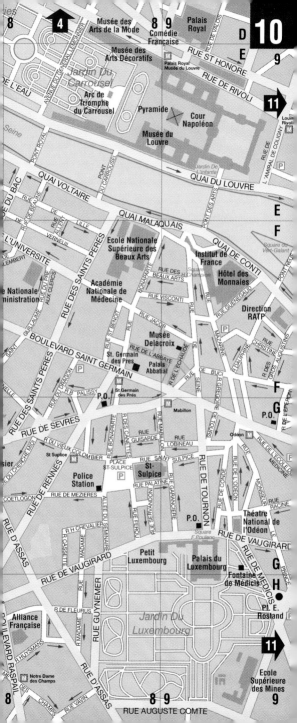

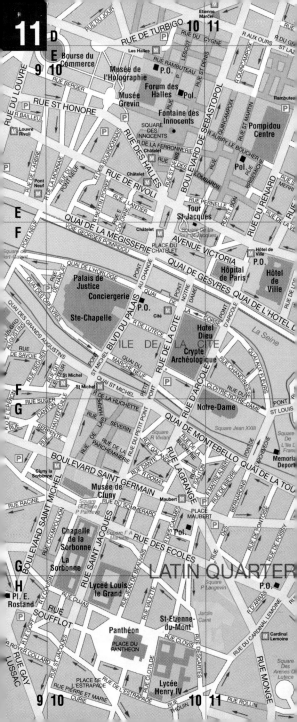

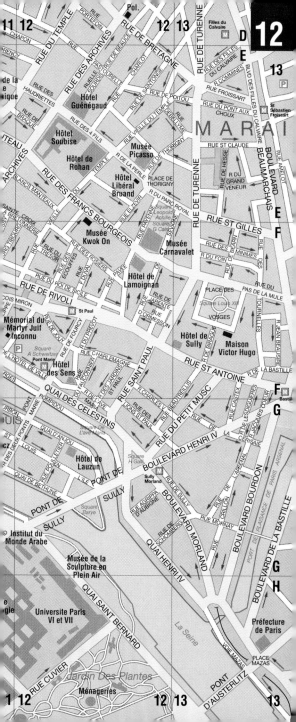

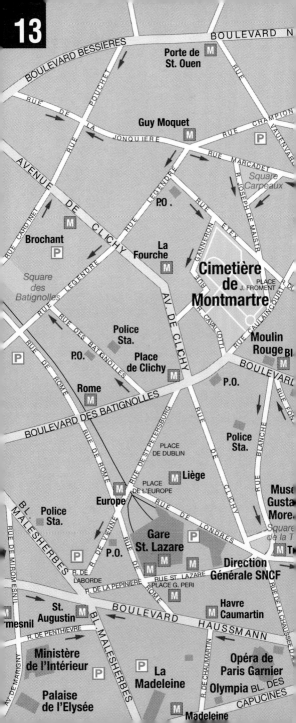